Maya and Spaniard
in Yucatan,
1648 – 1812

Maya and Spaniard in Yucatan, 1648-1812

Robert W. Patch

Stanford University Press
Stanford, California
1993

Stanford University Press
Stanford, California

© 1993 by the Board of Trustees of the
Leland Stanford Junior University

Printed in the United States of America

CIP data appear at the end of the book

Stanford University Press publications
are distributed exclusively by
Stanford University Press within
the United States, Canada, and Mexico;
they are distributed exclusively by
Cambridge University Press
throughout the rest of the world.

To My Mother and Father

Preface

Over the course of the years I have incurred debts to people and institutions too numerous to list. I would, however, like to mention some of them, even though many of the individuals are now deceased. First, I would like to thank my teachers: Stanley J. Stein and Joseph R. Strayer, of Princeton University, and Joseph L. Love, of the University of Illinois, Urbana-Champaign. Second, I thank the staffs of the Archivo General de la Nación, Archivo General del Estado, Archivo Notarial del Estado, Biblioteca "Crescencio Carrillo y Ancona," Archivo Histórico Nacional, and Archivo General de Indias, with special thanks to Luis López Rivas, Alfredo Barrera Vázquez, J. Ignacio Rubio Mañé, Miguel Civeira Taboada, and María Teresa Monforte de Menéndez. Third, I thank my friends and colleagues for their support over the years, especially Antonio Calabria, Gilbert Joseph, Cristina García Bernal, Sergio Quezada, Salvador Rodríguez Losa, Edward Kurjack, Rodolfo Ruz Menéndez, Juan Francisco Peón Ancona, Michael J. Fallon, Carlos Bojórquez Urzáiz, and Pedro Bracamonte y Sosa. I especially thank my wife Beatriz, not only for her support but also for constructive criticism. My debt to my mother and father is acknowledged in the dedication, but that to my brother Jim—one of my biggest obligations—is not, and I therefore acknowledge it here. Research was made possible in part by grants from the Henry L. and Grace Doherty Charitable Foundation and by a Foreign Area (Fulbright) Fellowship administered by the U.S.-Spanish Joint Committee for Cultural and Educational Cooperation.

Finally, a note about spelling. In order to simplify the identification of places, I have used the modern spelling of place-names. Hispanic surnames have also been modernized, but to retain some of the feeling of the past I have kept the older forms of given names (e.g. Joseph rather than José) and have used the original spelling in citing contemporary documents.

R. W. P.

Contents

Tables and Illustrations

TABLES

MAPS

FIGURE

Maya and Spaniard
in Yucatan,
1648 – 1812

Introduction

Latin America has usually been interpreted in European terms and measured by European standards. In modern historiography, this began in 1846, when Marx and Engels wrote in *The German Ideology* that the development of capitalism "received an enormous impetus through the extension of commerce which came with the discovery of America and the sea-route to the East Indies. The new products imported thence, particularly the masses of gold and silver which came into circulation and totally changed the position of the classes towards one another, . . . the extension of markets into a world-market, . . . called forth a new phase of historical development."[1] And a year later, in *The Communist Manifesto*, they wrote, "The discovery of America, the rounding of the Cape opened up fresh ground for the rising bourgeoisie. The East Indian and Chinese markets, the colonization of America, trade with the colonies, the increase in the means of exchange and in commodities generally, gave to commerce, to navigation, to industry an impulse never before known, and thereby, to the revolutionary element in the tottering feudal society, a rapid development. . . . Modern industry has established the world market, for which the discovery of America paved the way."[2]

Marx and Engels thus laid the basis of the historical analysis of Latin America in terms of its role in the development of Western capitalism. And this is still the dominant interpretation today. It is the cardinal tenet of dependency theory, which transformed the historiography of Latin America in the 1960's and 1970's.[3] It is also one of the key elements in the history of world capitalism put forth in the 1970's by Immanuel Wallerstein, who has had a major impact on recent European historiography.[4]

Latin America undeniably did play an important role in funneling money, precious metals, primary products, and raw materials to Europe, and eventually to the United States, once it had replaced Europe in the vanguard of capitalist development. Modern capitalism was stimulated and transformed as a result. But is that all there is to it? Should Latin America be viewed merely as the passive victim whose "open veins" are sucked by the vampires of colonialism, imperialism, and capitalism?[5] Does Latin American history have significance only insofar as it contributed to the development of Europe and the United States? The answer to these questions must surely be no. Latin America plainly has a history that can and should be understood primarily in Latin American terms.

This point must seem obvious. But in fact modern historians often avoid the obvious and attempt to force Latin America into a Western mold of analysis. For example, the noted French scholar Fernand Braudel, one of the most important historians of our time, uses an unabashedly Eurocentric framework in his famous history of world civilization and capitalism. He classifies the Aztec and Inca Empires as "semi-civilizations," that is, as cultures not quite up to the standards of a full-fledged civilization, because Inca and Aztec agriculturalists used the hoe rather than the plow, and lacked the technology of the wheel.[6] But in America there were no beasts of burden to be used with a wheel; and what would happen if, instead of the plow, irrigation were used as the criterion for defining a civilization? The efficient use of hydraulic resources, after all, requires systematic planning and the application of technology for the purpose of adapting the environment to human needs. It is, therefore, just as much a part of agricultural technology as the plow. Yet if irrigation is the major criterion, then most of Europe was well behind the Incas and the Aztecs in the development of civilization. Braudel's emphasis on the plow and the wheel is simply the arbitrary selection of Europe as the standard by which all other cultures must be judged.

Latin America must be studied as part of the world, but as a part of the world sui generis. For as Gabriel García Márquez has lamented, Latin American existence is ultimately made to appear meaningless by the Europeans' insistence "on measuring us with the yardstick that they use for themselves. . . . The interpretation of our reality through patterns not our own serves only to make us ever more unknown, ever less free, ever more solitary."[7]

Since the 1960's our store of historical knowledge about Latin America has increased substantially. This is due not just to the greater number of historians working in the field but also to a greater emphasis on social and economic history. That emphasis is the result of three factors. First, after the Second World War, the French historians of the *Annales* school began to transform research in the Western world. This resulted in an intellectual movement away from the traditional historiography, concerned overwhelmingly with political and institutional topics, and toward a broader conception of history as the study of societies. Historians, in short, became social scientists. Second, the problem of Latin American underdevelopment stimulated a search for explanations. That search naturally took social scientists into the field of history, especially into economic and social history. Third, this trend coincided with the rapid spread of Marxism, especially in Latin America but also in the United States, as a result of the breakdown of intellectual consensus in the 1960's. Since Marxists had always emphasized the economy and social classes, this ideological development gave added impetus to the study of social and economic history.

By the 1970's the new historiography had produced a flood of monographs.[8] Regional studies have been in the vanguard of this movement, and have revealed that many long-standing interpretations of past developments were based on generalizations derived from quite limited information. The traditional interpretation of the hacienda, for example, was based in part on firsthand acquaintance with the great estates as they existed in the late nineteenth and early twentieth centuries, when a landowning aristocracy ruled over vast properties pieced together over the years at the expense of smallholders and peasants. This latifundium conception was then projected backward in time and influenced the concept of the hacienda in colonial Latin America. But recent regional and case studies have revealed that colonial haciendas were in fact frequently small and burdened with debt, and that hacendados only sporadically gained profits from their properties. Moreover, peonage (long assumed to be the mainstay of the hacienda) was frequently not a major source of labor; indeed, landowners were sometimes indebted to their so-called peons. Finally, hacendados were not invariably members of the elites; non-elite people also owned haciendas, and estates rarely stayed in one family for a long period of time.

But even as the new research was helping to clarify some historiographical issues, it was also raising new questions by revealing the variety and complexity of regional social and economic structures. Indians, far from being simply the passive victims of colonial exploitation, were found to have fought back and defended their culture and their lands, and in some places the native peoples managed to retain possession of the resources necessary for their cultural survival. In many regions, therefore, the free village was just as important as, or even more important than, the hacienda. Moreover, it turns out that the supposedly nonexistent class of non-Indian small farmers, whose absence had long been used to contrast the history of the region with that of Anglo-America, was in fact present all over colonial Latin America. To be sure, their numbers were small in some places. But in others they were quite numerous, thus belying the old interpretation of Latin America as a society consisting only of rich landowners on the one hand, and slaves, peons, and poor Indian peasants on the other. Socioeconomic structure, in short, was found to be remarkably heterogenous.

Finally, the new historiography has led to a new interpretation of the nature of the colonial economy. Recent research in fact has revealed the existence of what Eric Van Young refers to as "a heretofore unsuspected economic vitality" at the local level.[9] Whereas most regions were assumed to have had "natural" (i.e., nonmonetary, barter) economies, the new historiography has found considerable evidence of production for local and sometimes distant markets. Haciendas, small farms, and peasant villages, in other words, were far from the self-sufficient entities that traditional historiography had imagined them to be. Local economies were usually monetized to a considerable degree, and interlocked with the regional, "national," and world economies.

Local or regional history, therefore, has proved to be a crucial part of the new historiography. And since this level of analysis requires a much better understanding of geography than was the case with traditional historiography, the new approach has opened up a fruitful dialogue with the increasingly important field of historical geography. In fact, geographers have come to play a major role in the study of Latin American history.[10]

This study of the history of Yucatan grows out of the new historiography of Latin America. It is an analysis of the historical development of a society, and as such it takes a broad, multicentury approach studying that society within the framework of a specific ecosystem.

The region analyzed is the colonial province of Yucatan, which in fact was a macro- or super-region made up of several smaller regions, or microregions.[11] This area, comprising what are now the states of Yucatan, Campeche, and Quintana Roo, has become one of the best-studied parts of all colonial Mexico.[12] Yet the structure of the colonial economy has received surprisingly little attention, and as this study will demonstrate, this failing has resulted in historical interpretations of limited validity. For example, it has been assumed that colonial Yucatan was well isolated from the world around it because of its almost total lack of exploitable resources, and that as a result the Maya, free from the full rigors of colonial exploitation, managed to survive better as a cultural group than many other native peoples. At the same time, Yucatan has frequently been interpreted in terms of its uniqueness, a condition that resulted, it is said, from the area's special geographic conditions.

The thesis of this study is that Yucatan was unique only in the sense that *all* regions are unique; that Yucatan's history differed from that of some regions but paralleled that of others; that Yucatan was not an isolated province, for it possessed resources that were exploited and used to effect integration into the world economy; and that the survival of Indian culture must therefore be explained not as the result of preservation from colonial exploitation but rather as a result of the nature of that exploitation. Finally, it will be demonstrated that the history of Yucatan, far from proving simply that the region was unique, helps contribute to a better understanding of the crucial articulation of relationships between local, regional, and world socioeconomic structures in colonial Latin America.

PART ONE

Yucatan to 1648

CHAPTER ONE

Geography and Civilization

WHEN AN EIGHTEENTH-CENTURY Treasury official sought to describe Yucatan to the government in Madrid, he wrote that the province reminded him of "the wharf of Barcelona." The comparison was as suitable as any, for northern Yucatan (where most of the people lived in the eighteenth century) is effectively a solid limestone rock, covered with broken stones, a thin layer of soil in some places, and dry, rugged forests. This was a country that did not delight the easily delighted minds of Renaissance Spaniards. Here there were no mountains, the rivers flowed underground, the climate was almost unbearably hot and humid, there was no gold, no silver, no precious metal or stones of any kind, and the Indians were poor, warlike, difficult to defeat, and rebellious, and were "settled on the rocky terrain without there being enough soil there even for a horse race."[1]

On the peninsula as a whole, the soil tends to be deeper as one moves south and east, thinner as one moves north and west. It is only six inches deep in most of the northwest, and in places there is no soil at all. Indeed, in the extreme northwest near the Gulf of Mexico, one can walk for hundreds of yards in places and encounter nothing but rock and thickets somehow growing out of solid bedrock. Even in the southeast, where the soil is deepest, it is often of poor quality. In fact, there is no truly good soil anywhere in Yucatan.

In the northern half of the peninsula, with its solid limestone bedrock, water filters rapidly through the soil and stone to the water table below, and rivers do not form. The northernmost river is the Champotón, and it is nothing more than a stream running west into the Bay of Campeche. Farther south, where there is more rainfall and less limestone, the Candelaria River runs out of the tropical rain forest of southern Campeche. On the Caribbean side of the peninsula, there are no rivers until one gets as far south as Chetumal Bay. Into that body of water flow two substantial rivers, the Río Hondo and the New River, and a few minor rivulets. The Río Hondo is navigable by large canoe to a considerable distance inland.

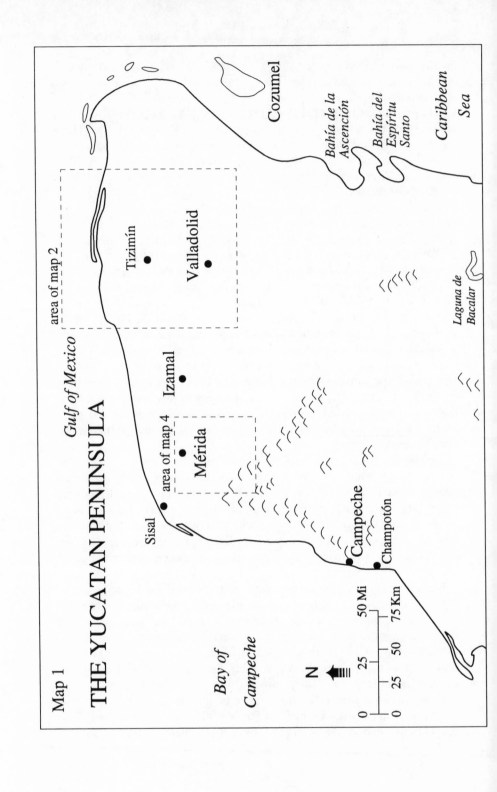

Map 1

THE YUCATAN PENINSULA

Gulf of Mexico

Bay of Campeche

Sisal

area of map 4

Mérida

Izamal

area of map 2

Tizimín

Valladolid

Cozumel

Bahía de la Ascención

Bahía del Espíritu Santo

Caribbean Sea

Laguna de Bacalar

Campeche

Champotón

N

0   25   50 Mi

0   25   50   75 Km

Finally, several minor rivers flow into the Caribbean in the central and southern parts of what is now the country of Belize.

But the northern, riverless part of the peninsula is where most of the Indian population has lived since Post-Classic Maya times, and therefore we shall concern ourselves primarily with this part of the country. Here the porous surface conditions make irrigation ditches impractical. Hydraulic resources for agriculture are therefore scarce, and as the City Council of Mérida put it in 1579, "the water that nourishes this land comes from the sky."[2]

Water can also be had from the natural wells called *cenotes*. These are cavities reaching down to the water table produced when the surface limestone over subterranean caves collapsed millions of years ago. Extracting water from these wells and then transporting it overland to farms are enormous tasks, and consequently cenotes are largely useless for agriculture. But they are useful and even necessary to the human population, because during the dry season (from October to May) they are practically the only sources of drinking water. Cenotes were the only geographical features of the land that enchanted the Spaniards, for these wells are frequently in beautiful settings made romantic by Indian legends. Some cenotes are 50 meters or more across.

In general there are more of these natural wells in the north than in the center of the peninsula. In the south, where the limestone has given way to soil and allowed rivers to form, there are no cenotes at all. Here lakes are even possible, and several exist in southern Campeche, southern Quintana Roo, and northern Guatemala. Most of these are heavily silted, and getting around in this area is difficult. But in the past, before the silting took place, it was probably rather easy to travel about by foot or light canoe.

Since the peninsula's elevation increases at the rate of about 20 centimeters per kilometer as one moves north to south, the water table in central Yucatan is far below the earth's surface. Because natural wells are very few here, access to water is difficult, for in the absence of cenotes, humans must dig wells—a difficult task for Indians lacking the metal tools necessary to cut through the thick limestone.

In the northern and central parts of the peninsula, the water for agriculture comes almost entirely "from the sky." Rainfall is distributed in Yucatan in the same pattern as soil: there is more precipitation in the east and south than in the north and west. A coastal strip four kilometers wide, including the town of Progreso (in the extreme northwest, 32 km north of Mérida), receives an average of only 50 centimeters of rain per year. A point eight kilometers south of Progreso has an annual average of 60 centimeters. By the time Mérida is reached, the average is from 90 to 100 centimeters. Northern Campeche and almost all of what is now the state of Yucatan receive between 110 and 130 centimeters annually, as does northeastern Quintana Roo. The northern and central parts of Quintana Roo average 130 to 150 centimeters, and as one moves farther south toward the tropical rain forests of Belize and Guatemala, precipitation surpasses 150 centimeters. By the time one gets to the Petén area of northern Guatemala, the rain forest has been reached, and the annual rainfall is 165 centimeters.[3]

However, precipitation is not evenly distributed throughout the year. It is concentrated in a rainy season lasting from the end of May or June until September. During those months precipitation comes from the Caribbean and passes over Yucatan from east to west. Rain usually falls in the afternoon. Some rainfall also comes in with the storms that blow in from the north off the Gulf of Mexico. Called *nortes*, or northers, these storms are most frequent between September and December, and were alleged to cause sickness and death. Finally, there are periodic fierce hurricanes. Though their "season" is from June to December, most occur during the rainy season, that is, from June to September. So, from January to May there is very little rainfall, and the temperature gradually increases in these months. April and May are usually extremely hot and dry.

To be sure, the weather is by no means as predictable as the above suggests. The rains may come early or late, in large or small amounts, and even during the "dry" season. For example, in 1902 Mérida received only 40 centimeters of rain (42 percent of the average during the decade 1960–70); in 1916 it got fully 160. Extremes for the Petén area are 89 centimeters (1928) and 236 (1929) centimeters. Also, there is a general tendency, as one moves south, for some rain to fall during the dry season; or to put this another way, the cycle of dry season–rainy season is more marked in the north than in the south. The important effects of climatic variations will be discussed as this work progresses.

Yucatan has three quite distinct vegetation zones. Northwestern and north-central Yucatan is a region of scrub forest. Since the area has been occupied by agriculturalists for over 3,000 years, what meets the eye is not "jungle" but rather a patchwork of crop land and forest in various stages of reforestation. Because there is very little rainfall outside the rainy season, the vegetation has to endure many rainless, scorching months in succession, with the result that as more and more greenery disappears, the forest takes on the appearance of kindling wood. In these conditions it is rare for a tree to reach a height of 10 meters, and most trees are a good deal shorter than that.

East and south of this vegetation zone is a region characterized by taller trees, though the forest is still rather dry in the months before the rainy season. At its southernmost point, this tall, dry forest almost reaches to the border between Mexico and Guatemala.

West, south, and east of this land of tall, dry forest lies the region of tropical rain forest, stretching from Chetumal Bay, through northern Belize and into the Petén region of northern Guatemala. This vegetation zone also embraces much of the Mexican states of Chiapas, Tabasco, and Campeche, though in these states the rain forest sometimes gives way to savanna. Trees grow very tall here, as high as 50 meters. In parts of northern Belize the forest has been replaced by sugarcane, and in Quintana Roo the trees are being cut down for timber and paper. Petroleum exploration and human colonization from Guatemala have recently invaded the Petén. But all of this activity is relatively new. During colonial times most of the rain forest was thinly populated. Before that, however—over 1,100 years ago—this area was very important to Classic Maya civilization. Tikal, perhaps the most splendid of all Maya cities, is found here.

On the entire peninsula there is only one geological structure that can accurately be termed mountainous. This is the small range called the Maya Mountains, in southern Belize, almost off the peninsula altogether. Other than this, there are only low hills. The most important of these is the group called the Sierra (or Puuc, to use its Maya name) in northwestern Yucatan. These hills, located to the east and northeast of Campeche City, are strung out over the landscape in the shape of an inverted V. This geological formation is much too low in altitude to affect climate, but other topographical features of the Sierra region did have an effect on human settlement. The soil on both sides of the Puuc is deep by Yucatan standards. On the northern side of the hills human settlement has always been dense. But not so on the southern side. Here there are few cenotes, and the water table is far beneath the earth's surface and protected by limestone. The Indians must have found it difficult to get water. Yet just south of the Sierra, near the point of the inverted V, is the abandoned Maya city of Uxmal, and farther south still are other ruined cities of the ancient civilization. How could the Maya have settled in this region of unfavorable living conditions? The answer is found in the system of cisterns built to catch and store rainwater.

Yucatan's geographic conditions have been discussed in some detail because they are an important part of its historical development. An approach that does not take physical reality into account will be misleading. Agrarian structures—the basis of all preindustrial societies—though not determined by geographic factors, are clearly limited by what is materially possible. Human beings must therefore be considered not only as individuals and as members of society, but also in the context of their environment. This will be demonstrated in the course of our study of Yucatan. If it appears less true elsewhere, this is only because these other places have not been studied with what Marc Bloch once called the "magic wand" of comparative history.

Agriculture and Animal Domestication

Agriculture was the most important factor leading to the rise of civilization in the Maya area. By 1500 B.C. this new method of food production—an innovation introduced from elsewhere in Mesoamerica—had spread to all parts of Yucatan and highland Guatemala. Substantial population growth, however, did not take place until some 700 years later. By the first century B.C. the Maya were constructing large-scale buildings and using a calendar (probably of Olmec origin) based on accurate astronomic observation. A great civilization was emerging.[4]

Maize was the most important crop of the agricultural revolution. As might be expected, the methods of cultivation varied throughout the Maya area. In southern Campeche, Quintana Roo, northern Guatemala, and Belize, the Maya, much like Andean peoples, developed a complex system of terraces for the cultivation of maize. The inhabitants probably also farmed on man-made islets in the small lakes that once existed in the area and that are now for the most part silted up. These would have been the Maya equivalents of the Mexican *chinampas*.

In the northern part of the peninsula, however, the area of our greatest concern, swidden (slash-and-burn) agriculture—or shifting cultivation—was more common. In this system, the peasants clear the land after the harvest, that is, sometime after October; burn it off in March and April, a process referred to as the *quemas* ("burns"); then commence planting right after the start of the rainy season. Sowing is carried out today exactly as it was thousands of years ago. As Diego de Landa described the process in 1560, "In cultivating the land they do nothing but clear the bush, and burn it to sow later . . . and with a pointed stick they make a hole in the ground and put into it five or six grains. . . . And when it rains, it is marvelous to see how it grows."[5] After sowing comes weeding and finally the harvest, which begins in September or later and lasts until the end of the year. This main, grain-producing agricultural cycle is complemented by the planting and harvesting of other, so-called minor but in fact essential crops like beans and chili peppers.

Of course, no agriculture is or can be absolutely changeless. The weather frequently interferes with the orderly cycle just described. If the rain comes too early it can dampen the fields and brush before they have been burned, making the quemas less complete and hence less efficient. Indeed, too much precipitation too soon can be disastrous. The rainy season sometimes stops right after the first rains, causing the planted seeds to die in the ground from lack of water. Even if precipitation begins on schedule, the total rainfall may be insufficient. And finally, any time from May to November a hurricane may destroy the best of crops.

The prosperity of society therefore depended on the weather. In addition, soil conditions had important effects on agriculture and on the so-cial organization of agricultural production. In the north the limestone lies so close to the surface that plows are useless, and the thin topsoil is quickly exhausted. In the southern half of the peninsula, in the area of the tropical rain forest, the soil is not of good quality at best, is extensively leached, and will lose its fertility and become hard and unworkable should the cover of plant life be removed permanently.

In these circumstances, land can be cultivated for only a limited time and then must be allowed to revert to forest for regeneration. In the south the fallow period lasts from four to seven years, in the north from eight to 20. Usually the land is worked for only two successive years, the first-year plot being called *milpa roza* (on freshly burned land), and the second, *milpa caña*. At any given time most land suitable for cultivation is in fal-low, in one of various stages of reforestation. If the land needs 20 years of fallowing, as it sometimes does in northern Yucatan, then for every newly burned plot that is cultivated, there must be one of second-year milpa and 20 plots in fallow. Although the situation, especially in the south, is usually less extreme than this, ecological conditions in Yucatan have important implications: agriculturalists depend on a large space for their survival, though only a small part of it is under cultivation at any one time.

Nineteenth-century liberals in Yucatan lamented this sad state of affairs because of its apparent inefficiency. Three centuries of Spanish domina-tion of the Maya, they complained, had done nothing to improve the bar-baric agricultural techniques in use since time immemorial. This negative assessment in fact served as the justification for policies facilitating the acquisition of Maya landholdings by Hispanic landowners.[6] But the tech-nical inefficiency is more apparent than real. Swidden agriculture, mod-ern research has shown,[7] can be quite efficient given the limitations im-posed by certain environments. Shifting cultivation historically has flour-ished in habitats with soil of very low fertility. The burning of primary and secondary growth is not done merely to clear the land for planting, as the Spaniards and their descendants have traditionally assumed. Rather, the forest is burned in order to return nutrients to the soil in preparation for cultivation. In fact, planting is done as much in the ashes as it is in the soil itself, which explains why productivity depends so much on the qual-ity of the "burn," that is, the degree of success in firing the forest. More-over, the very heating of the soil, as a result of slash-and-burn, raises pro-ductivity. Rainfall before or during the process dampens the wood and brush and makes the "burn" less successful, thereby lowering productiv-ity. In these ecological conditions, swidden agriculture is usually more efficient than any alternative technique. In Yucatan improving the soil was impossible for people lacking the technology to develop chemical fertilizers and the animals to produce manure, and in any case fertilizer is dangerous to use in an environment in which porous soil allows rain to wash organic materials into the water supply.

The Maya cultivated several kinds of beans, squash, and chili peppers. Chilis in fact were quite important, for their high vitamin content was a healthful addition to a largely vegetarian diet. Also of significance at times were the fruits, roots, and berries to be found in the forest. They probably saved many lives over the years, for whenever famine struck, the Maya took to the forest to look for anything to eat that might keep them alive.

The Indians also cultivated cotton. Pre-Hispanic Yucatan was a major producer of cotton textiles, exports of which tied the Yucatecan Maya into the greater Mesoamerican commercial system, linking Yucatan with present-day central Mexico and Honduras. This trade continued to flourish in the colonial era. Cotton cloth was produced in the form of *mantas*, or large mantles, which were sold in the cities and mining camps of central and northern Mexico. Textiles were the most important source of income for the Spanish colonists, and were such a significant part of tribute that mantas became the unit by which the Indian population was counted for fiscal purposes.

The invading Spaniards added to the base of resources for agriculture and stock-raising. The most important crops introduced in the Americas were wheat, barley, rye, sugarcane, and rice; cattle, horses, sheep, goats, pigs, and chickens were the most important animals. Ecological conditions, however, determined which crops and animals could be raised in which areas.[8] In Yucatan the Spaniards found what to them was one of the most inhospitable of environments. This was one reason why so many of them wanted to leave and why the early Spanish government forbade emigration.[9] Most importantly, the ecology of the peninsula would not allow wheat, barley, and rye to grow. Unlike the Mediterranean basin, with its wet spring followed by a warm, dry summer, Yucatan has a dry spring and a hot summer. These conditions proved to be fatal to the principal European grains. As the City Council of Mérida explained in 1579, "There is no wheat in this land, although with irrigation by hand it begins growing well and buds, but . . . lacking water it dries out because the earth is not humid [during the planting season], nor is there water to grow it using irrigation, and the water that nourishes maize comes at a time different from that required by wheat, because it comes along with many hot winds and heat, which cause the wheat to turn yellow and dry out."[10]

The climate does permit rice cultivation, but for some reason Spaniards made no attempt to grow rice until late in the colonial period. In the sixteenth and seventeenth centuries, therefore, Spaniards either imported wheat or ate maize. In fact they did both, but since the cost of importing grain was high, for the Spanish population as well as for the Indians, the "grain of first necessity," as it was so often called, was maize.

Despite the limited agricultural potential of Yucatan from the Spanish point of view, the colonists did find some resources to exploit and therefore the impact of colonialism on the countryside was by no means negligible. European grain crops may have done poorly, but a variety of fruits and vegetables prospered. The colonists introduced orange trees from Spain and such fruits as mango, tamarind, and banana from tropical Asia. It is likely that they also brought in garlic and new kinds of beans. More important, to provide meat and transport for the Spanish population, the colonists imported and raised pigs, horses, and cattle. To raise these animals the Spaniards set up ranches, called *estancias*. The ranchers, or *estancieros*, did compete to a certain extent with the Indians for land.[11] But many of them simply occupied unused land, large quantities of which were available because of the decline of the Indian population in the sixteenth and seventeenth centuries.

Since the Maya were capable of producing enough maize to feed themselves and the Spaniards, the newcomers did not find it profitable to engage in corn production during the sixteenth and seventeenth centuries. But the colonists did not stay out of agriculture forever. In the eighteenth century, they began to convert their ranches from stock-raising to producing rice and maize for the market. Also of long-term importance was the production of sugar and henequen. Sugarcane had been introduced as early as the 1540's. By the middle of the eighteenth century, sugar production and the distillation of cane alcohol—carried out despite royal prohibition—had reached significant proportions. The illegal liquor trade was eventually legalized, and after Independence cane production steadily expanded. The growth of this sector of the economy continued until the outbreak of the Caste War (1847), and in fact the expansion of the sugar industry was a major cause of that uprising.[12]

Henequen has a much longer history, for it is indigenous to the peninsula. It was used to make rope and sandals in the pre-Conquest era, and to make sacks and rigging for ships during the colonial period. But it was only near the end of the colonial era that an increasing world demand for fiber made henequen production commercially profitable. Further increases in demand came in the following century as the U.S. market for binding twine expanded with the development of the McCormick reaper.

Civilization

Maya society at the time of European contact was no longer the great civilization it once was. Nevertheless, it was still a civilization, for it was characterized by a highly complex social and economic structure. Indeed, had Maya society been anything but highly complex and developed, it could not have survived Spanish colonialism.

It was in the area of commerce, rather than in agriculture, that the Maya economy of the late fifteenth century reached its greatest development. The significant level of commercial activity, in turn, had a major impact on the social structure, as is demonstrated by the spatial distribution of society in Yucatan. Cook and Borah have estimated that some 800,000 people lived in the northern half of the peninsula in 1528 (that is, immediately before the Conquest): 50,000 in Acalán (the area southwest of the Laguna de Términos in western Campeche), 150,000 on the west coast of what is now northern Campeche, 300,000 on the east coast from Cabo Catoche (in the extreme northeast) to Chetumal, and 300,000 in the interior.[13]

These figures may overestimate the size of the pre-Hispanic population, but the settlement pattern described is probably accurate and is historically significant. The geographic distribution of the population reflects the orientation of the late Post-Classic economy. More than 60 percent of the people were settled along the major trade routes and made their living not only from agriculture but also, and in many cases more importantly, from fishing, salt gathering, and commerce.

Late Post-Classic Yucatan was part of a great Mesoamerican commercial economy, tied through trade to both lowland and highland Mexico, Chiapas, Guatemala, and points south. Two important trade routes, one maritime and one overland, connected the Gulf Coast lowlands with Honduras. The main entrepôt along the overland route was Acalán (i.e. southern and western Campeche); the major port for the maritime traffic was Cozumel, which came to possess an especially dense population.

This trading network was held together by a system of regional specialization and division of labor. Much of the trade was in luxury goods. Quetzal feathers were sent from Guatemala to Yucatan and central Mexico, ornamental gold went from Panama and Costa Rica to Honduras and Yucatan, and slaves and precious stones went in all directions. Yucatan's only contributions to this luxury trade were slaves and flint, which was mined in the Sierra region. The strength of its commercial activity lay instead in the production of goods for mass consumption, namely, salt, fish, and especially cotton textiles. Completing the list of important articles of trade were the finished goods coming from central Mexico (precious stones, jewelry, elegant cloth, tools, and weapons), and cacao.

Cacao, produced in Tabasco and Honduras, as well as on the Pacific coast of Chiapas and Guatemala, is especially noteworthy, for it was used not only as chocolate but also as the universally accepted currency of Mesoamerica. Since Yucatan had to import almost all its cacao (it produced only a small quantity itself, at Chetumal), the ready availability of this item, which was used even in the interior, is ample proof of the extent to which the late Post-Classic economy was market-oriented.[14]

There was also extensive interregional commerce within the peninsula. The coastal towns were not self-sufficient in food production because their immediate hinterlands were exceedingly barren. Therefore, villages in the interior provided the coast with the necessary food, as well as the above-mentioned flint, slaves, and cotton textiles. In return, the coastal towns and villages provided the interior with fish and, above all, salt. Salt was in such demand, indeed, that many pre-Conquest wars among the Maya were said to have been fought over the salt trade.

As might be expected, population density was by no means uniform on the peninsula in the late Post-Classic period. The littoral was densely populated, the interior relatively thinly. Moreover, there was great variation in population density even within the interior, for settlement patterns ranged from very large towns to small hamlets. Sometimes considerable concentrations of population were to be found, and formed the basis of Maya states. The Xiu state, occupying most of the Sierra region, is one such example. Another is Ahcanul, which included the large villages northwest of the western leg of the Puuc. Other centers of population included the area around what is now Mérida, a region controlled by the Sotuta state, and the Cupul towns between Valladolid and Tihosuco. In the rest of the northern and central peninsula, the population was not as concentrated but was nevertheless of significant size.[15]

At the time of the European invasion, the Yucatec Maya were organized politically into 18 independent states.[16] Some of these units were ruled by a lord called a *halach uinic* ("real man"), whom the Spaniards referred to as a *Señor natural*. The *halach uinic* lived in the principal town and ruled over the rest of the people through a local official called a *batab*. Other states, like Cupul and Ahcanul, were ruled by lineages that monopolized political power at the village as well as the state level. But in all cases, a political elite ruled over the mass of the population. This political system reflected the social structure, for the rulers were also part of the social elite. The latter also included priests and merchants. Many a *halach uinic* and batab participated in trading ventures, thereby demonstrating that commerce had no socially degrading connotation attached to it. Consequently, class lines were not rigidly drawn, as they were among the Aztecs, and the various political, social, and economic leaders tended to blend into one general upper class.

Below the elite were the Maya artisans, most of whom were probably part-time peasants. The extent of artisan activity is revealed linguistically by the existence of words for such craftsmen and occupations as "carrier, charcoal-burner, dyer, farmer, fisherman, flint-worker, mason, painter or artist, potter, salt-gatherer, sandal-maker, stone-cutter, tanner, and weaver."[17] This artisanry blended in with the peasantry, for all peasants, men and women, carried out some form of skilled or semiskilled nonagricultural labor. Finally, below artisans and peasants were the slaves, many of whom had been captured in slave-raiding expeditions organized by the elites. Others probably owed their lowly status to some economic misfortune that forced them to become dependent on the elite.

The basis of the elite's superior position is not well understood, but the general outlines are clear enough. Elite status was determined in part by inheritance and lineage, and was supported by the control of political positions and by a variety of economic activities. Upper-class wealth was based in part on commerce. Slave-owning was also a source of economic power, as was the control or ownership of land, although landed properties were likely to be held as prebends or owned by lineages or families rather than by individuals.[18] But political power was probably the most important basis of upper-class wealth, for it enabled the rulers to demand labor services and collect tribute from the peasant masses. The nature of tribute varied from region to region. Villages in the interior paid their rulers in maize, beans, squash, chili peppers, honey, wax, cotton textiles, and raw cotton, occasionally in flint, and sometimes even in cacao, which is to say, in cash. The people of the littoral sometimes rendered tribute in these goods but more often paid in salt and fish.[19]

The pre-Hispanic Maya were therefore organized in ways that were going to be of great significance for the future. The economy, far removed from the subsistence level, belonged to a wider multiregional economic block characterized by a division of labor and commercial interdependency. Moreover, within each region extensive commercial exchange took place. The political structure, although relatively undeveloped compared with that of the Aztec and Inca empires, was nevertheless characterized by rule by an elite whose legitimacy was widely recognized and accepted. Finally, the economy and society were organized in such a way that goods were channeled from producers to an elite in sufficient quantity to allow the existence of a non-producing upper class. Consequently, although the Spaniards were to introduce many changes in the organization of the Maya, they were also to find much that could be useful in the construction of the colonial regime.

CHAPTER TWO

The First Century of the Colonial Regime

For all the many changes the Spanish Conquest brought about in Latin America, it did not displace the native Americans from their traditional position as peasants. Thus one part or sector of the colonial regime, called in colonial terminology the *República de Indios*, or Indian Commonwealth, was composed entirely of the indigenous people, whose surplus production was channeled away to support and provide for the wider society. The Maya peasant communities were controlled and supervised by Spanish priests and bureaucrats and by Indian caciques, all of whom received a share of the tribute and taxes collected from the members of the República de Indios.

Imposed on this Indian sector was the *República de Españoles*, the commonwealth comprising all the Spanish elements of colonial society. These people were the principal beneficiaries of the colonial relationship between their República and that of the Indians. They conducted a variety of activities and eventually established their own agrarian system alongside that of the Maya.

The colonial regime, however, was not a dual society. Rather, it was a single system composed of two structures or sectors, one Indian and one Spanish.[1] The two Repúblicas, in other words, were intimately related, the historical development of the one affecting that of the other.

The Imposition of the Colonial Regime

The most obvious change introduced by the Spaniards was the phenomenon that had begun even before the Conquest was complete: rapid population decline resulting primarily from the sudden introduction of diseases brought by Europeans and Africans to a continent that had been epidemiologically isolated from the Eastern Hemisphere. This secular demographic decline was to have many important effects, but certainly the most immediate one was the severe weakening of Maya resistance to Spanish invasion. Yet it eventually affected Spanish fortunes as well.

As the following figures demonstrate,[2] contact had an instant and di-

sastrous impact on the Yucatec Maya, who at that point, it will be recalled, numbered as many as 800,000 people:

Year	Population	Year	Population
1550	232,576	1607	164,064
1586	170,000	1639	207,497
1601	163,625	1643	209,188

By 1550, the first year for which reasonably reliable information exists,
the figure had dwindled to some 232,000. Thereafter the rate of decline
slowed considerably. By 1601 the population was about 70 percent that
of 1550. A few decades of modest growth followed, bringing the 1643
population up to about 90 percent of the 1550 level.[3] In short, the Yucatec
Maya, after suffering an immediate demographic collapse, made a significant recovery in the early seventeenth century.

It is worth noting that all population counts based on fiscal data from
Yucatan are flawed. With an open frontier to the south, thousands of Indians periodically abandoned the areas under Spanish control and took up
temporary residence in places where they were not counted for fiscal purposes. This was especially common during epidemics and famines. Once
these crises were over, many thousands returned voluntarily to their original villages, and thousands of others were forcibly returned by Spanish-
organized expeditions sent south in search of runaways. Consequently,
population counts made in the wake of a social crisis underestimate the
total, and later demographic "recoveries" in part reflect the return of the
refugees. But despite these population movements, which had their counterparts in Guatemala but not in other parts of Mexico, the figures in the
tabulation have long-term validity and can be accepted as reasonable ap-
proximations of the demographic history of Yucatan during the first century of the colonial regime.

Although disease was the major cause of Maya population decline,
Spanish invasion and colonialism created conditions that made diseases
devastatingly mortal. Exploitation and cruelty, and the violence accompanying the Conquest, seriously disrupted the Maya way of life, thereby
making the natives more susceptible to the new diseases and exacerbating
their effects. The early colonists extracted as much wealth as they could
from the conquered population, and even the Franciscans, who shunned
riches altogether, contributed in their own way to the tragedy. The friars
not only exacted labor for the construction of convents and churches but
also forcibly relocated whole villages and thousands of Indians. This policy, called *reducción*, entailed the gathering of dispersed Indians into large
villages, thereby contributing significantly to the spread of contagious
disease. Colonialism itself, in short, was a major factor provoking the decline of the Maya population.

An important result of colonialism and epidemics was the almost total elimination of the Yucatec Maya living along the trade routes, where as much as 60 percent of the population had once been concentrated. The communications network undoubtedly contributed mightily to this development, serving as a mechanism for the spread of contagious disease. At any rate, by the early seventeenth century the coasts and Acalán were almost totally depopulated.[4] As a result, and since the population of the interior did not decline so drastically, the focus of Maya life shifted from the coast to the interior, where it has remained ever since. Fishing and salt gathering continued to be important activities, but only for the small number of villages in close proximity to the sea.

The colonial regime therefore came to be based on the Maya of the interior. There, as in all parts of Spanish America, a balance had to be struck between the demands of the colonists and the productive capabilities of the Indians. In some places the excessive nature of the invaders' demands resulted in such social dislocation that native society collapsed altogether and was eliminated as effectively as if exterminated by disease. But generally speaking, the more organized the Indian economy and society, the better the chance of the natives' ultimate survival.[5] The Maya of Yucatan for the most part had achieved a level of social and economic integration that allowed them to bear the burden of colonialism despite demographic crisis and have thus survived as a cultural group down to the present day.

It was in the interest of the Spaniards to see that the impact of colonialism did not result in extreme social dislocation. For this reason, the official policy was to preserve some elements of the Maya economy in order to counteract the disruptive effects of invasion. Consequently, Maya land tenure was legally sanctioned and protected, and although the colonists would have liked the Indians to pay their tribute in gold or silver money, the natives were permitted to continue paying in kind. Moreover, since the crown had little to gain by the establishment of Spanish-owned landed estates and a lot to lose by the diminution of the tributary population—both of which would have resulted had the colonists been given a free hand—the Spanish state and its dependent clerical arm together sought to protect the Indians from the Spaniards. A special court—the Tribunal de Indios—was created to provide the native communities with legal assistance in their conflicts with an ever-increasing Spanish population.[6]

The colonial regime also attempted to preserve important elements of Maya social structure. The Maya upper class, with the exception of the priesthood, was recognized as a legitimate nobility. Members of the elite, Indios Hidalgos in Spanish parlance, were permitted to use the titles of *don* and *doña*, were exempted from tribute and labor services, were supposedly preferred for honorable employment, were allowed to ride horses, wear Spanish dress, bear arms, and use coats of arms, and were given special status in courts of law.[7] The Maya nobility continued to hold this status throughout the colonial period, and its members always made a careful distinction between themselves, as Indios Hidalgos, and the *macehuales* (commoners, derived from the Nahuatl word for peasant). Only nobles could use the honorary *don* and *doña*.

Despite these efforts to maintain continuity, colonialism resulted in substantial change. For however much the law asserted legal equality between Maya and Spanish nobility, colonial reality demanded inequality. Thus, although many Indian nobles could and did exercise some of their special prerogatives, only a small number were ever permitted to own firearms. The inequality inherent in Spanish-Indian relations is also revealed by the absence of marriage between Maya doñas and social-climbing Spaniards. There had been a certain amount of this in central Mexico right after the Conquest as some of the invaders found they could improve their social status by marrying into nobility. But the practice quickly died out—except in the case of a particularly wealthy Indian heiress—because eventually for a Spaniard to marry *any* Indian meant downward social mobility. The conquest of Yucatan was completed significantly later than that of central Mexico, and consequently the colonial ambiance was already dictating inequality. For Spaniards, Indians of whatever class were people with a lower, never higher, status.

Moreover, the indigenous elite's position was being undermined even within the República de Indios. The gradual decline of the pre-Hispanic trading system meant the elimination of commercial wealth as an economic prop of social status. The abolition of slavery deprived the Indian elite of a whole class of dependents who had served as an important base of wealth and prestige. The Spanish policy of appointing village governors, or *gobernadores*, charged with political functions eroded the power of the old hereditary elite and created a new elite that owed its existence to Spanish, not Indian, authority. By the eighteenth century, the Spanish-appointed village governors had even appropriated the titles of cacique and batab, and the descendants of the old *halach uinic*, or territorial lords, had become indistinguishable from ordinary Indios Hidalgos. As a result, many members of the traditional class of lords were left without even high-sounding political positions. And finally, the Spaniards' imposition of new Indian village governments, or *cabildos*—instituted in most of the pueblos by the end of the sixteenth century—destroyed the traditional ties between lesser villages and larger ones and completely eliminated the political base of the traditional Maya territorial states. Consequently, political power—probably the most important base of the elite's position—was fragmented.[8]

A concomitant of the decline of the native elite was the lowering of the status of women. Before the Conquest, females had carried out important roles in Maya religion and at times had wielded some political power as *cacicas*. But Catholicism demanded that women be relegated to positions of insignificance in religious affairs. The Spanish priests once considered creating a native priesthood, but the experiment was for men only; the Church, then as now, could not even conceive of a female clergy. Moreover, as the native nobility was removed from power and replaced by officials appointed by the Spanish state, females were pushed out once more, for the colonial authorities again could not even conceive of women in positions of power; only males were appointed to serve as village governors.[9] In the future centuries of the colonial regime, there would be many Indias Hidalgas but no more cacicas.

Maya social structure continued to change in significant ways all during the course of colonial rule. In some parts of the Americas, the final result was the elimination of class differences within Indian society, as the upper class was pushed downward and the lower classes of serfs and slaves moved upward. Everyone thus met in the middle, and only minor distinctions between groups survived as the basis of social stratification among a generally impoverished peasantry.[10] But in other areas, the process was so slow that class differences within Indian society, although less marked, continued to exist throughout the colonial period. Only in the nineteenth century were all the native people finally reduced to the status of a mere peasantry.[11]

The latter was the experience of the Yucatec Maya. For despite the undermining of the old elite, the principle of class distinctions among the Indians did not disappear.[12] As old props of social stratification were eliminated, new ones emerged and were taken up by the new elites to preserve a stratified social order. The religious brotherhoods, or *cofradías*, offered the upper class the opportunity to continue to serve as the spiritual leaders of their communities, as they had done in pre-Conquest times.[13] And the Spanish system of property allowed the native elite to gain possession of land as private property and thus consolidate their superior status. This was made possible by the very complexity of pre-Hispanic Maya land tenure, for large quantities of land had been owned not by the village community as a group but by family and lineage units; after the Conquest, it became easy for the families and lineages to separate their lands from those of the community as a whole and thereby avoid being pushed downward into the mass of macehuales.[14]

A stratified Maya society thus survived the imposition of colonial rule. This is testimony to the resilience of the social structure, for in many additional ways the colonial regime introduced changes that would have led to societal collapse among less organized groups. One of the most notable of these challenges to the survival of Maya social structure was the co-

lonial policy of *reducción*, that is, the forced resettlement of the indigenous population. From the Spanish point of view, the scattering of the
population throughout the countryside meant the lack of civilization, and
therefore as part of their *mission civilisatrice*, both civil and religious authorities attempted to group the people of hamlets into villages, and the
people of smaller villages into larger ones. The resulting concentration of
the population was convenient for the Spaniards, for the Indians could in
this way be more effectively taxed, watched over, and Christianized. It
was also conducive to the spread of contagious disease, as already noted,
and thus contributed to the Maya demographic collapse.

Obviously many Indians did not want to move. In those cases force had
to be used, and settlements were burned in order to get the people to leave
and to discourage them from returning. Added to this element of disorder
was the confusion resulting from the resettlement of so many people into
new villages, where they were sometimes unwelcome.[15] In any case, the
colonial authorities were not entirely successful in their attempts to force
the Indians to live as the Spaniards wanted. For the Indians resisted, and
whenever the authorities relaxed their efforts, many people went back to
their own ways, moved out of their unwanted new residences, and re-
established their original settlements.[16] This was a problem that was to
plague the Spanish authorities throughout the colonial period.

Maya society was thus transformed but by no means destroyed during
the course of the first two centuries of the colonial regime. Even though
much of the traditional way of life was eliminated and the Indians were
relegated to a position of social and political inferiority to the Spaniards,
there remained a solid Maya core in the end. For the native people resisted
colonialism. On occasion the resistance was violent. More often, it was
covert, in the form of cultural expression and noncooperation. This
prompted Fray Diego López de Cogolludo to complain in 1656 that "in
general these Indians are so little inclined to give alms [i.e., pay religious
tribute] that if they had things their way, they would not even give us an
egg for our sustenance."[17] Perhaps most important of all was the Indians'
continued belief in the tradition that said the days of the Spaniards' rule
were numbered, and that eventually they, the Maya, would rise up and
destroy the alien regime.[18] This tradition was written down in the Maya
colonial chronicles, in which time was measured according to the ancient
calendar, and where just as the arrival of the white men and the defeat of
the Maya had been predicted by the movement of time, so too were the
end of Spanish rule and the liberation of the Indian foreseen.[19]

The Maya Economy

The economy was the aspect of Maya life that changed the least during
the first century of colonialism. As members of agrarian communities,

that is, as peasants, the Maya maintained their agricultural system intact. They continued to grow their traditional food crop; no evidence has yet been found of the Maya having attempted to grow European grains like wheat, barley, rye, or rice. They continued to practice traditional swidden agriculture, a system that was primitive but effective, and produced the food necessary for their subsistence and Spanish survival.

It was in the area of animal domestication that real changes were made. The Maya quickly learned to raise European chickens and pigs, and eventually took up cattle and horses. In fact, so many Indians came to own horses and even mules that they practically monopolized the transport trade.

Little is known about Maya stock-raising in the early colonial period. The available evidence suggests that at the start, in the early seventeenth century, most indigenous production of cattle and horses was carried out not by family units but by estancias belonging to the village sodalities, or cofradías.[20] Practically all villages established such ranches as cash enterprises and to provide meat and lard for community festivals. The proliferation of cofradía estancias demonstrates the Maya's willingness to change their traditional economy when it was in their interest to do so.

The other mainstays of the Maya economy were textile production and wax-gathering. As already noted, cotton textiles had been Yucatan's major export during the Post-Classic era, and they lost none of their importance after the Conquest. Exports of cloth and wax continued to be the basis of Yucatan's ties with the outside world during most of the colonial period.

Production of both these trade goods was characterized by local specialization and the sexual division of labor. Conditions were most propitious for the cotton plant in the eastern part of the peninsula, where it grew wild in abundance and was harvested, apparently, by males. But once collected, the cotton became the work of women and girls, who carried out the labor-intensive tasks of carding, spinning, and weaving. The villages of the central and western parts of the peninsula received their cotton supply from the eastern communities, and thus the whole province was integrated economically to become a cotton textile production and exporting platform. Wax, which was collected from wild bees all over the peninsula, was an exclusively male occupation. It was a task that required men to leave their villages for extended periods of time on treks through the bush in search of this valuable trade item.[21]

It was all the easier for the Spaniards to milk the Maya economy of these products because the institutions of colonialism were based in large measure on existing structures of production and the sexual division of labor. Long before the European invasion, for example, the Maya peasants had paid tribute to their rulers, and therefore to a great extent the tribute system imposed by the Spaniards was a continuation of an in-place mechanism for channeling goods from the peasantry to the elite. The colonial institution that accomplished this was the *encomienda*, that is, the right granted to a private individual to exact tribute from the conquered population. At first the conquerors extracted as much as they could get away with, but eventually the crown imposed schedules to limit payments to fixed quantities. The government also established controls over forced labor, which thereafter was allocated to individuals by the Spanish state.[22]

By the late sixteenth century, the tributary system had taken on the shape that it would retain into the eighteenth. Each married couple was responsible for the annual payment of one-half *manta* (a measure of cotton cloth), a *fanega* of maize, a turkey, and a chicken. Unmarried men between the ages of fourteen and sixty and unmarried women between twelve and sixty—widows and widowers, as well as bachelors and spinsters—were defined as half-tributaries and were required to pay half the quantity demanded of a full tributary. The value of these goods could vary substantially. In 1583 the total worth of a married couple's tribute was 18 reales (that is, two pesos, two reales), which was somewhat higher than the payment exacted in New Spain because of the high value placed on Yucatan's cotton textiles.[23] Some 25 years later, in 1607, the couple paid the equivalent of 31 reales (three pesos, seven reales), for mantas, maize, chickens, and turkeys had all risen in price. To overcome the problem of such fluctuations, in the 1630's the government assigned fixed values to tribute goods, at the rate of four pesos, four reales, per manta, four reales per fanega of maize (two reales per carga), two reales per turkey, and one real per chicken. Eventually fowl were uniformly evaluated at 1.5 reales each. Tribute was thereafter assessed at 25 reales per couple, a level maintained until the middle of the eighteenth century. By the late seventeenth century, however, there are some indications of a growing trend toward the commutation of tribute from kind to money.[24]

The other major mechanism employed in the sixteenth century to channel wealth to the non-producing Spanish society, the taxation imposed by the Church, also had its counterpart in the pre-Conquest period. Before the European invasion, Indians had to provide goods and labor for the maintenance of their religious establishment, and the same was true after the native cult was banned and replaced, to a certain extent, by Christianity. At first these payments were euphemistically called alms (*limosnas*), but they were decidedly not voluntary. Nor were they regulated as quickly as civil tribute, and for some time the quantities demanded were set by each parish priest as he saw fit. Apparently fixed schedules were not established until the early eighteenth century, by which time a new word, *obvenciones*, had been introduced to refer to religious taxes. These consisted of payments, once again, of mantas and thread, as well as maize, beans, chili peppers, honey, salt, and chickens. Eventually these were evaluated at 12.5 reales per male between the ages of fourteen and sixty, and nine reales per female between twelve and fifty-five. Like tribute, religious taxes increasingly came to be commuted to money payments. In addition to these obvenciones, Indians had to pay for the catechism classes of their children. This *doctrina* was eventually set at two reales per married couple, but both before and after the establishment of a tax schedule, it was customarily collected in the form of one egg paid to the priest every Thursday by every child.[25]

The obvenciones and doctrina were collected year in and year out, unlike another class of religious exactions called *obvenciones menores*. These were fees for the performance of the sacraments of baptism (three reales), matrimony (ten reales), confirmation (eight reales), and extreme unction (eight reales per adult, four reales per infant or child). Still more fees were collected for matrimonial inquiries and bequests, both of which cost four reales. Since these exactions were not made annually, total religious taxes varied from year to year, depending on whether the individual Indian had the financial misfortune to be married, buried, baptized, or confirmed. Nevertheless, the total collected by the Church must have rivaled and possibly surpassed tribute in importance.[26]

Indians were subject to two other exactions. In the late sixteenth century, one real was collected from each tributary as a community tax, called the *comunidad*, to provide the village treasury with revenue for municipal necessities. This was later raised to between four and five reales, before being set at four reales in 1668.[27] And in 1591 an impost of half a real per tributary was imposed to provide revenue for the Tribunal de Indios, the special court established to provide legal aid to the Indians.[28]

Undoubtedly tribute, minor taxes, and religious exactions channeled a significant quantity of goods and money to the Spanish colonists. But these were by no means the only ways in which the Indians were made to support the weight of the colonial regime. Labor services were also extracted. As in the case of tribute and religious taxes, these had their pre-Hispanic counterpart, and in fact at the village level the natives more or less continued to provide community labor as always, at the rate of one day a week. They worked in their villages constructing and repairing churches and at times serving their own native elite. In addition, the state exacted corvée labor for road-building and the construction of public buildings, letter-carrying, and the transport of goods and humans. Finally, labor drafts known as *servicios personales* were exacted more or less as the juridical equivalent of *repartimiento* labor in New Spain.[29]

In the second half of the sixteenth century, substantial labor services were demanded of the Indians to work the indigo plantations being developed by colonists. But so many died as a result of the dangerous conditions that the Franciscans eventually succeeded in getting the crown to

ban forced labor in this industry.[30] Since there were no other Spanish enterprises requiring large inputs of labor, the *servicios personales* eventually
came to consist of approximately one week of domestic service per tributary each year. Women were made to prepare tortillas and carry out
other domestic tasks, while men provided firewood and performed heavy
labor around the house for the Spanish colonists. The law required the
payment of wages, but these were set at a level much below what free
wage laborers would have earned, so in fact the *servicios personales* served
to appropriate Indian labor at bargain rates.[31]

Certainly the most effective mechanism for tapping Maya surplus labor
was the system known as the *repartimiento*.[32] Literally the term means the
process of distributing, allocating, or dividing something up. Historically it referred to the various kinds of commercial arrangements the
Spaniards had with Indians. In the New World, the best-studied system
is the one carried out in central Mexico and Peru, which consisted for
the most part of the forced sale of goods to Indian communities. Spaniards, usually government officials, were in charge of allocating or distributing the goods, which had to be paid for in money or in kind at a
later time. In practice, the highland repartimiento worked to incorporate
the Indians involuntarily into the colonial economy as both consumers
and producers.[33]

In other regions, the repartimiento involved only minor quantities of
goods forcibly sold to the Indians. Instead, in a large part of southern
Mexico and Central America (from Oaxaca and Yucatan to Nicaragua),
and in the Philippines as well, money and credit were advanced to the
Indians, and repayment was demanded almost exclusively in kind.[34] This
system incorporated the Indians into the world economy as involuntary
producers of raw materials, primary products, and manufactured goods,
which Spaniards acquired at bargain prices and then resold to make handsome profits.

The origins of this system in Yucatan are obscure. The first persons
reported to be carrying out repartimientos were encomenderos.[35] Priests
and other representatives of the Church eventually joined in the business
as well. But the people who fought most persistently to establish the system were the royal governors. To do so, they first attempted to institute
local magistracies (*corregimientos*) and have the magistrates carry out the
business with the Indians. But the crown and the Audiencia of Mexico
abolished the magistracies as fast as the province's executive officers could
institute them.[36] Only with the establishment of *capitanías a guerra* (war
captaincies), initiated in 1617 to meet the threat of attacks by pirates, did
the governors find the solution to royal interference in their business activities. The captaincies had military value and were therefore tolerated

by the crown; and at the same time, the captains carried out the reparti-miento for themselves and for the governors.[37]

The government officials' business dealings were multifaceted and sometimes involved the sale of goods to the Indians.[38] But for the most part the system was based on advances of money or credit for the purpose of paying tribute and other taxes. The whole point of the business was the acquisition of exportable goods. Eventually the system functioned al-most exclusively to procure wax and cotton textiles for other parts of the Spanish Empire. The repartimiento in southern Mexico and Central America came to have this function because of the decline of cotton and cotton textiles in the depopulated producing areas of central Mexico.[39] The resulting shortage necessitated a change in the highland Indian trib-utary system: payment could no longer be demanded in textiles because of the lack of raw cotton, and consequently payments were commuted to money.[40] At the same time, the rapidly developing mining communities generated even more demand for goods of all types, especially cloth.[41] The demand throughout New Spain became so great that even China, India, and the Philippines were incorporated into the Spanish imperial economy as producers of cotton textiles for the Mexican market.[42]

In short, the repartimiento system in Yucatan owed its existence to a great historical conjuncture: the catastrophic decline of the Indian popu-lation of Mesoamerica and the rise of the Mexican silver-mining econ-omy. The export of encomienda tributary goods, especially mantas, was also made possible by the demand for textiles in New Spain. Conse-quently, the nature of both the repartimiento and the encomienda in Yu-catan was determined to a great extent by the development of a colonial economy based on the export of precious metals.[43] Textile production was in part a backward linkage of mining. Colonial Yucatan was clearly far from being the commercially isolated area it has been held to be.[44] In the world economic system, it played the role of an exporter, not of raw ma-terials or primary products destined for European markets, but of man-ufactured goods demanded in the colonial heartland of New Spain, which together with Peru produced the precious metals accounting for over three-quarters of Spanish American exports to Europe.

The native communities of Yucatan were thus incorporated into the world economy through the encomienda, religious exactions, and the re-partimiento, all of which required payment in cotton textiles. At the local level, the Maya were also incorporated into a regional market economy. Here too there was considerable continuity between pre-conquest and co-lonial economic activities. In the *Relaciones* of 1579–81, many Spanish en-comenderos reported that the indigenous monetary system, based on ca-cao, continued to prevail throughout the peninsula, supporting the traditional trade in salt, cloth, honey, wax, and native foodstuffs, including venison, in village and urban markets. Moreover, some villages were said to specialize in a particular craft, such as sandal-making, wood-working, and canoe construction.[45] Cacao was the means of exchange among the Maya, and the Spaniards accepted the native monetary system because it facilitated the payment of wages and even purchases on the market in an economy suffering from a chronic shortage of metallic currency.[46]

Indeed, they not only accepted it but took advantage of the system to further their own interests. In fact, as Nancy Farriss has rightly argued, the colonists frequently used commercial exchange as a disguise for "appropriation by force." The repartimiento, after all, was in theory not extortion but business. And there is little doubt that peddlers and merchants often pressured the Indians into buying consumer goods and into selling foodstuffs at what were in effect confiscatory prices.[47]

But there is little doubt also that the Indians continued to carry on a thriving regional and local trade. As already noted, the encomenderos referred to the native people's many economic activities in their *Relaciones* of 1579–81. They are also described in an early-seventeenth-century work by Pedro Sánchez de Aguilar, a Yucatecan creole cleric who had been entrusted with an investigation into what the Spaniards referred to as idolatry, that is, the survival of Maya religion. He commented on the survival of the Indian economy as well, and noted that all the villages had mule drivers, blacksmiths, bridle- and saddle-makers, locksmiths, tailors, shoemakers, painters, fitters, joiners, and potters. Some of these professions had been introduced after the Conquest, but others are examples of traditional artisanry. Sánchez de Aguilar also noted that the Indians produced a large variety of goods, including cotton, meat, honey, and wax, "which they bring to this City [Mérida], to the plaza and market, from which activity they earn a lot of money."[48]

Putting aside the question of the morality of the methods the Spaniards used to extract wealth from Indian society, these methods were undoubtedly necessary for the maintenance of the colonial regime. It was therefore with considerable justification that the elite defended the institutions of colonialism as being essential for their survival. For in practice the first Spanish colonists found few productive enterprises to engage in. Production was almost a monopoly of the Maya.

Spanish Colonization

In the absence of precious metals and readily available natural resources in the region, the basis of the Spanish elite's wealth was Maya society itself. This fact helps explain why the encomienda lasted so long in Yucatan. That institution all but died out in most of Spanish America in the seventeenth century because the New Laws of 1542 had limited the inheritability of grants to two successive heirs after the death of the original encomendero, that is, for a total of three "lives"; on the death of the third holder, the encomienda was incorporated into the royal fiscal system. But the poverty of certain regions led the crown to modify the New Laws somewhat. In Yucatan, encomiendas were continually re-granted or distributed among a basic pool of recipients, that is, among the ruling class founded by the original conquerors. This modus vivendi between the crown and the elite continued until 1785, when the institution was finally abolished.[49]

Originally about 150 of the 200 Spanish conquerors of Yucatan received encomiendas. They settled themselves on the peninsula and founded cities in a pattern largely determined by considerations of their own security and of controlling the conquered population for the purpose of tribute collection. Thus on the west coast 30 encomenderos founded Campeche, on the east coast eight to ten settled at Bacalar, and in the interior 70 settled at Mérida and 39 at Valladolid. Within this semicircle of Spanish towns was enclosed the majority of the peninsula's Indian population.

As centers for the collection of the encomienda tribute paid by the conquered Maya, these towns tended to be established amid large concentrations of Indians. Bacalar is the exception to this rule, for after the Cupul uprising of 1546–47, and after the ravages of disease, the whole east coast was almost totally depopulated. Consequently, Bacalar never developed into a true urban center. But the other three early on became the focal points of economic exchange. Since almost no Spaniards participated in agriculture, all food except beef was produced by the Indians. The encomienda, therefore, served as an important mechanism for the provisioning of the urban population with foodstuffs.

Some Spaniards did of course attempt to develop sources of income other than encomiendas. Positions in the ecclesiastical bureaucracy were eagerly sought after, and consequently members of the local elite quickly challenged the Franciscans' monopoly of the Indian parishes. Eventually the crown gave in to this pressure and secularized some Franciscan benefices, thereby creating well-paying jobs for the creole clergy. But the secularization process was slow. In 1606 only 12 parishes were in the hands of the seculars, compared with the Franciscans' 28. More positions were created by dividing the benefices into smaller units, but even so by 1636 there were only 49 parishes, of which 35 were held by the Franciscans. By 1656 the total had risen to 52, but even then only 15 belonged to the seculars.[50] The Franciscans thus carried out a successful rear-guard action during the whole first century of the colonial regime. In practice, precious few positions opened up in the local Church. The Spanish colonists for the most part had to look elsewhere for sources of income.

Eventually, they found the solution to the problem in the land, in the establishment of ranches, plantations, and haciendas. But in the short run this was far from easy. Since geographic conditions did not permit the cultivation of wheat, barley, or rye, the small grain-producing farm, or *labor*, so typical of other parts of Spanish America in the sixteenth century,[51] never made an appearance in Yucatan. At the same time, Spaniards found it unprofitable to cultivate maize. The institutions of colonialism extracted all that was needed for domestic consumption from the Indians. As the City Council (*cabildo*) of Mérida explained in 1579, "Mérida is established in a region of four Indian provinces . . . and each province has many villages of native Indians with lords and governors who come to this city . . . and bring to it the necessary sustenance that the earth produces, with which we, the Spanish and foreign residents who live in it, sustain ourselves."[52] And Yucatan's distance from other Spanish American urban centers precluded production for export.

That is not to say that some of the first colonists did not make attempts to establish agricultural enterprises. As early as the 1530's the Adelantado (political-military commander) Francisco de Montejo founded a sugar plantation near Champotón, on the southwest coast. It was reported that he used the Indians of his encomienda of Champotón as laborers.[53] But when Montejo was stripped of his encomiendas in 1550, sugar production was abandoned. Because of the difficulty of acquiring cheap labor, little sugarcane was produced until late in the colonial period.

The scarcity of cheap labor was also the cause of the failure of the indigo (*añil*) industry. At first this seemed to be an enterprise with a great future. Commercial production by Spaniards, we are told by Cogolludo, was begun in 1550 by Fernando de Bracamonte, the encomendero of Tekit. Since the violet-blue dye was much in demand in Europe, other entrepreneurs followed suit and established their own *ingenios de añil* (indigo mills). By 1577 there were 48 such mills in operation, each reportedly worth between 2,000 and 3,000 pesos.[54]

The crown at first encouraged the industry, via a *real cédula* (royal order) of June 4, 1576. But then the horrors of indigo production came to light. Labor in the ingenios was strenuous, and the Maya died in large numbers. In fact, the native population decline seemed to be most acute in the indigo-producing areas. In response to protests lodged by the bishop, the Franciscans, and the Protector of the Indians (the head of the Tribunal de Indios), the crown on May 15, 1581, banned all Indian labor, voluntary or otherwise, in indigo production.[55] The political opposition of Church and state was too strong for the mill owners to overcome, and the indigo industry all but disappeared. As one Spaniard summarized the position of entrepreneurs in the early colonial era, "If the Indian is lacking, so is everything else."[56] Clearly, labor was the sine qua non of agricultural enterprise, and in sixteenth-century Yucatan there were precious few laborers who could be made to work on landed estates.

The Spaniards therefore had to limit themselves to activities that did not require a large labor force. The solution reached was probably the only one possible under the circumstances. The Maya population decline had resulted in a surplus of land, which the Spaniards began to put to use for stock-raising. Yet even here geographic conditions played a limiting role: since the hot and humid environment was unsuitable for sheep, the colonists had to concentrate on *ganado mayor*—horses, cattle, and mules. The enterprise proved to be relatively easy, for the barren land of Yucatan provides adequate pasture. Moreover, stock-raising was practical because it required very little labor. Finally, the sale of meat and hides provided a significant, although modest, income. As we will see, the establishment of estancias in the early years of settlement turned out to be the wave of the future.[57]

Nevertheless, during the first century of the colonial regime, the colonists engaged in little productive activity. With the exception of beef, subsistence goods were produced by the Maya. The same was true of trade goods, for the major exports—cotton textiles and wax—were again either exclusively or overwhelmingly the domain of the natives. This reality was well understood by contemporaries. As Diego de Contreras, encomendero of Nabalón, Tahcabó, and Cozumel, explained in 1579, "In this land there is a lack of all the things of Castile, namely, wine, oil, linens and other cloths, soap, and everything else . . . and the Spanish residents, encomenderos or otherwise, have no productive activities at all to carry out, because there are none . . . and were it not for the rent [*renta*] that the Indians give us, we would not live in [the land] . . . and we sustain ourselves with the maize that the Indians of our encomiendas give us, and some chickens, and every four months they give us some mantas of woven cotton, and these we sell to provide for our households, wives, children, and families."[58] The fundamentally parasitic nature of colonialism was also admitted by Cristóbal de San Martín, encomendero of Cansahcab, who after listing the tribute payments he received, went on to say that "all this the Indians acquire from what they harvest, which they sow and reap in their villages, [and] with these mantas and wax we pay the merchants for debts we owe them, and they [in turn] send all of this to New Spain in exchange for the merchandise they bring here."[59]

In other words, since the peninsula had neither gold nor silver to export, and since the Spaniards could not or would not produce anything themselves, they squeezed what they could out of the Maya. The goods thus extracted were exported to pay for imports of goods that could not be produced in Yucatan and that were earmarked exclusively for the Spanish population's consumption. The royal government entered the picture to get its share, by imposing taxes on the movement and sale of trade items and by collecting tribute from its own encomiendas.

In Yucatan, therefore, the major enterprise of the colonists was not production but commerce. Since the Spanish mercantile system required almost all goods to move from Yucatan to Veracruz and vice versa, and since Campeche was best situated to handle this trade, that city (technically, it was only a *villa*, or town) became the peninsula's major commercial center. As time went on, Campeche in fact came to rely overwhelmingly on commerce for its livelihood, for the native population declined much more severely in that area than around Mérida and Valladolid. The encomiendas of the Campeche jurisdiction eventually yielded very little income, and commerce was the only viable enterprise to replace what was lost through Indian demographic decline.

The Spanish residents of Campeche out of necessity learned to exploit the few commercial possibilities available. In addition to handling all the cotton textiles and wax exported and consumer goods imported, the merchants developed a small but significant commerce in salt and logwood (*palo de tinte*), both of which became, in the seventeenth century, substantial items of trade between Yucatan and New Spain. The dye extracted from the logwood in fact became the province's only direct export to European markets. To participate in this trade, ships were necessary, and the residents of Campeche soon discovered that the local wood was suitable for building oceangoing vessels. By the second half of the seventeenth century, Campeche's shipbuilding industry furnished some 6 percent of the merchantmen on the "Indies Run" between Spain and Spanish America. Though the local products were among the smallest of these trading vessels, Campeche's contribution to the carrying trade was significant.[60]

Not all Spanish cities in Yucatan prospered in the colonial era. Mérida, the provincial capital, did well because of government business and its ability to dominate internal commerce; most goods of the interior had to move through Mérida before going to Campeche. But Valladolid, isolated as it was from major maritime trade routes, stagnated. And Bacalar, near the east coast of Yucatan, had no possibilities at all as a port city, for apart from being far away from a sizable Indian population, it was on a dangerous lee shore. Ships did well to steer clear of that coast, and steer clear they did throughout the whole colonial period.

Commercial development in the colony took place within a distinctly Spanish mold. Not only was Spain's economy, like that of most European countries before the rise of modern capitalism, characterized by substantial governmental intervention regulating and directing commercial exchange, but the colonists brought with them a strong municipal tradition growing out of the uncertainties of extending settlement in conquered territory and controlling a potentially hostile people in the central and southern parts of their own country during the Reconquista. Consequently, city governments, though weakened politically by the time of Ferdinand and Isabella, had come to possess considerable economic power at the local level.

This was to be of special importance in Spanish America. First, the complex of economic regulations so permeated the economic structure that they eventually formed a kind of ancien régime—a body of obsolete practices and institutions that hindered modern economic development and would therefore eventually have to be eliminated, as they were in the nineteenth century.[61] Second, since many of these regulations even in Spain sealed the city's domination of its hinterland, the effect in America, with its Spanish urban centers and Indian hinterland, was to strengthen Spanish domination of the native people.[62]

In America, as in Spain, therefore, it was the cabildo that instituted controls over the surrounding countryside and over urban commerce. The restrictions on trade were rational attempts to solve the very real problem of an uncertain supply of the goods necessary for the very survival of the cities. The methods employed included export prohibitions, protective tariffs, curtailing the activities of hoarders, engrossers, and middlemen, and price-fixing for many articles of consumption. In time of need, municipal governments organized the purchase of grain from abroad, exacted loans from citizens to pay for such imports, granted bonuses and credits to importers, and instituted controls on consumption by prohibiting resales and hence speculation, ordering the stockpiling of goods, and instituting rationing. Finally, the goal of provisioning the city coincided with the policy of preventing fraud by enforcing quality controls on consumer goods, especially through the use of standardized weights and measures.[63]

This, then, was the framework in which commercial exchange took place in colonial Yucatan. Of course, the system did not always accomplish its goals, for in one important case—meat—the producers were Spaniards who had important political connections. Ranchers in fact were always well represented on the cabildo, the very institution responsible for the protection of consumers. But almost all other foodstuffs were produced by the Indians, and consequently it was relatively easy for the city councils to favor urban consumers over rural producers. Spanish rule in America was frequently shaped less by the purported functions of institutions than by the nature of colonialism, that is, Spanish domination of the Indians.

An analysis of the colonists' economic activities during the first century of the colonial regime thus demonstrates what all contemporaries frankly admitted: the Spanish Commonwealth lived overwhelmingly at the expense of the Maya. To be sure, the conquerors and their descendants, as well as later immigrants, did develop productive enterprises. But these would become significant only later in the colonial period. In the meantime, the essence of colonialism was taking from the Indian to give to the Spaniard. As the already cited encomendero had put it, "were it not for the rent that the Indians give us, we would not live" in Yucatan. And thus the situation would remain until the eighteenth century.

PART TWO

The Colonial Regime, 1648-1730

CHAPTER THREE

Maya Society

THE TIME HAS NOW come to refer to the calamities and hardships that this kingdom of Yucatan has suffered since the year 1648, and if one were to go into all the fine details, one could write an entire volume about nothing else."[1] So wrote the Franciscan Diego López de Cogolludo in 1656 as he reflected on the terrible impact of the epidemics that had begun to strike the peninsula in the previous decade.

The demographic history of Yucatan in the century after the European invasion diverged considerably from the pattern evident in central Mexico. In both areas (as everywhere else in the Americas), the native population diminished rapidly after the initial contact with Europeans. But in Yucatan the population began to recover in the late sixteenth or early seventeenth century, whereas in central Mexico the decline, though stopped, had not yet reversed. Then, in the mid-seventeenth century, the direction of the movement changed on both sides: a series of events began in Yucatan that resulted in a substantial decline of the native population, while the Indians of Mexico were entering a period of long-term demographic expansion. The trends in the two areas could not have been more different.[2]

Why did central Mexico and Yucatan follow diverging historical paths? Sherburne Cook and Woodrow Borah ascribe the difference in part to differences in rainfall and surface moisture.[3] But in fact the two areas have very similar rainfall patterns. They are different only with respect to climate and relative humidity: central Mexico has cool winters and dry air; Yucatan has warm winters and a relative humidity 10–20 percent higher than in central Mexico.[4] Science therefore confirms what any observer can plainly see: highland Mexico is semiarid and even has desertlike flora, while Yucatan, which in some years receives even less rain than the highlands, has a lush and green appearance throughout most of the year. The climate of the peninsula is not truly tropical for, as we saw earlier, the average rainfall in northern Yucatan is below 150 centimeters. The important factor is the high relative humidity.

These environmental conditions had an important impact on historical demography. First, since the mortality from smallpox tends to be greater in cold and/or dry climates than in warmer, humid areas, this disease probably killed a greater proportion of the population of the Mexican plateau.[5] It is also possible that the impact of the other epidemic diseases in sixteenth-century America—measles, typhus, pneumonic plague, and hepatitis—was determined to a certain extent by environmental factors. This could help explain why Yucatan's native population did not continue to decline into the seventeenth century, and why demographic recovery began earlier than in central Mexico. In any case, considering the wide variety of different environments in America, it is clear that the Mexican "model" of historical demography cannot be mechanically applied everywhere.

The Demographic Crisis of the Seventeenth Century

In the seventeenth century, a new disease that had no effect on central Mexico[6] devastated Yucatan. This was yellow fever, which had previously been absent from the Western Hemisphere because its vector, the *Aëdes aegypti* mosquito (of African origin), had not yet managed to infest the Americas. But it eventually succeeded in doing so, for it found an ideal breeding ground in the many American lowland areas of high humidity. Yucatan was one of the first places affected. Yellow fever, however, was not merely one more Old World disease. Till now, New World epidemics had devastated only the Indian population, for the invaders had developed some immunity to diseases infesting their own homelands. But few Europeans had any exposure to yellow fever, so that they were just as susceptible to the disease as the Indians. In fact, the Bight of Benin, the part of the African coast frequented by slave traders, became known as "the White Man's Grave" because of the heavy mortality caused by yellow fever. The disease was so fatal to non-Africans that it effectively prevented the European colonization of tropical Africa for over four centuries.[7] And in the New World, epidemics eventually broke out from Boston to Buenos Aires. Therefore Yucatan's demographic history, while diverging from that of central Mexico, may have converged with that of other parts of the Americas.[8]

With the outbreak of 1648, Yucatan embarked on a new historical era. Yellow fever appeared first in Campeche in June—just after the beginning of the rainy season. Presumably the rains had produced a swarm of mosquitoes, as they still do in Yucatan. The news of the pestilence was so ominous that the governor, thinking to beseech divine protection, ordered the image of the Virgin of Izamal brought to the capital. But neither the miraculous statue nor the prayers of the multitudes could stop this horseman of the Apocalypse. The plague was in Mérida by August, and in Valladolid by September. In its wake were thousands of dead, including the governor; the Provincial and two former Provincials of the Franciscans; the Guardians of both the Franciscan convents in Mérida, as well as 20 resident friars; more than half the priests of the Cathedral Chapter; and the rector of the Jesuit seminary, along with six of eight seminarians. The toll among the Spaniards was so heavy that at first it was thought the Indians would be spared. Inevitably, one of the natives began to proclaim that all the Spaniards would die, and the Indians would finally be left alone; he was quickly locked up, and in any case proved wrong. The epidemic spared no one and soon struck the villages with force.

Cogolludo, who survived a bout with the fever and believed that the pestilence was divine punishment for the sins of mankind, made what must be considered a classic description of the symptoms, and even noted the existence of different varieties of the disease: "Most commonly the victim came down with a severe, intense headache and an aching of the bones so violent that he felt he was disintegrating or being crushed by great weights. Shortly thereafter he ran a high fever, usually, but not always, causing delirium. This was followed by vomiting of what appeared to be rotten blood, which few people survived. Others did not vomit, but rather came down with severe colic, which ended up producing what is called dysentery, while others had no bowel movement at all, and many suffered fever with aching bones without any other symptoms." To make matters worse, the novelty of the disease caused confusion. "It is not possible to say what kind of plague it was," wrote Cogolludo, "because the doctors have no knowledge of it." Treatment, then, was improvised and was of such a nature at times as to hasten death.[9]

The epidemic lasted two years before abating. But another horseman of the Apocalypse—famine—rode in on its heels in 1652 after a poor harvest and caused many more fatalities. Then, in 1654, a smallpox epidemic broke out.[10] In the ensuing years, yellow fever continued to ravage the peninsula and was often followed, or preceded, by famine and malnutrition. Outbreaks of the plague were reported in 1694, 1698, 1699, 1711–15, and 1727–29 (although measles may have been the culprit in the last case).[11] Indeed, yellow fever continued to haunt Yucatan until the early twentieth century. The disease therefore played a long-term role in the demographic history of the peninsula. And in the short-run—the second half of the seventeenth century—the effects were devastating.

According to Cogolludo, approximately half the population died between 1648 and 1656.[12] This, of course, was merely a guess, but he may have been close to the mark. M. C. García Bernal has studied the seventeenth-century population decline in some detail. By her estimates, summarized in Table 3.1, epidemics and famine wiped out something on

TABLE 3.1
The Indian Population of Yucatan, 1643–1700

Year	Indian tributaries	Approximate Indian population
1643	61,526	209,188
1666	36,020	108,060
1688	33,314	99,942
1700	–	130,000

SOURCE: García Bernal, Yucatán: Población y encomienda, pp. 87–143, 159–63 (including Table 10, p. 160).

the order of 48 percent of the Indians between the 1640's and the 1660's. Moreover, the disaster caused a concomitant decline in the average size of Maya families.[13] The population then continued to diminish, reaching its nadir in the late seventeenth century; the level in 1688 was perhaps only 48 percent of that of the 1640's.[14]

As for the effects on the Spanish population, Marta Hunt has thrown some light on the subject by analyzing Cathedral baptismal records. These reveal that what had been a sharply rising curve of Spanish births flattened out between 1648 and 1660—the result, presumably, of the deaths of wives and husbands, the postponement of marriage, and miscarriages—and then began to move upward again.[15] The Spanish population therefore did not suffer the effects of the crisis for as long a period as the Indians. In part this was due to a steady stream of new immigrants, which helped the population to make up losses faster than the Indians could. But Spaniards also had a much better chance of surviving famine, because when the price of food rose sharply, only those with money could afford to buy. Supply and demand were thus balanced, and those without money—the poor Indians—simply starved.

Of course, as already noted, population estimates for Yucatan are always distorted to some degree by the migrations to and from the region to the south, which was beyond colonial control. Whenever plague or famine broke out, many Indians simply trekked to that area with whatever they could carry. This region also attracted many Indians who ran away from what contemporaries called the extortions of excessively greedy government officials and priests. Every now and then the colonial authorities organized Indian-catching expeditions, called entradas, to bring the runaways back. The entrada of 1652, composed of three different columns, netted some 22,000 Indians, who were brought back to replenish the depleted villages; but many of these returnees took flight at the first opportunity and again disappeared from the tribute rolls.[16] Other expeditions followed and perhaps had more success.

Despite the distorted nature of the data, the general outlines of Yucatan's demographic history are clear. The Maya began to recoup their losses near the end of the seventeenth century. The recovery in central Mexico thus antedated Yucatan's by almost half a century and presumably slowed down sooner as well.[17] Once again Yucatan followed a separate path.

The period under discussion, 1648–1730, ended as it began: in demographic crisis caused by plague and famine. Before the population could fully recover to its pre-1648 level, one last major epidemic struck. It followed in the wake of a famine stemming from the poor harvest of 1726. The disease was either yellow fever or measles, or possibly both. Together, plague and famine once more carried off a large number of people. The Tribunal de Indios reported in 1728 that 17,000 Indians had died in the past year.[18] The epidemic lasted into 1729.

All the same, the effects of this crisis were not nearly so severe as in the period after 1648. Even if 17,000 Indians died, this would have been less than 15 percent of the population of 1700. Cook and Borah, using fairly reliable data, estimate the 1736 population at 127,000.[19] As García Bernal points out, this is convincing evidence that the trend, evident after 1648, of diminishing Indian population had been reversed. This time plague and famine, rather than beginning a decline of *longue durée*, merely interrupted an ongoing trend of demographic expansion.[20] The 1727–29 epidemic thus signaled the end of an era. There would be outbreaks of pestilence in the future, but these would be largely local in scope. During the rest of the colonial period, the specter that would haunt Yucatan would be not plague but famine.

The Problem of Controlling the Maya

It had not been easy to conquer the Maya of Yucatan. It was even more difficult to control them afterward. To be sure, important changes were imposed by brute force, and the Indians were subjected to colonial authority whether they liked it or not. Nevertheless, within certain limits, the Maya exercised a kind of freedom. Since they were overwhelmingly agriculturalists, they frequently had to leave their villages to work in their fields to produce what both Spaniards and Indians needed for survival. Moreover, colonialism itself forced the natives to leave their villages for extended periods of time, for the wax repartimiento required people to wander in the bush for weeks on end in search of beehives. Finally, even in the Indian villages the Spanish presence was weak. Most pueblos did not have resident priests, for the clerics usually resided in the larger villages and visited the outlying settlements only periodically. Spanish civil authority outside the cities was practically nonexistent; the only perma-

nent officials who resided in the villages were the dozen or so war captains, whose presence would have affected only a very small minority of
Indians. In short, colonialism could not eliminate all vestiges of freedom.
The Maya in fact moved about with little interference from the authorities, and sometimes they failed to come back.[21]

The Montaña

Adding to the movement of the people, natural in a peasant economy,
was the existence of the open frontier to the south, beyond colonial control and an attractive haven for many Indians. The Spaniards called this
region the Montaña—a strange choice of word, given the area's almost
uniformly low terrain. In fact, except for the low mountain range in the
extreme southeastern part of the peninsula, in modern Belize, there is almost nothing even approximating a hill, let alone a mountain, between
the southernmost Yucatecan village of Dzibalchén (said to be "at the foot
of the Mountain") and the highlands of Guatemala, a distance of over 250
miles. Practically all the other villages were over 300 miles from real
mountains. The Montaña, rather, was in the mind of the Spaniards. To
people of Mediterranean culture, mountains were not exclusively topo-
graphic features. They were refuges, places difficult to to control, and, in
Fernand Braudel's words, regions of a "separate religious geography,"
wherein "devil worship" and "magic" were performed. Populations
were small, dispersed, and often inclined to banditry and other forms of
antisocial behavior. The mountains were a land of freedom.[22] And to
Spaniards, in Yucatan as in Europe, freedom was a bad word.

Southern Yucatan was independent of Spanish colonialism for more
than a century and a half after the conquest of the northern states. Nice
as it would be to impute that fact to the Maya's extraordinarily intense
resistance to colonialism, it is hard to avoid the conclusion that this independence, like that of the Amazon rain forest region east of the Andes,
was simply the result of the area's lack of attractiveness to Spaniards.
Conquest would have required the outlay of funds needed elsewhere and
would have produced no economic benefits beyond the capture of some
runaways from the north. The population was extremely dispersed and
so scant that a colonial settlement would have required subsidies to survive. Consequently, Spanish authorities entrusted the matter to the Franciscans, who undertook a purely spiritual conquest. But in the long run,
the spirit was not enough. Force was the sine qua non of the subjugation
of the Montaña.

The Maya of the region, although politically independent, were by no
means isolated from the Spanish colony to the north. Trade between the
two halves of the peninsula took place on a regular basis. The free Maya
traded cacao for various kinds of consumer goods and even Christian re-

ligious paraphernalia.[23] Moreover, the south was the constant recipient of northern runaways, who sometimes served as the leaders of the syncretic religious practices developing in this region of a "separate religious geography." The Montaña, then, maintained a symbiotic relationship with the colonial society to the north.[24]

Apart from the occasional entrada, the Spanish authorities left this zone to go its own way in the early colonial years; once these expeditionary forces withdrew, everything returned to normal.[25] In the second half of the seventeenth century, however, the problem of the unconquered Maya became more important to the Spanish government. Three developments accounted for the new interest. First, the epidemics and famine had increased the number of fugitives from the north escaping to the Montaña. Second, in the 1660's the Indians of the Sahcabchén region, south of the port of Campeche, fled their villages to escape from the excessive repartimientos imposed by the rapacious governor, Rodrigo Flores de Aldana.[26] This left part of the Campeche coast without an Indian society to sustain the colonial regime. Finally, this circumstance coincided with a renewed threat of buccaneer attacks and the possibility that the depopulated coastal area would become a base for pirate operations against Spanish shipping or for the exploitation of the area's logwood resources.[27]

The royal government therefore began to take more vigorous action. In 1678, after a frontier rebellion had caused the death of 14 Spaniards, including an encomendero, Governor Antonio de Layseca Alvarado sent a punitive expedition against the independent Maya capital of Tipu. This apparently was no ordinary entrada, for more Indians were killed than were captured. Tipu was forced to sue for peace, and the expedition then withdrew.[28] The Montaña was not conquered, but the natives thereafter made less trouble for the Spaniards. Governor Layseca also sent expeditions to dislodge French and English pirates from Dzilam (on the north coast) and from the Bay of Campeche.[29]

Another large-scale entrada was mounted in 1686–87. This was led by Captain Juan del Castillo y Toledo, a Spanish-born adventurer, soldier, and entrepreneur who had come to Yucatan in the 1660's as a hanger-on of Governor Flores de Aldana. The forces under Castillo's command totaled 132 Spaniards and 145 Indians, the latter consisting of two companies raised in Oxkutzcab and Tekax, as well as a complement of 23 *Indios Hidalgos*. The entrada lasted six months. In all, Castillo created eight new villages by "reducing" 14 settlements and appointing caciques to rule over the 956 Indians who were inducted into the colonial regime. The expedition then went home, presumably taking prisoners along. The entrada cost 3,073 pesos, a sum that helps explain why governors were reluctant to mount such essentially futile expeditions.[30]

Still, at the end of the century the crown authorized a massive com-

paign to conquer the last independent Maya states once and for all. Expeditions were launched simultaneously from Yucatan and Guatemala,
and in 1697 the Indians of Petén Itzá, the last holdout of the free Maya,
were finally forced to submit to Spanish rule.[31] But the elimination of the
independent Maya states and the founding of a string of missions to unite
the northern and southern halves of the peninsula did not put an end to
emigration and flight from the northern villages. The Spanish fort built
on the island in Lake Petén Itzá served less to control the Indians than to
punish Spaniards sent there from Guatemala to languish in what was essentially a penal colony. Indians moved into and about the region at will,
and would continue to do so for centuries. In the 1840's, for example, the
engineers constructing a road from Champotón to Bacalar, right across
the peninsula, reported that the area was filled with numerous small, clandestine settlements. The state government even appointed an official with
orders "to discover the occult settlements in the mountains" to the south.
In short, neither Spanish nor Mexican authority could stop the free movement of people to the frontier and beyond civil and ecclesiastical control.
The real subjugation of the free Maya would not come until the twentieth
century.[32]

Reducción and Dispersion

Colonial authorities thus found that the Indian society around them,
although conquered, would sometimes slip through their fingers. For colonialism attempted to make the natives live in a manner that was culturally foreign and economically impractical. It is well known that Spaniards
came to America with very specific and rigid ideas on what constituted
civilization. In essence, they adhered strictly to the etymological origins
of the word: civis meant, in Latin, city. For the colonists, whose cultural
origins were greatly influenced by the Greco-Roman tradition, civilization meant the polis, city life, the constant interaction between humans as
members of a society. This interest in humans was so extreme in the colonists' culture that of all the Europeans who visited America and East Asia
before 1650, Spaniards perhaps showed the least interest in observing and
describing the physical environment. They were, in the words of a modern Jesuit, "deficient in naturalistic observation."[33]

From this point of view, a settlement pattern in which people frequently chose to live in tiny hamlets scattered all over the landscape was
pure barbarism. But the pattern was hardly unique to the Maya; it was
typical of practically all of North, Central, and South America. Only a
few areas—such as the Valley of Mexico—were characterized by concentrated settlements.[34] Moreover, the American environment was so inviting to the dispersal of the population that it was capable at times of transforming European culture, as in the case of the English colonists in east-

ern North America. To this day Spaniards and Hispanic Mexicans find the frequent Anglo-American preference for living isolated from the city, on mountaintops, in the woods, and on ranches, positively perverse.

Consequently, as colonialists will always do, the Spaniards decided to impose "civilization" regardless of what the natives thought about the subject. This they sought to do through the policy of reducción, which began to be carried out in Yucatan sometime after 1552.[35] The Franciscans, who were entrusted with implementing the program, rounded up the people residing in hamlets and small villages and forced them to move into larger settlements, where they would be, as it was said, *bajo de campana* ("beneath the [church] bells").

In theory reducción was to affect only small settlements. In practice, however, this was not always the case. Villages of substantial size were sometimes destroyed, and the people moved to other sites for reasons known only to the friars. For example, a village in Campeche called Nunkiní, which in 1543 had 480 tributaries (about 2,160 people), was "reduced" sometime in the 1550's or 1560's, its inhabitants being moved to Calkiní. A settlement known as Chaltunhá, which had 550 tributaries (2,475 people) in 1549, was resettled in Izamal.[36] According to a 1582 list of parish *cabeceras* (chief villages) and *visitas* (auxiliary villages), 47 villages had by then been moved to a different site.[37] But this figure not only fails to include hamlets that were "reduced"; it is also incomplete in regard to entire villages that were relocated.[38]

Disruptive as resettlement was, reducción worked a worse hardship on its victims: it interfered with important elements of Maya culture.[39] Spaniards mistook settlement pattern for social structure and assumed that the natives belonged to a social unit embracing all members of a village or settlement. In short, they saw Indians fundamentally as villagers. But the Maya saw themselves only partially as members of villages. They also belonged to subdivisions of villages called *cuchteelob* (sing.: *cuchteel*), units that were frequently more significant to them than the village as a whole. Perhaps more important, the Maya saw themselves as members of lineages, or *ch'ibalob* (sing.: *ch'ibal*), that is, social units comprising people of real or fictive ancestry, and their allegiances to these too were frequently stronger than their allegiance to their villages. In fact, the Indians' ties to their villages were usually more than offset by their more important loyalties to cuchteel or ch'ibal. Maya settlements, therefore, were anything but homogeneous. Very rarely did all members of a ch'ibal live together at the same site; usually they resided in several villages. By the same token, settlements were made up not of one lineage but of several different lineages.[40]

This was the reality the colonialists did not understand when they imposed the reducción policy. To them, all natives were alike, and so it never occurred to them that the people who were "reduced" might not take kindly to the inhabitants of the settlements to which they were relocated, or that the people who were already inhabiting a settlement might not welcome newcomers. Only after the fact did the Spaniards discover that not all the "reduced" settlements were viable village units. In effect, they were forced to admit that all Indians were not alike, and that native society had organizing principles that could not easily be ignored. In the end, the colonial authorities often found it necessary to allow different social groups occupying the same site to maintain their independence from one another. These separate units, which became known as *parcialidades*, had their own churches and governments, and were considered individual pueblos. Some parcialidades had their origins in a pre-Conquest cuchteel that continued to occupy the same site after the Spanish invasion, and others resulted from the reducción policy of moving one entire pueblo into another. In both cases, their very existence demonstrates that the Spaniards had to adapt their policy to the reality of Indian society. Maya culture and social organization could not be obliterated at will.

An extreme case of this failed policy is Calkiní, a site to which nine different settlements were moved. Out of this chaos emerged six distinct parcialidades.[41] Of course, not all settlements survived as independent entities. Sometimes newcomers were absorbed by the original inhabitants, or perhaps the newcomers absorbed the original inhabitants. Still, as Table 3.2 demonstrates, at least 69 parcialidades—remnants of Post-Classic social and political units—continued to exist into the eighteenth century.[42]

The reducción policy's shaky foundation was further undermined by the Spaniards' failure to take account of the nature of the peasant economy, or better stated, agriculture carried out in the ecological conditions of Yucatan. As we have seen, then, as now, agriculturalists required large quantities of land but kept only a small proportion cultivated. As a result, they had to walk great distances to work in their fields. Inevitably people built temporary quarters near their milpas to avoid the long walk from their village to their fields. At some point, these temporary residences might then be converted into permanent satellite communities of the home pueblo, and those satellites could then serve as staging areas for colonization even farther from the home village.[43]

For this reason alone, the reducción policy was certain to fail in the long run. The dedicated Franciscans of the sixteenth century could gather up the people of the scattered settlements and make them live in nucleated villages. But only an army of occupation could have kept them there. Peasants had to move in and out of their villages in accordance with the natural rhythm of their agricultural economy, and once beyond the prying eyes of the priests, they could, if they so chose, build temporary,

TABLE 3.2
Village Parcialidades, 1700–1722

Village	Parcialidades	Source
Acanceh	Acanceh, Acanceh Cheltún	1
Bécal	Nohcacab Bécal, Bécal	
	Santa María	1, 2
Calkiní	Calkiní Kinlacam, Kucab,	
	Halachó Calkiní, Cihó	
	Nunkiní, Calkinillo	1, 2
Chichimilá	Chichimilá, Chibxul	1, 2
Cuzamá	?	2
Dzitbalché	San Antonio, San Joseph,	
	San Francisco	1, 2
Hecelchakán	?	2
Homún	?	2
Hunucmá	Hunucmá, Sihomchén,	
	Yabucú	2
Izamal	Izamal, Pomolché	1, 2
Kanxoc	Tulumché Kanxoc,	
	Kauván Kanxoc	2
Kinchil	Kinchil, Dzeme	2
Mama	San Antonio, San Juan	2
Nohcacab	Santa Bárbara, San Mateo	2
Oxkutzcab	Oxkutzcab, Yaxá-Kumché	
	Oxkutzcab	2
Pocmuch	?	2
Popolá	Popolá Duque, Popolá	
	Magaña	1, 2
Sacalaca	?	3
Sotuta	Sotuta, Yaxá Sotuta,	
	Sotuta Kom	2
Sucilá	Sucilá, Yokchec	4
Tahdzibichén	San Joseph, Santo Tomás	2
Tahmuy	Tahmuy, Yaxcabá Tahmuy	2
Tekit	San Francisco, San Pedro	2
Tekom	?	2
Temozón	Temozón, Temozón Braga	2
Tepakán	Tepakán, Mopilá Tepakán	2
Tixculum	Tixculum, Tixkoch	1, 2
Tizimín	Tizimín, Cacauché,	
	Dzonotchayl	2
Tunkás	?	2
Umán	Umán, Dzibikal, Dzibikak	2

SOURCES: (1) AGI, México 1035, Certificaciones originales de los agravios irreparables y Vejaciones impuestos . . . (1700), no fol.; (2) AGI, Escribanía de Cámara 327, Causa criminal . . . contra el Tesorero de la Santa Cruzada (1716), fols. 9–285; (3) AGI, Escribanía de Cámara 323A, Residencia de Fernando y Alonso Meneses Bravo de Sarabia, Pesquisa en Mérida (1721), fols. 529–44; (4) AGI, México 1039, Testimonio no. 4 (1722).

and eventually permanent, settlements without the knowledge of the Spanish authorities.

As a result, as time went on the Maya ever so gradually reversed the reducción policy imposed by their colonial masters. Many people simply moved from one settlement to another regardless of what the colonial authorities wanted them to do. Others moved beyond the pale of colonialism and took refuge in the Montaña. In short, the Maya of colonial Yucatan seem to have moved all over the place, in order to use their resources more conveniently, to seek opportunity elsewhere, or to escape from the colonial regime altogether.[44] Indeed, in the final analysis, we will surely never be able to account in full for the extraordinary geographic mobility of the Maya. The motives were sometimes known only to the Indians themselves.

In any event, the policy of reducción was gradually undone. As time passed the Spanish authorities realized that the Maya were slipping through their fingers. This had become obvious to Bishop Diego Vázquez de Mercado as early as 1605. Since the solution he proposed, that the natives be forced to plant their milpas "near and around their houses,"[45] was plainly impossible, the authorities put pressure on the caciques to stop the dispersal. But apparently this was beyond their power. As Cogolludo put it, the Indians "are extremely fond of passing their time in the bush and out in their fields," and would do so "for almost the whole year if allowed."[46]

By the late seventeenth century, many Maya had succeeded in circumventing Spanish policy. As Table 3.3, which includes information reported by the Franciscans for 23 of the guardianías, or parishes, under their control, shows, in 1700 about 12 percent of the Indians resided not in the villages but on estancias, sitios (less-developed cattle-raising estates), or ranchos (unauthorized settlements). The friars' report certainly understates the proportion of people living outside the villages, for though it includes those living on estancias, who to a certain extent could be counted, it leaves out most of the ones on the ranchos. Only 11 years later, the Tribunal de Indios reported that 33,764 Indians fourteen years of age and older were living fuera de campana, that is, in unauthorized settlements.[47] By the Spaniards' own reckoning, then, a sizable number of Indians, probably a fourth of the total, were now living outside of the authorized villages. The proportion living in dispersed settlements would of course have varied from region to region.

Information on this subject is hard to come by, for officials found it difficult to count the people in the unauthorized settlements. But some documents produced in the course of a thorough investigation of repartimiento abuses in 1716 give some insight into the settlement pattern of two areas, Valladolid and Tizimín. Since in those regions textiles tended

TABLE 3.3
Proportion of Indians Living Outside
Authorized Settlements, 1700

Franciscan parish (guardianía)	Indios de confesión	Indians living on estancias, sitios, or ranchos	
		No.	Pct. of total
Mérida	2,162	968	44.8%
Conkal	1,632	168	10.3
Motul	2,276	176	7.7
Cacalchén	880	48	5.5
Teya	848	8	0.9
Dzidzantún	1,138	228	20.0
Temax	900	176	19.6
Cansahcab	782	34	4.3
Izamal	1,352	139	10.3
Campeche	981	196	20.0
Bolonchén	1,167	172	14.7
Calkiní	2,264	194	8.6
Bécal	1,585	113	7.1
Maxcanú	1,729	107	6.2
Maní	2,379	173	7.3
Ticul	2,442	210	8.6
Oxkutzcab	3,112	474	15.2
Tekax	2,987	265	8.9
Muna	1,323	633	47.8
Sisal (Valladolid)	3,678	44	1.2
Uayma	1,573	222	14.1
Chichimilá	2,629	30	1.1
Tixcacalcupul	1,368	56	4.1
All 23 parishes	41,187	4,834	11.7%

SOURCE: AGI, México 1035, Matrícula y razón individual del número fijo de los indios tributarios . . . , 28 June 1700.

NOTE: The count covers only those old enough to make confession and receive absolution.

to be contracted primarily in the villages, we must turn to the data on the wax repartimiento, which was carried out in all settlements, to determine roughly what proportion of (male) Indians lived *fuera de campana*. Table 3.4 summarizes the information by parish.

Of course, the data are likely to be flawed, for it is certain that the repartimiento was not always carried out on a per capita basis, as it was supposed to be. But since the same person contracted the wax in all the settlements in Table 3.4, we can assume that even the abuses were fairly consistent. In short, it is likely that the information has internal consistency and is thus a fair, if rough, guide to the settlement patterns of the Indian population.

Even allowing for inaccuracies in the data, Table 3.4 illustrates a dispersed settlement pattern in the parishes of Navalam, Kikil, and Chemax,

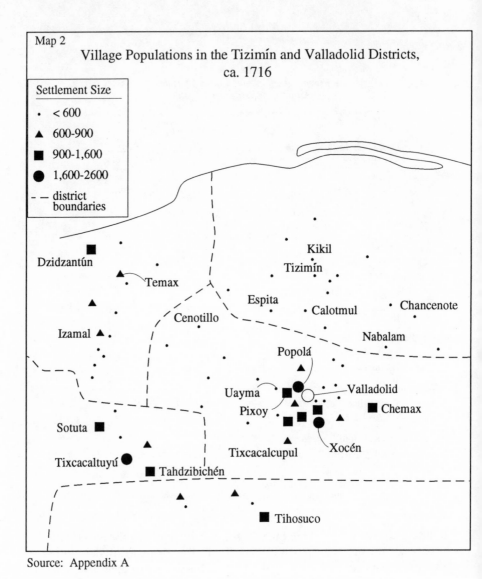

Map 2

Village Populations in the Tizimín and Valladolid Districts, ca. 1716

Settlement Size

- • < 600
- ▲ 600-900
- ■ 900-1,600
- ● 1,600-2600
- – – district boundaries

Dzidzantún

Temax

Kikil

Tizimín

Espita

Cenotillo

Calotmul

Chancenote

Izamal

Nabalam

Popolá

Uayma

Valladolid

Pixoy

Chemax

Sotuta

Tixcacalcupul

Xocén

Tixcacaltuyú

Tahdzibichén

Tihosuco

Source: Appendix A

TABLE 3.4
*Provenance of Wax Contracted in the Valladolid and Tizimín Regions Under the
Repartimiento of the Santa Cruzada, 1716*

Parish cabecera	Number of visitas	Villages		Estancias/ranchos	
		Pounds of wax	Pct. of total	Pounds of wax	Pct. of total
Chichimilá	4	1,950	89.0%	241	11.0%
Tixcacalcupul	1	700	77.0	209	23.0
Uayma	3	780	73.6	280	26.4
Cenotillo	2	775	72.1	300	27.9
Tizimín	4[a]	725	69.6	317	30.4
Nabalam	3	600	56.0	471	44.0
Kikil	4[b]	718	55.8	568	44.2
Chemax	0	400	51.6	375	48.4
Calotmul	2	550	47.5	608	52.5
Espita	0	250	22.4	866	77.6
Chancenote	2	125	15.0	699	85.0

SOURCE: AGI, Escribanía de Cámara 327, Causa criminal . . . contra el Tesorero de la Santa Cruzada (1716), fols. 65–208.
[a]Komilchén and Dzonot Aké, though called ranchos in the documents, are counted as visitas because of Cogolludo's classification.
[b]Loché, though called a rancho in the documents, is counted as a visita because of Cogolludo's classification.

and an extremely dispersed one in Calotmul, Espita, and Chancenote (Map 2). In these areas to the north and east of the villa of Valladolid, well over one-quarter of the Indians, and sometimes well over half, lived *fuera de campana*. At the same time, a concentrated settlement pattern was evident in the parish of Chichimilá, and to a lesser extent in Uayma and Tixcacalcupul. What the state of affairs was elsewhere cannot be determined, but one thing is certain: the dispersed settlement pattern was also of considerable concern to the Maya authorities. The native elite lost power and wealth when people of their villages emigrated. Moreover, those who stayed were forced to bear a heavier burden of taxes and labor services. Consequently, when given the opportunity, the Indian governments complained about dispersal and requested the Spanish authorities to carry out new rounds of reducción.[48] But the problem was even more vexing to the Spaniards, who saw great danger in people "living in their freedom, without being subject to Justice." Beyond the pale of civilization, the Indians were believed to engage in incest and ritual drinking, and to be dedicated to "idolatry" and to "killing each other in revenge as a result of their passions, throwing the dead bodies in caves, and raising their children without Christian doctrine."[49] Perhaps all this was true. But what could be done about it?

On occasion new reducciones were carried out. Governor Juan Joseph de Bárcena undertook one in 1688–89 in the Chancenote area, and his efforts were later praised at his *residencia* (trial for conduct in office). But as Table 3.4 shows, and as Governor Antonio de Cortaire testified 30 years later, the Indians soon dispersed, and the situation returned to normal.[50] Governor Cortaire in turn attempted reducciones, but with no better success. Cortaire blamed his failure in part on the refusal of local priests to cooperate in implementing the policy.[51] Bishop Juan Gómez de Parada thought the blame should fall instead on the Governor's abusive repartimientos. But he could not come up with a better solution than to promulgate a new synodical constitution for the diocese, in which he reminded the natives that they were forbidden to live in scattered settlements, and to recommend that the authorities "try to persuade [the dispersed Indians], and if necessary force them, by means of their caciques in accordance with what has been established by Royal Law and the [Episcopal] Councils of Lima and Mexico, to live together, in a concentrated manner, in unified villages, helping them to understand the benefits resulting from such sociable life."[52]

Moral exhortation, however, was no substitute for action. Governor Cortaire's successor, Antonio de Figueroa, reported that the situation had not improved at all. Indians continued to desert their villages to such an extent that he knew of cases in which the only people left in some pueblos were "the cacique, three or four old Indian men, and a few unhappy abandoned women, the young people living in the bush on estancias, sitios and *milperías* [unauthorized settlements], wherein they live free from the rule of a cacique, are not reprimanded by their *alcaldes* [magistrates], and are not even seen by the priests except when the latter collect their taxes."[53] But at least Figueroa, unlike his predecessors, recognized his inability to solve the problem and hence did nothing. The colonial authorities finally despaired of ever getting the Indians to live the way they wanted them to.

Settlement Patterns

Figueroa's cases notwithstanding, the Franciscans' survey of 1700 suggests that the great majority of the Maya lived in authorized villages.[54] By their count, 71,677 Indians then lived in the 105 rural settlements under their charge. Each village thus had an average of 683 people. But because of the relatively large number of small settlements, the median was only 571; and fully one-fourth of all villages had fewer than 250 people.

All the same, as Table 3.5 shows, most of the Maya lived in relatively large villages. Half lived in settlements of 902 or more, and a fourth in villages of 1,600 or more. At the other extreme, only one-quarter lived in settlements of 593 or less, and just 2.3 percent in villages with fewer than 200 people.

TABLE 3.5
Distribution of Indian Population in Authorized
Settlements by Quartile and Decile, 1700

Population	Range in settlement size (No. of inhabitants)
Quartile	
1	13–592
2	593–901
3	902–1,599
4	1,600–3,255
Decile	
1	13–373
2	374–547
3	548–627
4	628–737
5	738–901
6	902–1,228
7	1,229–1,559
8	1,560–1,679
9	1,680–2,684
10	2,685–3,255

SOURCE: AGI, México 1035, Matrícula y razón individual del número fijo de los indios tributarios . . . , 28 June 1700.

Certain regions, moreover, were home to many more Indians than others. The villages in the southern part of the Sierra district, an important agricultural region known as the Sierra Alta (see Map 3), contained 23 percent of all non-urban Indians under Franciscan jurisdiction, and tended to be much larger than the province-wide norm. The two largest villages in all Yucatan—Oxkutzcab and Tekax, with 3,255 and 2,974 inhabitants, respectively—were found there; these two settlements alone accounted for 38 percent of all the Indians in the Sierra Alta. The average size of villages was an extraordinary 1,169, and the proportion of people living in villages of more than 1,600 inhabitants was huge—70 percent, compared with just 25 percent for the province as a whole. In fact, more than 50 percent of the people lived in settlements of over 2,139 inhabitants. Even the lowest quartile of the population lived in villages ranging from 297 to 833 people.

At the other extreme were the areas near Mérida and Campeche. The five settlements around the provincial capital averaged only 190 inhabitants, the eight around Campeche only 95. Some of the latter settlements were relatively new, created by the reducciones carried out after the massive depopulation of the area in the 1660's.

With one exception, which we will come to shortly, the other regions (as far as can be determined) fell between these extremes. The Costa, for example, had no large villages; the most populous village, Baca, had only

Map 3

Political-Ecclesiastical Districts (Partidos) in the Eighteenth Century

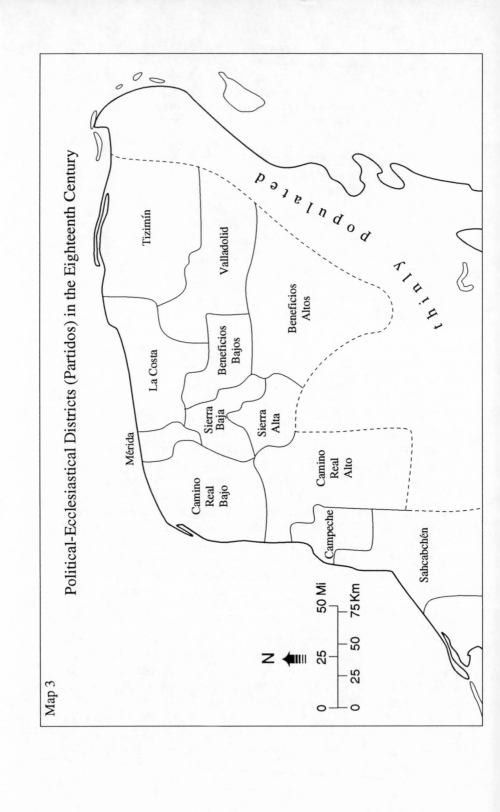

1,316 people. But small settlements were also uncommon, for three-quarters of the population lived in villages of 586 people or more. The Costa therefore was overwhelmingly a region of middle-sized villages: more than half the population lived in settlements of between 586 and 1,169 people, and one-quarter lived in villages of between 1,169 and 1,316. The average for the 39 villages was 604. A very large population lived in these villages, though. In fact, the Costa had more people than the Sierra Alta. Some 32.8 percent (that is, almost exactly a third) of all the Indians under Franciscan control lived there.

The Valladolid region tended to have larger settlements than the Costa. It contained Popolá, the third-largest village in the province, with 2,685 inhabitants. The average for the 19 villages was 764 people, and 59 percent of the population lived in middle-sized settlements of between 548 and 1,632 people. But the upper range was higher than in the Costa: the Costa did not have any settlement of more than 1,600 people, whereas almost 30 percent of the Valladolid Indians lived in villages of that size.

Evidence on the other districts is too fragmentary to analyze with precision. Important parishes of the Camino Real were under the control of the secular clergy, and consequently the Franciscan report covers only half the district. Fortunately, three of the parishes reported on were contiguous, stretched out along the Camino Real from Maxcanú to Calkiní, so the available information at least sheds some light on a compact section of the district. The villages tended to be much larger than the provincial norm, for the nine settlements of the three contiguous parishes averaged 958 people—the highest average in the province after the Sierra Alta. Moreover, 40 percent of the people lived in large villages. Consequently, like the Sierra Alta, the mid-section of the Camino Real contained a relatively concentrated rural population.

The Franciscans also reported on seven of the 13 villages of the Sierra Baja, the region to the south of Mérida, between the provincial capital and the all-important Sierra Alta. This seems to have been a zone of transition. The three villages of the northernmost parish of Muna averaged only 384 people, compared with 863 for the four in the parish of Teabo to the south. Moreover, all of Muna's settlements were relatively small—the largest had only 511 people—whereas in Teabo 79 percent of the population lived in villages of over 1,100 people.

Finally, what can be said about the districts of Beneficios Bajos, Beneficios Altos, and Tizimín? Here the Franciscans cannot help us, for these regions were entirely in the hands of the secular clergy. The sketchy data available, presented in Appendix A, suggest that like the Sierra Baja, Beneficios Bajos was a zone of transition, with predominantly small villages in the northwestern part of the district (the parishes of Hoctún, Hocabá, and Homún) and relatively large ones in the southeastern part (parishes

TABLE 3.6

Proportion of Non-Native Indians (Forasteros) and Women
in 22 Villages of La Costa and Beneficios Bajos, 1721

Parish and village	Adult Indians[a]	Total population[b]	Forasteros as pct. of adults	Women: as pct. of adults	Women: as pct. of forasteros
Motul	828	1,507	9.3%	55.4%	64.9%
Motul	319	518	12.2	56.1	59.0
Ucí	229	417	7.0	54.6	68.8
Kiní	216	393	6.5	56.9	85.7
Muxupip	64	116	12.5	50.0	50.0
Conkal	1,385	2,521	7.8	53.4	61.1
Conkal	122	222	19.7	54.1	66.7
Ixil	715	1,301	8.1	55.1	56.9
Chicxulub	356	648	7.3	51.7	65.4
Cholul	112	204	0.0	50.0	–
Sicpach	80	146	0.0	50.0	–
Telchac	1,509	2,746	14.2	57.3	50.0
Telchac	322	586	32.0	57.1	53.4
Dzemul	897	1,633	3.6	57.4	34.4
Sinanché	290	528	27.2	57.2	51.9
Hoctún	792	1,441	11.5	56.2	52.7
Hoctún	184	335	17.4	56.5	50.0
Xocchel	256	466	15.6	51.2	47.5
Tahmek	141	257	0.0	60.3	–
Seyé	211	384	9.0	59.2	68.4
Sotuta	1,510	2,748	36.2	52.7[c]	50.7[c]
Sotuta	589	1,072	29.4	51.8[c]	50.0[c]
Cantamayec	237	431	57.4	54.4	50.0
Uzih	99	180	3.0	51.5	100.0
Tabi	276	502	18.1	54.3	54.0
Bolon-Tabi	131	238	16.8	53.4	50.0
Tibolón Nuevo	178	324	91.0	50.0	50.0

SOURCE: AGI, México 1039, Testimonio no. 24, Testimonio de Seis Certificaciones dadas por los doc-
trineros seculares y regulares de Yucathan del numero de mantas de que se compone cada curato . . .
(1721).

[a]Includes males 14 years of age and older, and females 12 and over.

[b]Calculated by a conversion factor of 1.82, based on statistics from the Visitas Pastorales of Espita,
Yaxcabá, Sotuta, and Ichmul in 1784.

[c]Excludes one of the three parcialidades of Sotuta village.

of Sotuta, Tixcacaltuyú, and Yaxcabá), which included the large village
of Tahdzibichén. But the point is murky, for in the Beneficios Altos, still
farther south and southeast, the settlement pattern was probably one of
middle-sized villages. Tihosuco was clearly a village of some size, but
probably not in the same category as the settlements in the Sierra Alta.
As for the Tizimín region, the data strongly suggest that it was characterized uniformly by small villages. Even if the information significantly
underestimates the village population, it is virtually certain that the very
largest of its settlements were well under the Franciscan averages. This

region north and northeast of Valladolid, then, bore a close resemblance to the area around Mérida and Campeche, and differed sharply from the area west and south of Valladolid.

Of course, describing settlement patterns is easier than explaining them. Nevertheless, an attempt must be made, for settlement patterns are not of mere antiquarian interest, but help reveal factors that had a long-term impact on a people's history. In our own case, the data suggest, first of all, a correlation between settlement patterns and ecological conditions. The areas of greatest concentration tended to be in the south and southeast, which had the peninsula's deepest and best soil (especially in the case of the Sierra Alta) and most reliable rainfall; those of least concentration fell in the north and northwest, where the soil was thin, and the rainfall relatively unpredictable. Perhaps ecological conditions impeded growth in settlement size beyond a certain point and encouraged people to disperse or migrate.

To be sure, there were important exceptions to these ecological rules, and the existence of these exceptions reminds us that geography is a limiting, but not always a determining, factor in history. The mid-section of the Camino Real, for example, was an area of large villages even though the soil and rainfall were not as propitious for agriculture as they were in the Sierra. This abnormality was probably due to the region's access to the resources of the coast, especially salt, which was mined and traded in considerable quantities. Maritime resources, which were not available to villages of the interior, certainly provided many settlements of the Camino Real with a broadened economic base, thereby permitting the villages to outgrow the agricultural restrictions of the area. This conclusion is supported by the pattern of the Costa district: except for Motul, the Costa's largest villages—Chicxulub, Baca, Motul, Ucí, and Dzemul— were all located close to the coast and participated in the salt and fishing economies.[55] At the same time, even the coastal regions sometimes found ways to expand their agricultural resources. For example, in the 1840's the village of Pocmuch (just south of the Camino Real area reported on by the Franciscans in 1700) was using the land of Jaina Island, off the Campeche coast, for its milpas. This appears to have been a long-standing practice, for village leaders claimed that the island had belonged to their pueblo "since time immemorial," or more specifically "since even before the Conquest," and they presented seventeenth-century documents to prove that Pocmuch's possession of Jaina had been legally sanctioned and defended by the royal government.[56] In any case, it is certain that the Camino Real villages, as well as those in the northern parts of the Costa, had access to resources that were not available to the Maya farther inland.

Another exception was the Campeche area. This region has better soil and more plentiful rainfall than the northwestern part of the peninsula, but the settlement pattern was nonetheless one of very small villages. But, as already noted, this was the area from which the Maya population had fled in the 1660's. Moreover, demographic decline was most severe in Campeche, probably because the extreme humidity and abundant rainfall made the area almost perfect for the spread of yellow fever. In 1700 the settlements there were tiny; many were wholly new villages created by recent reducciones. These special conditions account to a certain extent for Campeche's deviation from the general trend.

The final exception to the rule was Tizimín. In this case, we can only speculate on what produced a settlement pattern of small villages and an extremely dispersed population. The area's agricultural potential is apparently no worse than that of the northwest, yet the Tizimín district had no settlements of even moderate size. The answer presumably lies more in the region's history than in its ecology, for in fact the northeastern part of the peninsula was thinly populated even before the Spanish invasion. The only settlement of any size had been the coastal city of Ecab, which had probably been an outpost of the Chontal (non-Yucatec) Maya and which was completely abandoned after the Conquest. Much of this region had been the domain of the Maya states of Chikinchel, Tases, Ecab, and Cupul. With the exception of the last, little is known about these states, but the ease with which they disintegrated on contact strongly suggests that they were socially and politically the least complex of the late Post-Classic Maya states in Yucatan. It is likely therefore that this area became largely depopulated after the Conquest not only because of disease but also because the degree of social integration was too low to withstand the demands imposed by colonialism.[57]

The Cupul state would seem to contradict this interpretation, for it was well integrated socially and politically, and its people survived the Conquest remarkably well. But in fact before the Conquest the Cupul were barely occupying Tizimín at all. The vast majority of these Maya people were settled in the large villages west and south of what was to become the town of Valladolid. In other words, the part of the Tizimín district occupied by the Cupul was characterized by small settlements even before the arrival of the Spaniards. Perhaps the Cupul presence was weak because the settlements were the result of northern and northwestern expansion from the state's main territory with the intention of acquiring access to the coast and to the salt beds. In any case, it is clear that the dispersed population and small-sized settlements of the area north and northeast of Valladolid in 1700 cannot be imputed to ecological conditions alone. Historical factors thus far unexplained were also responsible.

Geographic Mobility and the Village Community

Although much is known about Maya society in the colonial era, much more needs to be known. Though historians have used fiscal data to estimate total population, parish registers have yet to be analyzed to determine birth and death rates, marriage patterns, fertility, inheritance, and the like. Consequently, we shall have to be content with the mere glimpses into Maya social life that the documents occasionally give us.

Unquestionably, one of the most important features of village life was geographic mobility. In addition to dispersal and flight to the frontier, movement from village to village was quite common. Reports made in 1721 by priests in three parishes of the Costa district and two in Beneficios Bajos provide us with some insight into this phenomenon. The data, which are summarized in Tables 3.6 and 3.7, show non-native Indians (*forasteros*) residing in 19 of the 22 villages surveyed. Outsiders accounted for 17.2 percent of the adult Indians in these five parishes. But these newcomers were not evenly distributed in the villages. Motul and Conkal were not nearly so attractive to migrants as Telchac and Sotuta. Neither was Hoctún, which drew only 8.8 percent of them, though in an area that was thinly populated to begin with, the forasteros made up some 11.5 percent of the adults.

We can only speculate on why people chose to move around with such frequency. Maya patterns are so difficult to discern that Nancy Farriss has compared the Indians' trekking about to a kind of province-wide game of musical chairs. But the information in Table 3.6 does permit us to make some reasonable guesses about what was going on. According to the priests, 54.9 percent of the adults in these 22 villages were women. That finding is not especially surprising, for it was, and is, common for women to outnumber men in society. What is interesting is their disproportionately high representation in some areas. In Conkal and Motul, parishes of relatively few immigrants, women constituted over 60 percent of the outsiders. On the other hand, in the parishes of Sotuta and Telchac, the proportion of female and male newcomers was about equal, whereas the native residents exhibit the usual pattern of a female majority. The same was true, although to a lesser extent, in Hoctún.

These data demonstrate that there were at least two kinds of migrations under way. The villages that were on the whole less attractive to immigrants seem to have been the destination of migratory groups in which females outnumbered males, while the parishes of considerable inmigration attracted males and females in roughly equal proportions. This suggests that it was nuclear families that migrated into the areas of opportunity—Telchac and especially Sotuta, and to a lesser extent Hoctún—for colonization by individual males was almost certainly negligible, and the movement of extended families would have meant a greater proportion of females to males. By the same token, the less attractive areas may have tended to draw extended families, or alternately two separate groups, namely, nuclear families and individual women. But since the migration of individuals of whatever sex was almost certainly carried out

TABLE 3.7
Migration Pattern of Non-Native Indians
(Forasteros) in Five Parishes, 1721

	Forasteros	
Parish	No.	Pct. of total forasteros
Motul	77	7.4%
Conkal	108	10.4
Telchac	214	20.7
Hoctún	91	8.8
Sotuta	546	52.7
TOTAL	1,036	100.0%

SOURCE: Same as for Table 3.6.

to join relatives elsewhere, it is highly likely that the movement of people made up mostly of women was related in one way or the other to the extended family.

The search for opportunity, therefore, seems to have been one motive of migration, and tended to attract people who moved in nuclear family units. Areas of little opportunity were the destination of people belonging to extended families. That group's reasons for migrating can only be guessed at. Presumably, widows and orphans moved to join kin groups for material and psychological support. Also, relatives possibly moved to the communities of other family members to occupy land or other resources made available by the death of a member of the kin group. People probably moved closer to their relatives after a poor harvest or other natural disaster had necessitated out-migration. And finally, all sorts of personal as well as economic motives unknown to us must have existed to draw people to areas disdained by others.

The attractions of Telchac and Sotuta parishes are not hard to explain. Sotuta was not as densely populated as Conkal and Motul parishes, and consequently land was available for colonization. The name of one of the villages in the parish, Tibolón Nuevo, strongly suggests that it was similar to the numerous settlements called *villeneuve* in medieval France: a village founded by a whole group of colonists from another settlement. In fact, forasteros made up 91 percent of the population of Tibolón Nuevo. In-migration was also heavy in Cantameyec and in the village of Sotuta. Telchac, on the other hand, is not likely to have had a great deal of land to colonize. Its attractions were of a different sort. As will be recalled, the northern villages of the Costa district had easy access to coastal resources. Consequently, these settlements tended to be larger than those farther inland, which were limited to agriculture. Perhaps Telchac village and Sinanché grew in part because of in-migration. But even in the case of the maritime villages, other factors must have been involved, for not all the coastal settlements in the sample attracted immigrants. In particular, Ucí, Ixil, Chicxulub, and Dzemul—all villages with easy access to the sea—had relatively few forasteros. Consequently, until further research is carried out, the causes for migration from village to village must remain to a certain extent a mystery.

Nevertheless, geographic mobility was clearly an important feature of social life among the colonial Maya. The movement of people was on such a scale that many scholars, myself included, have called into question the validity of the time-honored anthropological concept of the Mesoamerican closed corporate community,[58] and have argued that in fact the communities were open; otherwise so many outsiders would not have been able to settle in villages other than those of their birth.[59] However, the evidence does not really support the thesis of an open Maya community. The problem lies in our definition of community. If by this we mean village, then the communities in the colonial period can be seen as open. But, as we have already noted, for the Maya membership in a village was only one, and by no means the most important, principle of social organization. Ties to cuchteel, ch'ibal, and family were usually more important. Thus it has been argued in the case of the highland Maya of Guatemala that in the colonial period the closed corporate community to which the Indians belonged was not the village but the lineage group or parcialidad, of which there were usually several settled at the same site, that is, in the same village.[60]

If the focus shifts from residential site to lineage group or parcialidad as the Indians' community, then it becomes more likely that the Maya of Yucatan belonged to closed corporate communities. There is no evidence that real outsiders—people who did not belong to one of the communities of a village—were in fact readily accepted by the residents of an established settlement. Moreover, there is considerable evidence that the Maya had a sense of corporate ownership, or at least exclusive right to the usufruct, of specific lands belonging to their family, ch'ibal, cuchteel, or even, in some cases, village.[61] Finally, the higher proportion of women among some of the forasteros strongly suggests that migrants were sometimes rejoining their kinsmen elsewhere. Consequently, the migration of people into a village may have been possible not because it was an open community but because the immigrants belonged to one of the family or lineage units already there, groups that would not have shared their resources with *real* outsiders.

More research needs to be done before we can understand Indian social structure. Nevertheless, it seems likely that the Maya did belong to closed corporate communities, although the communities in question did not coincide with the village or residential site in which they were located.

Immigrants probably were accepted into existing settlements because they already belonged to the community, paradoxical though this may seem. It should be remembered that the Spaniards confused residential sites with social structure, and we should avoid doing the same. After all, the Maya belonged to communities and social groups that cannot always be categorized, or even understood, by Western concepts of social organization.

CHAPTER FOUR

The Peasant Economy

ONE OF THE TRAGEDIES of European colonialism in America was the transformation of great civilizations into peasantries. Before the Spanish invasion, many Indian societies had achieved high degrees of social organization, economic development, political institutionalization, and cultural expression. They were complete societies, embracing a gamut of social classes that had emerged from a long-existing system of social stratification.

Colonialism eventually reduced the Maya to the condition of a part-society. With the gradual elimination of the native elite and of some of the bases for social stratification, practically all Indians were eventually pushed into a single social class. To the Maya was assigned the role of a peasantry, that is, members of rural communities producing the goods required for the survival of the higher social classes, which in Yucatan were composed of mixed-race people and Spaniards. The Indians, then, made up a part, but only a part, of a larger society. As a result, cultural expression ceased to be the product of a variety of classes, and instead became associated only with the peasantry. Maya culture became peasant culture.[1]

Of course, the change from a complete society to a part society did not take place overnight. In fact, not until the late nineteenth century can it be said with certainty that the Maya were almost exclusively peasants. The continued social stratification among the Indians in the colonial period helped delay the inevitable cultural impoverishment resulting from the European invasion.

Land Tenure

The survival of the Maya elite for more than two centuries after the Conquest was made possible in part by the preservation and adaptability of the Indian system of land tenure. It is important to note that property relations among the Post-Classic Maya were complex and are not yet thoroughly understood. It is clear that the kind of large landed estates owned as private property and worked by dependent serfs or renters found in highland Mexican societies did not exist in Yucatan or anywhere else in the Maya area.[2] On the other hand, it is inaccurate to subsume the system of land tenure under the term "communal," for there were many types of property besides the type that could be called communal.

Alfonso Villa Rojas and Elías Zamora Acosta have been able to distinguish a host of land-holding arrangements among the Post-Classic Maya: the state, the village, the parcialidad, the lineage, the nobility, and private individuals were all involved.[3] Unfortunately for our purposes, some of these forms of land tenure were similar enough to Spanish ones that the colonial authorities simply incorporated them into the legal system without clarifying the important differences that undoubtedly existed between Maya and Spanish concepts of property. As a result, in documentation the Indians appear to be operating on two levels: on the one hand, their property-holding conforms to Spanish principles, and consequently land is registered, bought, sold, and inherited in accordance with Hispanic law; on the other hand, there are sometimes just enough hints to suggest that at the same time some other (i.e., Maya) principles of property ownership are being maintained without any explanations given to, or asked by, the Spaniards. In the circumstances, the best way to approach the subject is by giving examples that demonstrate part of the reality of property relations.

First of all, in the extant documentation there are numerous examples of Indian village or communal property. The Titles of the Hacienda Tabi record a conflict between the villages of Dzan and Ticul in the mid-seventeenth century over lands claimed by both pueblos.[4] Village rights of ownership to specific properties were well understood, and consequently when Indians from Yaxcabá established a new settlement in an area belonging to Cuncunul, Tekom, and Tixcacalcupul, those pueblos vigorously defended their rights in the Spanish courts; Cuncunul and Tekom were then also disputing the ownership of other properties with Ebtún and Kauá.[5] Sometimes village land was actually used communally to produce agricultural goods for common ends: both Calotmul, in 1722, and Cisteíl, in 1761, possessed a "milpa de la comunidad."[6] The most numerous examples of village or communal property, however, are those involving sales of such land by pueblos to private individuals, especially to Spaniards. All of the hacienda deeds I have consulted include purchases of village properties by Spanish landowners. Some other examples, culled from notarial records, are shown in Table 4.1.

The documentation also shows numerous cases of property ownership by individuals or families. Ralph Roys found many instances of private land-holding in his study of the Titles of Ebtún.[7] Since this point is of considerable importance and is at variance with what is known or believed to have been the case elsewhere, the topic deserves some discussion.

TABLE 4.1
Sales of Village-Owned Property to Non-Indians, 1689–1737

Year	Village/ barrio seller	Purchaser	Source in Archivo Notarial del Estado, Mérida
1689	Sicpach	Br. Tomás Conrado	J. A. Baeza, 28 Jan. 1689, fols. 3–6
1692	Hocabá	Dr. D. Joseph de Ancona Hiniestrosa	Ibid., 8 June 1692, fols. 491–92
1700	Maxcanú	D. Clemente de Marcos Bermejo	J. M. de Mendoza, 8 Sept. 1846, fols. 242–46
1713	Calkiní and parcialidad Nunkiní	Tomás Trejo	M. Montero, 21 Apr. 1719, fols. 292–95
1713	Itzimná	Alférez Augustín de los Ríos	Ibid., 7 May 1721, fols. 107–10
1713	Tixpéual	Br. Joseph de Quero	Ibid., 30 Jan. 1719, fols. 206–7
1720	Campeche	Da. Juana Caballero	Ibid., 3 July 1720, fols. 107–10
1720	Opichén and Maxcanú	Teniente D. Ignacio Enríquez	Ibid., 5 Aug. 1720, fols. 156–60
1722	Chuburná	Paula Carranza	Ibid., 4 Oct. 1737, no fol.
1722	Huhí	Dr. D. Diego Leiton Tamudo	Ibid., 3 Aug. 1722, fols. 465–66
1728	Caucel	Esteban de Salinas	B. Magaña, 8 Apr. 1728, no fol.
1731	Tixkokob	Br. Juan Antonio Méndez	F. A. Savido, 4 Nov. 1735, fols. 157–60
1737	San Francisco (Campeche)	D. Joseph Claudio Méndez de Cisneros	N. F. de Córdoba, 4 Dec. 1737, no fol.
1737	San Francisco (Campeche)	Br. D. Santiago Fernández	Ibid., 4 Dec. 1737, no fol.

NOTE: Br. = Bachiller (an academic title awarded to secular clergymen).

The evidence for private or family property among the Maya dates back to the earliest days of the Conquest. In 1569, for example, the Pox family claimed that their ancestor Napuc Pox had been the first owner of certain lands that had belonged to them "long even before the Conquest of the Spaniards," and that boundary markers clearly separated their holdings from the milpa of an Indian named Ahmen Ek on the south, from the *montes* (uncultivated lands) of the Indians named Chim and the milpa or montes of Diego Chan on the southeast.[8] Here, then, we can see that the Indians must have known very well what lands were theirs and who their neighboring landowners were, and apparently placed boundary markers to demonstrate their ownership of property.

The documentation for the sixteenth century is so meager that one can do no more than prove the existence of individual or family ownership of property; and though we have more information on the late seventeenth century, it is still difficult to decipher the reality of Maya land ten-

ure. Nevertheless, it does seem clear that individuals and families continued to own property in ways that were clearly not communal. The documents of Spanish landed estates frequently make reference to the nearby
properties of Indians. In 1689 Estancia Tanlum (just to the northwest of
Mérida) was bordered by a plot of land with a well owned by Sebastián
Canché and by another plot owned by Francisco Chan.⁹ Sometimes the
documents explicitly identify the neighboring owners as Indians, as if to
leave no doubt about the reality: a sitio near Chuburná in 1692 was bordered by "los montes de Diego Chel y Juan Chan, yndios."¹⁰

It is also possible to see what were apparently communal and individual
or family properties side by side. One of the most detailed examples of
such complexities of Maya land tenure involves the sale of five properties
near the village of Bokobá between 1701 and 1707. The first of these was
owned by Captain Don Felipe May, the gobernador-cacique of Bokobá.
The land in question had belonged to the ancestors of May's grandfather,
Francisco Mutul, who had inherited it and then passed it on to his son,
Don Esteban May. The property, which bordered on a raft of other holdings—the milpa of Gaspar Tamay; a water well called Chac-choc (formerly owned by Felipe May's father and grandfather); the milpas of May's
older brother Don Fernando May; some lands "de los de Motul [a
pueblo]"; more properties belonging to Felipe May; "los montes de los
de Bokobá"; some *montes* belonging to Juan Chan of the village of Tekantó, Bentura Uitzil of Bokobá, Gaspar Ame of Bokobá, Francisco Uitz,
and Juan Pisté (identified as the *secretario* of Bokobá); and milpas of Francisco Mo of Bokobá—sold for 120 pesos, a considerable sum for the time.
May also owned other lands. As he put it, he could do without the property he was selling "because I still have a lot of land and *montes* to provide
for me and my children." Moreover, he appears as the owner of milpas
bordering on one of the other holdings being sold during these years. The
sellers of the other four properties were Ignacio Oxté, Juan Mo and Magdalena Dzib, Antonio Pat and María Noh, and Juan Mo, all identified as
Indians of Bokobá.¹¹

Note that two of these five properties were sold jointly by a man and
a woman. Possibly, the women owned the land in these cases, and the
men simply appeared in the transactions because Spanish law provided
that a married woman could not sell property without her husband's approval. But it is also possible that the couples had joint ownership, for
there are many cases of multiple Indian owners of property. In the Titles
of Tabi, for example, we find a holding belonging to Diego Mul in 1624
surrounded by "los montes de los Yndios Canules," "los montes de los
Yndios Yces," and "los montes de los Balamnaes."¹² In 1708 some lands
formerly belonging to Nicolás Tun (which would eventually become part
of Hacienda Tabi) was bounded by "los montes de los muchos h Caches";
a milpa belonging to the same people; some lands of "los indios h

Chimes"; a property of Juan Balam; the montes of the late Joseph Mo; some lands of "los indios h Cabes"; a property of "el indio h Cauich" and another belonging to Juan Tuin; a savanna; and the "montes de los Yndios h Taxes."[13] Finally, in 1733, another plot of land that would also become part of Tabi was owned jointly by Diego, Gaspar, and Francisco Uc.[14]

Similar cases appear in the records of Spanish notaries. Sometimes the multiple owners were obviously members of the same family. In 1712 a sitio near Sinanché was jointly owned by Andrés, Nicolás, Antonio, and María May.[15] In 1728 the cacique of Cuzamá, Captain Don Andrés Cocom, owned a property along with Gaspar, Juan, and Mateo Cocom, who were identified as Indians from Cuzamá.[16] Some land near Cholul was owned in 1730 by Felipe, Diego, and Manuel Mex, Indians of Itzimná.[17] A sitio near Tekit was owned in 1733 by Juan and Pedro Kantún.[18] And another property, near Cuzamá, was owned in 1737 by Mateo, Joseph, Joaquín, and Catalina Can, Indians of Cuzamá.[19]

At other times the relationship between the multiple owners is far from clear. Luis Yam and María May, who in 1713 owned Sitio Mukuiché, near Bokobá, were probably a married couple.[20] But what are we to make of the case of some "montes y tierras" near Temax owned in 1692 by Andrés Chan (the *maestro de capilla* of Temax), Juan Canul (identified as a *mayordomo*, presumably of either an estancia or a cofradía), and Diego Canul?[21] The last two were probably related, but there is no clue to the relationship between them and Chan. The same is true of Sitio Xuxá, a property owned in 1719 by Felipe and Buenaventura Chablé and Manuel Canché.[22]

Multiple ownership of land by Indians is significant, even if the relationship between the owners is not always clear, because it demonstrates the existence of principles of land tenure that were clearly Maya in origin. Among Spaniards, land was frequently inherited by several people, but such properties were always divided up as part of the process of probate. Consequently, sales and purchases of land by Spaniards were invariably made by individuals; not one case of true multiple ownership exists in the notary records until the emergence of companies and commercial corporations in the late nineteenth century.

The cases of multiple ownership by Indians thus demonstrate that the Maya did indeed act on two levels in their dealings with Spanish law. On the one hand, ownership was claimed, and properties were bought and sold. On the other, the Maya adhered to principles of ownership that were quite distinct from those of the Spaniards, and perhaps for this reason the Spanish officials declined to try to clarify what was for them a feature of a foreign culture. Some things were best left alone.

These examples of multiple ownership almost certainly are cases of family or lineage land-holding. Sometimes the documents themselves make it clear that the group of owners had inherited the land in question.

For example, in the Titles of Tabi, the aforementioned Diego Mul willed his property to his six children, Alonso, Gaspar, Pablo, Antonio, and Pedro Mul and María Canul, with the provision that "no one can take [the land] away from them because it is their inheritance."[23] In the late eighteenth century lands being acquired by the owner of Hacienda Tabi had belonged for generations to people named Couoh. As the Indian officials of the village of Dzan testified, "we state that since ancient times the Indians *h* Couohes have had possession [of the land] from their ancestors." But then these people "left it to their grandson Pasqual Ku, for so he is named, and upon the death of said Pasqual Ku, he left it in the hands of his son Antonio Ku, the grandfather of Nicolás Ku, Miguel Ku, and Felipe Ku, who are the true owners of these *montes* now, and their grandfather having died, [the land] remained in their hands, for which reason no one can take it away from them because they are descendants of the Indians Couohes, and so it was handed over to the Indians Kues because there are no other descendants of the Indians Couohes alive."[24]

The Maya system of inheritance therefore clearly provided for landed property being passed on from generation to generation. Sometimes this took on the appearance of Spanish-like inheritance, in which single individuals ended up as sole owners. For example, the site of what would eventually become the core of Hacienda Tabi was owned in the seventeenth century by the grandfather of Felipe Chel, who sold the property to a Spaniard at the end of the century. But in between Chel and his grandfather, the land had passed, also by inheritance, to Alonso Uc, whose relationship with Felipe Chel was not specified.[25] Perhaps the property had been inherited either by Uc or by Chel through the female line, for as is clear from many of the cited examples, women could and did inherit property. This was also true in the case of a well and surrounding land near Tekit owned in 1719 by Marcelino Tun, who specifically stated that he had inherited the property he had sold from his wife.[26] The same was probably the case in the sale of some land near Muna owned previously by Diego Balam. Balam's grandson, Diego Magaña (possibly a mestizo), inherited the property and sold it to a Spaniard in 1719.[27]

In all of these cases, land was inherited and disposed of by single individuals, as was done among the Spaniards. But again, there are hints in the documents that the Indians were in fact operating on different principles of land tenure. For among the Maya, family members seem to have had much more say about property than was the case among the Spaniards. For example, when a cacica named Doña Magdalena Hau bought the montes and milpas of Pedro Can in 1640, the Indian government of Oxkutzcab, after authorizing the transaction, added the comment that no one could henceforth dispute her ownership, "neither her children . . . nor her relatives."[28] Similarly, when Sebastián Mul sold some land to a

Spaniard in 1738, he specifically stated that "no one will be permitted to stand in the way of this transaction which I have formalized, nor may my children or my grandchildren impede it."[29] In this way possible claims by relatives were ruled out, a procedure the Spaniards were only too willing to accept.

Relatives were sometimes also given special rights over property. When Doña Cristina Chuel, a native of Samahil, resident of the parcialidad of Dzibikal of the village of Umán, and member of the Maya elite, made her will in 1692, she left her son, Andrés Jorge, all of her property, including the Estancia Dzidz. In the last he stood to gain a considerable holding, for though the estate had only four head of cattle at the time, it had 20 horses and 350 beehives. In addition, Andrés Jorge kept 50 hives of his own on the property, and Don Pedro Kumún kept another 200. Kumún was the uncle of Andrés Jorge and was probably Cristina Chuel's brother or half-brother. Doña Cristina's will contained the proviso that her son would inherit the property on the condition "that he not expel the said Don Pedro Kumún his uncle, but rather the two should live together honorably and in full accord with each other."[30]

The significance of these statements specifically excluding or providing for relatives and descendants is that they were made at all. Such provisions were never included in wills or sales made by Spaniards, for among the colonists property was truly private. There was no need to exclude people who had no rights. But among the Maya, family members apparently had, or felt they had, some say over the property owned by their relatives. It is possible, therefore, that the cases of apparent private property among the Indians hid a larger reality, or simply resulted from the death of all other relatives. And when documents were drawn up to seal the transfer of Indian lands to Spaniards, family members with potential claims were specifically disowned, thereby giving the purchasers undisputed possession.

Maya land tenure principles, in sum, were quite complex and are still somewhat mysterious. Since the Spaniards drew up documents with no intention of clarifying the matter, we can observe part of the system as it functioned but cannot fully understand its underlying principles. Nevertheless, it is clear that the Maya held property in a variety of different ways, and that the family or the lineage, or both, continued to play some role in ownership long after the Conquest. Of course, in the long run the Spanish system would overwhelm the Indian. But in the short run the basis of social stratification among the Maya was maintained. Even in the early nineteenth century some numbers of Indians, especially members of the upper class, still owned land and in a few cases landed estates.[31] With this basis of property to prop up its position, the elite's descent into the impoverished peasantry would take centuries to be completed.

Peasants, Markets, and the Regional Economy

The role of peasants everywhere in the world is to provide a surplus of agricultural goods to feed, and sometimes clothe, the nonpeasant population of towns and cities. In colonial Yucatan, part of the surplus of Maya agriculture was channeled away from the producers by the institutions of tribute and religious taxation. These institutions have already been discussed and need not concern us here. But we have not yet gone into detail on another important process mentioned earlier, how the Maya peasantry was incorporated into the regional economy through a marketing system, and it is to this subject that we now turn.

The regional marketing system that developed in Yucatan was affected to a great extent by ecological factors. Not only did the conditions in the area differ markedly from those in central Mexico, but in certain respects Yucatan had the better of it. Crop-killing frosts are never a threat in the peninsula, sparing Yucatan from a disaster like the great frost of 1785–86 that destroyed much of the harvest in central Mexico and led to mass starvation and social crisis.[32] On the other hand, the dry season, combined with the extreme permeability of the soil, made it impossible to irrigate fields; this in turn made it impossible to grow wheat, as was done in many parts of Spanish America, even in regions of large Indian populations like Oaxaca and Cuzco.[33] As a result, until the introduction of rice sometime in the eighteenth century, the people depended wholly on one grain— maize, or "the grain of first necessity," to use the phrase of contemporaries.

The topography of the peninsula also affected the marketing system. Given the almost uniform flatness of the terrain, there were no physical barriers to trade, but the total lack of rivers and even of streams meant that all internal transport had to go overland, and the rockiness of the terrain resulted in roads of such poor quality that even wagons were impractical. Nevertheless, Yucatan's system of communications—travel on horseback or litter, transport by mules or horses—though primitive, was adequate. In fact, conditions were such that the Maya gladly took over the transport system and organized grain purchases and mule trains to carry peasant produce to the urban markets. By contemporary standards, the peninsula's economy was well integrated, for cities and villages were tied together over considerable distances.

Yucatan's geography therefore was not without its advantages. But ecological factors also produced disadvantages, one of which had a major impact on the formation of the regional economy. The peninsula's high humidity is not only propitious for the breeding of fever-carrying mosquitoes. It also produces fungi that, combined with normally high temperatures, result in the rapid decomposition of all organic matter, including harvested maize kernels. At the same time, hosts of insects, which proliferate in hot, humid climates, invade every nook and cranny of houses and warehouses. As a result, maize stored for any length of time begins to decompose and be eaten by insects. Therefore, in the colonial era year-old corn was always called either simply *viejo* ("old") or *picado* (literally, "minced"), and had to be disposed of quickly.

The impossibility of storing maize for any length of time had an important impact on the structure of production. In central Mexico, with its lower humidity and less intense heat, grains could be stored for several years. Hacendados could thus withhold their supply from the market when prices were low and then release them when prices were high. Though large landowners would often lose money for several years in a row because the peasants provisioned the cities with maize during normal years, they could count on recouping their losses during one year of shortage. The long-term profitability of landed estates, therefore, depended on periodic grain shortages and the ability to store maize and sell it when prices were abnormally high.[34] In Yucatan, the impossibility of storing maize against a market rise helped keep grain production in Indian hands. Only when food shortages became practically endemic, in the middle of the eighteenth century, would Spanish landowners find it profitable to enter this field in a significant way.

Ecological factors thus contributed to the formation of a structure of production in which the Maya for all practical purposes monopolized agriculture. But demographic factors also played a role. Since Yucatan attracted far fewer European immigrants than central Mexico, the urban population, and consequently the size of the urban market, was comparatively small. Sheer numbers do not tell the full story, however, for if Mérida was no Mexico City, it was at least close to the size of a Guadalajara, and yet their market situations were not at all comparable. The Maya survived colonialism much better than the Indians of New Galicia, and therefore the ratio of Indian peasants to city dwellers was much greater in Yucatan than in the region of Guadalajara and its hinterland. Consequently, whereas in New Galicia Spaniards participated significantly in agricultural production in order to feed the city,[35] in Yucatan the colonists stuck mostly to stock-raising. In other words, although Mérida and Guadalajara were comparable in terms of the demand for goods they exerted within their respective regional economies, the smaller number of native suppliers in New Galicia made it necessary for Spaniards to carry out agricultural production too; in Yucatan the large number of Indians effectively kept the colonists out of agriculture for most of the colonial era.

In the period right after the Conquest, the city dwellers were able to survive on the grain acquired through the institutions of tribute and religious taxation. But these mechanisms soon proved inadequate, and consequently the city governments were forced to establish the typically His-

TABLE 4.2
Contracts of the Pósito of Mérida with Indian Villages
and Parcialidades, 1678–1727

		Cargas of maize[a]		
Year	No. of settlements contracted	No. contracted	No. undelivered from previous contracts	Total contracted and owed
1678	–	5,400	0	5,400
1680	–	5,407	0	5,407
1681	–	5,517	0	5,517
1682	–	5,718	0	5,718
1683	–	5,909	0	5,909
1684	–	5,832	0	5,832
1685	–	5,424	0	5,424
1686	–	5,496	0	5,496
1688	–	5,486	0	5,486
1689	–	5,178	0	5,178
1690	–	2,890	0	2,890
1691	80	5,133	0	5,133
1692	62	4,508	0	4,508
1693	65	4,865	0	4,865
1694	–	2,358	3,000	5,358
1695	–	2,210	3,044	5,254
1696	–	3,574	1,400	4,974
1697	–	4,739	520	5,259
1698	116	5,468	0	5,468
1699	125	5,182	0	5,182
1700	103	5,726	0	5,726
1701	–	6,098	0	6,098
1702	103	5,468	0	5,468
1703	99	5,490	188	5,678
1704	–	5,621	100	5,721
1705	100	4,609	620	5,229
1706	106	5,535	1,807	7,342
1707	100	5,118	86	5,204

panic urban institutions of the *alhóndiga* (granary) and *pósito* (grain fund). In practice these two functioned as a single unit, which was usually called simply the pósito. The institution was founded by the cabildo of Valladolid in 1594 with the stated purpose of providing a supply of maize at affordable prices for the urban poor, widows, and orphans. Mérida's city government took the same step at approximately the same time.[36]

Lack of documentation prevents us from studying the pósitos in the years shortly after their founding, but by the second half of the seventeenth century they were mentioned often enough that the system can be described in some detail. The pósitos accomplished their objective of providing grain for the cities by purchasing maize from the Indian producers. Usually the purchases were made a year in advance and were sealed by

TABLE 4.2 (*continued*)

Year	No. of settlements contracted	Cargas of maize[a]		
		No. contracted	No. undelivered from previous contracts	Total contracted and owed
1708	29	4,886	1,209	6,095
1709	119	5,717	137	5,854
1710	119	5,480	641	6,121
1711	119	3,365	2,469	5,834
1712	106	4,603	1,118	5,721
1713	89	5,332?	–	5,332
1715	–	6,162	26	6,188
1716	94	4,672	481	5,153
1717	107	4,934	624	5,558
1718	99	4,362	1,945	6,307
1719	94	6,201?	–	6,201
1720	98	5,464?	–	5,464
1721	100	4,773	0	4,773
1722	–	5,309	0	5,309
1723	–	4,932	453	5,385
1724	–	4,744	504	5,248
1725	–	4,744	504	5,248
1726	–	387	4,586	4,973
1727	–	–	–	7,300

SOURCES: AGI, Escribanía 321A, Residencia de Antonio de Layseca, Autos en Mérida (1684), fols. 78–115, Residencia de Juan de Arrechaga, Autos Generales (1684), fols. 52–53; Escribanía 321B, Residencia de Juan Bruno Tello de Guzmán, Autos en Mérida (1687), fols. 133–35, 141–45, 153ff, 162–64, 180–82; Escribanía 321C, Residencia de Juan José de Bárcena, Autos Generales en Mérida (1692), fols. 163ff, 211ff; Escribanía 322A, Residencia de Roque de Soberanis, Autos Generales (1709), fols. 123ff, 130ff, 102ff, 110ff, Residencia de Martín de Urzúa y Arizmendi, Autos Generales (1708), fols. 183–288; Escribanía 322B, Residencia de Alvaro de Rivaguda Enciso y Luyando, Autos Generales (1709), fols. 106–42; Escribanía 323A, Residencia de Fernando y Alonso de Meneses Bravo de Sarabia, Autos en Campeche y Mérida (1715–21), fols. 340–50, 361–402, 403ff; Escribanía 324A, Residencia de Juan Joseph de Vertiz, Autos Generales (1724), fols. 82–179, Residencia de Antonio de Cortaire, Autos Generales (1725), fols. 48ff; Escribanía 324B, Residencia de Antonio de Figueroa, Autos Generales (1734), fols. 108–97.

[a]A dry measure equivalent to approximately 0.275 hectoliters or 0.75 bushels.

signed contracts between the pósito administrator, or mayordomo, and the Indian village governments. The customary rate was two reales per *carga* (about 84–97 pounds, or as a dry measure, about 55.5 liters or one-half *fanega*). In the specific case of Mérida, the pósito tried to ensure a grain supply by signing contracts with a large number of villages in all the districts of central, western, and southern Yucatan, in effect hedging its bets against a failed harvest because of drought or some other disaster. As Table 4.2 shows, it was not uncommon for Mérida to make arrangements with more than 100 villages and parcialidades. Since there were only some 200 villages and parcialidades in the province, and since the

suppliers usually included all the large settlements, more than half the Indian population was incorporated into the marketing system of the provincial capital. Though comparable information from Valladolid and
Campeche is lacking, we do know that both likewise purchased grain
from many surrounding villages. On one occasion, for example, Valladolid's pósito signed contracts with as many as 24 pueblos.[37] Therefore,
the vast majority of the Maya were incorporated to some degree into urban markets through the pósito system.

Little is known about how the village governments arranged for the
grain to be delivered after the harvest. A clue is found in a statement made
by the cacique of Ticul in 1721. When asked at an official inquest if the
former governor Fernando de Meneses had ever confiscated grain in his
village, the cacique responded, in sworn testimony in Mérida, that maize
had never been stolen or confiscated by anyone; the only grain taken out
of Ticul "was that which, since time immemorial, is provided to the Pósito and Alhóndiga of this City at the price of two reales per carga, the
money being paid in advance to the village officials [justicias], who then
distribute it among the people."[38] Spaniards rarely, if ever, dealt directly
with individual Indian producers; they always worked through the Maya
authorities, whether to collect taxes, arrange for textile production, or
contract for grain. The village governments, then, were the indispensable
links in the economic chain tying peasant producers to urban consumers.

Some idea of the urban grain market's reach into the countryside is provided by the few surviving pósito records of deliveries and defaults on
contracts. Table 4.3 lists 85 villages and parcialidades known to have either
delivered or defaulted on grain contracts with the pósito of Mérida in
1681 and 1686. Information for Valladolid is scantier, for only some of
the settlements contracted for a given year are mentioned in the documents. The 12 identifiable villages and parcialidades contracted in 1717–
18 are listed in Table 4.4.

According to Table 4.3, Mérida was provisioned by the partidos of the
Camino Real Bajo, the Costa, the Sierra Baja, the Sierra Alta, and Beneficios Bajos. No information was found for the partidos of the Camino
Real Alto, Campeche, and Beneficios Altos, but the first two undoubtedly provisioned the port of Campeche, as they are known to have done
later in the century. Though Beneficios Altos seems to have been left out
of the grain market, it would probably be fair to conclude that the partido
was integrated into the provincial grain market on a somewhat irregular
basis.

The pósito of Mérida paid transport costs for its purchases by districts,
allowing so much for each horse or mule according to the distance traveled, and from these data we can piece out where it got its supplies of
grain. As can be seen in Table 4.5, the areas closest to the city accounted

TABLE 4.3
Villages and Parcialidades Contracted to Provide Maize to Mérida, 1681 and 1686

Partido	Village and parcialidad	Year	Partido	Village and parcialidad	Year
Camino	Hunucmá	1681, 1686	Costa	Izamal	1686
Real	Yabucú	1681, 1686	(continued)	Sitilpech	1681, 1686
Bajo	Sihunchén	1681, 1686		Pixilá	1681
	Kinchil	1686		Dzoncauich	1681
	Tzeme	1681, 1686		Buctzotz	1681
	Umán	1681, 1686	Sierra	Acanceh	1686
	Dzibikal	1681, 1686	Baja	Acanceh-	
	Dzibikak	1681		Chaltún	1686
	Tetiz	1681		Timucuy	1681, 1686
	Halachó	1681		Tecoh	1681, 1686
	Samahil	1681, 1686		Telchaquillo	1681, 1686
	Bolon-			Abalá	1681, 1686
	poxché	1686		Sacalum	1681
Mérida	Caucel	1686		Tekit[a]	1686
	Kanasín	1686		Teabo	1681
Costa	Conkal	1681, 1686		Sayá	1681
	Chicxulub	1686		Pencuyut	1681
	Cholul	1681, 1686		Chumayel	1681
	Ixil	1686	Sierra	Ticul	1681
	Sicpach	1686	Alta	Maní	1681
	Tixkokob	1686		Dzan	1681
	Euan	1681		Tipikal	1681
	Ekmul	1686		Oxkutzcab	1681
	Mocochá	1681, 1686		Yaxá	1681
	Tixkuncheíl	1681, 1686		Yotholín	1681
	Baca	1686		Tekax	1681
	Nolo	1681, 1686		Ticul	1681
	Tixpéual	1681, 1686		Tixcuitún	1681
	Motul	1686		Tixméuac	1681
	Kiní	1681, 1686	Beneficios	Hoctún	1686
	Muxupip	1686	Bajos	Seyé	1681, 1686
	Ucí	1686		Tahmek	1686
	Telchac	1681, 1686		Xocchel	1686
	Sinanché	1681, 1686		Homún	1686
	Cacalchén	1681, 1686		Cuzamá	1686
	Bokobá	1681, 1686		Hocabá	1681, 1686
	Yobaín	1681, 1686		Huhí	1686
	Cansahcab	1686		Sahcabá	1686
	Teya	1681, 1686		Sanlahcat	1686
	Tepakán	1681		Cantamayec	1681
	Tekantó	1686		Yaxcabá	1681
	Citilcum	1681, 1686		Mopilá	1681
	Kimbilá	1686			
	Tixculum	1686			
	Tixkoch	1686			

SOURCES: AGI, Escribanía 321A Residencia de Antonio de Layseca Alvarado, Autos en Mérida (1684), fols. 104–6; Escribanía 321B, Residencia de Juan Bruno Tello de Guzmán, Autos en Mérida (1687), fols. 145–46.
[a]Only the parcialidad of San Pedro was identified.

TABLE 4.4
Villages and Parcialidades Contracted to Provide
Maize to Valladolid, 1717–18

Partido	Village and parcialidad	Partido	Village and parcialidad
Tizimín	Espita	Valladolid	Kanxoc
	Tzabcanul	(continued)	Kauan
Valladolid	Yalcón		Tulunché
	Tahmuy		Temozón
	Yaxcabá		Chemax
	Tesoco		Chichimilá
	Xocén		

SOURCE: AGI, Escribanía 323 B, Residencia de Fernando y Alonso de Meneses Bravo de Sarabia, Autos en Valladolid (1721), fols. 48ff.

for only a small proportion of the deliveries. The majority of the grain supply in fact came from a relatively distant part of its economic hinterland. The Sierra Alta accounted for more than 70 percent of the deliveries in six of the ten years from 1709 to 1720, and no less than 59 percent in the other four. We can readily understand why that partido was called "the country's granary" in the colonial era. Only when supplies from the Sierra were diminished by drought did the share of any of the other districts, especially the Costa, rise to over 20 percent. On the other hand, the occasional failure of the Sierra to fulfill its contracts demonstrates that the pósito officials were indeed wise to let contracts in all possible producing areas.

TABLE 4.5
Provenance of Maize Delivered to Mérida as Indicated by Transport Costs, 1709–20
(Percent of total)

	Transport cost per pack animal (reales)					
Year	1	2	3	4	5	6
1709	0.6%	10.7%	14.4%	72.8%	–	1.5%
1710	0.2	11.0	15.7	71.2	1.0	1.0
1711	0.8	10.9	18.4	65.4	–	4.5
1713	0.4	11.6	16.6	69.0	–	2.3
1715	0.4	10.2	13.4	74.9	0.2	1.0
1716	0.1	9.5	12.6	66.1	1.2	10.4
1717	0.2	11.7	10.9	76.3	1.0	–
1718	0.7	15.2	22.1	58.9	1.4	1.7
1719	0.8	11.8	10.9	74.8	1.5	0.2
1720	1.0	12.0	12.7	70.8	2.3	1.1

SOURCES: AGI, Escribanía 323 A, Residencia de Fernando y Alonso de Meneses Bravo de Sarabia, Autos en Campeche y Mérida (1715–21), fols. 337–89; Escribanía 324 A, Residencia de Juan Joseph de Vertiz, Autos generales en Mérida (1723), fols. 84–178.

As already noted, Maya participation in the urban marketing system involved more than just the production of grain. Practically all of the transport system was run by Indians, who owned the horses and mules that carried the goods to market. This aspect of the economy was revealed during the *residencias* of Governors Martín de Urzúa y Arizmendi (1695–97, 1699–1703, 1706–8) and Antonio de Cortaire (1720–25), both of whom raised transport rates allegedly to benefit the Indians.[39] The Maya *arrieros*, or pack drivers, continued to control this sector of the economy until the end of the colonial period,[40] with the result that hard currency was continually infused into the peasant economy. When all market activities involving the transport of goods are taken into consideration, it is clear that these represented significant sums of money.

The important fair held annually in Izamal in December, to celebrate the Feast of the Immaculate Conception, also exerted market demand and led to the consumption of even more Indian produce. It also provided the opportunity for the Maya to spend their money, and consequently Spanish merchants regularly remitted merchandise to the fair, which the Indians attended in large numbers.[41] In short, the Maya were incorporated into the regional economy not merely through the confiscatory mechanisms of colonialism but also through their own voluntary decisions to sell grain and buy goods on the market.

The Maya and the World Economy

Despite the peasants' voluntary participation in the regional grain market, the confiscatory mechanisms of colonialism were undoubtedly of crucial importance in the economic relationships between Maya and Spaniard. In no area of Indian economic activity was this clearer than in cotton textile production. Here by far the most important institution was the repartimiento. Indeed, the repartimiento can be said to have been the "leading sector" of the economy of colonial Yucatan.

As the system worked in Yucatan, the Spaniards advanced money or credit to the Maya in return for future repayment in raw cotton, woven cloth, thread, or wax. Though the repartimiento began in the sixteenth century, it became firmly entrenched only in the early seventeenth century after the governors had succeeded in instituting the war captaincies in some of the major villages. The war captains theoretically provided for the military defense of the peninsula but in fact served to carry out the governors', and their own, repartimientos.

The governors and war captains were not the only people involved in the business. Encomenderos had been carrying out repartimientos since the late sixteenth century, and continued to do so throughout most of the colonial period. And since the profits to be made were substantial, soon all sorts of people tried to cash in on the opportunity by organizing their own repartimientos.

Besides the governors, the most successful of these practitioners was the Santa Cruzada (Holy Crusade). This was an ecclesiastical institution established in the fifteenth century to raise money to pay for Spain's war against the Moors through the sale of bulls of indulgence. Once established, however, the selling of indulgences continued for the next 300 years simply because the crown was no more willing than the Church to forgo its share of so profitable an enterprise. Accordingly, every four years saw a new indulgence proclaimed and made available to the faithful in return for cash.

Still, the Spanish government, aware of the ease with which Indians could be cheated, did attempt to prevent abuses by prohibiting the sale of indulgences in Indian villages.[42] Any native who wanted one, the reasoning went, could purchase it in a Spanish city. But in Yucatan a Basque immigrant named Pedro de Garrástegui had other ideas. Around 1675 Garrástegui bought the post of Treasurer of the Santa Cruzada for 14,000 pesos. Included in the purchase price was the right to pass the position on to his heirs.[43] The investment proved to be well worth the money, for the enterprising Basque quickly learned to exploit his post by selling indulgences to the Indians in exchange for future deliveries of cloth and wax.

While one can only speculate on the eschatological validity of indulgences sold on credit, there can be no doubt about the material rewards collected by the Santa Cruzada Treasurer. In fact, shortly after buying the post, Garrástegui purchased the title of Count of Miraflores, thereby making himself and his heirs the only family of titled nobility in Yucatan. No record was kept of most of the first officeholder's business activities, but when the second Count of Miraflores got involved in a political dispute with the governor in the early eighteenth century, a detailed investigation of the Cruzada's accounts was made by officials of the Royal Treasury. It was found that during the ten-year period from 1704 to 1714, the Cruzada's exports from the port of Campeche had totaled 112,590 cotton patíes (each of which measured 2 varas by 0.75 vara, i.e. about 1.67 meters by 0.63 meter), 3,355 mantas, 2,912 *arrobas* of thread (about 72,800 pounds) of various qualities, 154,750 pounds of wax, 800 dozen hair combs, and about 400 cloth sacks. The goods, worth between 187,440 and 255,529 pesos f.a.s. Campeche, were sold in Mexico City for 345,269 pesos, 4 reales. The indulgences sold during that ten-year period were worth only 80,000 pesos, the sum that the Count had to deliver to the Santa Cruzada office in Mexico City to pay for the bulls; this meant that, at top price, the Count's annual gross revenues came to some 17,552 pesos. Since his costs, including the provision of the raw cotton for spinning and weaving, came to less than 2,000 pesos a year, at least 15,000 pesos were left as profits, to be divided between the Count, his family, and his repartimiento agents, many of whom were members of his family.⁴⁴ The position of Treasurer of the Santa Cruzada was very lucrative indeed.

As before, we will turn to the Franciscans for a detailed picture of the workings of the repartimiento system. (Although the data do not cover villages under the secular clergy, as noted, less than a quarter of the Maya lived in those settlements.) According to the friars, in 1700 all of the people carrying out repartimientos contracted the Indians for between 43,539 and 44,354 patíes, 1,028 mantas, 15,705 pounds of thread, and between 68,282 and 68,882 pounds of wax, for a total value of between 101,103 pesos, 5.5 reales, and 102,488 pesos, 2.5 reales. If the repartimiento was carried out in the villages under the secular clergy in the same proportions, then the total value of the contracted goods would have been about 135,000 pesos.

The most important of all the entrepreneurs involved in this business with the Indians was the Governor, Martín de Urzúa y Arizmendi. Urzúa controlled about 57 percent of all the textiles contracted, 6.5 percent of the thread, and 80.5 percent of the wax. Of the total value, the Governor's share, then, was almost an even 60 percent. Urzúa did not pocket all the profits, for he had to work through middlemen who of course received their share of the revenues. Nevertheless, his income from business with the Indians was considerable, and helps explain why politics in Yucatan in the late seventeenth and early eighteenth centuries revolved around the governor's role in the repartimiento system.

The rest of the business was controlled almost entirely by people holding official positions in the Church or the state, or exercising the powers of magistrate as alcalde. The Santa Cruzada and its agents received 11 percent of the revenues, the war captains got around 10 percent, and other important government officials received almost 10 percent. Included among these officials were Francisco de Avila (the Secretary General of the Government, or Secretario Mayor de Gobernación y Guerra); Clemente de Marcos Bermejo (accountant of the Royal Treasury and husband of the Treasurer of the Tribunal de Indios, i.e. the very institution created to defend the Indians against the Spaniards); Captain Blas Gutiérrez (junior alcalde of Valladolid; the senior alcalde always worked directly for the Governor); Captain Francisco de Solís (junior alcalde of Mérida; the senior alcalde, Captain Pedro de Cepeda y Lira, was an encomendero who carried out repartimientos in his own encomienda); Juan Joseph de Castro (a Spanish-born soldier who was *sargento mayor* (major), or second in command, of the provincial militia); and the various tithe collectors, who did business with the Indians on the side.

Next in importance were the encomenderos, whose share of the value of the repartimiento was 8 percent. The remaining 1 percent was shared by six private entrepreneurs. Though at the time of the survey these people did not hold important offices or work for important officials, they were by no means lacking in political influence. Maestre de Campo (Colonel) Manuel Bolio was the Governor's brother-in-law. Lucas de Villamil (a name that we shall see frequently in this study), a *regidor* (city councilman) of Mérida, had worked as chief repartimiento agent for a previous Governor; he was also the son-in-law of the senior alcalde of Mérida. Francisco de Valdés was an important member of society in Valladolid: he was the son-in-law of a powerful former senior alcalde and regidor, and the father-in-law of another regidor, and would soon be an alcalde, regidor, and high-ranking militia officer in his own right. Of the remaining individuals, Mateo de Cárdenas was a Basque immigrant who had been elected as mayordomo of the pósito of Mérida a few years before, had served as a tithe collector, and had married into a prominent family that included encomenderos, regidores, and militia officers; his son Domingo Cayetano would eventually become the chief official of the Tribunal de Indios and would administer the governors' repartimientos in the 1750's. In other words, four of the six private parties carrying out the most important kind of business with the Indians were identified in one way or another with former or current offices or officeholders or with encomenderos.

The repartimiento system in Yucatan, then, was intimately related to the colonial institutions of Church and state. For political power or protection was not only useful but essential for carrying out business with the Indians. Encomenderos actively intervened at times to keep everybody but the Governor's and the Cruzada's agents out of the villages of their encomiendas, and the Governor's people frequently used their positions to corner the market on raw cotton and keep other people out of the repartimiento business.[45] Everyone who thought he could get away with it tried to get into the business, and consequently once the agents of the Governor or the Cruzada, or tithe collectors, or anyone else, got access to the villages, they invariably carried out their own repartimientos. So too did the secular clergy in the villages not under the administration of the Franciscans.[46]

As already noted, the total value of the goods acquired through the repartimiento was considerable, given the relative poverty of Yucatan compared with the silver-producing regions of the Empire. The total yielded by the encomiendas was said to be only some 40,000 pesos, which would have meant that total tribute, both royal and encomienda, would have been only some 50,000 pesos.[47] Even assuming that this figure underestimates the total, it is still clear that the repartimiento system was of far greater economic importance than tribute, and probably close to being as important as tribute and religious taxes combined. In short, of all the mechanisms used to extract a surplus from the Indians, the repartimiento was primary.

In fact, it is possible that at times tribute became merely a branch of the repartimiento. Tribute had to be paid twice a year, at the Feast of Saint John (June 24) and on Christmas Day. Not surprisingly, most repartimiento contracts were arranged on exactly the same dates. One suspects that the frequent inability to pay tribute was turned to the advantage of the entrepreneurs, who could extend credit to the Indians by paying their tribute debts in return for repayment in kind at a later date. It is known, for example, that at least one encomendero used his revenues immediately to carry out repartimientos in the village of his encomienda, and that the Secretary General of the Government and the Treasurer of the Tribunal de Indios both arranged for their business on the very days when the Indians had to pay their taxes.[48] Perhaps secular clergymen did the same when their parishioners found it difficult to pay their religious obligations.

A detailed analysis of the repartimiento reveals important features of the economic structure of Yucatan in the late seventeenth and early eighteenth centuries. Involvement in the system required capital investment, because both cotton and either cash or credit had to be given to the Indians in advance. Investment capital was sometimes acquired from the Church or churchmen. For example, in the 1670's Bishop Juan de Escalante loaned either his own or the Church's money to Governor Antonio de Layseca to get the business going. Later, when the Bishop denounced the Governor for exploiting the Indians through the repartimiento, the investigating judge sent by the Audiencia of Mexico did not fail to point out the source of Layseca's capital, and noted that Escalante's change of heart was due not to "Christian zeal" but to personal enmity.[49] Bishop Juan Gómez de Parada also authorized the Church's lending of money for the repartimiento; in 1716 or 1717 he approved a loan of 3,800 pesos, taken from the Nunnery's endowment, to Governor Juan Joseph de Vertiz's commercial agent,[50] and in 1721 he authorized a loan of 8,011 pesos, taken from the Chantry Fund and again from the Nunnery, to Governor Antonio de Cortaire's agent, the regidor Lucas de Villamil.[51] The Church in fact played an invaluable role in the system by routinely providing the governors' commercial agents with the information they needed on the number of Indians in each village.

Capital could also be acquired from the merchant community in Yucatan. In 1700 Governor Urzúa apparently borrowed some of the money necessary for his business activities from Juan de Ugartena (or Huartena), a merchant who just happened to be the man who ran Urzúa's repartimientos for him.[52] In 1721 the senior alcalde of Valladolid borrowed 4,000 pesos from two regidores of Mérida who were also deeply involved in business affairs; one of them, Lucas de Villamil (whom we met earlier as a practitioner of the repartimiento in 1700), had by now become Governor Cortaire's local repartimiento agent.[53] Here, then, we see a close alliance between businessmen and government officials, or better, between business and the business of government.

Documentation does not permit a detailed analysis of the sources of investment capital for the repartimiento. But it is clear that at times people outside of Yucatan were involved. Governor-designate Alonso de Meneses, while still in Mexico City prior to his assumption of duties, borrowed some 50,000 pesos from two residents of the viceregal capital, and received an additional 21,000 pesos in loans from people in Veracruz and Campeche.[54] In fact, as we shall see, people outside the peninsula were often deeply involved in the repartimientos. For that reason, Governor-designate Cortaire, while still in Mexico City, had little trouble learning the best person to contact in Yucatan to arrange his business activities for him. People in the know told him to deal with Lucas de Villamil.[55]

Once the capital was available, it was advanced by way of middlemen to the Indians for future payment in kind. The going rate for raw cotton was four reales per carga (32 pounds). The material needed for weaving was always contracted in the Valladolid and Tizimín districts, which specialized in the production of cotton. The most important primary product after cotton was wax, which was produced in most parts of Yucatan. However, it varied in quality from district to district. The poor, black wax from Valladolid, Tizimín, and Beneficios Altos (the eastern half of the peninsula) fetched one real per pound, compared with one and a half reales for the high-quality yellow wax produced in the Sierra, the Costa, Beneficios Bajos, and the Camino Real.

At times some innovative entrepreneurs tried to contract for other goods, like vanilla, *achiote* (a condiment and food coloring), cochineal, copal (in the Bacalar area), *contrayerba* (a medicinal root), and henequen fiber thread and sacks.[56] But royal policy frowned on such practices, and the repartimiento was usually restricted to cotton and wax.

Once the raw cotton was acquired from the eastern producing regions, it was distributed throughout most of the peninsula, along with cash or credit. Supposedly this was done on a per capita basis, at the rate of one-half patí per female. But as we have seen, some people are known to have extracted more from the Indians than they were supposed to, and the women might end up heavily burdened with work. Each patí required six pounds of raw cotton to be spun and woven, and the women were paid four reales for their labor. The result was a piece of cloth measuring slightly more than one square meter. Mantas, less frequently contracted, required 16 pounds of raw cotton, and the labor cost was two pesos each.

A pound of thread required four pounds of cotton and was paid for at the rate of one real a pound.[57]

The 1700 Franciscan report clarifies to a great extent the relative importance of all branches of the repartimiento. Textiles accounted for some 66 percent of the value of the goods, thread for 7 percent, and wax for 27 percent. Clearly, then, the production of cloth and thread was the main function of the repartimiento. But the various people involved in the business specialized in different branches of production. The Governor, who received 60 percent of the total value of the goods, received 57 percent of the textiles, only 6.5 percent of the thread, but 80–81 percent of the wax. Everyone else's share of the wax was correspondingly reduced, while the slack in the thread was picked up by the encomenderos (who got 26 percent) and above all by other government officials (54 percent), or more specifically, by two of them: the senior and junior alcaldes of Valladolid, who together accounted for only 5 percent of the total value of the repartimiento but for 53 percent of the thread.[58] Certainly those officials' dominance in this branch of production was the result of their ability to exercise extensive political power in the prime cotton-producing region of the peninsula.

The repartimiento yielded considerable profits for the simple reason that entrepreneurs acquired their raw materials for much less than the market price and then manufactured them into merchandise worth many times that acquisition cost. In the 1670's, for example, when raw cotton was acquired from the Indians at four reales per carga, the market price was between eight and 12 reales. By the 1720's the market price seems to have declined to six reales, but the repartimiento still yielded a profit because the businessmen continued to pay only four reales to the Indians.[59]

Even more profits were realized because the labor of spinning and weaving was also underpaid. For each patí, the entrepreneur invested four and three-quarters reales (four for the labor, the rest for the cotton), then sold the cloth for eight to 11 reales. A manta required an investment of two pesos, two reales (two pesos in labor costs), and sold for from three pesos, two reales, to five pesos. And thread cost the businessman one and a half reales per pound (one real for labor) and sold for between two and three reales. In short, profits were between 68 and 132 percent of invested capital for patíes, between 44 and 122 percent for mantas, and between 33 and 100 percent for thread. Finally, for the laborious task of collecting wax, Indians got one or one and a half reales per pound, which the entrepreneur could then sell at two reales, for a profit of between 33 and 67 percent. On top of this, many of the Spaniards passed a large part of the transport costs on to the Indians by requiring them to deliver the goods in Mérida. The repartimiento was very good business indeed.

Not content with these healthy profits, entrepreneurs often used their own political power or their connections both to protect themselves from losses and to carry out even more obviously fraudulent business activities at the expense of the Indians. In 1678 the Governor's agent in Valladolid was able to corner the market in raw cotton by forcing the producers to accept contracts for the entire crop of over 16,000 cargas, thereby cutting into everyone else's profits. At the same time the Governor, Antonio de Layseca, arbitrarily declared an increase in the size of the patí, thereby acquiring more cloth without any increase in investment. For the purposes of wax collection, various governors simply declared that a pound consisted not of 16 but of 18 or 20 ounces. When wax was scarce because of drought, the entrepreneurs would sell it to the Indians at inflated prices so that payments could be made, as specified in the contracts, in kind. Governor Layseca's agents in the 1670's required the Indians to contract for cochineal, which could not even be produced in Yucatan; the whole purpose of the contract was to force the Indians to commute their obligations either by paying in cash two or three times the amount originally advanced or by delivering wax worth more than the alleged value of the cochineal.[61]

Besides Layseca, the Governor most notorious for such abuses in this period was Fernando de Meneses Bravo de Sarabia. In addition to increasing the sheer quantities of goods contracted, Meneses officially increased the size of the patí, the weight of a carga of cotton (from 32 to 40 pounds), and the ounces in a pound of wax (to 19). Moreover, after contracting the Indians of the Tizimín jurisdiction for raw cotton at four reales a carga, he then sold it to them at three pesos after a drought had destroyed the crop and prevented them from paying their debt in kind. In other words, the Indians paid in cash six times more than what they had received from the Governor's repartimiento agents.[62]

Meneses was exceptionally greedy, apparently, but according to the Franciscans, the system was abusive even when kept within normal limits. Indian men had to go off on wax-gathering expeditions lasting months, causing them to miss the sacraments and to die and be buried in the wilds without the proper last rites. Females were said to be so overburdened with work that fatigue resulted in numerous spontaneous abortions. Worst of all, force generally had to be employed to make the Indians accept the advance payments, and they were then frequently punished with the lash if they defaulted.[63]

What kept the repartimiento going, of course, was its enormous profitability. The merchandise acquired through this kind of putting-out system was used locally to a certain extent, but a very large proportion was exported. As we have seen, the Santa Cruzada alone shipped more than 100,000 patíes, 3,000 mantas, 36 tons of thread, and 77 tons of wax, as well as small quantities of combs and cloth sacks, to Mexico City between

1704 and 1714.[64] (At the same time, the repartimiento activities of the Santa Cruzada and of the *alcalde mayor* in Tabasco enabled them to import thousands of pounds of cacao into Yucatan, where it was used as currency as well as for making chocolate.)[65] Governor Antonio de Cortaire is known to have forced the Indians to supply 18,921 patíes and 1,593 arrobas (about 20 tons) of wax every six months, and during his brief tenure (1720–21), he sent 70,716 patíes and 6,043 arrobas of wax to Mexico City and 4,686 patíes and 482 arrobas of wax to Puebla.[66] A Spanish-born merchant operating out of Mérida in the 1690's is also known to have shipped repartimiento goods to Puebla, though according to Cortaire, Mexico City was the principal destination of such goods.[67] The Count of Miraflores also identified the Mexico City area (called simply "México" in colonial parlance) as the destination of the goods of Governors Fernando and Alonso Meneses. In a complaint against their excessive repartimientos, he alleged that the brothers had caused the price of mantas to fall in the viceregal capital in 1708–15.[68]

Once in New Spain, the goods moved through various mercantile channels before reaching the consumer. Some of the wax undoubtedly passed into the hands of the *alcaldes mayores* and *corregidores* of the Valley of Mexico, for those officials are known to have used wax in their own repartimientos with the Indians of their jurisdictions.[69] Since those repartimientos consisted not of the forced purchase of Indian products but of the forced sale of goods to the Mexicans, an item of trade that passed through both systems, first in Yucatan, where the Maya were made to sell their product at low prices, and then in New Spain, where the Mexicans were forced to buy it at high prices, brought profits at both ends of the economic chain.

A large part of the Yucatecan products flowed out of the viceregal capital into the hands of consumers all over Mexico. As already noted, textiles and thread manufactured in Yucatan were to be found in Puebla. They also turned up as regular items in the stock of stores in Zacatecas and Parral, where they were identified as products from Campeche, which of course was the port from which the goods were shipped.[70] Textiles in fact played an important role in the mining economy, for wages were often paid in cloth. Consequently, manufactured goods from Yucatan regularly made it into the commerce of the northern Mexican mining economy, and to do so, the cloth and thread had to travel a long way from the Maya villages of the Sierra, the Costa, Beneficios Bajos, and the Camino Real, and even farther away from the cotton-producing region of Valladolid and Tizimín.

Yucatan, then, far from being commercially isolated, was in fact an integral part of the world economy, for it was directly tied into the most important branch of the colonial Spanish American economy, namely, silver mining. The peninsula therefore had a major role in the international division of labor in the seventeenth and eighteenth centuries. The colonies in theory and in practice served to provide the mother country, and through it the Western European economy, with raw materials and primary products, the most important of which were gold and silver. But in an unexpected twist resulting from economic integration, Yucatan, as well as Oaxaca, Chiapas, Guatemala, Nicaragua, and even the Philippines, produced manufactured goods—cotton textiles—for the exporting regions of Spanish America because it was too expensive to import them from Europe.[71] It was cheaper to manufacture the textiles under conditions of colonialism, that is, where the materials could be purchased at confiscatory prices, and the labor was compulsory.

On closer examination, then, the repartimiento had considerable historical significance beyond the mere exploitation of the Indians. Exploitation, after all, took place everywhere and therefore should surprise no one. The repartimiento in fact was the most important mechanism developed by Spanish colonialism in the seventeenth century for the extraction of a surplus from the Yucatec Maya. Moreover, by extracting goods that could be exported, it was the major mechanism integrating Yucatan into the world economy as a producer of manufactures for consumption by the poor of silver-rich Mexico. Contemporaries understood what was happening. In fact, in 1678 an encomendero denounced the system because, as he put it, "the 272 pueblos in this Province [are] in a continuous *obraje* [textile mill]."[72] Yucatan had in effect become a sweatshop.

The repartimiento also served to integrate Yucatan's own regions into an economy geared for export. Cotton was acquired where it was best produced and was then shipped to where it could best be woven into cloth. Moreover, the system relied on a marked division of labor, not merely by region but also by sex: the spinning and weaving were carried out exclusively by Maya women and girls, while harvesting the cotton, gathering the wild wax, and transporting the goods back and forth across the peninsula were exclusively male domains. In short, males and females were integrated into productive units. This point bears emphasizing, for it is often forgotten that the colonial system of forced labor involved women just as much as men. The success of the repartimiento rested on its ability to get the entire peasant community involved as laborers in one capacity or another. Its genius was in the organized way in which the surplus labor of adults and children of both sexes was tapped to the fullest.[73]

Finally, the repartimiento system was historically significant for political reasons. For it was illegal. Governors were not only prohibited from engaging in business activities in the areas under their jurisdiction; by the late seventeenth century, they were specifically forbidden to carry out the repartimiento. Yet they did so on a grand scale, and even the most rapa-

cious of them—Antonio de Layseca and Fernando de Meneses—on con-
viction for their abuses were given only minor punishment and were then
formally declared to be fine Christian gentlemen fit to hold even higher
office. The sale of indulgences in Indian villages—on credit, of course—
was also illegal and was sometimes even opposed by the Governors. But
the Counts of Miraflores got away with it by taking advantage of archaic
features of the law: each Count, starting with the first, got himself named
alguacil (constable) of the Holy Office of the Inquisition, and as an alleged
member of the clergy, he was not under the Governors' criminal jurisdiction. The Counts eventually succeeded in extending their special protection to all of their repartimiento officials. Businessmen were thus
passed off as ecclesiastics.

The structure of Church and state resulted in acceptance of the repartimiento. In fact, politics even necessitated it, for once the office of Governor began to be sold—the post sold for 9,000 pesos in 1707 and for
12,000 in 1711[74]—the repartimiento was inevitable: it was the only viable
business the Governors could engage in to recoup their investment and
make a profit from public office. Only in 1731 did the Spanish government stop pretending that it was illegal and authorize the Governors to
carry out business with the Maya.

Consequently, the repartimiento was one of the most important economic and political facts of seventeenth- and eighteenth-century Yucatan.
Yet for all its abuses, it did not end up destroying the Maya. In the end,
the people who carried out the repartimiento had to accept the Maya for
what they were without trying to change them. Indians had been harvesting cotton, spinning thread, weaving textiles, and gathering wax before the European invasion. The colonists simply demanded that the
Maya keep it up, and do more of it. In short, the economic function of
Yucatan in the world economy did not require new structures of production at the local level.

To be sure, coercion had to be used to maintain Yucatan as an exporter
of manufactured goods. The caciques, who were forced to distribute the
raw cotton and money to the people of their villages, were sometimes
whipped for their failure to deliver the requisite quantity of goods. The
repartimiento was not merely a putting-out system of the late medieval
European sort. The free population of Europe could not be subjected to
forms of coercive labor recruitment and repression the way the Indians
of the Spanish Empire were. Force was a sine qua non of the system, for
the Maya actively resisted the repartimiento. Sometimes they did so with
success. For example, many of the villages around Campeche were exempted from the repartimiento after the 1660's because the Indians in the
area had simply run away beyond the frontier to escape the abuses of Governor Rodrigo Flores de Aldana; to encourage people to return and live

in the villages, the government relieved the Indians from the reparti-miento.[75] As the cacique of one of these settlements had bluntly explained to the local curate in 1700, his pueblo "has defended itself by saying that, should repartimientos be introduced, the Indians will run away, being, as they are, at the foot of the Mountain, and moreover the village is newly founded."[76] This threat of flight was taken so seriously by the Spaniards that the villages of the Campeche jurisdiction successfully avoided repar-timientos until the 1770's.[77]

The rest of the Maya were not so fortunate. They were forced to work so that Yucatan could serve as an export platform providing Mexico with cheap cloth, thread, and wax. The demand for these goods was so great that even India, China, and the Philippines exported cotton textiles to New Spain; the Philippines also provided Mexico with some of its im-ported wax.[78] Long-distance trade therefore was not limited merely to luxury goods.[79] The Maya were thus dragged into the world economy against their will. Nevertheless, the labor of the repartimiento was known and understood; nothing new, like work in silver or mercury mines, was involved. Spanish colonialism succeeded in Yucatan because it lived off Indian society without destroying it.

This reality helps explain the survival of Maya culture in Yucatan. If it is true that some indigenous societies were destroyed by colonialism be-cause of the excessive demands placed on them, it does not follow that the others survived only because they were isolated from the core colonial economies and hence free from substantial exploitation. The native people of Yucatan, Chiapas, Oaxaca, and Guatemala were all subject to a very demanding repartimiento system, yet these are the most "Indian" parts of Latin America today. Native cultures survived in part because in these areas the colonial regime employed existing structures of produc-tion to accomplish its ends. Whereas in most Western societies the posi-tion of the ruling classes was based on their ownership of the means of production and on the need of the propertyless to pay rent or sell their labor, in colonial Spanish America the Indians frequently maintained con-trol of the means of production, that is, the land, but could not control the relations of economic exchange between themselves—the peasant sector—and the larger society.[80] They did exercise some control over the grain economy in Yucatan, but the most important mechanisms for ex-tracting wealth from the Indians were repartimiento, tribute, and reli-gious taxation. Brute force exercised by the state ensured that these worked to the Spaniards' advantage. Social stratification and economic inequality were therefore the result not of property relations but of co-lonialism.

In short, the Spaniards' status as the elite did not depend on the exercise of economic power emanating from their ownership of the means of production. Rather, the colonists received the benefits of colonialism because the state imposed the rules of economic exchange between Spaniards and Maya, and although the crown did take measures to protect the natives from the colonists, it did not change the nature of exchange relations between peasants and city dwellers, that is, between Spaniards and Indians, until the end of the colonial period. When the effort was finally made, the colonial regime was already in crisis.

CHAPTER FIVE

Hispanic Economy and Society

Spanish society in Yucatan began with the 175 *vecinos* (heads of households) who founded Mérida, Campeche, Valladolid, and Bacalar in the middle of the sixteenth century. Natural growth and a slow but steady stream of immigrants pushed the number to 600 by the early seventeenth century, which would have signified a total of about 3,000 men, women, and children. By 1639 the urban centers had 878 vecinos, or some 4,390 people. The society was plainly growing rapidly, although in that year the Maya still outnumbered Spaniards by about 47 to one.[1]

The importance of the Spanish colonists, however, is only partially measured by their numbers. Their presence also resulted in the growth of a mestizo population that was counted as neither Spaniard nor Maya. Of course, some mestizos were absorbed into the native population, especially if the Indian mother maintained her ties to her family and community. But many of the mixed-race people came to occupy a social and racial middle ground between the Spanish and Maya societies, and as time went on they became thoroughly Hispanized, significantly increasing the size of the non-Indian society.

Another large component was added to that society with the forced migration of Africans. Black people commonly accompanied Spanish exploration and conquest in America, and it is therefore no surprise to find Africans in Yucatan from the very beginning of the colonial period. By 1582 Bishop Gregorio de Montalvo was reporting that many blacks and mulattoes were living in the Indian villages and marrying the natives in spite of royal prohibitions against both activities.[2]

Over time, natural growth and the continued importation of slaves produced a distinctive African-American society in Yucatan. Not all of these people were called simply "blacks," for Spaniards tended to distinguish between *negros* (who were of unmixed African ancestry) and *mulatos* (descendants of black Africans and whites). In Yucatan no term was ever used to specify someone of African and Indian ancestry. But as time went on, and as more and more racial mixing took place, the term *pardo* (dark person) came into use. Eventually all people who were partially or wholly descended from Africans were called collectively pardos. Nevertheless, the terms *negro* and *mulato* continued to be used, presumably because African slaves continued to be imported until the early nineteenth century. *Negro* usually implied a slave, pardo or mulato a free person.

Eventually a significant number of free African-Americans lived in Yucatan. These pardos tended to be employed in particular occupations. In the cities they were usually artisans; in the countryside they were frequently found as peddlers and foremen (mayordomos) of estancias, and less often as owners of farms dedicated to raising pigs and chickens. Some pardos became rather important people, a handful managing to hold positions as war captains and militia officers. In one notable case, a mulatto became regidor of Valladolid.[3]

But for Africans in Yucatan, history almost always began the hard way, in slavery. Most slaves probably came directly from Africa—from "Mina" (the Slave Coast), "Caramantin" (West Africa), or Angola. Others apparently were acquired from English colonies, for some slaves were said to be from Belize and one was simply identified as English. In fact, we are left to guess at all this, for Spaniards were not usually interested in these matters, and few buyers and sellers bothered to comment on where the slaves' homelands were.[4] Since most of the slaves brought to Yucatan worked as domestic servants, they were probably not treated as badly as their counterparts in the fields and mines. Nevertheless, the system was notoriously inhumane: practically all the slaves whose sale was documented in the notary records in the early eighteenth century had been branded, usually on the face. Almost all of them had been brought to Yucatan by the English merchants who controlled the Real Asiento (the exclusive right to provide African slaves to the Spanish Empire). To carry out this business, English factors resided in both Campeche and Mérida.[5]

It is impossible even to guess at the number of people of whole or part African origin in Yucatan in the mid-colonial era, but it must have been substantial, for in the early eighteenth century a large part of the urban militia was made up of mulattoes. One barrio of Mérida—Santa Lucía—was inhabited overwhelmingly by people of African descent. In 1722 Bishop Juan Gómez de Parada even complained that many Indians were being forced to perform labor services for some of Mérida's pardos. The Bishop thought this altogether inappropriate because, as he put it, black people "should serve rather than be served."[6] Some pardos in the countryside also were exacting labor from the Indians.[7] But for the most part, in both town and country, African-Americans were, in Gómez de Parada's words, "commonly extremely poor," though they nonetheless "disdained to be equated with Indians."[8] In fact, the two groups were noted for disliking each other. In 1725 the procurator of Mérida reported that the presence of mulattoes in the Sierra region greatly increased the danger of open conflict there between the African-Americans and the Maya, as well as the possibility that the mulattoes would abuse the Indians.⁹

The people of African descent ended up speaking Spanish and becoming Hispanized in culture, although certain elements of African culture may have been preserved for some time. Like African-Americans in other parts of the Spanish Empire, those in Yucatan soon founded their own cofradías, or religious brotherhoods, and participated in Christian or quasi-Christian religious rituals. Because of the small number of African women brought in, males usually married or formed unions with women of racially mixed ancestry, and as time went on the retention of African culture became all but impossible.

In sum, sharply divided as African-Americans were from other classes in Hispanic society, they belonged to the República de Españoles that would eventually overpower the Maya culturally as well as politically. In the mid-colonial era, of course, Yucatan was still overwhelmingly Indian. Moreover, cultural change was not entirely unidirectional, for elements of Maya culture penetrated the creole communities and made them less Hispanic in nature. Acculturation, in short, worked both ways. Nevertheless, the Spanish commonwealth represented the wave of a future in which people of Maya culture would become a minority in their own land.

The Encomienda and the Formation
of Hispanic Society and Economy

Thanks to growing royal restrictions and a declining Indian population, the encomienda had already lost much of its importance in Yucatan by the late sixteenth century. Nevertheless, the institution held on there well into the era of the Bourbon monarchy, a century or more after most of the encomiendas in the core areas of the Spanish Empire in America had been incorporated by the crown. The encomienda, therefore, is one feature that clearly distinguishes Yucatan's history from that of much of the rest of Spanish America.

After the late sixteenth century, the encomenderos' rights were largely limited to exacting tribute from the Indians of the villages that fell under their grants. Labor services seem to have ceased altogether, although in practice encomenderos, like all members of the local elite, succeeded in getting domestic laborers at artificially low wages or for no payment whatsoever. Even so, encomiendas were far less lucrative than they had been in the early colonial period, for not only were there fewer tributaries, but grants were now much more burdened with taxes and with obligations to provide nonencomenderos with a share of the tribute. García Bernal has estimated that taxes took away between 29 percent and 31 percent of tribute revenues from resident encomenderos in the early eighteenth century. The rate of taxation for absentee encomenderos was 39 percent.[10] At the time of the final incorporation of encomiendas in 1785, the rate of taxation was 35 percent, and another 15 percent had to be paid to pensioners. Thus encomenderos were losing one-half of encomienda tribute throughout the eighteenth century.[11] The early encomenderos had paid neither taxes nor pensions.

For all this, the encomienda was still an institution of considerable social importance, for history had contrived to make the possession of an encomienda a sign of prestige in the colonial society of Yucatan. At the time of the Conquest, some 150 encomiendas were distributed among the conquistadores, and since there were only about 200, and possibly even fewer, conquerors, most of the first colonists became encomenderos. But the gradual incorporation of some grants by the crown and the distribution of others to people residing in Europe cut the number of available encomiendas to about 115 by the early eighteenth century,[12] thus ensuring that only a small proportion of families in the rapidly expanding Spanish community could boast this status. As a result, more and more prestige came to be associated with the holding of a grant, and elite families on the termination of their grant immediately scrambled to get another one. *Arrivé* families frequently succeeded in being granted encomiendas, and those in decline tended to be removed from the pool of potential recipients. By the early eighteenth century, in fact, some elite families had managed to solidify their social position by acquiring several encomiendas. In colonial society, therefore, the tributary grants became not merely a means of extracting a surplus from the Indians but also an important element of social stratification among Spaniards.[13]

In the mid-colonial period the encomienda also had a military function. To be sure, from the very beginning the grants had entailed the recipients' obligation to provide military service to the King upon request. For this reason, grants ought to go only to men, the Council of the Indies had argued in 1549; women were unsuited to be encomenderos "because they do not defend the country, nor can they have or use arms and horses to defend it."[14] In most parts of the Empire the requirement to perform military service became a dead letter after the last of the major Indian rebellions following the Conquest, but because of Yucatan's exposure to pirate attacks, which occurred with some frequency in the seventeenth century, the crown was inclined to make this a consideration in bestowing encomienda grants. Military service was actually demanded of encomenderos, even in the eighteenth century. For example, the cabildo of Campeche reported that when the city was threatened by the English in 1742, Mérida's "Mounted company of Encomenderos, accompanied by squires and servants," came to the rescue.[15] Moreover, to raise funds for the defense of the Caribbean and the Gulf of Mexico, the crown regularly collected a special tax, called *escuderaje*, from all encomenderos who were unable to perform their military service. Of course, this financial burden fell especially hard on female holders of encomiendas. The Royal Exchequer thus benefited in a very real sense from a cultural tradition that denied women knowledge and responsibility in domains defined as appropriate only for males. In any case, the encomienda in Yucatan closely resembled a fief, for escuderaje was of course scutage, and the special taxes placed on tributes were essentially a form of feudal aid. Since the grants were made to provide holders with the revenue necessary to maintain themselves and provide military service, the encomienda was the equivalent of the medieval European money fief.[16]

Despite the great decline in the number of tributaries, the encomienda in the seventeenth and eighteenth centuries was still a valuable asset. The holder of a grant annually collected from each tributary a certain quantity of cotton cloth, maize, and hens. The monetary value of the tribute from the 115 encomiendas existing at the beginning of the eighteenth century was about 40,000 pesos.[17] This was a far cry from the 150,000 pesos collected in the middle of the sixteenth century, but in a province in which the average landed estate could be bought for less than 1,500 pesos, and in which the most valuable estates were worth less than 4,000 and yielded only a few hundred pesos of income a year, the encomienda remained of considerable economic importance to the local elite. An encomendero might gain up to 600 pesos from his grant.[18] This certainly compared favorably with the income generated by a major landed estate. Even when the encomiendas were finally incorporated by the crown in 1785, some were still profitable enterprises. Though the net median income (after taxes) of the 73 encomiendas was 323 pesos, 1 real, two holders were then receiving more than 1,000 pesos, and 12 had incomes of over 500. At the other extreme, seven grants yielded less than 100 pesos each.[19]

But tribute was only one of several ways in which the provincial elite profited from encomiendas. As we have seen, encomenderos frequently used their positions to carry out repartimientos in the Indian villages. For the realities of power were such that once someone had the right to extract anything from the Indians, he or she soon tried to extract everything. Relatives of encomenderos were able to use their family ties to carry out repartimientos as well.[20] Encomenderos who were also cabildo officers are known to have extracted corn from "their" Indians (the holder of an encomienda always displayed his or her superior position by referring to the natives as "my" Indians) for the purpose of selling it to the pósito of Valladolid, and the same is likely to have been the case in Mérida. Merchants frequently got themselves appointed as administrators of encomiendas held by absentees specifically to carry on business with the villagers.[21] Some encomenderos forced "their" Indians to provide them with food-stuffs without payment; others avoided paying tithes by requiring the natives to make the payments for them; still others made the villagers pay tribute in kind during food shortages in order to sell the goods at a great profit.[22]

One of the most important ways in which encomiendas could be made to yield wealth beyond their tribute revenues was through the acquisition of land and the concomitant exaction of labor to work in the encomenderos' enterprises.[23] In fact, as we shall see, the encomienda allowed Spaniards to get a foot in the door, so to speak, in rural Yucatan, and to set up landed estates.

For all these reasons, then, the encomienda continued to be of considerable economic importance even in the eighteenth century. And in fact because of these other activities, encomiendas had one more valuable aspect: they could be mortgaged.[24] Moreover, they could frequently be mortgaged for much more than their worth in tribute. For example, in 1721 Captain Pedro Calderón Robles, who had come to Yucatan in the late seventeenth century to serve a royal Governor as war captain and local repartimiento agent, was able to mortgage his encomienda for 4,211 pesos, a grant that had provided a revenue of only 670 pesos 19 years earlier, and that was certainly yielding less than 1,000 pesos a year at the time it was mortgaged.[25] In 1722 Francisco de Sosa y Cámara mortgaged his encomienda for 3,958 pesos, 2 reales; yet in the late seventeenth or early eighteenth century, its annual income was only 631 pesos, 2 reales, and in 1756, when it at last passed the 1,000-peso mark, that was because other encomiendas had been combined with it.[26] Finally, in 1729 Lieutenant Manuel de Carbajal mortgaged his encomienda for 1,374 pesos, a grant that had yielded a mere 347 pesos, 2.5 reales, in 1708 and whose current worth was certainly less than 500 pesos.[27] On the other hand, an encomienda alone was not always enough to secure a loan, and some encomenderos had to mortgage their houses and estancias in addition to their tributes.[28] An encomienda, in other words, was an asset just like any other form of property.

Apparently, many encomenderos ended up mortgaging their grants to pay debts. But others used the money for business ventures, as Captain Antonio de la Helguera y Castillo did in 1728. The then-regidor, a native of Burgos who had become so accepted into local society that eight years earlier he had been elected Procurator of Mérida and sent to Spain to plead for the continuation of encomiendas, invested the proceeds from a mortgage in a company in Veracruz.[29] Still other encomenderos used the money raised through mortgages to provide dowries for nuns, found chantries, or even post bond for associates.[30]

The sources of mortgage capital were varied. Some people raised money by mortgaging their encomiendas to the Church's Chantry Fund or the Nunnery.[31] But whereas landed property owners usually borrowed from the Church, encomenderos appear to have relied heavily on mercantile sources of credit. The great majority of such cases in the notarial records involved advances of money, credit, or goods by powerful entrepreneurs, who in return received the right to collect the debts directly from the Indians of the encomiendas.[32] These local merchants in turn sometimes paid off their own debts, in cash or kind, to creditors as far away as Mexico City and Madrid.[33]

Transactions of this sort were concluded for one reason: to gain access to Maya society. Why else would businessmen be willing to loan more money than the encomiendas were worth? In fact, the most important of the lenders were Lucas de Villamil, Francisco de Solís, and Eloy Clemente de Cuenca—all of whom were longtime practitioners of the repartimiento for themselves and for royal Governors. The encomienda therefore had one more thing in its favor: it opened the door to the mercantile interests that organized, financed, and reaped the profits from the most important commercial activity being carried out in Yucatan.

The possession of an encomienda, then, gave the holder a considerable boost in the *sauve-qui-peut* competition for wealth and status in colonial society, and local encomenderos understandably fought vigorously to preserve the institution. For example, when the crown attempted to incorporate all the encomiendas in America in 1717, the cabildo of Mérida, after being informed of the law in 1720, held an emergency session and elected to send its Procurator, the above-mentioned Antonio de la Helguera y Castillo, to Spain to persuade the government to exempt Yucatan from the law. Helguera was instructed to remind the Council of the Indies that "the principal reason for introducing them [the encomiendas] was to reward the people who gave their services to conquer, pacify, and populate, at their own expense, without any cost at all to the Royal Exchequer, shedding their blood and purifying their lives."[34] The Procurator accomplished his mission, for in 1721 the crown exempted Yucatan from the incorporation decree, thus allowing the institution to survive even longer. It would fade from history only when the colonial regime itself had become obsolete.

The Age of the Estancia

Because land eventually became the basis of upper-class wealth in Yucatan, the process of property acquisition by Spaniards is a topic of considerable historical importance. For the great nineteenth-century haciendas developed out of existing landed estates that had paved the way for the growth of export agriculture. The colonial estancias and haciendas were essential stages in the long-term development of privately owned landed estates in Yucatan.

The Encomienda and the Landed Estate

Since the colonists' early efforts to carry out agricultural production on a large scale failed for lack of labor and markets, most of the early landed estates were cattle ranches. But there is evidence that some were founded in part for the purpose of aiding in the collection of encomienda tribute. For example, in 1630 Juan de Montejo Maldonado, the great-grandson of the Adelantado, and encomendero of several villages just to the east of Mérida, stated that in the area of his encomienda he owned Estancia Chichí, "where ordinarily I stay most of the year and occupy myself in the administration of the said Estancia and in the collection of my tribute, from there effecting the capture of those people who have fled from the villages of my encomienda, and there are many such people."[35]

Here, then, is a clear-cut connection between the encomienda and the landed estate. Recent historiography has clarified that, although the one did not evolve from the other in an institutional sense, in fact the two were sometimes related. Encomenderos frequently were the first people to establish landed estates in the countryside and often located their enterprises close to the villages of their encomiendas. Moreover, they invariably tried to make use of "their" Indians as laborers and frequently succeeded in doing so despite laws prohibiting the practice. True, most haciendas were founded by people other than encomenderos, and encomiendas in any case did not develop into landed estates. Nevertheless, there were at times socioeconomic and political relationships between the two. The encomienda, in short, was not merely an institution for extracting tribute from the Indians but part and parcel of the process by which Spaniards extracted a surplus from the countryside.[36]

It is virtually impossible to demonstrate a relationship between all encomiendas and landed estates in a given region. To do so, one would first have to identify both all the encomenderos and their family members and all the owners of landed estates, then systematically correlate the two sets of names to find a possible overlap, and finally link the encomienda to the founding or operation of the landed property. Failing more documentation, it is unlikely that anyone will ever even attempt such a task.

Nevertheless, in the case of Yucatan it is possible to trace at least some connections between the encomienda and the hacienda. García Bernal has helped make such a study possible by identifying practically all the encomenderos, and Valdés Acosta has carried out the genealogical research necessary for identifying the family members of most encomenderos and many landowners.[37] What is lacking is complete information on the ownership and location of landed estates. Notarial documents, the best source for this topic, are not to be found before 1689 and are fragmentary thereafter, so that a thorough study of any one period of time is impossible. Nevertheless, the extant notarial records are sufficient in quantity and quality to provide at least some insight into the connections between the encomienda and the landed estate in mid-colonial Yucatan.

Study of this topic is complicated by the fact that in both cases ownership did not stay in one family over time. An encomienda had to be turned over after two generations; the notarial documents suggest that estancias and haciendas also were rarely owned by the same family beyond the second generation. In other words, both landed estates and encomiendas changed hands so frequently that one might be tempted to conclude, as Marta Hunt has done, that connections between the two were tenuous at best and in any case broken very quickly.[38]

Under the circumstances, the number of cases that can be cited of encomendero families owning estates within the jurisdiction of their encomiendas is quite astonishing. For a start, there was Nicolás Carrillo de Albornoz, regidor of Mérida, who owned Estancia Holactún, near Cuzamá, in 1700, when he was the holder of the encomienda of Homún-Cuzamá. Moreover, while Carrillo was still encomendero of those villages, someone named Juan Manuel Chacón, probably Carrillo's father-in-law, established Sitio Pixixá in the same area, and in 1720 Carrillo purchased that sitio upon the death of Chacón. By that time, however, Nicolás Carrillo de Albornoz was no longer encomendero of Homún and Cuzamá, for he apparently had traded that grant for the encomienda of Tixkoch. The new encomendero was Carrillo's son, Cristóbal Carrillo de Albornoz y Chacón. Nicolás Carrillo thus continued to own property within the jurisdiction of the family's encomienda.[39]

Another example is provided by the encomienda of Tekit and the Ancona family. The founder of this prominent colonial family was Francisco Antonio de Ancona, a native of Seville who settled in Yucatan with his wife and several brothers in the middle of the seventeenth century. His children intermarried with the local elite, and as a result his son Pedro was named encomendero of Tekit in 1678, became regidor of Mérida in 1692 or 1693, and was senior alcalde in 1702 and 1707. Pedro de Ancona's son, also named Pedro, eventually succeeded his father as encomendero, and because both survived into old age, the encomienda of Tekit stayed in the Ancona family until about 1750.

Soon after Pedro senior got his encomienda, we find members of his family owning property nearby, and in fact the Anconas eventually had a long-term relationship with Tekit. His sister, Catalina de Ancona, wife of an important member of the prominent Salazar family, founded or purchased Estancia Halalchán, in the jurisdiction of Tekit. The second Ancona encomendero, Pedro de Ancona y Barbosa, and his wife, Doña Jacinta de Castellanos, came to own Estancia Susulá (Dzudzulá?), located within the jurisdiction of Tekit, and one of the encomendero's two brothers, Francisco, actually established residence in Tekit and owned nearby Sitio Lomcab. Gregorio de Ancona y Barbosa, his other brother, founded or purchased Estancia Santa Teresa and Sitio or Estancia Tekax; both of these estates were in the jurisdiction of Tekit and stayed in the Ancona family at least until the 1770's.[40]

An even more complicated, and interesting, case is that of the abovementioned Salazar family. The founder of this family had come to Yucatan in the sixteenth century, and like the Anconas the Salazars intermarried with elite families. Among their ancestors through the female line was the Adelantado Montejo. As descendants of the original conquistadores, the family was favored with encomiendas. In 1664 Francisco de Salazar y Córdova was given the encomienda of Muna, and in 1675 he married María Rodríguez de Villamil y Vargas, encomendera of Nolo and sister of the oft-mentioned Lucas de Villamil, encomendero first of Kucab-Kinlacam, and later of Xocchel-Tzanlahcat-Sacalum. Francisco's son, Simón de Salazar y Villamil, eventually inherited his mother's encomienda of Nolo, and his grandson Joaquín de Salazar y Valverde got Muna.

Meanwhile, Francisco de Salazar's brother Gaspar de Salazar y Córdova became encomendero of Ucí and married Catalina de Ancona, of the Tekit connection, and their son, Gaspar de Salazar y Ancona, inherited Ucí and married into the Casanova family, which held the encomienda of Chuburná. Francisco's other brother, Martín, married into the branch of the Carrillo de Albornoz family that held the encomienda of Yalcón. Francisco's oldest son, Simón, married María Manuela de Valverde, the daughter of the first member of that family to hold the encomienda of Cacauché-Dzonot-Aké and the sister or aunt of the second Valverde encomendero. And finally, Francisco's second son, Buenaventura, and grandson Joaquín married the Solís y Barbosa sisters, Inés and Antonia, who were the daughters of the encomendero of Chicxulub, nieces of the encomendero of Umán, and sisters of the encomenderos of Motul-Tekax and of Tzeme-Tixculum-Teya. In short, the Salazars either held encomiendas directly or were married into encomendero families.

They also developed important political connections. Gaspar de Salazar y Córdova served as junior alcalde of Mérida in 1684, held the office of regidor and *alférez mayor* (titular leader) of the cabildo between 1684 and 1704, and was elected senior alcalde in 1703. His brother Francisco served as senior alcalde in 1686 and 1695, acted as the legal defender of former Governor Urzúa during Urzúa's residencia in 1708, and was one of the *fiadores* (bondsmen) for Governor Alonso de Meneses in 1713. Francisco's and Gaspar's sons, grandsons, and nephews served as alcaldes or other elected officials of the cabildo in 1716, 1719, 1720, 1727, 1728, 1732, and 1733.

These connections undoubtedly created great opportunities, although the documentation does not permit us to investigate all of them. But a few cases do appear in the records. Francisco de Salazar y Córdova, encomendero of Muna, owned and probably founded Estancia San Antonio Caxquí, in the jurisdiction of his encomienda. This property passed to his son Simón de Salazar y Villamil. The father also purchased Estancia Uxmal (the site of the famous ruins), which was also in Muna. The son, Simón, came to own both Uxmal and Estancia San Joseph, located between Muna and Sacalum, the encomienda of his uncle Lucas de Villamil. Simón's son, Joaquín de Salazar y Valverde, owned still another estate, Santo Domingo Yuncú, located near Muna and Sacalum. Meanwhile, within the jurisdiction of Ucí, Gaspar de Salazar y Ancona purchased Estancia Nuestra Señora de Kancabchén at a time when either he or his father was encomendero of Ucí. The Salazar family may have used their connections with in-laws as well, for Simón de Salazar y Villamil owned Sitio Tzcab, near Chuburná, when his cousin Gaspar de Salazar y Ancona was married into the family of the encomendero of the village.[41] On the other hand, that may have been mere coincidence.

But coincidence cannot account for the other cases cited. In fact, enough encomenderos had landed estates in the jurisdiction of their encomiendas to provoke criticism of their practice of exacting labor services from the villagers. This was of course illegal, but labor continued to be demanded by encomenderos until the abolition of the encomiendas in the late eighteenth century.[42]

Obviously, therefore, a motive for the establishment of landed estates by encomenderos near their encomienda villages was to get at a source of labor denied to other landowners. At the same time, the estate could facilitate the collection of tribute, as we have already seen in the case of Estancia Chichí of Juan de Montejo Maldonado. And the encomenderos could use their power to acquire land at the expense of the villagers.

The last cannot of course be documented, because no records were kept of what was after all the abuse of power. But there is no question that encomenderos wielded real power within their jurisdictions and felt free to interfere with the lives of the Indians in all sorts of ways, including imposing their own candidates as caciques and prohibiting the villagers from marrying people "belonging" to other encomenderos.[43] Indians had to behave in a deferential manner before their encomendero, who was addressed as *amo* ("master"), and the encomenderos in turn demonstrated their superior status, as we have seen, by referring to "their" Indians. Moreover, the caciques understood perfectly well that their *amo* was a personage of power and influence, and therefore solicited his or her aid in time of need. For example, in the 1690's Doña Juana de Vargas Mayorga, encomendera of Nolo and mother of Lucas de Villamil, supported, and possibly even instigated, the attempt by the Indians of her encomienda to have the village of Nolo established as a parish seat (*cabecera*). Acting on reports that the curate of their current parish, Tixkokob, had been abusing the people of Nolo, Vargas began litigation "as the said encomendera and as the legitimate defender of the said Indians of Nolo."[44] People like Vargas who possessed power and influence at the provincial as well as the local level were undoubtedly those most able to acquire land near their encomiendas.

In any case, the very presence of so many estates owned by encomenderos in the jurisdictions of their encomiendas provides at least circumstantial evidence for relatively easy land acquisition by encomenderos. The real proof, however, is negative in nature: encomenderos were almost certain to complain to higher authority should an outsider try to establish an enterprise too close to "their" Indians, and therefore the easiest and safest way to get land was to do so within one's own encomienda. This was true all over the Spanish Empire, for encomenderos did not take kindly to intrusions by other Spaniards and fought at all costs to maintain their own prerogatives.[45]

This was certainly the case in Yucatan in the seventeenth and eighteenth centuries. A notable example is the conflict resulting from the establishment of Estancia San Bernardo del Buenretiro by Bernardo Magaña, a direct descendant of the conquistador Juan de Magaña and a member of a powerful colonial family. In 1657 Magaña bought some land from the villagers of Maxcanú for the modest sum of 200 pesos, requested a license to raise cattle, and began stock-raising on a large scale even before he had the legal right to do so. The encomendero of Maxcanú, Ignacio de Vargas, brought suit against the owner of the new estancia. Magaña was able to get the Jesuits to testify in his behalf because he had borrowed money from them and had used his cattle to guarantee the loan. The Indian Defender (Defensor de los Indios), who headed the Tribunal de Indios, at first hesitated to take action "out of respect and fear for the said Captain Don Bernardo Magaña, for he is a powerful and influential [*valido*] man, and the Indian Defender depends on him for his salary." Indeed, Magaña had at least two different royal Governors on his side, for he loaned money to Rodrigo Flores de Aldana and Antonio de Layseca to help finance their repartimientos. He was also regidor and *alférez mayor* of the cabildo of Mérida, and had served as senior alcalde in 1682.

As it turned out, these connections were not enough to save Magaña. In the end the Defender and the Tribunal de Indios did take up the case. When the Franciscans and others testified that Magaña's stock-raising would be prejudicial to the villagers of Maxcanú, the Tribunal sided with the encomendero. The crown finally ruled against Magaña, and the livestock of San Bernardo del Buenretiro had to be liquidated. The estancia never recovered its past glory as one of the largest cattle ranches in Yucatan.[46]

This case was cited in subsequent years by other encomenderos attempting to prevent the establishment of estancias in the vicinity of their encomiendas. In 1700 Nicolás Francisco Carrillo de Albornoz, the aforementioned encomendero of Homún-Cuzamá, and Francisco de Avila, administrator of the encomienda of Seyé-Hocabá (it had an absentee encomendero), both cited the ruling in the Magaña case to argue against the founding of an estancia near their encomiendas by Juan Baptista de la Cámara, a mestizo. But Cámara not only had the backing of the Governor—he had rendered valuable service in the conquest of the Petén—but perhaps more tellingly, called into question the motives of the encomenderos. He pointed out that both Carrillo de Albornoz and Avila owned estancias in the same area and argued that his opponents, far from defending the Indians of their encomiendas, were in fact protecting their own ranching interests. Neither opponent denied the allegation, and Cámara eventually received his license, although he never succeeded in raising the capital to stock his ranch and ended up selling his property to someone who could come up with the means.[47] In 1694 the encomendero Francisco de Salazar y Córdova protested an outsider's attempt to establish a new estancia within the jurisdiction of his encomienda of Muna, and he too cited the example of Estancia San Bernardo del Buenretiro to argue his case. Salazar, like Carrillo de Albornoz and Avila, owned an estancia in the area of his encomienda, and also like the other two encomenderos, he lost his case.[48] So too did Pedro de Ancona, who in 1701 protested the granting of a stock-raising license to the owner of Estancia Timul, located in the jurisdiction of Ancona's encomienda of Tekit.[49]

If encomenderos sometimes failed in their efforts to prevent the establishment of estancias within their encomiendas, this was always due to the power of those who supported the intruders. In all the cases cited, the Governors sided with the would-be ranchers, and although this did not always result in victory for the outsider, it clearly helped. By the same token, someone without the help of the Governor had little chance of success. And of course, the vast majority of non-Indians could not hope to get support powerful enough to fly in the face of the certain opposition of the affected encomenderos and ranchers. It is in this sense, then, that the development of the landed estate was closely connected with the encomienda. Encomenderos had great political as well as material advantages over practically everyone else when it came either to founding or to preventing the founding of rural enterprises.

The Land Tenure Aspects of Estancias

Spanish colonists in America established estancias to carry out ranching because stock-raising was one of the few branches of production that was both profitable and practical. In Yucatan, where productive activities were even more limited than elsewhere, ranching was almost the only branch of the economy in which the colonists could successfully engage. To begin with, in this endeavor they faced no competition from the Indians, as they did in agriculture; ranching was an activity quite unknown to the Maya but wholly familiar to the would-be entrepreneurs, for the economy of Spain had a large and well-developed stock-raising sector.[50] Moreover, since Spaniards, in Spain and America alike, consumed meat in prodigious quantities, colonial cities provided markets for the sale of one of the major products of stock-raising. Hides could also be sold locally for leather-making, and be exported to other colonies and to Spain itself, for the mother country's demand for leather was greater than its domestic supply.[51] Later, new markets for cattle products, and even for cattle on the hoof, would open in Havana and Veracruz.

Obviously, this was not an activity that all Spaniards could aspire to. First of all, stock-raising required a considerable investment in animals, equipment, buildings, and the like. Second, assuming money was no impediment, a would-be rancher in theory had to have an official license, or *licencia*, to raise cattle, for the crown, in order to protect the Indians' milpas from invasion by cattle, opposed the uncontrolled expansion of the ranching economy. And finally, of course, the rancher needed land.

In practice, land was easier to acquire than a licencia. In part this was due to the poor quality of the soil, for whether one judges value by utility or by price, land was not worth very much in Yucatan. At the same time, there was a great deal of land available as the Maya population dwindled and Indian holdings were abandoned.

Spaniards acquired legal title to land either by royal land grant (*real merced*) or by purchase from Indians.[52] Surviving hacienda titles suggest that many estates began as royal land grants and then expanded through the purchase of surrounding properties. Spaniards bought land from Maya villages, families, or even individuals. As we saw in Chapter Four, Indian cabildos frequently sold village land. The native leaders undoubtedly had their reasons for agreeing to the sales, but the documents rarely disclose what they were. The few documented cases are revealing. In 1652 the village government of Maxcanú sold land to Bernardo Magãna, owner of the newly established Estancia San Bernardo del Buenretiro, because the Indians needed money in the midst of a famine.[53] Sixty-eight years later the same village, along with Opichén, sold a well called Kankixché to Teniente Ignacio de Enríquez for 40 pesos because the Indians

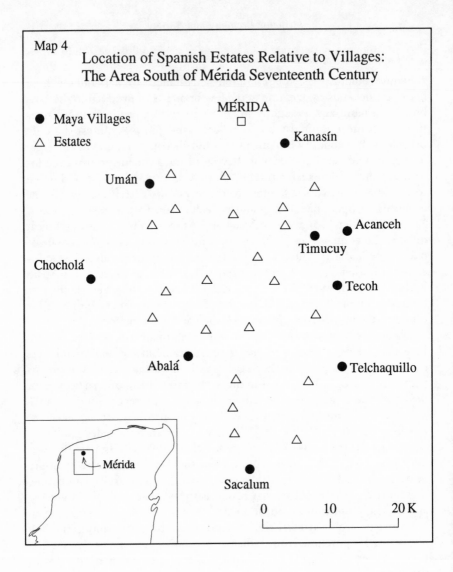

Map 4 Location of Spanish Estates Relative to Villages: The Area South of Mérida Seventeenth Century

needed money for unnamed village expenses.[54] The Indian cabildo of the barrio of San Francisco, of the villa of Campeche, was more specific: it sold the property called Cucultún to the priest Santiago Fernández for 100 pesos because the villagers needed the cash to pay their tribute.[55] Clearly, the vicissitudes of a peasant economy put some Indian property into the hands of outsiders.

On the other hand, not all villages came out losers in these transactions. Many estancias in the area between Sotuta and Valladolid were founded either on sites disputed by two or more villages or along boundaries that were likely to be the source of future disputes. Apparently Indian cabildos would sell land at the interstices of villages, thereby gaining cash while passing on past and future lawsuits to often unsuspecting Spaniards.[56] This tendency to establish landed estates on the fringes of village lands is evident elsewhere. Estancia Dzibilchaltún (now known as San Antonio de Peón) bordered on Ekmul, Tixpéual, and Tixkokob, but the sale of the property to a priest named Juan Antonio Méndez in 1731 was done by the cabildo of Tixkokob alone; the other two villages were not even consulted.[57]

It is hard to attribute all such cases to the Indians' clever sale of what was not rightfully theirs. More likely, the cabildos disposed of village property because they realized that, with their diminished population, they no longer needed as much land as before. This is almost certainly what happened in the case of the concentration of landed estates within a circle formed by Mérida and the pueblos of Umán, Chocholá, Abalá, Sacalum, Telchaquillo, Tecoh, Timucuy, Acanceh, and Kanasín (see Map 4). These villages are far enough apart (the distance between Chocholá and Tecoh, opposite each other on the circle, is almost 40 km) that the Indians could not effectively occupy all the territory in between, as they had undoubtedly done before the demographic collapse of the sixteenth century. The villages therefore sold large tracts of land to Spaniards. Many of the estancias founded here eventually developed into some of Yucatan's greatest latifundia and most profitable henequen plantations, of which the best known are Yaxcopoíl, Xtepén, Lepán, Uayalceh, Temozón, Mukuyché, and Xcanchakán.

Private property owned by Indians was also acquired by Spaniards eager to establish or expand landed estates. Most if not all of this land, as we have seen, was probably owned by families or lineages rather than by individuals. Whatever the case, Spanish purchasers found these holdings much to their taste because the Indian sellers could dispose of their property without the approval of the crown's representative, the Governor, or the Tribunal de Indios.

One landed estate produced by such a transaction was Hacienda Chumul, located in the jurisdiction of Kimbilá, near Izamal. The estate's titles show that the land belonged to Don Gerónimo Komún, an Indio Hidalgo, in the sixteenth century and was inherited by Bartolomé (or Bernardino) Komún, a resident of one of the Indian barrios of Mérida. Komún passed the property on to his relatives, Gregorio, Martín, Pedro, Domingo, and Pablo Komún, who in turn apparently passed it on to one or more of their heirs in 1611. Sometime later Chumul came to be owned by Doña María Balei, an India Hidalga, and her husband, Juan Pérez de la Paz, possibly a mestizo. The estate then was sold, sometime in the late seventeenth century, to Joseph Rivero, a Spaniard. Chumul remained in non-Indian hands until part of the property was taken away during the agrarian reform of the 1920's.[58]

Several other examples can be cited: the sale of some land near Cacalchén by Ignacio May, an Indian, to Joseph de la Peña, a Spaniard, in 1707 (the origin of Hacienda San Francisco Tzon); the sale of Sitio Ya (near Sinanché) by Andrés, Nicolás, Antonio, and María May, Indians, to Alonso Pacheco and his wife Paula Aguilar, Spaniards, in 1712; the sale of Sitio Xuxá (Cholul, just to the east of Mérida) by Felipe and Buenaventura Chablé and Manuel Canché to Alférez Ignacio Domínguez in 1719; the sale of the water hole and surrounding land called Kalax (Tekit) by Marcelino Tun to Alférez Salvador Solís in 1719; the sale of Sitio Xaxá (Cholul) by Felipe, Diego, and Manuel Mix to Alférez Ignacio Domínguez in 1730; and the sale of Sitio San Antonio Hiciná by Juan and Pedro Kantún to Marcos de Avila in 1733.[59]

Since caciques were in a good position to set themselves up as private landowners, it comes as no surprise to find them prominent among the individual Indians who sold property to Spaniards. The cacique of the barrio of San Cristóbal in Mérida, Captain Don Melchor Ki, who because of his military rank must have been an important Indian official, sold some land outside the city to Manuel Ramírez in 1707.[60] The cacique of Cuzamá, Captain Don Andrés Cocom, who also must have been rather important, sold a property named Anicabil, near his village, to Joseph Rodríguez de Ocampo in 1726, and two years later he sold another plot, called Balché, which he owned jointly with Gaspar, Juan, and Mateo Cocom—certainly relatives of his—to Francisco de Salazar.[61] A final example is Estancia Xukú, near Homún and Hocabá, a property that was owned in the late seventeenth century by the cacique of Hocabá, Hernando Yah, who passed it on to his nephew Juan Baptista de la Cámara. Cámara, it will be recalled, was the mestizo who had succeeded in getting a licencia to run cattle on Xukú despite the opposition of nearby encomenderos but failed to raise the capital necessary to stock his estancia. Cámara then sold Xukú to a Spaniard, Alférez Joseph de la Peña.[62]

Spaniards interested in buying land probably had little trouble finding Indian sellers, though some surely found it easier than others. As we have seen, many encomenderos were able to acquire land within their jurisdictions because of the power they exerted at the local level. Parish priests also seem to have had advantages when it came to property acquisition. Since clerics were generally of elite background and were an important monied interest in the colony, it is to be expected that they would become landowners. But just as encomenderos found reasons to establish estancias near their encomiendas, so too did some curates found estates within their own parishes, even though this practice expressly violated Church policy.[63]

One of these violators was Bachiller Francisco Gómez, the pastor of Peto ("Bachiller," abbreviated "Br.," was an academic title granted to secular clergymen). The two estates Gómez founded within the jurisdiction of his curacy—Hobonil and Bitunul—eventually developed into two of the largest haciendas of colonial Yucatan.[64] Another who saw fit to go against policy was Dr. Diego Leyton Tamudo, the curate of Sotuta, who in 1717 owned Sitio Kancabkú, located within his parish's jurisdiction. He later sold that sitio in order to acquire the even more important Estancia Chiló, also near Sotuta. Leyton's presence in the parish was strongly felt, for eventually his brother, Br. Nicolás Leyton Tamudo, came to possess an estate of his own—Estancia San Joseph Dzulché—near Sotuta. The second Leyton Tamudo later went on to become curate of Peto, and presumably went on to develop enterprises there as well.[65]

At least some priests, then, were in the vanguard of the Spanish invasion of rural Yucatan. Fortunately for the Maya, most parishes were under the care of the Franciscans until the middle of the eighteenth century, and the Franciscan order shunned the ownership of rural estates. Moreover, the Society of Jesus, which had no such inhibitions, never owned more than a handful of estancias, and none of these was exceptionally large or important. Consequently, the acquisition of land by churchmen was almost entirely the work of the secular clergy.

Parish priests possibly established or purchased estancias within their curacies because they could use their position to acquire labor in ways in which nonclerical landowners could not. But there were undoubtedly real economic advantages to close-hand supervision of estate management in any event, and for this reason, many estancieros took up residence in the villages near their estates. Though this was officially prohibited, the landowners got around the law by claiming to be *vecinos* of Mérida and only *residentes* of the villages. Non-Indian village residents who owned nearby estancias and sitios were reported, between 1690 and 1730, in Umán, Motul, Cacalchén, Mama, Teabo, Oxkutzcab, Dzidzantún, and Izamal.[66]

There are few records of *reales mercedes* in Yucatan, but the available examples clarify to a great extent how landed estates could be put together through a combination of purchase and royal land grant. The outstanding case is Estancia Chichí, located just to the northeast of the outskirts of Mérida, which was founded in 1558 as a *real merced* granted to Alonso Rosado, one of the original conquistadores. Six sitios, or undeveloped pieces of land, were added to the estancia's core area in the seventeenth century, and numerous additions in the next 200 years made Chichí one of the largest estates in the immediate vicinity of the capital; by 1912 its holdings totaled 1,908 hectares.[67]

At the same time, a *real merced* was not necessary for the formation of a latifundium, as the case of Estancia Uayalceh demonstrates. This estate, located 35 kilometers south of Mérida, was founded in 1653 when Iñigo de Mendoza y Magaña, an encomendero and regidor of Mérida, bought a sitio from the village of Tecoh for 50 pesos. Four years later Mendoza paid 100 pesos for 11 more sitios, which were sold to him by one of his in-laws, also an encomendero, who had just purchased the land from Tecoh, probably to serve as a cover for the owner of Uayalceh. In 1659 four more sitios were acquired, this time directly from the nearby village without the use of a go-between, for 60 pesos. Apparently no other acquisitions were made in the seventeenth century, and so the core of Uayalceh was assembled in six years through purchases totaling 210 pesos.[68] More land was probably added in the eighteenth and nineteenth centuries, and by 1911 the estate's holdings totaled 9,152 hectares, making it one of the largest latifundia in Yucatan at that time.[69]

In theory, the government awarded two kinds of stock-raising licenses, for *ganado mayor* (literally, "major cattle," horses and bovines) and for *ganado menor* (goats and sheep). Though some of the early settlers did attempt to raise *ganado menor*,[70] Yucatan's hot and humid climate made it impractical to produce either goats or sheep on a significant scale. In any event, at that point the distinction between *ganado mayor* and *ganado menor* tended to be ignored by the government, as well as by the ranchers, as indeed the phenomenon of the landed estate itself was. The result was illegal cattle-raising. For example, Estancia Chichí's original *real merced* did not specify that the estate was licensed for *ganado mayor*. Yet in 1626 the owner arbitrarily declared Chichí to be an "estancia de ganado mayor," and in all subsequent sales the estate kept that status, with buyers and sellers claiming that it had been a cattle ranch ever since its founding in 1558.[71] Estancia Uayalceh has a similar history. At the time of its founding in 1653, Iñigo de Mendoza did not have a license to raise cattle. Nevertheless by the 1660's he was running them there, and when he sold Uayalceh to his son Andrés, the terms of the sale specified that the estancia was of *ganado mayor*.[72] Clearly the crown was not enforcing the law rigorously. Nor was it encouraged to do so, for during the first century of the colonial regime there were apparently so few people with the capital to establish ranches that the legitimate cattle ranchers in general did not feel threatened enough by competition to pressure the government into enforcing the law.[73]

In the mid-colonial period, for reasons of their own, both the crown and the stock-raisers wanted to tighten things up. Established ranchers eventually felt the need to limit competition by preventing the founding of more estancias, and the government saw a way to profit from a strict enforcement of the law. Back in 1591, Philip II had attempted to raise revenue by offering to give legal sanction to irregular or outright illegal property acquisitions in America in return for the payment of a special fee. This *quid pro quo*, called a *composición* of land titles, was successfully resisted by landholders, backed by the Audiencia and royal officials, for a half-century or more. The 1591 *real cédula* was finally implemented in New Spain in the 1640's, but the composición fees were not wholly discontinued there until 1675–76.[74] It is perhaps no accident that just as the last payments were being made in New Spain, they were apparently beginning in Yucatan. In the late 1670's, both Chichí and Uayalceh had to pay a fee to get their titles legalized.[75] In 1711–13, during the war in Europe, the crown succeeded in raising a handsome 9,240 pesos, 5 reales, in composición fees from landowners whose titles were in need of legalization.[76]

By the late seventeenth century, then, estancieros and government officials had begun to pay close attention to what was happening in the countryside. It became more difficult to convert estates from *ganado menor* to *ganado mayor*. Moreover, as the case of Estancia San Bernardo del Buenretiro shows, it became even more difficult to begin stock-raising on a massive scale without a license to do so. We may recall, in this connection, that the encomenderos who opposed intruders in their jurisdictions objected not to the outsiders' ownership of land but to their cattle-raising. Some encomenderos, in mounting their cases against would-be ranchers, went so far as to voice a more general opposition to any further expansion at all of stock-raising estates. For example, in 1700, when Francisco de Avila and Nicolás Carrillo de Albornoz tried to stop Juan Baptista de la Cámara from raising cattle on his Estancia Xukú, Avila stated that "experience is showing that there is already a sufficient number of estancias," and Carrillo de Albornoz argued that there were already so many ranches in the vicinity of Mérida that "in just the jurisdiction of the said City the number of *estancias de ganado mayor* exceeds one hundred twenty-five, and there is not a hand's breadth of land that does not have cattle and horses." Resistance to cattle-raising on Xukú continued as late as 1728, when the estanciero Francisco Xavier Márquez led the opposition, and argued once again that there were too many stock-raising estates in Yucatan.[77]

The situation was exacerbated by the proliferation of estancias belonging to Indian cofradías. In 1723 Governor Antonio Cortaire reported that most of the damage to Indian crops was being done not by the cattle of the Spaniards but by those of the Indians themselves. Governor Antonio Figueroa made the same point in 1729.[78] Although much of the Indians' stock production was oriented toward their own consumption, the cofradías, as we shall see, did sell enough meat in the Spanish cities to intensify the competition in the all-important urban meat markets.

Opposition to the founding of new estancias soon resulted in conditions being imposed on the use of land being bought and sold. When the Indian cabildo of Maxcanú sold some rural property to Clemente de Marcos Bermejo, part-owner of the Estancia San Bernardo del Buenretiro (which Bernardo Magaña had passed to his daughter Magdalena as her dowry when she married Marcos Bermejo), the sale was made contingent on the buyer's agreement never to use the land for stock-raising. Moreover, the Indians even retained the right to pasture their horses on the site in the future.[79] A provision in the title of Sitio Tóo, without a license to raise cattle, specified that the owner of nearby Estancia Citincabchén (near Teabo) had first purchaser rights should the sitio be sold.[80] Nicolás Carrillo de Albornoz imposed the same conditions on his small estate named Pixixá when he sold it in 1720: all future owners who wished to sell the estate had to offer Pixixá first to the owner of Estancia Holactún (near Cuzamá), who just happened to be Nicolás Carrillo de Albornoz.[81]

Predictably, people resorted to various subterfuges to get around the efforts to keep them out of the business. Br. Pablo Asson de Evia, the curate of Umán, for example, allowed his sister-in-law, Juana Cervera, to keep 70 head of cattle and between 15 and 20 horses, as well as 400 beehives, on his Estancia Nuestra Señora del Rosario Ocán, located about 20 kilometers east of Mérida.[82] It is possible that other license-holders likewise served as fronts for people without legal permission to carry out stock-raising.[83] The resistance to new estates of ganado mayor may also account for some renewed efforts in the late seventeenth century to raise ganado menor.[84] But judging by the quick disappearance of sheep and goats from estate inventories, those efforts failed.

Eventually opposition to the expansion of cattle-raising wrought important changes in the value of rural property. Estates with licencias came to be worth much more than those without. In other words, the rights attached to the land were valued more than the land itself. This development had an impact on a considerable number of people—Indians, mestizos, Africans, mulattoes, pardos, and non-elite Spaniards—who had established themselves as owners of estancias of ganado menor. In an earlier age, these people could have entertained hopes of developing their estates into full-fledged cattle ranches. But the enforcement of the law in the late seventeenth century, followed by the crown's decision in 1731 to prohibit outright the granting of any further licencias to raise cattle,[85] froze the historical development of the estates of *ganado menor*. To be sure, the 1731 law was to be violated often in the future. Nevertheless, it had a "chilling effect," and many owners of estancias of *ganado menor*, realizing their lack of opportunity, sold out to the owners of estancias of *ganado mayor*. All of the great twentieth-century haciendas were built through this process of absorbing surrounding small estates that had failed to become full-fledged estancias.

In other words, the change from the relatively open system of the six-teenth and early seventeenth centuries, when restrictions on cattle-raising were not strictly enforced, to the more rigid one of the second half of the seventeenth century facilitated the growth of latifundia in Yucatan. Since cattle ranches were now the only estates with motives for expansion, the rights attached to the land were crucial in determining which estates would become latifundia and which would not.[86]

As might be expected, the spatial distribution of estancias was largely determined by their functions. Some, as noted above, were founded to serve as centers for tribute collection, and these were sprinkled around the countryside, in or near the encomiendas of their owners. But the vast ma-jority were established for the purpose of producing meat for the urban markets, a function that demanded that they be built as close as possible to those markets. Consequently the Spanish cities came to be ringed by cattle ranches. As early as 1579, the cabildo of Mérida reported that there were numerous estancias in the immediate vicinity, and Fray Ponce re-ported the same in his inspection of Yucatan in 1588.[87] So far as can be determined, all the landed estates still operating in the Mérida area in 1900 had been founded by the end of the sixteenth century.[88] We have no spe-cific information about the Campeche area, but estancias were certainly established there as well. As for Valladolid, although the cabildo of that villa made no mention of estates in its relación of 1579, we do have the observations made by Ponce in 1588. He saw only one estancia in the im-mediate vicinity of Valladolid, but found six or seven estates in operation near Tizimín, some 50 kilometers north.[89] These undoubtedly provided Valladolid with meat, though it is likely that they produced hides for ex-port via the coastal hamlet of Río Lagartos as well.

The pattern of estancias being established around cities and along the roads leading to the urban centers was reinforced in later years by the con-tinued growth of the Spanish communities of Campeche, Mérida, and, to a lesser extent, Valladolid. The provincial capital's Spanish population increased from about 1,500 people at the end of the sixteenth century to about 4,000–5,000 by the end of the seventeenth.[90] This growing popu-lation naturally generated an increasing demand for meat, which in turn stimulated the continued expansion of the cattle industry. Thus through-out the colonial period, more and more estancias were established, especially along the main roads. A large number of these ranches were strung out along the Camino Real connecting Campeche and Mérida. Also, by the early seventeenth century, Spaniards were founding estancias along the road from Mérida to Valladolid via Tixkokob and Izamal. Soon even the secondary thoroughfares leading out of Mérida—to Hunucmá, to Dzidzantún and Dzilam via Motul and Temax, to Hoctún and Hocabá via Acanceh, and to the Sierra towns of Ticul and Maní via either Umán and Muna or Acanceh, Tecoh, Tekit, and Mama—were straddled by cattle ranches.

Ranchers also rushed to fill up all the unoccupied lands relatively close to the cities. Just to the south of Mérida, enclosed by the circle of villages depicted on Map 4, was one such area. Others include the land north of Mérida between the swamps bordering on the Gulf of Mexico and the villages of Ucú, Caucel, Chuburná, and Chablekal; the territory west of Mérida enclosed by Caucel, Ucú, Hunucmá, Tetiz, Kinchil, Samahil, and Umán; and the area west of the arc formed by the villages of Kinchil, Samahil, Chocholá, Kopomá, and Maxcanú. In the case of Valladolid, ranchers confronted with a city surrounded by Indian villages moved into the thinly populated area to the north, around Tizimín, where there was a great deal of unoccupied land. Finally, in the Campeche area, with its relatively small Indian population, cattlemen had little trouble finding land to ranch. Spaniards thus occupied a variety of different sites, especially those having easy access either to the Camino Real or to the villa itself. In short, once again there took place a complicated interplay of geography, demography, and economy, the result of which was the emergence of the landed estate in a landscape once used exclusively by the Maya.

The Estancia Economy

The estancias of early and mid-colonial Yucatan were simple institutions. Stock-raising was not labor-intensive, and most ranches employed only a few permanent workers, typically a steward, called a *mayoral*, and a few cowboys, or *vaqueros*.[91] And record-keeping seems at best to have been confined to the most rudimentary accounting procedures. Although there are a number of surviving land titles, or *títulos*, from sixteenth- and seventeenth-century estates, researchers have yet to discover a single account book detailing or summarizing production, expenses, or marketing. Probably none was kept.

As a result, we have only a hazy idea of the Yucatecan landed estate in the early colonial era. The situation is much improved for the late seventeenth and early eighteenth centuries, when the documentation—especially notarial records—yields a reasonably clear picture of the Spanish-owned rural properties before the agrarian changes of the middle and late eighteenth century. At this stage, they still fell into two categories, at least by name, estancias and sitios. The latter were either small, newly founded, and growing ranches or estates of any size that raised cattle without a government license. Economically, there was no difference between the two kinds of properties, both being dedicated primarily to stock-raising and secondarily to apiculture.

Agriculture was not yet common on Spanish-owned properties, as an analysis of notarial records dating from the early eighteenth century clearly shows. In the 54 surviving inventories of estancias registered with notaries between 1718 and 1738 (the years for which almost continuous records exist), agricultural production—in all cases cropland planted with maize—was listed in only three. Similarly, there were only two cases in the 68 sitio inventories recorded during that period.[92] Moreover, agriculture was of little economic significance on the few estates that engaged in it. For example, the cropland on Estancia Chiló, near Sotuta (80 km southeast of Mérida), which had the largest area under cultivation of the three estates—17.5 hectares—was evaluated at only 55 pesos, representing but 5 percent of Chiló's total value of 1,093 pesos, 4 reales. What most determined this estancia's worth was the *planta* (the combination of buildings, equipment, and legal rights attached to the estate), assessed at 800 pesos, or 73 percent of the total value. The other assets listed were 14 head of cattle (worth 70 pesos), 10 horses (50), two mules (30), and 177 beehives (80).[93] Unused pasture was not assigned any specific monetary figure because it had value only if the estanciero already had or stood to obtain the legal right to use it.

Likewise, the 12.5 hectares of cropland on Estancia Hobonil (125 km south-southeast of Mérida, in the jurisdiction of Peto), one of the most valuable estates in Yucatan, were worth only 12 pesos, 0.5 real, and the 543 cargas of harvested maize listed in the inventory were worth 135 pesos, 6 reales. The total value of agricultural land and produce, 147 pesos, 6.5 reales, was only 4 percent of Hobonil's net worth of 3,580 pesos. The estancia's most valuable assets were the livestock (135 head of cattle, 182 horses, two mules, eight donkeys, and 13 hogs, worth 1,911 pesos, 2.5 reales, or 53 percent of the total value) and the planta (1,300 pesos; 36 percent).[94] The third estancia with cropland, San Joseph Kibá (15 km northeast of Mérida, jurisdiction of Conkal), had 10 hectares, valued at 32 pesos, 5 reales. This represented only 3 percent of Kibá's net worth of 1,138 pesos, 5 reales. Again, livestock (90 head of cattle, 18 horses, a mule, and a donkey, valued at 516 pesos) and the planta (500 pesos) were the estate's most valuable assets; they accounted for 45 and 44 percent of Kibá's net worth.[95]

As for apiculture, though more widely practiced than agriculture, it did not figure large on these estates; only 37 percent kept bees.

These inventories can be taken only so far, however. Though agriculture shows up as an unimportant pursuit on these estancias, it was probably more widely practiced on estates in the Sierra (which had some of the best soil in Yucatan), in the Campeche region, and around Valladolid. Since the Indian population had diminished radically, and permanently, in the southwestern part of the peninsula, some estancias near Campeche and along the Camino Real may have produced maize on a regular basis for that villa. According to the *matrícula* of 1688, Estancia Nohkakal, located some 28 kilometers southeast of the town of Campeche, had a resident population of 22 Indian laborers, as well as 11 vaqueros.[96] The matrícula also identifies 112 Indians as living and working on the estates near Hecelchakán (a large village along the Camino Real).[97] These Indian workers were seemingly among the first members of a social class in the making, namely, a peasantry dependent on masters for access to the land needed for survival. But in 1688 they were a small minority in a society made up overwhelmingly of independent peasants.

Agriculture also was carried out to some extent in the Valladolid region, which produced a large part of the province's cotton. There are indications that in the late seventeenth century some estancias, especially around Tizimín, took up cotton-growing because the expanding repartimiento system demanded more raw material than the Indians alone could produce.[98] Also, when famine threatened, the pósitos of Mérida and Valladolid sometimes loaned seed corn to Spanish estate owners to produce an emergency supply of maize. However, such practices normally involved no more than a handful of people, and once the crisis passed, grain production on estancias usually ceased.[99]

The development of agriculture on estancias was impeded by the lack of a permanent market demand for grain. Food shortages were still too infrequent for Spanish landowners to risk engaging in grain production on a significant scale. A shortage of workers must also have hindered the growth of agricultural estates. Significantly, a large part of the agricultural labor mentioned in the sources in this period was involuntary, exacted by war captains, encomenderos, and priests, that is, by people who because of their special positions had access to a labor supply not available to most landowners.[100] There are just a couple of hints, one in Tizimín and one in the Campeche region, suggesting that a few people rented land in return for labor services, usually performed on each Monday of the week.[101] These *luneros* (from *lunes*, Monday), as we shall see, were the wave of the future. But conditions were not yet ripe for the emergence of a whole social class of landless people willing to work for others in return for land. Labor accordingly remained scarce in the mid-colonial period.

The inventories in the sample reveal still another important characteristic of the Yucatecan landed estates of the period, namely, their low value. Of the 46 estancias sold between 1718 and 1738, the average selling price was only 1,471 pesos, 2.5 reales. The median selling price was even lower, 1,175 pesos. Two estancias fetched a mere 420 and 200 pesos. A full two-thirds of the estates were worth less than 2,000 pesos. At the other end of the scale, the most valuable estate in the sample—Estancia Hobonil—was assessed at 3,580 pesos. It was one of only three estates worth more than 3,000 pesos.[102]

Since meat, cowhides, and tallow were the most important products of stock-raising in Yucatan, the quantity of cattle on the estates is a good indicator of the level of their economic activity. It also permits comparisons between Yucatan and other areas of Spanish America. Over the years 1718–38, the median number of cattle on the sampled estancias (not counting abandoned, i.e. nonfunctioning, estates) was a meager 87. One-fourth of all operating estancias possessed 21 or fewer head, and the ones in the top quartile had between 180 and 263 head. This, of course, was a far cry from the thousands in the great herds of New Galicia and New Vizcaya.

Interestingly, the Yucatecan estancias of an earlier day seem to have possessed more livestock than their early-eighteenth-century counterparts. Two estates with 400 head of cattle were noted in chantry records dating from 1639 and 1645.[103] Other sources indicate that Estancia Nohpat had fully 1,700 head in 1611, that Teya had 400 in about 1625, and that Chichí had 300 in 1640.[104] It is noteworthy that all these cases are found in the years before the great crisis that began in 1648. As will be seen later in this study, socioeconomic crisis led to a depletion of estancia livestock in the eighteenth century. Perhaps the mid-seventeenth-century crisis had the same effect.

The estancias of Yucatan in the early 1700's may have had small quantities of livestock compared with other areas of Spanish America, but they partially made up for this in sheer numbers. The surviving notarial records alone make reference to well over 100 estancias and 80 sitios within a 25-kilometer radius of Mérida, as well as to over 100 estancias and 50 sitios elsewhere. Documents of the late colonial period record an enormous number of estates in Yucatan. The tithe records of 1790, far from complete for the province as a whole, list 115 estancias, 16 sitios, four *cabríos* (goat farms), three *quintas* (fruit farms), and nine unidentified properties within the jurisdiction of the parishes of Mérida alone. At the same time, the nearby curacies of Conkal, Acanceh, Umán, and Mocochá contained 22, 22, 24, and 21 estates, respectively, while the more distant Izamal had 52. In the 1770's, the parishes of the city of Campeche contained 30 estates within their jurisdictions. The census of 1795 reported a total of 859 estancias and 229 ranchos (agricultural estates) in the three regions of Mérida, Campeche, and Valladolid.[105] These figures, of course, are for the late eighteenth century, after a period of considerable growth of the livestock economy. Still, even if only half the estancias of 1795 had come into existence by 1718–38, Yucatan clearly had an extraordinary number of landed estates in the mid-colonial period, far more than in any region of comparable size in New Spain, New Galicia, or New Vizcaya.

Why should Yucatan have had all these Lilliputian estates, and northern Mexico a comparatively small number of Brobdingnagian ones? Part of the answer certainly lies in the many Indian villages that survived in Yucatan, restricting the estancias' room for expansion. To offset this limitation, a powerful estanciero, rather than establishing one huge estate, commonly came to own several small estancias in different locations, thereby creating a noncontiguous complex of landholding and production. Ecological conditions also contributed to the differing patterns of estate formation. Though water was scarce in both regions, Yucatan did have many cenotes; ranchers, like the Indians, were understandably attracted to places where water was available during the long dry season. In short, the numerous but scattered sources of water encouraged the formation of numerous and scattered landed estates.

Whether because of the estates' modest proportions or for some other reason, peonage was a rarity in the 1718–38 sample. The debts of peons were included among estancia assets in only five of the 53 estates for which information is available. Even then, the debts were very small in three of the cases: the "Yndios sirvientes" or "criados" of Estancias San Joseph Kibá, Katzcupó, and San Joseph Tiholop collectively owed only 10, 25, and 39 pesos, 5.5 reales, respectively. Substantially more money was owed in the other two cases. The peons of Hobonil and San Gerónimo Bolonpich—two of the most valuable estates in Yucatan—owed 170 and 142 pesos, 6.5 reales.[106] Since four of these five estates were worth considerably more than the average or median estancia, the incidence of peonage may be related to their size. It is also possible that peonage was more common, and more important, in Campeche, Tizimín, and the Sierra, that is, where more landed estates engaged in farming. Nevertheless, it is significant that so few of the estates in the sample had debt peons. Even allowing for errors of omission by buyers, sellers, or notaries, we can reasonably assume that peonage was not as important as free labor on most estates in early-eighteenth-century Yucatan.

Since the economic activities of most estancias were not labor-intensive, their work forces tended to be small. A case study of one ranch revealed that in the 1730's one mayoral and two or three vaqueros sufficed to carry out the stock-raising and apicultural labor on an estancia that was slightly larger than average at the time.[107] With the demand for labor so low, few estancias had a resident population of any size. Nevertheless,

TABLE 5.1
Debt Structure of 29 Estancias, 1718–38

Creditor	Percent of total debts
Chantries	61.5%
Convent of nuns	17.0
Private individuals	10.0
Franciscan convents[a]	6.7
Society of Jesus	3.3
Cofradía[b]	1.4

SOURCE: ANEY, Notarías 1718–38.
NOTE: Percent column does not total 100 because of rounding.
[a]Convents of San Francisco and La Mejorada.
[b]Cofradía de las Varas del Patrón, of the Cathedral of Mérida.

some estates had enough permanent workers to justify the construction of *oratorios*, or chapels, to provide for their immediate spiritual needs.[108]

Finally, the notarial records of 1718–38 reveal that Yucatecan estancias, although of modest value compared with those of other regions of Spanish America, were in general deeply in debt. Forty-one of the 46 estates for which information is available had obligations of one sort or another, and no fewer than 16 had liens equaling or even surpassing their entire net worth. The 41 estancias together were evaluated at 61,333 pesos, 2 reales, and their total debts came to 45,083, or a debt-to-value ratio of 73.5 percent. The median ratio was an even higher 87.9 percent. If the five unencumbered estates are included to form a sample of "typical" estancias, the median debt ratio of the 46 estates is still no less than 77.7 percent.

To whom were these relatively enormous obligations owed? The identifiable creditors, from 29 estancias, are shown in Table 5.1. Clearly, the most important obligation by far was to provide for *capellanías*, or chantry fees. These were not outstanding loans, though, but amounts that the estate owners were legally obliged to pay the priests (amounting to 5 percent of the *capellanía* value annually) for a specified number of masses to be said for the souls of people specified by the chantry's founder. Since a large part of estate revenues was channeled away from the landowners to priests in return for spiritual benefits, and not in repayment of loans, the estancias' large debt ratios are misleading. Loans had to be repaid with interest. A *capellanía* generally represented a permanent burden on estate revenues.

Once chantries are removed from the debt structure of the estancias, we have a more realistic view of debt ratios. One lien held by private individuals was also removed from the sample because the debt was not the balance due on a loan but a permanent charge placed on the property. As it turns out, only 10 of the estancias had outstanding loans. These 10 estates had a net value of 14,375 pesos, 6 reales, and had debts totaling 8,513 pesos. Consequently, the debt ratio was still high—59.2 percent—but far lower than the figure with which we began. Yucatecan estancias in general, therefore, were over-burdened with capellanía obligations but not with debts to be repaid with interest. Moreover, indebtedness was even less frequent for Yucatecan sitios. In the 1718–38 notarial records, only 16 of 66 sitios had debts of any kind, and most of the obligations were to chantries.

By far the most important creditor of the 10 encumbered estates was the Convent of the Nuns of the Immaculate Conception, which accounted for 59.7 percent of the landowners' debt. Second in importance, significantly, were the Franciscan convents of San Francisco and La Mejorada, which had lent 23.4 percent of the total; apparently the Franciscans, while shunning the acquisition of landed estates, did not refrain from moneylending. The other creditors were the Jesuits and a Spanish religious brotherhood, or cofradía, with 11.7 percent and 5.1 percent, respectively.

The estancias thus reflected characteristic features of the Spanish American economy and of Spanish culture. Yucatan did not have any banks until the late nineteenth century, so the Church was practically the only source of investment capital in the colony. At the same time, by instituting chantries the Church provided an outlet for the fear of the unknown. The fees to maintain them were certainly not as burdensome as outright loans, but they did mean that capital flowed away from estate owners with only spiritual rewards in return. The cost of salvation was high.

The Struggle for the Surplus

The landed estate would eventually become the basis of the upper class's wealth in Yucatan. But in the mid-colonial period, as we have seen, capital accumulation was based overwhelmingly on tribute, religious taxes, and the repartimiento. To get a share of the surplus extracted from the Maya, a family or individual had to be granted an encomienda, a benefice, or permission to carry out business with the Indians. Wealth, in other words, was prebendal in nature: it resulted from awards granted by the state. This dependence on the state was, in the words of Mario Góngora, "one of the historical elements of longest duration in the Hispanic American aristocracies."[109] It meant that for a long time economic position was the result rather than the origin of political power. Politics therefore overlapped with economics, and consequently capital accumulation took place within a highly politicized context.

The struggle between the secular and the regular clergy is one example of this intertwining of politics and economics. In theory, the issue was whether or not the Franciscans, having accomplished their goals of evangelizing and civilizing the Indians, should be made to abandon the pacified area to the secular priests. But in reality this was not the only, or even the major, issue. The two branches of the Church were in fact fighting to decide who should be allowed to benefit economically from the Maya, for the Indians supported the clergy through religious tribute, tithes, and extralegal contributions.[110] This was one of the major themes of colonial politics.

Because parishes were such valuable sources of income for Spaniards, they were frequently divided in order to create more positions. The 30 parishes of the early seventeenth century had expanded to 52 by the 1650's, and by the late colonial period they would number over 70. The struggle for control over these positions was intense. By the middle of the seventeenth century, the Franciscans had been made to give up 15 of the 52 benefices to the seculars. They lost six more in 1680, and three others in 1711. The friars were on the defensive on other fronts as well, for the seculars were also bringing charges against them for alleged immoral actions in their dealings with the Indians.[111] Consequently, by the early eighteenth century, though the Franciscans still administered the majority of the parishes, the seculars were in a position to shift the balance when the next round of secularizations took place. The priests belonging to creole society would soon be receiving the lion's share of the Indians' surplus earmarked for the clergy.

The struggle for control of the parishes was important because the secular clergy represented an important economic force in the countryside. Since many curates founded estancias within their jurisdictions, the retreat of the Franciscans meant the advance of the landed estate. Moreover, the clergymen often were deeply involved in business activities, especially moneylending.[112] And finally, the priests' collection of religious taxes was in practice the ecclesiastical equivalent of an encomienda, for the curates not only received a steady income but also looked on their posts as their own personal property, to be used as they wished. For example, when Dr. Simón de Argaíz, the curate of Mama, made his will in 1692, he included among his assets "whatever my alms in *patíes* and wax are worth."[113] The pastors of Hoctún, Nabalam, and Chancenote all mortaged their "alms" (religious taxes in kind) against a cash loan from the former Collector General of Diocesan Tithes, Diego de Rivas Talavera, a prominent businessman and rancher.[114] Nowhere was the mercenary attitude toward benefices more clearly stated than in the mortgage agreement between Andrés Vázquez Moscoso, a prominent businessman-repartimiento agent, and Br. Matheo de Arce. The priest borrowed money to purchase his clerical garb, using the "tributes from my spiritual and temporal rents" as collateral.[115]

The political battle over the encomienda was no less hard fought. As we have seen, this institution had already disappeared in many regions of Spanish America by the late seventeenth century. But whenever the crown moved to abolish the encomienda in Yucatan, or to impose new taxes on encomenderos' incomes, the provincial elite mobilized to defend its interests. The government sometimes succeeded in raising taxes but always gave in to the arguments in favor of continuing the encomienda.[116] The basic structure of the colonial regime was to survive even longer.

The provincial elite's success in defending the encomienda was due in part to its ability to present a united front against the crown's program. This was not the case with the controversies over the repartimiento system. Conflicts over the encomienda and the secularization of benefices could be resolved through royal rulings, but the crown could hardly be asked to divide the spoils of what was an illegal activity. Conflict therefore had to be worked out at the local level, and as a result the repartimiento became the most important political issue in mid-colonial Yucatan.

During the first century of the colonial regime, considerable controversy took place over whether the repartimiento should be established at all. Once that issue had been resolved and the system was institutionalized, conflict arose over how to divide the profits. The first major controversy erupted in 1665, when the new Governor, Rodrigo Flores de Aldana, attempted to increase the quantity of goods contracted and to monopolize the profits as well. Since his policy coincided with the period of Maya demographic collapse, Flores de Aldana was in effect trying to get more labor out of fewer people. One result was the wholesale flight to the Montaña of the villagers of the region south of the city of Campeche. Minor uprisings also occurred. News of the Governor's unrestrained avarice traveled far and fast, and Flores de Aldana, barely three months in office, was deposed by viceregal order. But not far enough, as it turned out. Thanks to his personal acquaintance with Philip IV, he was restored to his post in 1667. Flores de Aldana held on to the governorship until 1670, when he was again deposed, this time by royal order. His abuse of power eventually became too notorious even for his royal patron to tolerate.

Flores de Aldana's downfall was caused by his own greed. But he had been allowed to perpetrate his abuses not only because of his influence with the King but also because some members of the local elite, such as Regidor Bernardo Magaña, chose to collaborate with him rather than oppose him.[117] Nevertheless, enough of the elite had opposed Flores de Aldana to cause him innumerable problems.

Controversy over the repartimiento erupted again within a decade. Although Flores de Aldana's successor, Sancho Fernández de Angulo, kept his business activities within certain limits, Governor Antonio de Layseca, who took office in 1678, was less restrained. Once again a swarm of the Governor's hangers-on descended on the Maya, and local people for the most part were denied a share of the profits. Their complaints brought a judge of the Audiencia of Mexico to Yucatan to investigate, and Layseca was deposed in 1681. He defended himself not by denying what he had done, but by arguing that the repartimiento system was good for the Indians because it kept them from resorting to their customary "laziness" and "drunkenness," because it enabled them to pay their taxes, and because there was nothing wrong with it; moreover, he stated, "in this province carrying out repartimientos with the Indians has never been considered a major crime," and "there are few if any governors who would not be so charged in their residencias." Layseca was restored to power the following year, but unlike Flores de Aldana, he then accepted the limits on his repartimientos and ended his term without further ado.[118]

The residencia of Antonio de Layseca was carried out by Juan Bruno Tello de Guzmán, the incoming Governor. This set a pattern that would last for several decades, and that gradually solved many of the political problems regarding the repartimiento. Tello de Guzmán in turn was judged by incoming Governor Juan Joseph de Bárcena, who in turn was judged by incoming Governor Roque de Soberanis. Political instability and war then interrupted the process, and the next residencia was delayed until 1708, when incoming Governor Fernando de Meneses judged a grand total of three former Governors (Soberanis, Martín de Urzúa y Arizmendi, and Alvaro de Rivaguda). In these circumstances, each newly arrived chief executive learned all that there was to be learned about business opportunities, made contacts with the local elite, and found his predecessor guilty of carrying out the repartimiento. The previous Governor then defended himself by at once arguing that the repartimiento was good and useful and disclaiming having any hand in it: the business, it seemed, had always been carried out by someone who was mistakenly assumed to be working for the Governor. The new chief executive then accepted this reasoning, absolved his predecessor from punishment on the grounds that the system was necessary, and ended the proceedings by declaring the man to be a "good, exact, and prudent Governor and Captain General," and "worthy to be honored by His Majesty with higher posts."[119]

This political expedient worked because each Governor found himself in need of help from the local elite. The crown required the chief executive to post a surety bond of 6,000 pesos against the costs of his residencia. This put him under obligation to local business and political leaders, who served as *fiadores*, or guarantors, of the bond. Is it unduly cynical to suspect that the bondsmen received something in return? In 1683 Sargento Mayor Francisco Guerrero, the commander of Mérida's militia companies, served as fiador for Governor Tello de Guzmán; the following year he was elected senior alcalde of Mérida.[120] Juan de Madrid, who had already served as repartimiento agent for Governors Fernández de Angulo and Tello de Guzmán, and who had held elected municipal offices in Mérida in 1680, 1689, and 1690, acted as bondsman for Governor Soberanis in 1693; he managed to carry out his own repartimientos, with no governmental interference, throughout the last three decades of the seventeenth century.[121] Governor Bárcena's guarantor in 1688 was Diego Cano Maldonado, an encomendero, who served as alcalde of Mérida in 1679 and Procurator in 1692.[122]

Martín de Urzúa y Arizmendi, a Basque who served as Governor on three different occasions before his transfer to the Philippines, and who used his repartimiento profits to buy the title of Count of Lizarraga, called on several men to act as fiadores. In 1695 his bond was guaranteed by Maestre de Campo Manuel Bolio, the commander of the provincial militia and Urzúa's future brother-in-law, and by Juan de Vergara, a Basque merchant involved in the repartimiento whom the Governor appointed to the post of war captain of Dzidzantún, that is, the local repartimiento agent. In 1699 Urzúa's bondsman was Juan del Castillo y Toledo, a Spanish-born war captain who had served as one of Governor Flores de Aldana's repartimiento agents and had been elected senior alcalde of Mérida in 1693. He was also the father of Juan del Castillo y Arrúe, who was elected junior alcalde of Mérida in 1701, became regidor and *alférez mayor* in 1705, was elected senior alcalde on seven different occasions, served as repartimiento agent for Governor Alonso de Meneses, acted as fiador for Governor Juan Joseph de Vertiz in 1715, was the most powerful local political figure in Yucatan during the three decades in which he was the titular leader of the cabildo of Mérida, and through thick and thin defended the Governors and the repartimiento system that was the basis of his own wealth. Governor Urzúa's final set of bondsmen included once again his brother-in-law Maestre de Campo Bolio, as well as three men who between them served as elected officials of the municipal government of Mérida 16 times between 1700 and 1730.[123]

Incoming Governors also found it expedient on occasion to reach an agreement with the cabildo of Valladolid regarding the operation of the repartimiento. Flores de Aldana and Layseca had tried to monopolize the business by appointing a hanger-on to the post of *teniente de capitán general* in that villa. In practice these appointees preempted the city fathers' jurisdiction over the Indians, thereby depriving them of the power to make the Indians accept repartimiento contracts. Not surprisingly, the cabildo, disgruntled at this usurping of its prerogatives, joined in the denunciations of the abuses perpetrated by Flores de Aldana and Layseca. Later Governors frequently found it politic to defer to the cabildo by appointing Valladolid's senior alcalde as teniente. Rotation in office, then, was a scheme by which members of the local elite could divide the profits of the repartimiento among themselves. And as will be remembered, the alcaldes of Valladolid controlled a large part of the contracts forced on the Indians for the production of thread. But this was illegal, and the officials had to answer for their activities during the Governors' residencias. A neat solution was found: the incoming Governors either absolved the alcaldes of all guilt or routinely found them guilty and fined them 30 pesos each.[124]

As noted earlier, cooperation with local interests was sometimes made easier by advance contacts between a future Governor and the provincial elite. This was clearly the case of Maestre de Campo Martín de Urzúa y Arizmendi, who despite his military rank was a practicing lawyer in the viceregal capital when he was appointed Governor. In that capacity he had handled lawsuits and business affairs for many people from Yucatan. Among his clients in 1689 was Juan de Madrid, who currently held the post of Procurator of Mérida, was to move up to junior alcalde the next year, and had served two earlier Governors as chief repartimiento agent.[125] Urzúa also represented the interests of the chief Treasury official in Yucatan; a member of the merchant elite of the provincial capital (and, like Urzúa, a Basque); a mulatto militia captain seeking a promotion; a regidor of Mérida; and several other elected officials. In fact, the few extant records show that the future Governor had dealings with people who served either as alcaldes or Procurators of Mérida in 1682, 1683, 1685, 1689, and 1690.[126] Contacts like these undoubtedly smoothed the way for a working relationship between the local elite and Martín de Urzúa.

Finally, it was important for the new Governor to avoid conflict with the Bishop. Antonio de Layseca, as we have seen, so antagonized Bishop Juan de Escalante that he began an inquest into the Governor's abuses. The secular priests, under the Bishop's authority of course, were among the most hostile witnesses against Layseca. Later chief executives managed by one means or another to avoid repeating this mistake. One way to get on the Bishop's good side was to support him in the struggle with the Franciscans over control of benefices. This was clearly the strategy of Martín de Urzúa, who joined with the Bishop in denouncing the Franciscans for their alleged immoral and fraudulent activities.[127] The friars retaliated in 1700 with an investigation into the repartimiento and its abuses. But 1700 was a bad year to expect action from the crown. The Franciscans' findings were ignored in Spain.

Through an array of expedients and strategies like these, the Governors and the local elite achieved a modus vivendi on the repartimiento. But the arrangement broke down once the governorship was put up for sale in the late seventeenth century. By 1707 the price had risen to 9,000 pesos; only four years later the post sold for 12,000.[128] The annual salary, however, was only 1,600. Moreover, since the position was widely reputed to be lucrative, some candidates were willing to buy the office years before it would become vacant. Juan Joseph Vertiz, for example, bought the governorship in 1707 but did not assume power until 1715.[129] The wait was something of a gamble for the purchasers. What if they should die before their turn came? The crown's solution was to make the office heritable. Thus Antonio de Cortaire inherited the governorship when his brother Domingo, the original purchaser, died while still on the waiting list.[130]

The Governors' attempts to make their investments pay off probably made conflict over the repartimiento inevitable. Matters were brought to a head by the misfortune of incoming Governor Fernando de Meneses, whose family was captured by pirates. Meneses had to pay a ransom of some 14,000 pesos. Pressed for cash, he paid himself an exorbitant salary as judge in the residencias of former Governors Soberanis, Urzúa, and Rivaguda. In effect, he was overcharging his Sovereign. Meneses also began to sell some war captaincy posts. He even created a new position, that of Treasurer and Judge of Indians in Valladolid, then sold it to one of the villa's leading citizens and repartimiento practitioners.[131] Finally, he decided to increase his own share of the repartimiento by extracting more cloth and wax from the Indians. In only four and a half years, he contracted for 127,049 patíes (worth somewhere between 127,000 and 175,000 pesos in Yucatan, over 30 percent more in Mexico City) and for 13,283 arrobas (about 166 tons) of wax (worth around 83,000 pesos). Meneses' repartimiento agent was Sargento Mayor Francisco Medina Cachón, who had held the same position for former Governor Rivaguda. And the methods employed for these heavy repartimientos, it will be recalled, included fraud and coercion.[132] After he had accumulated all the money that he thought he could get away with, Fernando Meneses handed over power to his brother Alonso in 1712, and then, illegally and in violation of his orders, he sailed with the fleet to Spain.

Although Alonso Meneses tried at first to conciliate opponents by cutting back on his brother's repartimientos, he eventually had to resort to some rather heavy-handed measures to stifle dissent. The problem for both brothers was that the Maya were already producing all the textiles they could, so the only way to get more was for someone else to get less. The Meneses brothers did not attempt to monopolize the business. They did not deprive the Secretary General, Diego Méndez Pacheco, of his share; Méndez, after all, had paid 23,100 pesos for his post, which, unlike the governorship, was a lifetime position.[133] The Meneses also got along well with several members of the cabildo of Mérida, especially with the alférez mayor, Juan del Castillo. Castillo, as we have seen, even served as repartimiento agent for Alonso Meneses.

The Governors had to cut into someone's share, however, and the someone they selected was the Treasurer of the Santa Cruzada, the Count of Miraflores.[134] To justify this action, Fernando Meneses informed the King of the abuses being perpetrated by the Count. The Ecclesiastic Cabildo of Mérida quickly counterattacked, denouncing the Governor in a letter to the King in 1710.[135] The Bishop, Pedro Reyes de los Ríos y la Madriz, entered the fray in 1711 by conducting an investigation into the Governor's own abusive repartimientos. In the following year, by which time Alonso Meneses had taken office, the Bishop denounced the Meneses brothers at a meeting of the cabildo of Mérida. The Governor responded by informing the cabildo that he had been instructed by a *real cédula* to carry out an investigation of the abuses being perpetrated by the Santa Cruzada. In the resulting report, he blamed the exploitation of the Indians not only on the Count of Miraflores but also on the parish priests, who cooperated with the Cruzada in the sale of the indulgences. Meneses also impounded the Count's encomienda and removed him from the cabildo of Mérida.

Throughout the controversy, the Meneses brothers were supported by the *alférez mayor* Juan del Castillo and several other regidores. The opposition was led by the Second Count of Miraflores and his uncle, the oft-mentioned Lucas de Villamil. Both Castillo and Villamil had served as repartimiento agents for former Governors, and the First Count of Miraflores, of course, had invented the device of using the repartimiento to sell the Santa Cruzada's bulls. The Second Count continued his father's business. The fact that the Church was financially hurt by the decline of Cruzada revenues certainly figured in the Bishop's decision to support the Counts. In short, while both sides in the struggle portrayed themselves as the defenders of the Indians, both had been involved in the repartimiento business for a long time. The real struggle was over the division of the spoils.

Word of what was happening in the province soon spread to Spain. The King, noting that abuses resulted when an incoming Governor was the person who sat in judgment on his predecessor's performance in office, ordered the Viceroy to appoint someone else to serve as residencia judge for the Meneses brothers. In 1715 the crown appointed a new Bishop, Juan Gómez de Parada, a Mexican cleric from New Galicia, who came armed with a *real cédula* empowering him to depose the Governor should that step be necessary to put the province in order.

The appointment of an impartial judge to carry out the residencia of the Meneses brothers appeared to be a good solution. But the reform measure was effectively sabotaged. The person Viceroy Linares selected, a militia officer serving in New Spain named Juan Francisco Medina Cachón, just happened to be the son of Fernando Meneses' chief repartimiento agent. The judge's residencia promised to be a whitewash. No hostile witnesses were called, and at times the Indians, who normally participated in the proceedings, were left out entirely. But the "cover-up" was never concluded. The new Governor, Juan Joseph Vertiz, took measures to stop the proceedings on the grounds that Medina Cachón's writ had expired. He was supported by a majority of Mérida's regidores, who now joined forces against the Meneses supporters after years of intimidation. Medina Cachón was forced to stop, and all sides awaited a decision from higher authority.

In the end, Vertiz was the one who carried out the Meneses residencia, though legal delays prevented the proceedings from beginning until 1721, by which time he had left office. It was also decided that Vertiz in turn would be judged by someone other than his successor. This suggested that the residencia system would be changed, and in fact in 1720 the cabildo of Mérida had written to the crown requesting that incoming Governors not serve as residencia judges for their predecessors.[136] Nevertheless, after Vertiz, there was a return to the old system of new chief executives judging the outgoing Governor. Real reform would require more commitment on the part of the higher authorities.

In any case, Vertiz, who like previous Governors had bought his position and counted on a return on his investment through repartimientos, had no desire to see the system reformed. In fact, among his fiadores was Juan del Castillo, who now cut his losses, changed sides, and joined his former opponents on the cabildo. Castillo also served later as legal defender at Vertiz's residencia. The adroit alférez mayor always knew which way the wind was blowing. Vertiz's choice of a repartimiento agent was another sign of continuity: he chose Juan de Huartena, who had held the same position during the governorship of Urzúa. And when Vertiz had to post bond in order to return to Spain before the completion of his residencia, Huartena served as the bondsman, along with Juan del Castillo and the regidor Antonio de la Helguera, one of his original fiadores. The new Governor also continued his predecessor's conflict with the Second Count of Miraflores over the repartimientos of the Santa Cruzada, and desisted only when threatened with punitive action by the Inquisition. He even paid himself an exorbitant salary as residencia judge, just as Fernando Meneses had done.[137]

Nevertheless, the residencia Vertiz conducted of the Meneses brothers permitted the airing of many grievances. The two former Governors were charged with 12 offenses, and some lesser officials, including Juan del Castillo, with five more. The most serious charges against the Governors concerned their abuse of power and their carrying out of repartimientos in a fraudulent and excessive manner. Juan del Castillo was charged with participating in the repartimiento while holding office as regidor and alférez mayor. The Meneses brothers defended their repartimientos with the same old arguments. The business was good for the Indians because it kept them busy and thus counteracted their natural "laziness." It also enabled them to earn the money to pay their tribute. And even though the repartimiento was illegal, "it is universally tolerated throughout the Indies and especially in this Province out of consideration for the Governors' low salary and few perquisites, which do not even cover the expenses and costs of maintaining themselves befittingly."[138]

The verdict handed down by Vertiz blamed all the repartimiento abuses on Fernando Meneses alone. Since Juan del Castillo and Alonso Meneses had defended themselves on the grounds that a controlled, moderate repartimiento was good, Vertiz in effect came down in support of the system as such. This is hardly surprising, since he himself had carried out repartimientos and fully expected to be exonerated in turn. It is also not surprising that Vertiz absolved Castillo from guilt: as we have seen, Castillo was one of Vertiz's bondsmen, and would soon be defending him at the next residencia proceedings. Vertiz was less charitable toward Alonso Meneses, who was found guilty on two counts of abuse of power and fined 2,200 pesos. Fernando Meneses was fined a healthy 14,554 pesos, 3 reales, all but 1,000 pesos of which had to be paid as reparations to the Indians. Vertiz then praised the brothers for their loyal service to the crown; they were "good Ministers, whom His Majesty can use in His service" and to whom His Majesty could "grant favors and rewards."[139] The records do not reveal whether or not the fines were ever paid.

It seemed, then, that things were back to normal in the wake of the Meneses governorships. Vertiz carried out his repartimientos, and to raise the necessary investment capital, he borrowed money from the Church with the authorization of Bishop Juan Gómez de Parada. His successor, Antonio Cortaire, also borrowed money from the Church, again with Gómez de Parada's approval, for his business dealings with the Indians. But then the Bishop suddenly declared his shock at discovering that the repartimiento exploited the Indians. Using the special powers granted him in the *real cédula* he brought to office, Gómez de Parada ordered the suppression of the repartimiento system. At the same time, he abolished the so-called *servicios personales*, that is, the domestic work the Indians were required to perform for the Spanish elite. Finally, after encountering enormous resistance to his reforms, the Bishop, again using his special powers, deposed Governor Cortaire. Another political crisis was at hand.[140]

The Spanish community in Yucatan, with the exception of a few Church leaders, was convinced that both the repartimiento and the *servicios personales* were crucial to its survival. The cabildo of Mérida sent a Procurator to Mexico City to present its case to the Audiencia. There they got a friendly reception, at least by the Fiscal, who argued that the repartimiento was not merely just, but essential, for "if that kind of buying and selling is not carried out, commerce will doubtlessly cease alto-gether."¹⁴¹ Everyone in Mérida said the same thing; indeed, everyone in-sisted that commerce was already being adversely affected. Governor Cortaire argued that the system was necessary to provide the war captains with some income in lieu of a salary, and that the war captaincies in turn were necessary for the defense of the province. Even the Tribunal de In-dios argued in favor of the repartimiento because without it the Indians would be unable to pay their taxes.

In 1726 a new Governor, Antonio de Figueroa, arrived in Yucatan and carried out the residencia of his predecessor. Cortaire was absolved for having carried out repartimientos during his first two years in office, and Figueroa officially noted that the chief executive's salary was inadequate. He also absolved all others involved in the business, including the ever-present *alférez mayor* Juan del Castillo. Once again Castillo had positioned himself well: he had been one of Governor Figueroa's fiadores. And later, on the Governor's death in 1733, he would be the executor of Figueroa's estate.¹⁴²

By then the repartimiento had been restored. Governor Figueroa, who had been ordered to investigate the matter, reported his findings to the King in 1729. He emphasized that in fact it was only because the repar-timiento advanced cash to the Indians in return for labor that they were able to pay their tribute and religious taxes. Using the same argument, he also defended the repartimientos carried out by encomenderos.¹⁴³ The crown finally made a ruling in 1731. After baldly admitting that the re-partimiento had been conducted in Yucatan "since the time of the first Governors," the King stated that Figueroa's report had convinced him that the system not only was not "inconvenient . . . but was very useful for the preservation of the Indians." Besides, the payment of tribute and religious taxes depended on it. He was accordingly ordering that the re-partimiento be reintroduced.¹⁴⁴ Yucatan thereupon became the only prov-ince in the Spanish Empire in which the repartimiento was legal. Later, attempts would be made to regulate the quantities of goods the Gover-nors could contract, but a limited repartimiento would prove to be just as difficult to enforce as its total prohibition.

The *servicios personales* were also restored under Governor Figueroa. The famine of 1726–27, coming as it did after the abolition of the repar-timiento, had led to further economic decline in Yucatan. Then the epi-demic of yellow fever or measles broke out. In the midst of this crisis, Figueroa reported to the crown that the Indians themselves caused the famine, for on hearing that their *servicios personales* had been abolished, they refused even to work their own milpas. This was patently absurd, but the crown was again convinced: the King declared the Indians to be "by their nature lazy and very fond of idleness," and he attributed the province's problems to the Indians' "never very prudent laziness." But when it came to explaining why Spanish women could not, or would not, grind corn and make tortillas themselves, Figueroa fell back on a different argument: white women were physically too weak to carry out such hard labor. Consequently, the *servicios personales* had to be exacted from Maya women as well as from men if the Spaniards were to survive. The logic of colonialism convinced the King, who approved Figueroa's decision, made in 1729, to restore the *servicios*.[145]

The crisis of the 1720's reveals the continued strength of the colonial regime. The repartimiento, encomienda, religious taxes, and minor domestic service all forced the Maya to work for others and produce a surplus. Coercion, in the form of colonialism, was what incorporated the Indians into the regional and world economies. The Spaniards, like all colonialists, mistook resistance and reluctance for laziness. In truth, the colonized people simply preferred to produce only for their own subsistence. When compulsory economic participation in the form of the repartimiento was removed, the Maya reverted to simple subsistence production. There was no surplus. The restoration of the repartimiento system, and to a lesser extent of the *servicios personales*, was therefore necessary for the preservation of Spanish colonialism in Yucatan. Small wonder that colonial politics often revolved around what for the colonists was the sine qua non of their existence.

PART THREE

The Regime in Decline, 1730-1812

CHAPTER SIX

Economic and Social Change

THUS FAR COLONIAL Yucatan has been analyzed as a dual society composed of Maya and Spaniards. This is a reflection of historical reality, for the colonial regime, in theory and in practice, consisted of a República de Indios and a República de Españoles, that is, Indian and Spanish commonwealths. Since these were legal as well as social classifications, each república was in fact an estate, that is, "a legally defined segment of the population of a society which has distinctive rights and duties established by law."[1] To be sure, the estate system was flawed from the start because mixed-race people, whose existence was after all inevitable, did not easily fit into the two-commonwealth schema. But in practice many mestizos were incorporated into Maya society, and mulattoes and Africans, though less than completely, into Hispanic society. So though the basis for the two-república system was undermined, society in the early and mid-colonial periods did consist, to a great extent, of two estates, one Maya and one Hispanic.

This estate system survived with only minor contradictory features (most of which, in any case, were present in the cities but not in the countryside) so long as Spanish colonialism continued to be based on the parasitic institutions of tribute, religious taxes, and repartimiento, which is to say, so long as the independent peasantry—the people of the villages, who were neither slaves nor serfs—were at the center of the provincial economy. Through the mid-colonial period capital accumulation by Spaniards was based only to a limited extent on property ownership; most wealth was acquired by getting a share of the surplus produced by the peasant communities. The two-estate system, therefore, was supported by, and reflected, the economic structure.

But in the eighteenth century the estate system began to break down. Spaniards came to use private property as the primary mechanism of capital accumulation. The independent peasantry lost its overwhelming importance, and many Maya people became part of a new and growing social class of dependent tenants. The estate system was gradually replaced by a class system, in which the Indian's inferiority to the Spaniard was defined in terms of property relations rather than colonialism.[2] To be sure, the process of change was both slow and uneven, at first affecting only the Maya in certain areas, especially the northwest and west. In the east and south, in fact, the estate system was still viable after Independence, and it remains so to this day in some of the more remote sections of the modern states of Yucatan, Campeche, and Quintana Roo.

Nevertheless, in the course of the last seven decades of the eighteenth century, Yucatan was transformed from a colonial to a neocolonial society. Two developments were at work here: first, the rise of the hacienda; and second, the decline of the encomienda and the repartimiento. Two props of the colonial regime would be destroyed by 1800. A third prop, religious taxes, would collapse between 1813 and 1840. The very existence of the independent peasantry would be called into question after Independence, when legal changes denied the Maya control over much of the peninsula's land.[3] Thereafter, the future of Yucatan, at least until the 1930's, would rest on neocolonialism, a system in which the province's economic base was to consist, not of peasant communities, but of Spanish-owned haciendas producing raw materials and primary products for local and foreign markets.

The Rise of the Hacienda

The establishment of Spanish estancias in early and mid-colonial Yucatan had taken place during a period of Indian population decline. The ranches had largely occupied lands being abandoned by Indians. As long as the native population continued to decline or at least did not grow, the development of Spanish-owned properties in the countryside presented no major problem for the Indians or the colonial economy. The Maya maintained control over enough land to sustain themselves and still produce a surplus for the colonists.

In the eighteenth century, however, the situation changed dramatically. By then the Indians were no longer as susceptible to the devastating diseases of the first century of the colonial era. And yellow fever, which had worked such havoc in the seventeenth century, was only a now and again thing during the last century of Spanish rule. That disease may have been the culprit in the epidemic of 1727–28, but after that the sources make no mention of the horrible *vómito prieto* until 1796, when yellow fever was reported in Champotón.[4] Even then, no province-wide epidemic followed. Other epidemic diseases were also contained: smallpox (reported in eastern Beneficios Altos in 1759), measles (reported in several locations after the outbreak of the famine of 1770), and an unspecified illness reported by the cabildo of Mérida in 1806.[5] The scourge of the late colonial era would be not plague but famine.

Once free of the threat of serious epidemics, the population had an op-

TABLE 6.1
The Population of Yucatan, 1700–1809

		Indian population			
Year	Tributaries	Inferred total	Non-Indian population	Total population	Source
1700	–	130,000	20,000	150,000	1, 2
1710	–	156,788	–	–	3
1736	–	126,897	34,000	161,000	2
1761	–	184,998	–	–	3
1761	56,060	207,422[a]; 224,240[b]	–	–	4
1765	57,539	212,894[a]; 230,156[b]	–	–	5
1773	35,317	130,673[a]; 141,268[b]	–	–	5
1779	–	158,994	59,389	218,383[c]	6
1794	59,306	237,224[b]	–	–	7
1794	–	254,000	103,000	357,000	2
1806	–	272,925	–	–	3
1806	–	281,012	–	–	2
1809	72,774	291,096[b]	–	–	3

SOURCES: (1) García Bernal, *Yucatán: Población y encomienda*, pp. 137–38; (2) Cook and Borah, *Essays*, 2: 75–114; (3) Farriss, *Maya Society*, pp. 59, 424–25; (4) *DHY*, 3: 10; (5) AGI, México 3057, Año de 1775, Testimonio del Primer Quaderno de autos formados sobre la falta de Tributarios de la Provincia de Campeche a causa de la Langosta y hambre que allí se ha padecido, fols. 49–50; (6) AGI, México 3061, Superior Govierno, Año de 1785, Testimonio no. 10 del Expediente que trata sobre poner en la Villa de Córdova una fabrica de Chinguirito para proveer el Estanco de Yucatán, fol. 15; (7) Censos de población de la intendencia de Yucatán, 1789–95, in Rubio Mañé, ed., *Archivo*, 1: 205–50.

NOTE: I have used two factors, 3.7 and 4.0, to arrive at the estimated total Indian population from the tributary counts of 1761, 1765, and 1773. The lower figure is suggested by Farriss for the whole of the century, but she does not provide any data in support of that decision. In my view, a higher figure is justified by the legal change that removed women from the tributary category in 1760, thereby inflating the family unit. Moreover, the figure 4.0 is used by Cook and Borah for the 1790's and by Farriss herself for 1809.

[a]Figure based on a 3.7 conversion factor.
[b]Figure based on a 4.0 conversion factor.
[c]Figure derived by adding data from each partido. The total given in the document is 214,974.

portunity to grow, and grow it did. Although the details of that development have yet to be worked out, the available data, summarized in Table 6.1, clearly demonstrate that by the early decades of the century the Maya population was beginning to recover. Famine and plague temporarily interrupted the trend in 1727–28, but growth resumed in the 1730's, and in the next three decades the Indian population swelled from about 127,000 to well over 200,000, the highest level since the middle of the sixteenth century. Most of these gains were lost in 1769–73, when famine resulted in the death or flight of an estimated 70,000 people. But a rapid recovery followed. By the 1790's, the Indian population had grown to between 237,000 and 254,000, and in 1809 the figure reached 290,000. By then it can be said that the Maya had recovered from the European invasion.

In the face of this demographic recovery, Indians needed to expand their landholdings. This presented little problem in the thinly populated eastern half of the peninsula, where there were few Spanish-owned estates to bar peasants from simply radiating out to establish new settlements. Where the possibilities of expansion were limited, however, as in the western half of Yucatan, peasants had to make arrangements to use the lands owned by non-Indians. Since a process of expanding Maya holdings at the expense of the Spanish-owned estates—in other words, an agrarian reform—was out of the question, population growth resulted in the rise of tenancy. It also of course meant that there were more mouths to feed. Some villages became the equivalent of small cities. The Sierra pueblos of Oxkutzcab, Tekax, and Ticul, for example, had 7,000, 5,600, and 4,500 inhabitants, respectively, in 1803.[6] Plainly, if peasant production could not keep pace with the Indian population's increase, there would be less food available to Mérida, Campeche, and Valladolid.

It was an intolerable situation for the cities, whose rate of growth was even faster than the Indians'. In fact, Yucatan's non-Indian population increased by something like five times over the course of the eighteenth century. Mérida proper expanded only moderately—from 4,000–5,000 in the *casco*, or inner city, in 1700 to 5,358 in 1794—but the barrios exploded. Data for two of them show the population rising from 3,612 to 17,416 between 1700 and 1794. In 1807, by the Governor's estimate, approximately 30,000 people lived in the capital, making Mérida one of the major urban centers of the Spanish Empire. The eastern city of Valladolid did not change much; by 1794 it had a population of 11,860. But Campeche grew considerably, and replaced Valladolid as the peninsula's second city. In 1794 the seaport had a population of 16,940.

The Development of Spanish Agricultural Production

By mid-century it was clear that the Maya peasantry's grain production was not increasing rapidly enough to meet the demand of a provincial population that was on its way to doubling and more, from 150,000 in 1700 to 350,000 in 1794.[7] To be sure, there had been shortages earlier in history, but before 1750 only general crop failures had caused scarcities. After that date, anything less than a good harvest resulted in a grain shortage; and crop failure produced famine.

The colonial government took measures to counteract the crisis, but at best it succeeded only in alleviating some of the effects of the food shortages. To encourage agricultural production, the government issued proclamations reminding the Indians that every adult male was required to plant at least 60 *mecates* (2.4 hectares) of milpa per year.[8] What effect, if any, these reminders had is not known. The cabildos of Mérida and Campeche dealt with the problem by rationing grain, paying bounties to importers, and sending out agents to purchase grain. These officials, entrusted with substantial quantities of cash, scoured the countryside in search of not only maize but rice (a grain first mentioned in the sources during the crisis of 1727–28). The purchasing agents were often sent as far away as Veracruz, Tuxpan, Charleston, and New Orleans in search of food for Yucatan.[9]

To a certain extent these measures alleviated urban hunger, but the problem of insufficient production remained unsolved. To make matters worse, the incidence of natural catastrophes, in the form of locust plagues and especially droughts, climbed in the second half of the eighteenth century, the result, apparently, of a climatic shift toward hotter, drier conditions.[10] Chronic grain shortages then set in. Between 1750 and 1809 no fewer than 18 severe shortages and two full-scale famines occurred; only six abundant harvests were reported in the course of almost 60 years. This trend continued right up to the Caste War in 1847 and resulted in the quadrupling of maize prices between 1813 and the 1840's.[11]

In the face of the increasing demand for food, non-Indian landowners began to grow maize on small farms or on landed estates. To be sure, some grain production had taken place on estancias before, but this had been sporadic in nature, and rarely became a permanent part of the estancia economy. After the famine of 1727–28, however, some of the estate owners enticed to enter the field by the pósitos of Mérida and Valladolid stayed in it. Soon the pósitos were making regular purchases of grain from non-Indians even during years when there was no shortage. What began as a temporary measure taken to profit from extraordinarily high maize prices ended up as a permanent step into the field of agricultural production on Yucatan's landed estates.[12]

The demand for food also stimulated the production of rice. This grain was grown exclusively in Campeche and the Sierra Alta, that is, the regions of greatest humidity and most plentiful rainfall. Much of the produce was shipped to Mérida for sale, especially when the harvest of maize was insufficient to feed the capital. During the severe food shortage of 1800, for example, 312.5 tons of locally produced and imported rice were shipped to Mérida from Campeche, and another 25 tons were received from the Sierra.[13] The port of Campeche was thus ideally suited both to import rice from New Orleans and Charleston and to export the local product to New Spain or Cuba in the rare event of a plentiful maize harvest and a surplus of food in Yucatan.[14]

The occasional export of rice draws attention to the role that the demands of the world economy played in bringing about economic change in Yucatan. Internal demand was not the only economic influence at work. Yucatan traded regularly with the outside world, and consequently it was affected by changes in the world market. Rice exports are one example of how local producers took advantage of the existing external demand for a product that could be sold in local markets as well. Another is offered by the livestock economy. There, too, the development of external markets, in Veracruz and Havana, combined with the increasing internal demand for meat, stimulated considerable growth in the second half of the century.[15]

This combination of internal and external demand was also evident in the case of cotton. Already grown, albeit on a modest scale, in the eastern part of the peninsula since at least the late seventeenth century, cotton was now taken up by producers throughout Yucatan.[16] The crop was sold to merchants, encomenderos, and the Governors' agents, and then delivered through the repartimiento system to the Indians for weaving. The finished material was exported to New Spain in large quantities, but it also had a considerable local market, for cotton cloth was purchased by practically everyone in the cities. Landed estates quickly responded to the growing demand of urban consumers by expanding their production, and numerous small farms, owned and worked by mestizos and mulattoes, sprang up around Valladolid and Campeche. Again, it was the interaction of internal and external factors that brought about economic growth.

Nevertheless, evidence from one of the most important branches of production demonstrates that growing internal demand was the most important cause of economic change. Sugarcane cultivation was second only to maize in importance in the agricultural economy of the landed estates, and in some places, especially in the south, it clearly surpassed maize in value of output. But production, which dated from the sixteenth century, seems to have been limited through the late seventeenth century and beyond.[17] Land planted in sugarcane, called *milpas de caña dulce* or *cañaverales*, does not appear in estate inventories in notarial records before the 1750's. Of course, there already existed considerable demand for sugar and its byproduct, *aguardiente* (cane alcohol). Indeed, statistics for the 1750's and 1780's indicate that the two together usually accounted for 40 percent of the imports arriving in Sisal bound for Mérida and the rest of the interior. Both sugar and aguardiente continued to arrive in Campeche in large quantities in the 1790's and in the first decade of the nineteenth century, but at no time were exports of either ever recorded. Local production (which in the case of aguardiente was in fact illegal) was exclusively for internal consumption.[18]

To meet this internal demand, landowners, especially in Campeche, in the Sierra, and even in Beneficios Bajos and Beneficios Altos, began to cultivate cane on their estates. Production was even carried out on small farms owned by the racially mixed population. A dramatic increase in the incidence of cañaverales in notarial records in the second half of the eighteenth century attests to this development. By the 1770's, local producers were so firmly established that the crown, responding to complaints by competing producers elsewhere in the Empire, tried to limit production through the introduction of a state-run monopoly, the Estanco de Aguardiente. But the goals of that policy were never achieved, for local producers were so numerous that the royal officials were unable to prevent the widespread evasion of controls and the illegal sale of cane alcohol.[19] In 1781 the government estimated local aguardiente production at 8,000 barrels annually.[20] A few years later, when the labor demands of the expanding sugarcane industry exceeded the local supply of workers, Campechano planters requested the massive importation of African slaves.[21] The request was denied, but the matter was raised again in 1791 by one of the spokesmen of the commercial-landowning elite, who also recommended that "vagrants" be forced by law to become part of the permanent work force of the sugar plantations.[22] Clearly, cane production was one of the leading sectors of economic growth in late colonial Yucatan.

Internal demand, then, was clearly the major cause of the introduction or expansion of agriculture on the landed estate in Yucatan. Since this economic activity was more labor-intensive than stock-raising, landowners needed to attract workers; as a result, the estancias developed into centers of population with mixed economies of ranching and agriculture. The nomenclature in use soon reflected these social and economic changes, for around the middle of the eighteenth century, the term *hacienda*, till then used to refer to wealth in general or to the Royal Exchequer, began to denote a rural property used for ranching and agricultural activities.[23] A new terminology was developing in response to historical change.

The transition from estancia to hacienda was slow. As late as 1773, the cabildo of Mérida reported that few non-Indians were involved in grain production, and that in a normal year (i.e., one without a grain shortage), the city was supplied with maize by the Maya peasantry.[24] Yet by the 1780's the haciendas were transforming the countryside. In one well-documented case, the parish of Umán, just to the southwest of Mérida, only 44 percent of the Indians lived in the four parish villages; the rest were residents of the 38 private estates.[25] In 1786 an official of the Royal Exchequer noted this trend and reported that the Maya villages "are becoming depopulated and almost barren at the same rate that the haciendas are becoming like populous villages."[26]

The Hacienda Economy

The rise of the hacienda represented the second stage of the Spanish occupation of the soil. To a certain extent the emergence of this new agrarian institution can be demonstrated statistically. Whereas only three of the 54 estates in the 1718–38 notarial records carried out agricultural production, 21 of 54 estancias and haciendas sampled for 1756–1803 listed cropland in their inventories. Moreover, the trend was toward still greater agricultural production, for between the years 1792 and 1803, exactly half the estates were found to be engaged in agriculture.[27]

Estate values also rose as agriculture became more important. Compared with the earlier period, the average value of estates rose 58 percent, and the median value 67 percent.[28] Moreover, a considerable number of these estates—15 of the 49 recorded—were worth over 3,000 pesos, and seven were worth 4,000. The most valuable of all the estates in 1718–38 had been worth just 3,580 pesos, and only two others were worth over 3,000.

Inflation was not the cause of this jump in values, for of all the components figuring in an estate's worth, only horses increased substantially in price over the century, their numbers thinned out by two equine epidemics. And in fact the evaluations put on some items declined considerably.[29] In short, though there was probably some inflation in Yucatan over the period, it was surely not substantial enough to account for the 58 percent rise in average estate values in the second half of the eighteenth century.

The major cause of these rising values was increased production and capital investment. The expansion into farming alone resulted in a massive increase—1,319 percent—in the agricultural component of estate values. Apiculture also expanded significantly; the average number of hives on the estates rose from 79 to 161, and the proportion of estates carrying out apiculture rose from 37 percent to 69 percent.

The third sector of the hacienda economy, stock-raising, also reached higher levels of production and investment. The average number of cattle increased by 66 percent (from 98 to 163), and the median number by 48 percent (from 87 to 129). Even more impressive—and significant—was the increased number of mules. In 1718–38 the average estancia had only 2.7 mules, and 49 percent had none at all. The 1756–1803 average was 8.5 mules, an increase of 215 percent, and the proportion of estates without mules fell to 25 percent.

The larger number of mules is of twofold importance. First, like cropland and apiaries, but unlike cattle, mules were capital goods, and as such their increasing number signified capital accumulation and investment. This was reflected in prices, for mules cost three times as much as cattle; stud donkeys cost nine or ten times as much. Second, since mules were used primarily to transport heavy, bulky goods to market, and since by volume, grain was by far the most important product to be transported, the larger number of animals points to the great importance of grain production on Yucatecan estates.

An indication of the balance among the agricultural, apicultural, and stock-raising sectors of the hacienda economy—in other words, the structure of production—is offered by tithe records. Although these are too imcomplete to permit the study of secular trends, extant data from 225 estates in the years from 1778 to 1796 give at least a glimpse of the structure of the hacienda economy in the last quarter of the century. A summary of these data is presented in Table 6.2.[30]

This table shows that the agricultural component of hacienda production was greatest in the Campeche area (partidos of Sahcabchén, Campeche, and Camino Real Alto), where maize, fruit, sugar, and rice were all extensively cultivated. The parish of Pich (southeast of Campeche city; see Map 5), located in a swamp-infested, thinly populated area, was an exception to this rule. So was Calkiní (northeast of the port), which included the largest concentration of Indians in western Yucatan. This circumstance undoubtedly made it more difficult for Spaniards to acquire land in the area. Stock-raising was more important than agriculture on the few landed estates in Pich and Calkiní. Apiculture was almost non-existent in most of the Campeche–Sahcabchén–Camino Real Alto region, although it did reach significant levels in the northern parishes of Hecelchakán and Calkiní.

The Camino Real Bajo was a zone of transition from agriculture to ranching. Agriculture was dominant in the southern parishes of Maxcanú and Kopomá but was only slightly more important than ranching to the north, in Umán. In the northernmost parish of Hunucmá, close to the provincial capital, stock-raising was by far the most important branch of estate production. The same was true in the partido of Mérida and in the parish of Mochochá, located close to the capital city in the western extreme of La Costa.

Economic diversification was evident in the eastern part of La Costa, around Izamal (70 km east of Mérida and 90 km west-northwest of Valladolid). Here for the most part ranching and agriculture were evenly balanced, and apiculture was highly developed as well. Maize was the mainstay of the agricultural economy of the haciendas, although beans and even some indigo (añil) were grown. A balanced hacienda economy was also generally evident in the partidos of the Sierra Baja and Beneficios Bajos (southeast and east-southeast of Mérida, respectively). However, in Beneficios Altos (farther to the southeast) landed estates were overwhelmingly enterprises devoted to stock-raising. Maize was practically the only agricultural product of landed estates in the three partidos of the Sierra Baja, Beneficios Bajos, and Beneficios Altos.

Agriculture was the mainstay of haciendas in most of the rest of the partidos. Since data on stock-raising are lacking for the Sierra Alta, there is no way to measure the relative importance of the three branches of production. But existing information leaves no doubt that agriculture was the major sector of the economy. Sugarcane was far and away the most

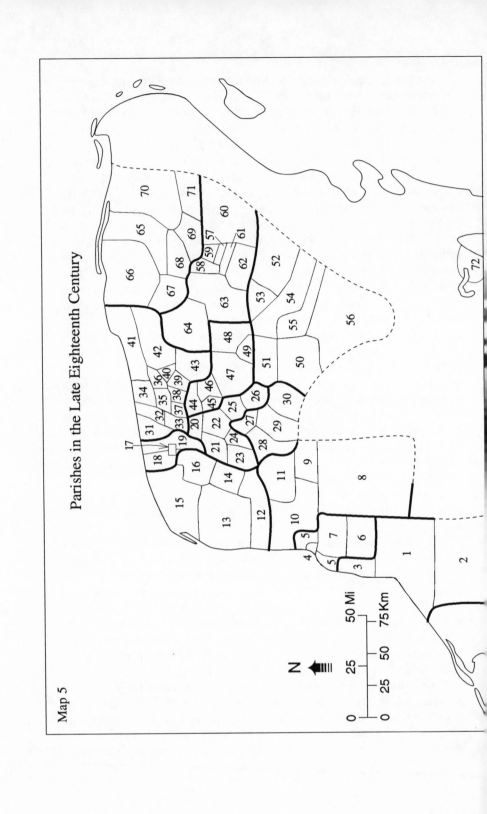

Map 5

Parishes in the Late Eighteenth Century

TABLE 6.2
TABLE 6.2
The Structure of Production on Selected Haciendas, 1777–96

Partido and parish	Pct. of total value of production			No. of estates
	Stock-raising	Apiculture	Agriculture	
Sahcabchén				
Sahcabchén, 1777–78	0.8%	0.0%	99.2%	4[a]
Seyba Playa, 1778–79	9.2	0.4	90.4	5
Chicbul, 1777–78	1.9	0.0	98.1	1[a]
Campeche, 1777–78				
Pich	61.7	2.2	36.0	4
Campeche villa	33.5	4.4	62.1	19
Campeche Extramuros	16.4	0.6	83.1	7
Camino Real Alto				
Hopelchén, 1777–78	7.1	0.0	92.9	1[a]
Bolonchenticul, 1777–78	6.3	0.3	93.4	2[a]
Bécal, 1777–78	1.6	0.0	98.4	1
Hecelchakán, 1778–79	35.7	7.5	56.9	10
Calkiní, 1778–79	52.9	5.9	41.2	4
Camino Real Bajo, 1777–78				
Maxcanú	40.7	8.1	51.2	9
Kopomá	27.6	8.6	63.8	2
Umán	41.7	14.7	43.6	11
Hunucmá	71.7	22.3	6.0	7
Mérida, San Cristóbal, 1778–79	60.8	11.4	27.8	8
La Costa				
Izamal:				
1790–91	42.3	12.4	45.3	49
1791–92	46.0	4.6	49.4	37
1792–93	47.9	8.4	43.7	37
Mocochá, 1790–91	78.3	5.1	16.5	11
Beneficios Bajos				
Hoctún, Hocabá, and				
Homún, 1777–78	34.5	18.2	47.4	18
Hoctún, 1795–96	43.7	8.0	48.2	25
Hocabá, 1795–96	54.9	6.5	38.6	26
Yaxcabá, 1777–78	32.0	14.7	53.3	3[b]
Tixcacaltuyú, 1777–78	88.9	11.1	0.0	1
Beneficios Altos, 1777–78				
Peto	27.5	0.0	72.5	4
Tihosuco	0.0	0.0	100.0	1[a]
Chunhuhub	21.3	1.4	77.3	1[a]
Sierra Baja				
Mama, 1778–79	41.3	21.6	37.2	5
Teabo, 1778–79	44.4	0.0	55.6	1
Teabo, 1795–96	53.8	23.9	22.2	5
Valladolid, Valladolid villa, 1787–88	39.6	7.7	52.7	18[a]
Tizimín, 1787–88				
Tizimín	0.6	1.5	97.9	3[a]
Espita	12.4	4.9	82.8	4[a]
Bacalar, Petén Itzá, 1778–79	61.6	0.0	38.4	?

SOURCES: BCCA, Manuscripts, Diezmos, 1778–79, 1783–88, 1791–93, 1795–96; AAM, Diezmos, Libros 19, 1791–94, 20, 1795–98; AGEY, Iglesia, exps. 4, 1795, 7, 1796.

NOTE: Percentages were fixed by the monetary value of the tithe payments. Where payments were made in kind, monetary values were based on what the tithe collectors got for the produce on the market.

[a]Data derived from payments made by individuals, not from payments made for estates.

[b]Payments were made for two estates and by one individual who may have owned more than one estate.

important crop in the Sierra Alta. Maize was dominant in the Valladolid district, although cotton was clearly important as well. It was here in the nineteenth century that Yucatecan entrepreneurs established a modern cotton textile factory.[31] Finally, cotton was king in the Tizimín district.

The Labor Force

If landowners were to devote their holdings to crops, they had to count on a reliable and fairly substantial labor force. How did they solve this problem? Certainly not by a large-scale peonage system, for they lacked the social and political controls to maintain such a system. Landowners in fact had great difficulty enforcing existing peonage laws, and peons reportedly left their masters at will.[32] Indeed, not until the late nineteenth century did an oppressive peonage system become workable.

In the late colonial period, farmworkers had to be recruited in other ways. One method was the old system of government-controlled labor drafts of free peasants, that is, the Maya villagers who juridically were neither serfs nor peons. This corvée began to be revived on a considerable scale in the late eighteenth century, when the government responded to recurring food shortages by authorizing *subdelegados* (local Spanish magistrates) to order caciques to supply landowners with laborers. In reality, however, this was merely a subterfuge, for the labor force recruited in this way was put to work in the cane fields. Indeed, in Beneficios Altos and Beneficios Bajos these labor drafts, called *mandamientos*, were a major component of the cane-producing haciendas. They were also important in the Sierra.[33]

Another method of securing workers, especially in areas where cane was not a major product of the estates, was the arrangement touched on earlier, in which Indians, or *luneros* as they came to be called, exchanged their labor for a plot of land. As a royal official explained in 1786, "The name *luneros* results from their being obligated to work every Monday [*lunes*], with no payment whatsoever, for the owner of the hacienda, and normally this work is interpreted so that each Indian works on ten *mecates* [0.4 ha] of *milpa* belonging to the *hacendado* each of the 52 Mondays of the year . . . ; other owners collect in firewood or whatever is convenient, and still others, not having tasks in which to occupy the [Indians], are accustomed to collect in money. To this general practice should be added the benefit to the owners of various labor services and cattle-tending, care of the beehives, and other minor tasks."[34] In return for this work, the landowners "assist them with as much land as they choose for their *milpas*, and [provide] the water they need."[35]

It is not known when this tenancy system began; even royal officials had trouble classifying it. Luneros were not day-laborers or salaried workers; nor were they sharecroppers or renters, because they usually did not pay anything, in money or in kind, for the use of the land. Rather in the words of one official, they were "those who, taking leave of their villages, . . . take shelter or seek protection on . . . the ranches that they freely choose. . . . These circumstances suggest that this class of Indians be considered emphyteutae [*enfiteuticarios*] . . . because they contribute a moderate pension to the landlord in recognition of the real ownership that he maintains of the land and water of which they have usufruct."[36] Under this arrangement, landowners had no rights over the person of a lunero; the worker could be neither punished nor forced to make cash payments.[37] Presumably the landowner's only recourse when the system failed was to expel the lunero from the land.

The agricultural economy, then, was not based on debt peonage. Luneros were not indebted to the landowners; what debt peons there were worked mainly in ranching activities. It was a distinction that the landowners themselves insisted on when, in 1786, the government attempted to make them pay the tribute owed by their luneros. With some exaggeration, the hacendados claimed that they had always paid the tribute of their peons, but they denied any responsibility for the luneros' tribute, because the luneros could not be forced to make good the money.[38] Paying someone's tribute, of course, was one way of getting, and keeping, the person in debt. "The Yucatecan . . . knows perfectly well what kind of system is used on the rural estates of the country regarding the Indians who serve on them," wrote a Yucatecan liberal in the 1870's. "The landlord is the one who pays the taxes to which the [Indian] is subject, and they are added to his account, which is constantly kept open."[39] Yet instead of jumping at this golden opportunity of extending the net of peonage around a whole class of free peasants, the hacendados protested the measure and predicted total ruin for the province if it was enforced.[40] Clearly, in 1786 landowners had little use for so many potential peons. The supply of labor, in short, was generally sufficient to make unnecessary the massive expansion of peonage.

Nancy Farriss has suggested that the settlement of Indian tenants on landed estates in eighteenth-century Yucatan represented only a minor change in the Maya way of life.[41] This was probably true in the short run, for many of the estates continued to concentrate on stock-raising, which required only a small work force and, in any case, did not involve the luneros at all. Moreover, to the extent that many haciendas had their own chapels and resident Indian populations as large as those of many villages, they were almost indistinguishable from other Maya communities. Several haciendas even achieved the religious status of full-fledged visitas, that is, auxiliary villages. This was especially true in the Sierra Baja and Sierra Alta, regions in which large estates proliferated.

Furthermore, many of the largest estates were located on territory that

Map 6   Distribution of the Indian Population on Landed Estates by Parish, ca. 1800

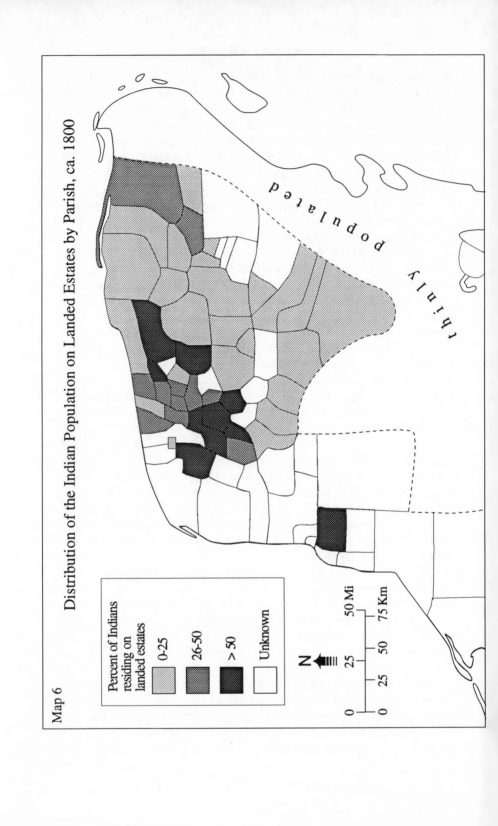

Percent of Indians
residing on
landed estates

0-25

26-50

> 50

Unknown

thinly Populated

N

0   25   50 Mi

0   25   50   75 Km

had been abandoned by Indians as a result of depopulation, so that in some sense the lunero system represented a reoccupation of the land by Maya agriculturalists[42] and, initially at any rate, a return to the traditional, pre-Hispanic Maya settlement pattern, which had been disrupted by the colonial policy of reducción. The Yucatec Maya resisted this policy of forced concentration by establishing clandestine hamlets and villages.[43] In the eighteenth century this was no longer necessary, for the haciendas provided the Indians with the opportunity of establishing agricultural communities without fear of more reducciones. In effect, the settlement of Indians on private estates as agriculturalists represented the officially sanctioned establishment of new Maya hamlets and villages. In the short run, therefore, for the Indians the haciendas were probably more like other Maya communities than units of production dominating their lives.

In the long run, however, the rise of the haciendas did represent a substantial social change, for eventually the hacendados did succeed in dominating the lives of the Indian residents on their estates. A century was required for the process to complete itself, but the direction of the change was becoming clear by the end of the colonial period. Rapid economic growth in the last decades of colonial rule generated an increased demand for labor, and since the government went ahead in 1786 with its program of collecting tribute from hacendados for their luneros, the landowners eventually exacted more labor from their tenants. By 1813 labor services were twice as heavy as in 1786.[44] They were heavier still in 1840, and by 1843 a government official noted that the luneros had become practically indistinguishable from debt peons.[45] So what had begun as a fiscal measure taken "with particular consideration for the interests of the Indians" (or so wrote Governor-Intendant Lucas de Gálvez in 1789[46]) ended up by pushing a whole class of free peasants into peonage. The tenants eventually became the equivalent of medieval European cotters: resident rural proletarians with the right to plant on small plots. The beneficiaries were the plantation owners who dominated Yucatan until the Mexican Revolution.

Innocuous as the lunero system seemed at the start, then, it was to work an enormous social change. The extent of that change by the late eighteenth century can be measured by comparing the relative proportions of village and hacienda Indians as revealed in the records of *visitas pastorales* (episcopal visitations) for the years 1781–87 and 1803–5. Data from these visitas are presented in Map 6.[47]

As the map demonstrates, the effects of the rise of the hacienda were not randomly or evenly distributed throughout the peninsula. In the northwestern quarter of Yucatan, within a 70-kilometer radius of Mérida, haciendas were important centers of Maya population. In many of the parishes around the capital, in the partido of La Costa, and in the

northern Sierra (Sierra Baja), more than half the Indian population resided on private estates. This was also true for some of the Camino Real
area between Mérida and Campeche.

The southern Sierra, or Sierra Alta, a region in which some of the most
valuable and productive haciendas were located, had substantial concentrations of estate Indians but also contained the most populous Maya villages in all of Yucatan. Consequently, large as their numbers were in absolute terms, estate Indians represented only a small percentage of the total Maya population.

In the eastern half of the peninsula, a significant proportion of the Indians lived on landed estates in two thinly populated cotton-producing
parishes northeast of Valladolid. However, for the most part eastern Yucatan was a land of free Maya peasants living in independent villages. This
was true both in the thinly populated area east of Izamal and northwest
of Valladolid, and in the more densely populated partidos of Beneficios
Bajos and Beneficios Altos. In some parishes of Beneficios Altos there
were no haciendas at all; the Indians lived exclusively in villages and hamlets.

Agrarian change in Yucatan thus resulted in substantial differentiation.
In the western half of the peninsula, a large proportion of the Maya population resided on haciendas. Although this did not initially have cultural
and political implications, in the long run the Indians of the west became
less like those of the east in both their settlement pattern and their economy. When the Caste War broke out in 1847, most of the western Maya
did not join the uprising. Rather, like the *peones acasillados* in some parts
of Mexico after 1910, they tended to be *indios pacíficos*, who chose, as it
were, to sit out the revolution. Some even fought on the side of their masters. The rebellion was carried to the outskirts of Mérida by the free Maya
peasants of the east, who received little or no support from anyone except
the Indians of the Chenes region (southwest of the Sierra, and again outside the influence of the colonial haciendas). Consequently, regionaliza-
tion in the colonial era, as well as in the post-Independence period,[48]
played a huge part in the great social upheaval of the nineteenth century.

Agrarian change in Yucatan demonstrates the complex relationship
among geographic, social, and economic factors in the development of
the landed estate in Spanish America. As Eric Van Young has noted, all
too often geography is treated as a given, to be mentioned in passing as
"background" but ignored as a causal factor.[49] In fact, however, every region's unique environment contributes to its historical development. This
is clear in the case of Yucatan, for geographic factors prevented certain
kinds of economic activity while encouraging others. Moreover, regional
differences in soil and rainfall caused local variations in historical development and the structures of production. At the same time, the things

that could be done under given ecological conditions were in fact done only when social conditions—such as an increasing population in need of food and with a desire for alcoholic beverages and sugar—made it *historically* possible. In short, socioeconomic change was part of the broader context of the development of the ecosystem, that is, of the "biotic community of interrelated organisms together with their common habitat."[50]

On the whole, the socioeconomic changes of the eighteenth century did not bode well for the long-term survival of that ecosystem. The intensified cultivation of maize began a process of overexploitation of the soil as more and more land was brought into production before being properly fallowed. Moreover, and more serious in the long run, the expansion of sugarcane led to the eventual destruction of large tracts of forest land. In maize production, at least, forests were burned for the purpose of returning nutrients to the soil. The new sugar mills and distilleries felled trees solely to fuel their cauldrons and returned nothing to the soil. To be sure, the impact of this destruction would hardly be noticed in the eighteenth century, and in any case cane production would largely cease after 1847. But a precedent—the unrestrained destruction of the environment—had been set, and it would be followed by the henequen plantations in the nineteenth and twentieth centuries. The results can be seen today: the impoverished land, and the impoverished people, of the henequen zone.

The rise of the hacienda in Yucatan is also significant because the historical causation reveals the nature of some of the forces that have shaped modern Latin American history. Dependency theory emphasizes the role of the world economy in stimulating the colonial, neocolonial, and imperialistic relationship between the modern capitalist countries and the Third World.[51] In the case of Yucatan, at a later time—after 1870—there is no question that world demand produced an export economy based on the gross exploitation of the labor force, a skewed distribution of income, and domination by the external forces of world capitalism. In fact, even in the colonial period the world economy played an important role in Yucatan's development. The hacienda was certainly encouraged by a growing world demand for rice and for beef and its by-products. And although the market for cotton textiles tailed off, Yucatan continued to export cloth in the late colonial period.

The major causes of the rise of the hacienda in Yucatan were nevertheless internal. The increasing demand for food made it profitable for local landowners to raise maize and, to a lesser extent, rice on their estates. At the same time, a process of import substitution *avant le mot* was at work in the production of sugar and cane alcohol. The demand that had made these products major imports since the early colonial period and that was eventually met by local producers owed nothing to external factors. The suppliers did need imported technology, it is true, but this was readily available in nearby Spanish colonies, and its importation did not result in any foreign involvement in the productive process. Agrarian change, in short, was for the most part caused by local social and economic factors.

The Decline of the Encomienda and the Repartimiento

The rise of the hacienda undermined the existence of the encomienda and the repartimiento. Those parasitic institutions of colonialism had been tolerated by the crown because they were seen as essential to the survival of Spanish rule in Yucatan. Once the landed estate had developed as the colonists' principal economic base, the Spanish government was in a position to bring Yucatan into line with imperial policy elsewhere by eliminating the encomienda. And once new sources of governmental revenue emerged, in Yucatan and elsewhere, in the last decades of the eighteenth century, the crown was in a position to end the repartimiento system; royal officials would earn money in new ways, and a new labor system would develop.

The Institutions of Colonialism in the Mid-Eighteenth Century

Just as the hacienda emerged gradually, so the encomienda and the repartimiento were undermined in a gradual manner. Both institutions remained firmly entrenched during the middle decades of the eighteenth century. The encomienda, for example, continued to be an important asset for those in need of ready cash. In 1756 Tomás Ceballos mortgaged his encomienda of Chuburná to Domingo Cayetano de Cárdenas, the Protector of the Tribunal de Indios and son of one of the people identified as carrying out the repartimiento in 1700. In return for an unspecified sum of money, Cárdenas was given the right to collect the encomienda tribute directly from the cacique and justicias of Chuburná.[52] In 1767 Estanislao del Puerto, a militia colonel, mortgaged his encomienda of Ekmul-Kantunil to Diego de Lanz, a resident of Campeche who would soon be an official of the Royal Treasury, for 550 pesos, which Lanz was allowed to collect directly from the Indians until he had recovered the capital plus costs.[53] In both cases the moneylenders gained access to the village and presumably carried out other business with the Indians on the side.

The encomienda, moreover, was still defended as vital to the province's survival. As late as 1765 even reformist royal officials could recommend to José de Gálvez, Visitor General of New Spain (and future Minister of the Indies), that the crown should preserve an institution that it had rightly preserved in the past, for "if the Spanish colonists had not been aided by the grant of encomiendas, Yucatan would have been depopulated by the conquerors and their descendants, because the country is . . . so poor that only with these subsidies from the Royal Munificence could they maintain themselves on this soil."[54]

As for the repartimiento, it not only continued to be the most important single mechanism for capital accumulation in Yucatan but even flourished, at least briefly, in this period. For the legalization of the system in 1731, far from recognizing the inevitable, resulted in an increase in the quantity of goods demanded from the Maya. In 1735 the Tribunal de Indios made an official protest against the increased demands made on the Indians, and this resulted in attempts to regulate the amount of goods the Governors were permitted to contract. In 1737 the limits were set at 10,000 patíes and 500 arrobas (6.25 tons) of wax per repartimiento, and the Governor was allowed to carry out two repartimientos a year, for an estimated annual income of between 22,000 and 24,000 pesos.[55] By 1765, the legally sanctioned limit had been raised to 12,000 patíes per repartimiento, a rate that remained in effect until the system was suppressed in 1782.[56]

Unfortunately for the Maya, the Governors did not always observe these limits. Writing in 1792, Governor-Intendant José de Savido charged that previous Governors and war captains had taken advantage of the legalization to expand the quantities of goods demanded from the Maya and to carry out additional business activities at the Indians' expense. It was hardly a new charge: the same points had been made repeatedly in the residencias conducted between 1740 and 1770. Furthermore, as some witnesses testified in the course of these proceedings, even the legalized repartimiento defrauded the Maya. For example, when wax was scarce because of drought, the Indians not only had to buy it on the market for much more than they had received in advance from the repartimiento agents, but got shortchanged again by having to repay the agents in kind. On top of this, as in the past, debt collectors used a "heavy" pound, of between 20 and 22 ounces, to extract even more wax out of the Indians. Indeed, the abuses extended to making the Indians pay out-of-pocket expenses, as when agents delivered cotton of bad quality to be woven into cloth, so that the women had to buy more or better cotton to fulfill their contracts; or as when the Indians were required to take the patíes and wax from their villages to the distant provincial capital without compensation for the labor and transport costs incurred.[57]

For all this, the system was defended by most of the colonists because it was the single-most-important branch of commerce in the colony. For example, in 1744 Maestre de Campo Simón de Salazar y Villamil, the leader of the powerful Salazar clan, testified at the residencia of former Governor Manuel Salcedo that the repartimiento "has never caused, nor does it cause, any harm whatsoever to the Natives; on the contrary, it benefits them because with the money they receive for the wax and the weaving of *patíes* . . . they pay their tribute, alms [religious taxes], and the other charges that burden them."[58] Even the Maya caciques were required to join the chorus of praise for the system. At the same residencia Don Lucas Tus, cacique of Pixoy, stated that the repartimiento did not cause any harm to the Indians of his village "because with the stipend they received, they had the means to pay their tribute, alms, and other expenses." The same words are to be found in the testimonies of Don Pedro Chan, Don Cosme Balam, and Don Antonio Chan, caciques of Sisal, Yalcón, and Sismopó.[59]

Nevertheless, enough abuses were reported to warrant a change. In the 1750's supporters of the system decided that it would be more defensible if it were run by the Tribunal de Indios, that is, by the special court created to protect the interests of the Indians. As a result, Domingo Cayetano de Cárdenas, who served as Protector, or chief official, of the Tribunal, took over the operation of the repartimiento. He was certainly qualified for the task for, it will be recalled, he was the son of one of Governor Martín de Urzúa's repartimiento agents. Shortly after this change was instituted, Cárdenas conducted a special inquest designed to prove that the reform had eliminated all conceivable abuses. All the witnesses, Maya as well as Spaniards, dutifully swore that the system, far from harming the Indians, was good for them. The cacique, justicias, scribe, and principales of Xocén were the first to be questioned, and they declared that the advance payments, through the repartimiento, "are very useful to them, because without them they could not pay their tribute and other annual burdens," and that in fact the Indians were eager to accept repartimientos "since it is hard cash which they receive." The Indian cabildos of many other villages then gave the same testimony, usually using the exact same words.[60] But even these rigged proceedings could not cover up everything; many Indians reported on past abuses, thereby casting doubt on all the testimony given since 1731 praising the fairness of the legalized repartimiento. In the end, Cárdenas had to reduce the allotments of many villages because the quantities demanded were too burdensome.[61]

It is of course difficult to know what the Indians really felt about the repartimiento. But the statements of participants in an uprising in 1761 are illuminating. Jacinto Canek, the self-proclaimed King who led the rebellion, denounced the repartimiento as an injustice and ordered its suppression. This action was remarked on by several of the rebels who were captured and later interrogated by the Spanish authorities. One Indian said specifically that he joined the movement because he had heard the leader would abolish the repartimiento, as well as religious taxes and the Santa Cruzada's bulls. (He was apparently misinformed about the last, for Canek had authorized the continued forcible sales of indulgences, the proceeds of which were to come to him.) The repartimiento was such an everyday feature of life for the Maya that the cacique of Tiholop, who took part in the rebellion, testified that he had first met Canek when returning to his home after collecting patíes from the Indians of his village. Ironically, Captain Cristóbal Calderón de la Helguera, war captain of Tihosuco and commander of the militia forces that crushed the rebels at Cisteíl, had been away from his post when the rising began because he was taking care of his family repartimiento business, namely, the sale of Santa Cruzada bulls.[62]

The governors' repartimientos escaped severe criticism in the next 20 years. Not so the repartimiento of the Santa Cruzada, which continued to be run by the House of Miraflores. In 1757 the new Bishop of Yucatan, Fray Ignacio de Padilla, became suspicious of the business of forcibly selling indulgences to the Indians on credit and ordered Dr. Joseph Martínez, the Dean of the Cathedral and Subdelegate General of the Santa Cruzada, to investigate the matter.[63] The Treasurer of the Santa Cruzada, Pedro Calderón Garrástegui, who would soon become the Fourth Count of Miraflores, avowed that he welcomed the opportunity to demonstrate the fairness and honesty of his administration of the business. His optimism was undoubtedly influenced by the fact that Dr. Martínez was the *compadre* of his son, Santiago Calderón de la Helguera, the future Fifth Count of Miraflores, who along with his brother Cristóbal administered the sale of the bulls in the partidos of Camino Real, Beneficios Bajos, and Beneficios Altos. The resulting investigation exonerated the administrators of the Santa Cruzada of any wrongdoing. But Bishop Padilla then accused Dr. Martínez of being partial to the Calderón family and ordered another inquest.

The second investigation was more revealing, and gives us some insight into how the sales were organized. The indulgences were offered in the villages literally with great fanfare: a procession made its way into the village to the sound of a band composed of various trumpeters and players of *chirimías* (a reeded wind instrument). The sales were announced and the Indians dutifully bought their allotments. As in the case of automobiles, there was a bull for every pocketbook: the most expensive ones, sold only to Spaniards, cost two pesos; moderately priced indulgences could be bought for one peso or four reales; and the cheapest bulls, sold to the Indians, cost two reales.

Many of the parish priests questioned at the inquest defended the actions of the Santa Cruzada. As some were quick to point out, not all bulls were sold on credit; Indians occasionally paid in cash. In any case, the curate of Chunhuhub declared, Indians could never pass up the opportunity to buy anything on credit, and consequently entered joyfully into the contracts to get bulls now and pay later in wax or patíes. Other priests pointed out that repartimientos were necessary to get the Maya to pay their tribute and religious taxes. Still others argued that the difference between the assessed value of the wax and cloth and their real market value was justified because the business entailed some risk. Besides, it faced the unfair competition of the Governors' repartimientos: the chief executives could force the Indians to deliver the goods freight free in Mérida, whereas the Santa Cruzada had to pay transport costs to get its wax and cloth to market.

But many other priests were prepared to testify against the Santa Cruzada, and their revelations led to the dismissal of at least one of the bull sellers. Several priests complained about the fraudulence of making the Indians repay their debts in goods worth far more than the money value set in their contracts. Sometimes the agents of the Santa Cruzada added extra fees onto the sales, which effectively raised the price of the bulls by 25 percent. Worst of all, despite the lip service paid to the voluntary nature of the practice, the Indians were in fact being compelled to buy the bulls. Some priests simply sided with encomenderos in opposing the business on the grounds that the sale of the bulls took the Indians away from their work, thereby interfering with the payment of tribute and religious taxes. This suggests that Indian surplus labor was being utilized to its fullest. There was little room left for the biennial sale of indulgences.

After the second inquest, Bishop Padilla informed the King of his concerns about the Santa Cruzada's abuses. He also promulgated new rules for the sale of bulls. Henceforth, parish priests were to inform the Indians that the purchase of indulgences was completely voluntary. The buyers could pay cash if they so desired. On the other hand, since the Church benefited financially from the sales, Padilla instructed the priests that sales on credit, with future payment in kind, were still permitted. And in fact the Bishop was determined to ensure that the Indians had the opportunity to benefit spiritually from indulgences. Priests were under no circumstances to do anything that would discourage people from purchasing bulls; hinting that the parishioners should not buy them was specifically prohibited.

The Treasurer of the Santa Cruzada appealed to the Viceroy to get the Bishop to withdraw his reforms, and as a result Padilla was censured. But he in turn appealed to the King, who then censured the Viceroy and commended the Bishop for his efforts to protect the Indians from abuse. The Santa Cruzada thereafter was administered without major complaint, but the emphasis on the voluntary purchase of the bulls had its effect. By the 1770's the business of indulgences was so bad that the Count of Miraflores had to return thousands of unsold bulls to the Cruzada administration in Mexico City.[64] Eventually the enterprise ceased altogether.

The End of the Repartimiento and the Encomienda

In the 1780's the royal government, headed by Charles III and the reformist Minister of the Indies, José de Gálvez, ended the repartimiento in Yucatan and incorporated the encomiendas into the royal tributary system. The Spanish state was thus ultimately responsible for abolishing the institutions of colonialism that had once been the basis of the economy and society of the Spaniards in Yucatan. But other factors contributed to the demise of some of the basic instruments of colonialism, and in the final analysis, it is certain that the repartimiento would have come to an end, and the encomienda would have declined greatly in importance, sometime in the early nineteenth century regardless of Spanish policy.

For both institutions depended on exports for profits, and the markets for those exports were shrinking. In the 1740's the price of patíes in Mexico was depressed,[65] and the same was true in the 1760's. Valera and Corres, the reformist officials who inspected Yucatan in 1765, reported that this circumstance was causing Yucatan's exports of cotton textiles to fall off and was resulting in declining incomes for encomenderos. Yucatan in fact was now suffering from competition not only from its traditional rivals—i.e. Oaxaca, the Philippines, China, and India—but also from Puebla, New Galicia, Michoacán, and Chiapas.[66] Then, in the late eighteenth century, Catalonia entered the market in a big way, and in 1797 Great Britain—the toughest competitor of them all—began to overwhelm all the producers still using the antiquated technology of pre-Columbian days.[67] Sooner or later, therefore, Yucatan's traditional cotton textile industry was certain to disappear, although at the time the state eliminated the repartimiento and the encomienda, it was still an important sector of the provincial economy.

Wax production was also in decline. In part this was the fault of Yucatan's own merchants, who in the 1740's tried to take advantage of high prices in Mexico by mixing pebbles in with the wax for added weight. When the ruse was discovered, demand for Yucatan wax fell off sharply, and the market had still not fully recovered 20 years later.[68] But the problem was also structural, for the high prices in Mexico were in part due to declining production in Yucatan. The supply was so scarce in the 1740's that Governor Antonio de Benavides was forced to suspend his wax repartimientos.[69] The scarcity continued in the 1750's and was commented on during the inquests carried out by the Protector of the Tribunal de Indios, Domingo Cayetano de Cárdenas, and Bishop Padilla. Only in the partido of the Camino Real Alto was wax still in good supply.[70]

In the case of the repartimiento wax, at least, the problem likely lay in the Indians' expanding numbers. As they cleared and colonized more and more land, they would inevitably have driven the wild bees they depended on farther away from the settled areas. It is significant that the Camino Real Alto was the best wax-gathering area, for at this time it still had a very small population. Whatever the case, the trend seems to have been irreversible, for when efforts were made in the 1790's to revive the repartimiento system, the resumption of wax-collecting was considered to be impossible and therefore out of the question.

Both the encomienda and the repartimiento, then, were based in part on declining sectors of the economy. In any event, by this time royal policy had clearly turned against the encomienda. Though the crown had bowed to the encomenderos' pressure and exempted Yucatan from the general incorporation of encomiendas in America in 1718, in practice the government pursued a policy of gradual incorporation. Of the 115 encomiendas in Yucatan in the first half of the eighteenth century, only 77 survived into the 1780's.[71]

The famine of 1769–72 had accounted for some of the losses. According to official records, the number of encomienda tributaries declined 39.6 percent between 1765 and 1773.[72] This resulted in a drastic reduction in encomienda revenues, for not only did the number of tributaries diminish; the surviving Indians simply could not pay their tribute, and would not be able to do so for years. Encomenderos, however, were expected to continue to pay royal and religious taxes, as well as their encomienda pensioners. Since no one could pay, the Royal Exchequer began to impound some of the encomiendas. The crown also granted tax relief to the Indians to stimulate economic recovery, as well as to encourage runaways to return to their villages. Consequently, encomenderos received practically no income at all for several years in a row.[73]

The cabildo of Mérida, responding to the complaints of the encomenderos, petitioned the crown to cancel the debts of holders of encomiendas. This was suggested as a measure to help put the province back on its feet.[74] The encomenderos also requested an extension of their grants for another generation, or "life," beyond that already stipulated. However, all the Spanish government would do, in a ruling made in 1778, was to extend possession for five years after the second holder's death.[75] One suspects that the economy's strength in the face of this crisis was what finally convinced the crown that the encomienda was no longer necessary for the survival of the elite.

It was only four years later that the crown abolished the repartimiento. The decision to take that step grew out of a policy review of the problems presented by the repartimiento system throughout the Empire.[76] The crown had always been concerned about the corruption resulting from the connections between public office and private commerce but had tolerated the business activities of its officials as a necessary evil. In the middle of the eighteenth century, reformist elements within the imperial bureaucracy had called attention to the evils of the repartimiento system and had urged its suppression. In an effort to eliminate abuses, the crown resorted to the solution it had employed in Yucatan in 1731: it permitted legalized but controlled repartimientos in Peru (1751) and the Kingdom of Guatemala (1777). But this solution did not lead to a less exploitative system, and consequently, in the era of Charles III and José de Gálvez, reformers again called for the end of the repartimiento. The attack on the system focused not merely on the corruption resulting naturally from the alliance between officials and merchants, but also on the economic disadvantages of maintaining the system. For in practice the local officials set themselves up as monopolists who prevented competitors from carrying out legal commerce. The reformers argued that doing away with the repartimiento would stimulate the economy by introducing commercial competition into the rural areas inhabited primarily by Indians.

While this issue was being debated, events in the colonies inspired the highest officials to make quick decisions on the subject. First, in 1780 the rebellion of Tupac Amaru broke out in Peru; Viceroy Agustín de Jáuregui responded by immediately abolishing the repartimiento.[77] Then, Minister of the Indies José de Gálvez began to be bombarded with reports from Yucatan accusing the acting Governor, Roberto Rivas Betancourt, and his repartimiento agent, Enrique de los Reyes, of a host of frauds and of mistreatment of the Indians. Their methods in fact were the same as those employed in Yucatan for the past hundred years: the quantity of patíes demanded was excessive; the cotton provided was either insufficient in quantity or of poor quality, compelling the Indians to use their own money to buy cotton on the market; the weight of the pound was arbitrarily increased to more than 16 ounces; the Indians had to make up shortages of wild wax by purchasing it at the full market price; agents tried to acquire all sorts of goods besides cotton cloth and wax; violence was used to make the Indians accept repartimientos or to make them pay their debts; and the acting Governor made extra money by selling the positions of war captain.[78] In addition, Reyes, who was war captain of the Sierra, as well as the Governor's repartimiento agent, was using his position to extort money or goods from the Indians. For example, they had to pay him for permission to take hogs to Campeche to sell.[79] The reformed repartimiento foreseen in legalization turned out to be not so reformed after all.

Perhaps more important was the sudden interest the Spanish military took in the repartimiento in Yucatan. The Intendant of the Army in Mexico, Pedro Antonio de Cosío, on hearing that canvas and cables made of henequen could be produced very cheaply in Yucatan, thought this might be a good source of supply for the Havana Squadron and the port of Veracruz. Diego de Lanz, a Treasury official in Campeche, was ordered to find out whether the province could increase its production of these items. Lanz reported that, as things stood, it could not. The Governors, he pointed out, had already cornered the labor market through the repartimiento, for "they bring all the Natives of the Province into this incessant weaving" of patíes. Production of more cables and canvas would be impossible so long as the Governors had this power. In short, what the Treasury official was trying to make clear was that all Indian surplus labor was being appropriated under the existing system, leaving none for anyone else to tap. Lanz went on to identify the war captains as part and parcel of the problem. These cronies of the Governors spent their entire time "in overseeing the punctual conclusion and collection of the repartimientos and [arranging] the purchase in advance [of the harvest] of all the cotton that is needed to carry them out." Thanks to them, if the crown were to try to buy any cotton, "it would be at best whatever is left over." Since the Governor's salary was only 4,000 pesos, the search for money was "the primary objective of his office"; the incumbent, Rivas Betancourt, Lanz said witheringly, thought of nothing but money and lived "gloating in the relish of absolute rule."

The only solution to this state of affairs, Lanz reported, was to pay the Governors a higher salary so that they would not have to get involved in the business. Such a policy would also be beneficial to the Indians because they could then sell their labor freely, rather than be forced to accept the Governors' terms. Lanz's report was sent on to the Viceroy and then to José de Gálvez, along with commentary by the Intendant of the Army in Mexico. Cosío concurred with Lanz on the need to increase the governors' salaries in order to get them out of the repartimiento business. He also recommended the establishment of an intendancy in Yucatan to root out the abuses once and for all.[80]

It appears, then, that what sealed the fate of the repartimiento in Yucatan was the direct involvement of the Minister of the Indies, José de Gálvez. Important decisions were made quickly. Rivas Betancourt, who had ruled as acting Governor since 1777, was replaced by José Merino y Ceballos, a soldier of considerable experience. The new Governor was assigned a salary of 7,000 pesos, and his appointment title specifically stated that he was being paid the higher salary because he was absolutely forbidden to engage in repartimientos. The problem at hand was also attended to at once. The *real cédula* of 1731 authorizing repartimientos was revoked, and Rivas Betancourt, still acting Governor, was ordered to abolish the repartimiento system. He complied, and the Minister of the Indies reviewed the case to ensure that his orders were followed. When Merino arrived in Yucatan to assume his duties in 1783, he immediately issued a proclamation informing the public that the Governor and war captains were absolutely forbidden to carry out repartimientos. Finally, in 1788 the crown instituted the Intendancy of Mérida. The reforms were complete.[81] Meanwhile, in 1785 the crown had ordered the incorporation of all remaining encomiendas. The old order was rapidly fading.

Still, it would take more than mere orders from the bureaucracy in Spain to root out these institutions once and for all. Efforts had to be made to guarantee enforcement in the face of considerable opposition from the Yucatecan elite. In the case of the encomienda, a compromise was reached. The dispossessed encomenderos were to be paid pensions based on the annual average yield of their encomiendas in the past five years. They did not accept this solution without complaint. As they saw it, their pensions should be pegged to the current Indian population, a method that allowed for the income they would have received from an ever-growing number of tributaries. But the crown got its way, and the encomenderos had to content themselves with fixed pensions, which continued to be paid until the early nineteenth century.[82] Significantly, much as the encomenderos protested against the crown's action, for the first time ever they did not make the argument that the encomienda was essential to their existence in Yucatan. Now that the hacienda had become the basis of elite wealth, the traditional argument for retaining one of the most important institutions of the colonial regime was simply not credible.

The repartimiento was much more difficult to eliminate. In the wake of the crown's actions, commerce between Yucatan and New Spain fell off badly, and it was not long before powerful interests moved to get the system restored. The stage was set during the residencia of Rivas Betancourt in 1786, when the abuses perpetrated during the last years of the repartimiento's legality were carefully blamed not on the acting Governor but on his agent, Enrique de los Reyes, whose property was impounded for several years as a result of the charges against him. Even the caciques were somehow recruited to defend Rivas Betancourt.[83] Once again, the tactic used was to blame abuses on bad officials, especially underlings, rather than on the system itself, which was said to be both fair and necessary.

Then, in 1789, the cabildos of Mérida and Valladolid turned to Lucas de Gálvez, the province's first Intendant, for help. The suppression of the repartimiento had been disastrous for commerce, they told him. It was already clear that since the Indians were given to idleness, were not motivated by money or a desire for improvement, and were content with poverty, a degree of coercion had to be used to get them to work and produce. (Enrique de los Reyes, it is worth noting, had argued in his defense in 1786 that although he had never given orders for anyone to be flogged, in fact whipping was necessary to make the Indians carry out their contractual obligations.) The repartimiento was simply "a form of habilitation," the councilmen claimed, an infusion of capital to spin the wheels of commerce. The Governor's role, it was said, was that of a go-between connecting the Indians to the merchants who invested in the business; without government involvement, the Indians could not be made to repay their debts. Finally, the repartimiento had enabled the Indians to pay their tribute and religious taxes; now that it was ended, the natives had trouble making those payments. In sum, the cabildos argued, restoration of the system was necessary to bring about economic recovery.[84]

The cabildos found a sympathetic ear in Gálvez. In a report to the crown, he pointed out that since the suppression of the system, Yucatan's commerce had declined in volume by more than two-thirds. It was the Indians who were to blame for this, Gálvez wrote, elaborating on the cabildos' theme: "The Indian by his very nature is given to idleness and slovenliness. There is no incitement that can move him to be employed, nor is he excited by money or by the comforts that human life can provide. He is not interested in improving his house and doing himself honor with esteemed possessions; he hardly dresses enough to hide his nudity. He does not think about the future of his family. None of his goods are invested in anything, and he never considers doing any business, not even what is necessary for his survival and subsistence." The only way to achieve economic recovery was to restore the repartimiento, for the Indians' participation was crucial to commerce. To eliminate possible abuses, Gálvez recommended that the system be run by the officials of the Tribunal de Indios, with the participation of the caciques and Indian officials. The subdelegados and *jueces españoles* (new positions created under the Intendancy to replace the war captains) would have the task of overseeing the operation to ensure its fairness.[85]

The arguments of the cabildos and of Intendant Gálvez were reiterated in 1791 by Captain Eugenio Rubio, a Spanish-born professional soldier who had married into a prominent local family and served as the spokesman of the new commercial-landowning elite in the Age of Enlightenment. Rubio, the author of several tracts arguing for fewer governmental restrictions in order to stimulate commerce, helped chart the course of economic Liberalism in the next century by recommending that the new commercial economy be based on tighter enforcement of peonage and vagrancy laws. In the matter of the repartimiento, Rubio recommended that the old system be reintroduced as a mechanism necessary for the commercial recovery of the province. He even suggested the usefulness of the repartimiento as a means of reviving Yucatan's exports of wax.[86]

Meanwhile, the highest echelons of the imperial bureaucracy were also debating the repartimiento, which had been brought to an end all over Mexico with the establishment of intendancies. The Viceroy of New

Spain, the Second Count of Revillagigedo, took a position contrary to that of his father 40 years earlier and supported the outright prohibition of the repartimiento, as did five of the ten Intendants who expressed an opinion on the subject.[87] But the Audiencia of Mexico, in its report of 1797, was divided over the issue, and Revillagigedo's replacement, Viceroy Branciforte, argued strongly for restoring the system. The proponents of restoring the repartimiento dredged up the same argument that had been used to defend the system in Yucatan since the seventeenth century: it was the only way to bring the Indians into the economy as producers and consumers.[88] The essence of the repartimiento was stated to be simply the extension of credit, which was absolutely necessary to make the Indians work.[89] Abolition had destroyed commerce and resulted in lower tax revenues. To support these arguments, Branciforte, in a report submitted after he had left office, even cited Yucatan as an example of the ill effects of suppression and the necessity of restoring the system.[90]

But in the end the crown did not rescind its order suppressing the repartimiento in Yucatan. In any case, the evidence suggests that by this time the business was being conducted on a much smaller scale than in the past, and that it had disappeared altogether in many parts of the province. In 1791, during the residencia of Governor Merino, it was reported that he and the cabildo officials of Valladolid had refrained from carrying out repartimientos after the abolition. Only a year or two later, a new textile factory was established in Mérida; this would have been inconceivable had the Governors still maintained their control over labor, marketing, and the supply of raw cotton. In 1795 the cabildo of Mérida informed the King that Governor-Intendant Arturo O'Neil was not engaged in any business with the Indians, a contention that was backed up by former Intendant Savido, who reported that no repartimientos were then being carried out in the partido of the Camino Real.[91]

On the other hand, in the same year the cabildos of Campeche and Valladolid, engaged in a power struggle with Governor-Intendant O'Neil, denounced the chief executive for tolerating repartimientos by the subdelegados, the officials who had replaced the war captains in the villages. But the only specific cases cited were of officials contracting for henequen sacks near Valladolid and Tizimín, and for firewood and pottery in Lerma, near Campeche.[92] In the following year, however, the *juez español* of Chunhuhub (a village right on the frontier with the Petén) apparently was found to be carrying out old-style repartimientos, and was fired.[93] Meanwhile, several priests reported that after the assassination of Intendant Lucas de Gálvez in 1792, the subdelegados had in fact restored the repartimiento. The claim is suspect, however, for they could only cite a single case, involving some contracts for wax near a small village in Campeche, and Bishop Luis de Piña y Mazo is known to have pressured the priests into reporting unfavorably on Governor-Intendant O'Neil. The Bishop, who during his many years in Yucatan ended up fighting bitterly with every Governor, was taking revenge on O'Neil for arresting his nephew as the prime suspect in Gálvez's assassination.[94]

All of these informants did agree on one point: the subdelegados were exacting forced labor from the Indians under their jurisdiction. This was cited as an abuse. But in fact it was a countenanced solution to a problem created by the ending of the repartimiento, namely, providing alternate sources of income for government officials. The crown had anticipated and solved the problem in the case of the Governor-Intendants, who now drew a salary of 7,000 pesos. But finding revenues for the new subdelegados was not so easy. A proposal put forth by Viceroy Revillagigedo to provide them with a decent income was ultimately rejected as too costly. These lowly officials were finally allowed to keep 5 percent of the tribute revenues collected in their jurisdictions, but usually this amounted to a very small salary indeed. As a result, in many parts of the Spanish Empire the lowest-level government officials continued to carry out repartimientos. The subdelegados, in the words of one scholar, were the Achilles' heel of the intendancy system in America.[95]

In Yucatan, however, the repartimiento was not strictly speaking revived. This was not because the subdelegados were paid any better there. In fact, the 5 percent of tribute collected yielded an annual income of only 170 pesos for the subdelegado of Bolonchencauich, and a paltry 70 for the man in Sahcabchén.[96] Rather, the new officials soon discovered that they were in a position to organize and allocate labor drafts (*mandamientos*), and quickly found ways of working this to their own advantage. A 1796 inquest into the subdelegados' economic activities revealed that by then practically all of them had land under cultivation within their jurisdictions and were assigning draft labor to themselves as well as to other landowners. The use of forced labor was especially evident in the sugar regions. The officials profited by charging landowners a fee in return for laborers, as well as from the sale of the produce of their own lands, which were worked, of course, by the very Indians the officials were supposed to protect. At first, the legality of this practice was unclear, but the province's Attorney General, Lieutenant Governor Fernando Gutiérrez de Pineres, ruled that it was indeed legal, and this opinion was supported by both Governor-Intendant O'Neil and the chief official of the Tribunal de Indios, Agustín Crespo.[97]

The new officials were thus allowed to replace the labor of the repartimiento with a forced labor draft. Ironically, this meant that what had been called the repartimiento in the early colonial era—a labor draft—was resurrected in the late eighteenth century under a new name—mandamiento. It could not go by its old name because repartimientos were now illegal. So far as the Indians were concerned, this was a mere sleight of hand: involuntary labor in weaving and wax-gathering was now replaced by involuntary labor in agriculture, especially in the hard work of cane-cutting.

The truly significant development, then, was not the formal end of the repartimiento as such, but the replacement of one labor system by another. For it should be remembered that the repartimiento was not merely corruption in government; it was a system designed to get the Indians into debt and then make them work to pay their debts, and it resulted in their incorporation into the world economy against their will. This is proved by the Maya's reaction on the two occasions when the repartimiento was suppressed: they refused to accept contracts for wax and cloth, resisted efforts to get them to work voluntarily, and tried to withdraw from the market economy by returning to pure subsistence production. Had this state of affairs been tolerated by the colonial authorities, there would have been little or no surplus to extract to support the Spanish colonists. Coercion, in short, was the sine qua non of colonialism.

The Spanish state did not fail to provide that coercion. It authorized government officials to use Indian labor for their own benefit. But this meant a different kind of labor system. In the past, colonialism had lived off the natives by siphoning off a large part of their surplus production. Then, in the last two decades of the eighteenth century, the transition was made to a system in which native labor was directly exploited by Spanish producers carrying out production on their own landed estates. The rise of the hacienda, in other words, made possible the elimination of the repartimiento as well as the encomienda because it created a new way to use Indian labor. It also permitted government officials to bolster their incomes in new ways, and thus laid the basis for the political changes of the late eighteenth century. The Bourbon Reforms in Yucatan, in short, were possible only because of social and economic changes that were fundamentally internal in origin.

By the end of the eighteenth century, the major mechanism of capital accumulation in Yucatan was ownership of productive, private property. This meant that the social and economic structure of Yucatan was no longer based on the colonial regime. Upper-class wealth ceased to be the result of prebends, that is, favors granted by the state. Instead, the late colonial elite was, in Weberian terms, a class of owners. All that was now required to accumulate capital was private property, markets, and a state to help provide labor and to make land available even if that meant taking it away from the Indians. All these could be had without colonialism.

In fact, land and labor could be had better without colonialism. The Mexican and Yucatecan governments of the post-Independence era would no longer adhere to the paternalistic ideology maintained by a distant monarchy; rather, they would represent the interests of the local upper class. Yucatan, therefore, was passing from colonialism to neocolonialism. It would produce raw materials and primary products for export, and would import manufactured goods from the industrialized core areas of the world economy. The colonial regime, already crumbling, would soon collapse altogether.

CHAPTER SEVEN

The Structure of Production

By THE LATE COLONIAL period, the Indians' near-monopoly of agricultural production had been broken. The basis had been laid for a new agrarian structure that would endure, with only minor modifications, until the middle of the twentieth century. There was much more involved here than the rise of the hacienda. In many rural areas a whole new class of producers who were neither hacendados nor Indian peasants emerged. In some places, indeed, the new group, largely mestizo and mulatto, would outnumber the indigenous people. Conspicuous as the hacienda was in the structure of production, then, the rural economy was in reality variegated and marked by a growing social complexity.

Geography and Economy

One of the measures of the socioeconomic change taking place in eighteenth-century Yucatan is the increasing value of tithe revenues. Since Indians contributed very little to this fund, tithes can serve as rough guides to the agricultural, apicultural, and livestock production of haciendas and farms, and can also be used as indicators of regional specialization, the geographic distribution of the units of production, and the division of labor.

Table 7.1 lists the gross revenues derived from tithes in the eighteenth century and in two earlier years, 1564 and 1635. The jump in revenues after 1775 is striking. By 1787 the Church was receiving twice as much income from this source as it received in 1713; and by 1809 tithe revenues were 84 percent higher than in 1777. These figures, however, can be used only in a most general way, for it is obvious that the secular trend was not without reversals. Especially noteworthy are the effects of the famines of 1727–28 and 1769–72. An added complication is that the diocese included Tabasco, whose share greatly inflates the total. In 1795, for example, Tabasco accounted for over 31 percent of the total tithe income.[1]

Finally, some variations in the data are almost certainly due to collec-

TABLE 7.1
Tithe Revenues of the Diocese of Yucatan, 1564–1815
(Pesos)

Year[a]	Revenue	Year[a]	Revenue
1564	700	1775	12,546
1635	11,223	1777	25,857
1713	17,892	1784	33,507
1738	15,864	1787	35,550
1757	17,406	1794	35,032
1764	16,992	1809	47,673
1766	28,000[b]	1815	44,608
1774	11,475		

SOURCES: Scholes and Adams, Don Diego Quijada, 2: 71; Farriss, Maya Society, p. 368; DHY, 3: 74.
[a]The year of production, which was one year before the revenue was collected.
[b]Estimate of royal officials looking into the province's affairs.

tion and accounting procedures. For the first three-quarters of the century, a general tithe collector was in charge of administering the entire diocese, and apparently the people holding this post carried out their functions with varying degrees of dedication or indolence. In fact, collection was quite lax at times, and according to Fray Luis de Piña y Mazo, who became Bishop of Yucatan in 1780, people generally shirked their responsibility because they believed that tithing was voluntary.[2] They were soon disabused of that idea by the zealous Piña y Mazo, who vigorously supported tithe-farming, the new method of collection introduced the year before he became Bishop. Under the new system, entrepreneurs paid the Church for the right to collect the tithes in specific parishes and then carried out the collection; whatever was received beyond what had been paid to the Church was pure profit for the tithe-farmer. This system quickly improved diocesan finances, as well as the fortunes of Piña y Mazo, who received a percentage of tithe revenue as his personal income.

Tithe-farming also resulted in better recordkeeping, and the data, submitted at times in a parish-by-parish format, can be used to study the historical geography of production by the non-Indian population. The records of the purchase prices of tithe-farms shed considerable light on the value of production, for the amounts paid were based on the collectors' perceptions of the profits to be made from their curacies. Table 7.2 lists the parishes in rank order of the prices paid in 1795; Map 7 locates these curacies and categorizes them by perceived value.

One of the most striking features of these data is the lack of correlation between a parish's perceived value and its population. The most expensive

TABLE 7.2

Purchase Prices of Tithe-Farming Rights for the Years 1795–98

(In round pesos)

Parish and partido	Price	Parish and partido	Price
Seyba Playa, Sahcabchén	5,582	Telchac, Costa	1,105
Pocyaxum and		Abalá, Sierra B.	1,105; 1,260
Campeche city,[a]		Bolonchencauich	
Campeche	5,493; 5,489	(Pich), Campeche	1,055
Izamal, Costa	4,510	Temax, Costa	1,055
San Cristóbal, Mérida	4,000	Bolonchenticul, Camino	
Tekax, Sierra A.	3,795	Real A.	1,050
Maxcanú, Camino Real B.	3,575	Sacalum, Sierra B.	1,045
Umán, Camino Real B.	3,150	Tekantó, Costa	1,025
Muna, Sierra B.	3,060	Cacalchén, Costa	1,010
Sahcabchén, Sahcabchén	2,956	Mocochá, Costa	970
Hecelchakán, Camino		Hopelchén, Camino	
Real A.	2,910	Real A.	900; 1,125
Calkiní, Camino Real A.	2,725	Homún, Beneficios B.	900
Oxkutzcab, Sierra A.	2,700	Cansahcab, Costa	885
Kopomá, Camino Real B.	2,315	Sotuta, Beneficios B.	865
Campeche Extramuros,		Presidio del Carmen	
Campeche	2,310	and Sabancuy,[a] Carmen	800
Hunucmá, Camino		Hocabá, Beneficios B.	680
Real B.	2,266	Teya, Costa	615
Tecoh, Sierra B.	2,200	Palizada, Carmen	500
Ticul, Sierra A.	2,150	Ichmul, Beneficios A.	400; 455
Dzidzantún, Costa	2,030	Sacalaca, Beneficios A.	275; 265
Motul, Costa	2,000	Presidio de Bacalar	
Conkal, Costa	1,925	and Chichanhá,[a] Bacalar	200
Tixkokob, Costa	1,860	Tihosuco, Beneficios A.	200
Mama, Sierra B.	1,700	Chunhuhub, Beneficios A.	200
Santiago, Mérida	1,600	Tixcacaltuyú,	
Hoctún, Beneficios B.	1,600	Beneficios B.	130
Petén, Bacalar	1,600	Yaxcabá, Beneficios B.	105
Acanceh, Sierra B.	1,530	Tahdziu, Beneficios A.	100
Peto, Beneficios A.	1,402	Cathedral and Jesús,[a]	
Bécal, Camino Real A.	1,375	Mérida	70
Maní, Sierra A.	1,265	Chicbul, Sahcabchén	65
Teabo, Sierra B.	1,245	Chikindzonot,	
Nolo, Costa	1,150	Beneficios A.	60

SOURCES: ANEY, M. Palomeque, 3 Jan.–17 Apr. 1795, fols. 1–60, 67–78, 88–89, except when a second figure is given, from AGEY, Iglesia, vol. 1, exp. 3, Diezmos, Cuadrantes de los diezmos del Obispado de Yucatán, 1795–97.

NOTE: "Baja" and "Alta" and all their variants are abbreviated "B." and "A."

[a]Two separate parishes.

Map 7

Value of Tithe Farms of 72 Parishes, 1795-98

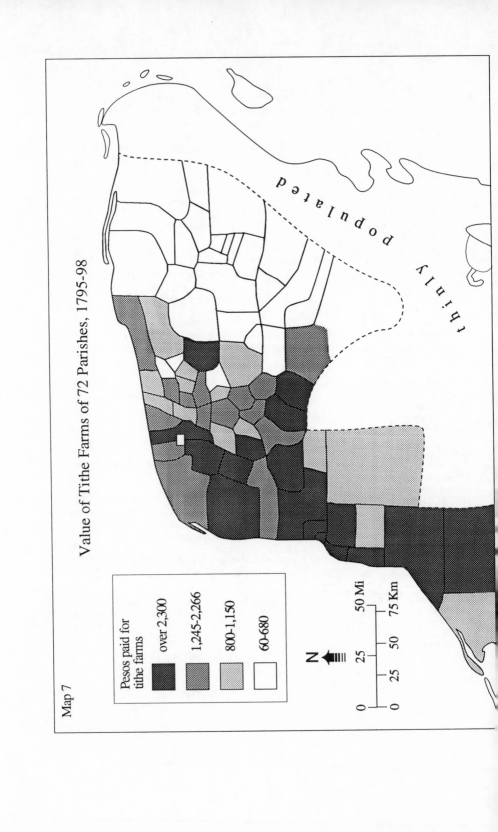

Pesos paid for
tithe farms

over 2,300

1,245-2,266

800-1,150

60-680

thinly populated

N

| 0 | 25 | 50 Mi |
| 0 | 25 | 50 | 75 Km |

curacy—Seyba Playa (near the Bay of Campeche), which was farmed out for 5,582 pesos, 4 reales—had only some 3,995 residents in 1794.[3] Yet Tihosuco, one of the largest parishes in the area south of Valladolid, with a population of 4,723, was purchased for a mere 200 pesos.[4] This phenomenon is easily explained: outside of the cities, large concentrations of population were usually composed of Indians, who paid very little in the way of tithes; from the tithe-farmer's point of view, what was important was the wealth of the non-Indians.

The sources of that wealth can be pieced out in a rough way from Table 7.3, which shows the relative value of the various crops. Clearly, despite the high value of sugarcane and indigo, the most important product among the non-Indians, as among the Maya, was maize. The only exceptions were the cotton parishes of Tizimín and Espita, and the cane-growing parish of Tekax. Indigo was produced in only three parishes, but in two of them, Hoctún and Maxcanú, the quantities reported were minuscule. Even in the third, Izamal, it accounted for only slightly more than 6 percent of the total value of agricultural production.

After maize, cane and cotton were plainly the most important crops. Though sugar was the more valuable of the two, it was not nearly as widespread as cotton, for it required more rainfall and deeper soil. Therefore it tended to be cultivated throughout the Campeche jurisdictions, the Sierra Alta, and Beneficios Altos, but not around Mérida or Tizimín, that is, the northern districts of the province. In the next 20 years, cane production would spread into Beneficios Bajos. It also expanded in Beneficios Altos, though as the ratios of cane to maize land demonstrate, maize was still the preferred crop in 1796. The ratio was 1:9.8 in Peto, 1:22.1 in Sacalaca, 1:25.2 in Chunhuhub, 1:239.2 in Ichmul, 1:332.6 in Tahdziu, and a minuscule 1:1,696.6 in Tiholop. No cane production at all was reported for the parishes of Tihosuco and Chikindzonot.[5] The northernmost limit of cane seems to have been Maxcanú, in the west, and the outskirts of the villa of Valladolid (the parish of Sisal) in the east. People tithed for cane production as far south as the Petén.

Cotton was grown all over Yucatan. It was the major cash crop of the non-Indians in the region north and northwest of Valladolid, especially in Tizimín and Espita. Cotton was able to adapt to a more varied environment than cane, but it was also of declining value in the period under study. The abolition of the repartimiento in 1782, as we shall see, caused the price of cotton to drop precipitously and probably led to the decline of the small farmers who had dominated production in the cotton-growing region.

Though rice was still a minor crop at this juncture, production was expanding. By the 1790's rice had boomed to such a point in the area south and southeast of Campeche that the ratio of rice to maize land reached

TABLE 7.3
Agricultural Production of Non-Indians by Crop, 1777–95
(Percent of total value)

Partido and parish	Maize	Cane	Cotton	Rice	Indigo	Other[a]
Sahcabchén						
Sahcabchén, 1777–78	80.2%	10.5%	1.4%	2.2%	0.0%	5.7%
Chicbul, 1777–78	92.3	0.0	0.6	0.0	0.0	7.3
Seyba Playa,						
1778–79	68.4	28.3	0.6	0.0	0.0	2.7
Campeche, 1778–79						
Campeche city	78.2	4.6	0.06	10.0	0.0	7.2
Campeche Extramuros	70.0	18.2	3.2	0.7	0.0	7.3
Camino Real Alto, 1778–79						
Hecelchakán	72.0	6.3	0.9	0.0	0.0	20.8
Calkiní	91.5	0.0	1.7	2.8	0.0	4.0
Camino Real Bajo, 1778–79						
Maxcanú	89.3	0.7	0.5	2.3	0.2	7.0
Sierra Baja, 1778–79						
Mama	91.1	0.0	0.3	0.0	0.0	8.5
Sierra Alta						
Maní, 1778–79[b]	92.6	0.0	0.3	0.0	0.0	7.1
Tekax:						
1790–91	21.0	77.5	0.7	0.0	0.0	0.9
1791–92	24.0	67.5	0.5	7.1	0.0	1.0
1792–93	37.4	50.0	1.0	2.5	0.0	9.0
La Costa, 1790–91						
Mocochá	88.9	0.0	0.0	0.0	0.0	11.1
Izamal	80.6	0.0	0.6	0.0	6.2	12.6
Beneficios Bajos						
Hoctún, Hocabá, and						
Homún, 1777–78	86.9	0.0	0.0	0.0	0.0	13.1
Hoctún, 1795–96	94.4	0.0	0.0	0.0	1.3	4.3
Sotuta, 1777–78	85.2	0.0	0.8	0.0	0.0	14.0
Beneficios Altos, 1777–78						
Peto	61.3	18.1	14.9	0.0	0.0	5.6
Tahdziu[c]	81.4	0.0	10.5	0.0	0.0	8.0
Tihosuco	92.7	0.0	3.3	0.0	0.0	4.0
Chunhuhub	87.3	0.0	2.9	0.0	0.0	9.7
Valladolid, 1787–88						
Valladolid	59.0	0.0	33.4	0.0	0.0	7.6
Sisal	56.1	40.9	0.0	0.0	0.0	3.0
Chemax[c]	96.2	0.0	0.0	0.0	0.0	3.8
Tizimín, 1787–88						
Tizimín	40.6	0.0	54.3	0.0	0.0	5.1
Espita	30.2	0.0	68.8	0.0	0.0	1.0
Bacalar, 1778–79						
Petén Itzá	87.3	7.0	7.0[d]	0.0	0.0	1.3

SOURCES: See Table 6.2. Tables 7.4–7.9 are based on the same sources.
[a]Beans, squash, chili peppers, and fruit and vegetables in general.
[b]Excludes the village of Chapab.
[c]No private estates in the parish.
[d]Includes minor quantities of squash and vegetables.

1 : 2.2 in the partido of Bolonchencauich (1797), and an even higher 1 : 1.7 in Sahcabchén (1795).[6] Rice had also come to be of great importance in Tekax (Sierra Alta) by then and was even being cultivated to some extent in the Camino Real parishes of Hecelchakán, Bécal, Calkiní, and Maxcanú. It was also to be found in Peto in Beneficios Altos, though the ratio of rice to maize land was only 1 : 42.[7]

In many parishes minor crops—beans, squash, chili peppers, and fruit—were more important than cane, rice, or cotton. Most bean growers concentrated on two varieties: lima beans (called by their Maya name, *ibes*) and especially the large black beans, or *frijoles*. A third type, small black beans, or *xpelones* (another Maya word), were occasionally mentioned. Squash, which was reported as seeds (*pepitas*; perhaps because the seeds were used to make cooking oil), came in two varieties, thick (*gruesa*) and small (*menuda*). Chili peppers of two types were grown, *escurre* and *bobo*, though the sources rarely make a distinction, simply referring to *chiles*. Fruit was usually mentioned generically as well; the only fruits specifically reported were watermelons, bananas, oranges, mangoes, and mameyes.

In Hecelchakán (Camino Real Alto), Hoctún-Hocabá-Homún and Sotuta (Beneficios Bajos), and Mocochá and Izamal (La Costa), such products accounted for over 10 percent of the value of agricultural production. With the exception of Hecelchakán, these parishes produced little or no cane, and the people apparently chose to cultivate little or no cotton. This suggests that the production of beans and squash—by far the most important of the minor crops—was resorted to where conditions were not conducive to more valuable crops. What proportion of land was diverted from maize to these two crops is not known.

Still, when agricultural production is broken down by sector, it is quite clear that the choice of crops was not wholly determined by geographic factors. Tables 7.4 and 7.5 show that hacendados were much more likely to be engaged in cane and rice cultivation than the village vecinos.[8] Indeed, only in Peto (Beneficios Altos) and in Campeche Extramuros did any rural vecinos at all engage in cane production; and none, apparently, cultivated rice. Cotton, on the other hand, was very much a product of the small producers, who in fact accounted for the total output in many of the parishes.

The contrast between sugarcane and cotton is easily explained. Both crops were extremely labor-intensive, but only in the case of high-value goods like sugar, molasses, and cane alcohol was it profitable to employ slave labor. In fact, with the boom in the industry, as we have seen, the slave trade picked up, especially in the Campeche region. To be sure, the number of Africans used as plantation slaves in Yucatan was never very large; and the owners of sugar plantations usually had to resort to another

TABLE 7.4
Agricultural Production of Hacendados by Crop, 1777–96
(Percent of total value)

Parish[a]	Maize	Cane	Cotton	Rice	Indigo	Other[b]	No. of estates
Sahcabchén[c]	60.7%	30.1%	0.0%	2.0%	0.0%	7.1%	4
Chicbul[d]	91.7	0.0	0.7	0.0	0.0	7.7	1
Seyba Playa	40.7	56.2	0.0	0.0	0.0	3.2	5
Pich	73.5	0.0	0.0	21.6	0.0	4.9	4
Campeche city	70.8	6.4	0.0	13.9	0.0	8.9	21
Campeche Extramuros	59.9	27.2	5.2	1.3	0.0	10.6	7
Hopelchén[d]	90.0	0.0	0.0	0.0	0.0	10.0	1
Bolonchenticul[d]	39.8	33.0	25.7	0.0	0.0	1.5	2
Bécal	94.2	0.0	0.0	0.0	0.0	5.8	1
Hecelchakán	57.7	16.0	0.3	0.0	0.0	25.9	10
Calkiní	84.1	0.0	1.8	8.7	0.0	5.4	4
Maxcanú	82.3	2.5	0.0	8.5	0.0	6.8	9
Kopomá	97.0	0.0	0.0	0.0	0.0	3.0	2
Umán	89.5	0.0	0.6	0.0	0.0	9.9	11
Hunucmá	93.1	0.0	0.0	0.0	0.0	6.9	7
San Cristóbal	78.7	0.0	0.0	0.0	0.0	21.3	8
Mama	69.8	0.0	0.0	0.0	0.0	30.2	5
Teabo	96.0	0.0	0.0	0.0	0.0	4.0	1
Tekax:							
1790–91[e]	7.0	92.1	0.6	0.01	0.0	0.3	52
1791–92[e]	15.3	75.8	0.5	7.9	0.0	0.4	52
1792–93[e]	26.1	60.6	1.2	3.1	0.0	9.1	49
Mocochá	86.4	0.0	0.0	0.0	0.0	13.6	11
Izamal:							
1790–91	74.1	0.0	0.7	0.0	11.7	13.5	49
1791–92	69.2	0.0	0.04	0.0	22.4	8.3	37
1792–93	62.2	0.0	1.9	0.0	14.4	21.5	37
Hoctún, Hocabá, and Homún	88.2	0.0	0.0	0.0	0.0	11.8	18
Hoctún	92.3	0.0	0.0	0.0	2.2	5.4	25
Sotuta	95.6	0.0	0.0	0.0	0.0	4.4	1
Yaxcabá[e]	87.9	0.0	2.4	0.0	0.0	9.7	3
Peto	62.2	27.3	1.8	0.0	0.0	8.7	4
Tihosuco[d]	95.9	0.0	0.0	0.0	0.0	4.1	1
Chunhuhub[d]	83.3	0.0	3.7	0.0	0.0	13.8	1
Valladolid villa[d]	53.7	0.0	38.0	0.0	0.0	8.3	18
Tizimín[d]	33.2	0.0	57.1	0.0	0.0	9.6	3
Espita	18.6	0.0	80.4	0.0	0.0	1.0	4
Petén Itzá	87.3	7.0	7.0	0.0	0.0	1.3	?

[a]For the partidos of these parishes and the pertinent dates, see Table 7.3.
[b]Beans, squash, chili peppers, and fruit and vegetables in general.
[c]Based in part on payments made by individuals, not on payments made for estates.
[d]Based wholly on payments made by individuals.
[e]Based wholly on payments made by individuals. Omits those made in cash, which are assumed to be for livestock.

TABLE 7.5
Agricultural Production of Hacendados and Village Vecinos by Crop, 1777–96
(Percent of total value)

Parish[a]	Maize		Cane		Rice		Cotton		Total value	
	Hacendados	Village vecinos	Hacendados	Village vecinos	Hacendados	Village vecinos	Hacendados	Village vecinos	Hacendados	Village vecinos
Seyba Playa	29.9%	70.1%	100.0%	0.0%	–	–	0.0%	100.0%	50.4%	49.6%
Campeche city	65.3	34.7	100.0	0.0	100.0%	0.0%	100.0	0.0	72.0	28.0
Campeche Extramuros	48.2	51.8	84.7	15.3	100.0	0.0	93.6	6.4	56.8	43.2
Hecelchakán	31.8	68.2	100.0	0.0	–	–	15.4	84.6	39.5	60.5
Calkiní	29.8	70.2	–	–	100.0	0.0	33.3	66.7	32.9	67.6
Mama	27.2	72.8	–	–	–	–	0.0	100.0	32.8	67.2
Tekax:										
1790–91	28.0	72.0	100.0	0.0	100.0	0.0	76.5	23.5	84.1	15.9
1791–92	56.9	43.1	100.0	0.0	100.0	0.0	100.0	0.0	89.0	11.0
1792–93	57.5	42.5	100.0	0.0	100.0	0.0	98.4	1.6	82.6	17.4
Mocochá	79.0	21.0	–	–	–	–	–	–	81.3	18.7
Izamal	40.5	59.5	–	–	–	–	47.3	52.7	44.1	55.9
Hoctún, Hocabá, and Homún	43.7	56.3	–	–	–	–	–	–	43.0	57.0
Hoctún	58.4	41.6	–	–	–	–	–	–	59.7	40.3
Peto	26.9	73.1	39.9	60.1	–	–	3.1	96.9	26.5	73.5
Tihosuco	26.2	73.8	–	–	–	–	0.0	100.0	25.3	74.7
Chunhuhub	66.9	33.1	–	–	–	–	88.9	11.1	70.8	29.2

[a]For the partidos of these parishes and the pertinent dates, see Table 7.3.

form of forced labor, namely, the mandamiento. But only large land-owners commanded the power and influence to be allocated mandamientos. Even then, given the small Indian population of Campeche, there was an insufficient supply of forced labor to meet the demands of the cane producers, and consequently a third labor system—peonage—was also employed. But in all cases—slavery, draft labor, and peonage—the large landowner had clear advantages over the small producer, who lacked the capital to buy slaves, the influence to get mandamientos, and the cash to get peons into debt. In any event, the small producer did not have the wherewithal to buy the expensive milling and distilling equipment that allowed large landowners to achieve economies of scale. In short, sug-arcane production in Yucatan, as elsewhere, was dominated by large-scale producers with capital, power, and influence.

In cotton cultivation, small producers had some advantages over larger competitors. Since the gin had yet to be invented, they could compete on an even footing with large landowners in terms of the costs of equipment. And since they managed and usually worked their properties themselves, their costs of production were lower. They could also apply as much of their own labor to production as they wanted to, and consequently sur-plus labor could be more effectively mobilized by the farmers than by the hacendados.

The farmers also were successful as producers of maize. In fact, even when this grain was the major crop of the haciendas, the village vecinos as a group frequently outproduced the large estates. In Izamal (one of the most valuable parishes from the point of view of tithe-farmers), the 49 haciendas produced significant quantities of maize and even some indigo, yet the small farmers still accounted for almost 60 percent of the total value of agricultural production. On the other hand, the farmers were relatively insignificant as stock-raisers. Their production was mostly lim-ited to pigs and chickens, and although these animals were important in the diet of all classes in Yucatan, they were not nearly as profitable as cat-tle. Cattle-raising was still largely confined to the Spanish-owned landed estate, and as was demonstrated in Table 6.2, it was in many places the most important branch of the hacienda economy.

Valuable as the tithe data are for demonstrating the considerable im-portance that the small producers had in agricultural production in late colonial Yucatan, they are somewhat misleading, for they are based on the value of goods produced. Though the price of sugar, cane alcohol, and molasses did not change much from year to year, the price of maize fluctuated wildly. The farmers in effect specialized in the production of a good of radically varying value. But even the haciendas, despite their typ-ically more diversified production, were greatly affected by the volatility of maize prices. Table 7.6, which shows the tithe payments of 145 ha-

TABLE 7.6
Fluctuations in the Value of Tithe Payments
of 145 Haciendas in Five Parishes, 1790–92

Parish	No. of estates	Percent change		Total change, 1790–92
		1790–91	1791–92	
Conkal	19	−10.6%	−2.5%	−12.7%
Acanceh	20	−22.8	+11.0	−13.6
Izamal	23	−13.8	−17.3	−28.7
Mérida (2 parishes)[a]	83	−8.3	−13.4	−20.6

[a]Santiago and San Cristóbal.

ciendas over a three-year period, demonstrates their economic vulnerability. If the hacienda economy was so drastically affected by falling maize prices, then the impact on the farmers who specialized in this most volatile of products must have been devastating indeed. In short, the importance of the rural vecinos, as well as of the hacendados, in the regional economy changed substantially from year to year depending on market conditions, which is to say, depending on the harvest of "the grain of first necessity."

One of the most remarkable economic changes in the whole colonial period took place in the Valladolid and Tizimín area, and took place not in maize but in cotton. With the government's suppression of the repartimiento in 1782, cotton prices promptly fell by half, from two pesos a carga (32 lbs.) to one peso. Production plummeted. As Tables 7.7 and 7.8 show, tithe payments in cotton fell from 34,289 pounds in 1782 to only some 2,922 a year later, and the monetary value of all tithes paid in Tizimín, the most important cotton-producing parish in Yucatan, fell from 877 pesos to only 88 pesos—a decline of 89.9 percent. Every parish was dragged down in the course of a year that saw the total value of tithe payments from all seven of the major cotton-producing curacies drop 67 percent. Cotton production and prices never recovered from this disaster, and by 1787, the last year for which tithe data are available, payments in cotton were down to 26.8 percent of the 1782 level. The monetary value of tithes collected in the seven principal cotton-producing parishes declined by 69 percent over the five years.

Meanwhile, the Maya of the villages south of the cotton-producing region suffered an even greater disaster. A bad harvest in 1786 caused near-economic collapse, and made it impossible for the villagers to pay their religious taxes. Tithes collected from the Indians (who were required to pay small sums for all their domesticated animals except turkeys) declined by 83.7 percent between 1783 and 1786, and the former year was by no

TABLE 7.7
Tithe Payments in Cotton from the Valladolid-Tizimín Jurisdictions, 1782–87

(In pounds)

Parish	1782	1783	1786	1787	Pct. change, 1782–87
Tizimín	12,900	872	1,527	1,595	−87.6%
Chancenote	5,182	855	312	313	−94.0
Kikil	5,012	252	754	1,253	−75.0
Espita	3,110	224	411	2,186	−29.7
Valladolid	2,447	412	894	1,376	−43.8
Cenotillo	2,322	160	250	894	−61.5
Calotmul	2,307	42	456	1,279	−44.6
Chemax	469	0	3	0	−100.0
Nabalam	244	102	43	273	+11.9
Xcan	144	3	1	22	−84.7
Sisal	128	0	0	0	−100.0
Tikuch	24	0	0	0	−100.0
Tixcacalcupul	0	0	5	2	−
Uayma	0	0	0	1	−
TOTAL	34,289	2,922	4,655	9,193	−73.2%

NOTE: Payments are rounded to the nearest decimal.

TABLE 7.8

Peso Value of Tithe Payments from the Valladolid-Tizimín Jurisdictions, 1782–87

Parish	1782	1783	1786	1787	1782–87
Tizimín	877.71	88.56	127.72	96.72	−89.0%
Chancenote	363.06	91.84	45.63	35.09	−90.3
Kikil	452.69	129.92	182.19	181.33	−59.9
Espita	266.94	102.75	95.70	119.13	−55.4
Valladolid and Tikuch	404.50	301.44	199.07	240.13	−40.6
Cenotillo	247.38	176.19	83.69	100.56	−59.3
Calotmul	227.45	55.06	43.42	100.95	−55.6
Chemax	79.00	45.88	6.64	9.81	−66.4
Nabalam	50.94	34.19	14.59	27.66	−45.7
Xcan	29.00	21.28	6.72	15.31	−47.2
Sisal	58.75	72.06	6.44	14.75	−74.9
Tixcacal-cupul	46.94	38.25	14.66	26.56	−43.4
Uayma	79.50	84.88	11.75	16.85	−78.8
Chichimilá	83.44	85.88	1.38	5.88	−93.0
TOTAL	3,267.39	1,328.18	839.58	990.73	−69.7%

means a good one, for the tithes of 1783 were down 10.6 percent from the year before. The 1786 level, then, was only 14.5 percent of the level of 1782. Fortunately, the 1787 harvest was better, but even so that year's tithe payments were still 72.7 percent below the 1782 level.

There was to be no quick economic recovery from this decline. In 1795 the tithes of the whole Valladolid-Tizimín area, composed of 15 parishes, were farmed out for a four-year period for 4,120 pesos, that is, an average of only a little over 1,000 pesos a year.[9] Since this area had contributed 3,267 pesos to the Church in the year preceding the collapse, 1782, the tithe-farmer was estimating that at this point taxable production had fallen off by about two-thirds. The collapse of economic activity in this region lasted well into the nineteenth century. The first and only sign of life came in the 1840's, when an entrepreneur attempted to establish a steam-powered cotton textile factory.[10] But by then the supply of raw cotton was uncertain, and in any case the Caste War ended the project. Only in the twentieth century would this region, especially Tizimín, recover from the effects of the collapse of the 1780's.

Sectors and Units of Production

Thus far we have analyzed the producing sectors in terms of the three neat categories of landed estates, farms owned by rural vecinos, and the Maya peasant economy. In practice, however, the distinctions between hacendados, rural vecinos, and Indian agriculturalists were not always clear-cut; they were often based wholly on legal definitions, not on economic activities. Indians were the people who were ruled by native authorities and were under the jurisdiction of the special laws for the Indian Commonwealth. They owned land as Indians, were subject to forced labor drafts, and paid tribute, other civil taxes, and religious *obvenciones*. Though subject to the tithe, they did not have to pay on their maize or any other goods native to Yucatan; they paid, in other words, almost exclusively for cattle, pigs, and chickens.

Rural vecinos were legally distinct from the Indians. They almost always were people of mixed race and were under the jurisdiction of the special laws for the Spanish Commonwealth. Their civil tax burden was lighter than the Indians', but they were subject to heavier tithes, for in theory they were supposed to pay one-tenth of all their production to the Church. Changing from one legal category to another (which in fact happened quite frequently) meant trading one class of legal obligations for another. But in terms of economic production, Indians and vecinos apparently did about the same thing. The difference between the two was probably marked only at the higher levels, for in practice the better-off farmers were more like hacendados than Indians. Beyond that, the vecinos' standard of living was probably higher on the whole than the Indians' because most of them operated in areas of sparse population and abundant resources.

At the very top of the rural vecino class the economic distinction between vecinos and lesser hacendados was also blurred, for many owners of small haciendas did not raise livestock but instead, like vecinos, were engaged in agriculture and apiculture. Once again, the distinction between the two groups was at times more legal than economic. In this case, the crucial factor was land tenure: hacendados owned land legally, that is, they had land titles and usually had licenses to raise cattle; vecinos sometimes were renters or sharecroppers, and often were probably nothing more than squatters, that is, people with no legal rights to the land. Nevertheless, as often happens, custom tended to override law, and vecinos were usually allowed to keep and even sell their lands as their de facto long-term owners. There is no evidence that large numbers of squatters were dispossessed during the colonial period. Though many were probably pushed off their land with the expansion of the henequen hacienda after 1870, I suspect that further research will demonstrate that a class of small and medium-sized Yucatecan farmers survived into the twentieth century.

The Maya Peasantry

Unfortunately, there is little information available for the study of the central element of the Maya economy—the milpa. But we may suppose that the Maya of colonial times worked their land much as their descendants do today. In current practice the basic unit of production is the extended family unit, for the labor of clearing and then weeding the land is best done by a group, but work in the milpa is considered to be the exclusive preserve of the male members of the family; female activities are carried out close to the place of residence.[11]

There is some indication that this sexual division of labor was rigorously maintained in the eighteenth century. As already noted, spinning and weaving were always associated with Maya women, and repartimiento textile quotas were routinely based on the number of females— girls as well as women—in a village. On the other hand, from the names of the people who sold maize to the agents of the pósito of Mérida in 1773 and 1774, it is pretty clear that the milpa was the exclusive preserve of males; of the more than 500 Indians listed, not one was female.[12]

Another important branch of the Maya economy was stock-raising. Animal husbandry is almost always practiced by peasants, and in Yucatan this activity had added importance because the ownership of pack animals enabled the Maya to participate in the market economy as intermediaries carrying goods to market. In fact, transportation was practically monopolized by the Indian *arrieros* (muleteers) and must have contributed significantly to total peasant income.

Tithe records are not very illuminating in this regard. Although the collectors reported receiving money from the natives, they usually simply stated that they had collected a lump sum from the village government as payment "for the animals of the Indians." However, in 1790 one tithe-farmer, in order to make sure that he received his full due, carried out a detailed investigation into Indian livestock holdings in the village of Mocochá (15 km northeast of Mérida, in the partido of La Costa). His records reveal that of the 104 Indians who tithed for their livestock—and in theory Indians were required to tithe for all animals except turkeys, which were native to Yucatan—five paid for mules and 37 for horses. Some 40 percent of the tithers, then, paid for either a horse or a mule. Even more commonly owned were cattle, for 85 people paid for calves. Only 19 villagers tithed for nothing more than hens or pigs. The documents record 18 sitios—each with its own name—owned by Indians, and several others owned by people who could have been Indians. All told, the villagers of Mocochá tithed for seven mules, 41 horses, and 113 calves, as well as for an unspecified number of the lesser animals.[13] Even if this village was somehow atypical of either its region or the province as a whole, small-scale stock-raising, even of cattle, horses, and mules, was probably not uncommon among the Maya. Nor was it uncommon among other Indian societies in America.[14]

In any case, Indians participated in the ranching economy in an important way through the cofradía estates. There were reportedly 158 such estancias in Yucatan in 1780, and although they were apparently administered like private haciendas, the profits belonged to the Indians, who used the money for their own religious ends. That is not to say all of these estates were devoted solely or even mainly to stock-raising. As can be seen in Table 7.9, showing tithe data for 77 of them, agriculture was often the main pursuit. Agriculture was the predominant activity in nine of the parishes or groups of parishes in the table, as against stock-raising in eight and apiculture in two. The products of this enterprise, however, were exclusively maize and beans, that is, the same crops the Indians themselves cultivated. None of the cofradía estates ever undertook to grow cane, rice, or cotton. Sugarcane, of course, usually involved either African slaves or drafts of Indian laborers, and the Indian-owned estates never employed those labor systems.

The cofradía estates are of particular interest to the historian because they provide the only detailed records of stock-raising on estancias over a long period of time. In the eighteenth century the Church began to require the sodalities to keep better records of their activities, and as a result it is possible to get considerable insight into the actual functioning of the

TABLE 7.9
The Structure of Production on 77 Cofradía Estates, 1777–96

Parish	No. of estates	Total production (in pesos)	Share of total Stock-raising	Share of total Apiculture	Share of total Agriculture
Sahcabchén	2	4.38	22.9%	0.0%	77.1%
Seyba Playa	3	7.44	57.1	2.5	40.3
Chicbul[a]	3	5.88	21.3	0.0	78.7
Bolonchen- cauich (Pich)[a]	3	13.81	65.2	13.1	21.7
Hopelchén	7	31.55	78.5	0.8	20.8
Bolonchen- ticul[a]	2	11.00	59.1	0.0	40.9
Bécal	2	10.49	19.1	15.5	65.5
Calkiní[b]	2	30.63	63.7	2.9	33.5
Maxcanú	6	132.29	6.8	3.5	89.7
Kopomá[a]	3	56.35	0.0	1.3	98.7
Hunucmá[a]	9	35.66	56.8	8.2	35.0
Mama	2	6.25	64.0	26.0	10.0
Hoctún, Hocabá, and Homún	20	47.08	30.3	40.6	29.1
Hoctún	5	14.04	35.6	14.2	50.1
Sotuta	1	3.44	36.4	29.1	34.5
Yaxcabá[a]	2	3.46	14.5	0.0	85.5
Tixcacaltuyú[c]	3	2.50	0.0	100.0	0.0
Tahdziu	1	1.77	0.0	28.2	71.8
Chikindzonot[a]	1	5.88	17.0	2.1	80.9

NOTE: For years not otherwise indicated, see Table 7.3.
[a]1777–78.   [b]1778–79.   [c]1795–96.

cattle economy. To be sure, there were some important differences between cofradía and private estates, including, as we have just seen, areas of agricultural specialization. But stock-raising was carried out in almost exactly the same fashion on the two kinds of properties, for both used the same labor system, both were oriented overwhelmingly to cattle, and both produced for the same markets. Even in terms of the quantity of production, the two were alike, for the cofradía estates, like most of the Spanish-owned estancias, were modest operations.

One of the most detailed cases of an Indian-owned stock-raising estate is Estancia Locá, belonging to the Cofradía of the Immaculate Conception of Euan, a village 30 kilometers east of Mérida in the parish of Tixkokob, partido of La Costa.[15] The first accounts of Locá date from 1745 and are fairly complete until the 1770's, when the great famine early in that decade caused the virtual collapse of stock-raising and administration on this and many other estancias in Yucatan.

Both agriculture and apiculture were practiced on Estancia Locá, but stock-raising was by far its most important activity. Table 7.10 shows the

TABLE 7.10
Sales of Livestock by a Cofradía Estate, Estancia Locá, 1746–75

| Year(s) | Number sold | | Income from sales (in pesos) | | |
	Cattle	Horses	Cattle	Horses	Total
1746	15	–	90	–	90
1747	23	1	123	12	135
1748	34	4	186	36	222
1749–51	47	3	208	15	248[a]
1752–53	36	3	188	32	220
1754	24	1	120	10	130
1755	10	–	54	–	54
1756	12	–	57	–	57
1757	26	–	118	–	118
1758	25	–	109	–	109
1759	8	–	35	–	35
1760	17	–	74	–	74
1761	11	–	47	–	47
1762	26	–	122	–	122
1763	18	–	81	–	81
1764	32	–	168	–	168
1765	32	–	163	–	163
1766	31	–	151	–	151
1767	30	–	144	–	144
1768	14	–	60	–	60
1769	16	–	71	–	71
1770	18	–	86	–	86
1771	37	–	180	–	180
1772	1	–	8	–	8
1773	1	–	7	–	7
1774	1	–	8	–	8
1775	2	–	12	–	12

SOURCE: AME, Libros de Cofradías, no. 16 (1727–75).
[a]Includes 25 pesos from the sale of one mule.

quantity of animals sold over the period 1746–75, as well as the income derived from the sales; and Table 7.11 provides basic data on the estancia's stock-raising activity from its founding in 1727 until its collapse in the mid-1770's. By 1755, cattle had become the estancia's only money-making product. Apiculture, though carried out throughout the entire period, shows up as only a minor activity.

Agricultural production is worth mentioning even though sales on the market were insignificant. There was reference to agriculture from the very beginning of recordkeeping, in 1745, when 161 cargas of maize had been harvested "from the *milpa* of the *estancia*." Just who did the harvesting is not specified, but all the maize was given to the estancia's *mayoral* (foreman) and two *vaqueros* (cowboys) as part of their "ración de maíz." The workers were thus paid partially in kind. In fact, in that same year the administrator had to purchase an additional 20 cargas to pay the

TABLE 7.11
Livestock of Estancia Locá, 1727–75
(Cattle [C], horses [H], and mules [M])

	Inventory			Livestock branded[a]			Inventory			Livestock branded[a]	
Year	C	H	M	C	H	Year	C	H	M	C	H
1727	35	22	–	–	–	1761	228	33	3	44	2
1737	135	48	–	–	–	1762	213	26	3	29	2
1746	96	78	2	–	–	1763	222	27	3	35	1
1747	–	–	–	25	5	1764	232	32	3	55	6
1748	–	–	–	24	4	1765	196	28	3	32	1
1749	143	26	2	26	1	1766	190	37	3	39	10
1752	153	37	2	50	5	1767	192	36	3	39	3
1753	166	42	2	29	1[b]	1768	191	33	3	26	3
1754	195	49	2	68[c]	–	1769	172	20	3	17	2
1755	–	–	–	–	–	1770	148	16	3	8	0
1756	210	31	2	42	4	1771	26	14	3	0	0
1757	207	29	3	41	1	1772	24	11	0	3	3
1758	163	20	3	28	1	1773	25	13	0	6	2
1759	190	21	3	30	3	1774	31	14	3	9	4
1760	205	31	3	45	3	1775	27	14	2	8	1

[a]The estate kept few mules and branded only 4 altogether, one each in the years 1747, 1748, 1749, and 1760.
[b]During the years 1753–55.
[c]During the years 1754–55.

full amount owed the labor force. There are several other instances of the estate purchasing maize to pay its workers. This estancia was clearly a net consumer, not a producer, of grain.

If the estate had any agricultural workers as such, the records do not name them. Careful account was kept of those who worked in stock-raising, however. In the 1740's the mayoral was one Melchor Canul, and the two vaqueros were Francisco Canul and Juan Cituk (or Quituk). Melchor got a cash salary of 15 pesos a year, and the cowboys got 10 pesos apiece. The total "ración de maíz" was 181 cargas (i.e. about 7,430 kg), which would have been worth 45 pesos, 2 reales (at the standard two reales per carga) at a minimum and even more during years of poor harvest in the province. Payment in kind, then, was more significant than the money wages. In any case, this was much too much grain for the annual consumption of three active males; they presumably sold part of it, or gave it to family members, or probably both. All three of the workers were nevertheless in debt to the estancia. They were, that is, debt peons, and as their surnames testify, they were Indians.

By the 1750's Locá had a new mayoral, Lorenzo Baeza, and the vaqueros were Melchor Canul (probably the former mayoral) and a man identified only by the surname Cituk (probably the Juan of the previous decade). Both of the Indians were still indebted to the estate; the foreman, whose racial or cultural origin is uncertain, was not. By the 1760's the work force had changed again. The mayoral was Juan Cituk (presumably the same mentioned above), whose annual salary was 18 pesos, 3 reales. The vaqueros were Juan Baptista Canul (perhaps a relative of Melchor Canul) and Vicente Cituk (perhaps a relative of Juan). The cowboys' wages were still 12 pesos. Juan Cituk remained in his position as foreman until 1770 or 1771, when he ran away ("se huyó") during the crisis of those years. The vaquero Vicente Cituk stayed on at least until the 1770's and took over as mayoral on the flight of Juan Cituk. Nothing is known of the fate of Melchor Canul, the other cowboy of the 1760's, but at the end of the decade a certain Felis Canul, perhaps a relative, was employed at the estancia as a cowboy. He stayed during the crisis of 1770–71. The final employees mentioned in the estancia's records were the vaqueros Juan Huh (or Kuh) and Gregorio Cituk, both of whom were first referred to in 1770. Gregorio stayed during the crisis, but Juan, who had been advanced eight pesos by the estate, ran away at the same time as the mayoral Juan Cituk.

After the crisis of 1770–71, which saw the estancia's livestock almost entirely liquidated by sale and theft, there is no further mention of any vaqueros. At the time recordkeeping ceased, however, the estate did still have a mayoral (unnamed but clearly an Indian, since he was obliged to pay the holpatán, a tax to support the Tribunal de Indios). Apparently, the estancia administration tried hard to keep the last foreman in its service, for in addition to paying him wages, it also paid his tribute and holpatán for him.

Estancia Locá is one of the few estates whose labor force can be charted by name for an extended period of time. What is of particular interest here is the employment of people of the same surname over several decades. We cannot be sure, of course, that these workers were related, but supposing they were, which is certainly a good possibility, then it could well be that the cowboys, like the unidentified agricultural workers, were neither social outcasts nor perennial rootless migrants but rather people who maintained family ties and/or raised families of their own. On the other hand, cofradía estancias may have been exceptional in this regard; intimately linked as they were to the local Indian sodalities, it was undoubtedly easier for the residents to maintain ties to the local village community.

Unfortunately for the Maya, the social and economic disaster of 1770–71 dealt a fatal blow to this important sector of their economy. Bishop Fray Luis de Piña y Mazo, who arrived on the scene soon after, quickly directed his attentions to the Maya sodalities. In a report submitted to the crown in 1782,[16] the Bishop pointed out that because of the great antiquity of these institutions, notable abuses had been creeping in. Most important was the confusion between cofradías and estancias or haciendas, for whereas in theory the one organized and owned the other, in practice the estates had appropriated the name of cofradía and thus everyone referred to the estancias as if they, and not the brotherhoods, were the real sodalities. On examining the matter in detail, he had found that only 42 of the 158 so-called cofradías were really sodalities; the others were merely estates. Moreover, many of the properties did not really belong to the Indian sodalities, because most of them had only usufruct rights to the land. Also, the actual functioning of the estancias occasionally proved injurious to the Indians, for the cattle sometimes destroyed milpas; but since the animals did not belong to individuals, the peasants could not sue anyone for damages. Finally, since the Indians did not actually manage the estates, which were run by administrators, supervised by "ecclesiastical judges," and interfered with by local priests, the Maya did not profit from their properties; the fruits of the estates were taken by others.

For these reasons, Piña y Mazo tried to impose order on a chaotic situation by eliminating as many of the cofradía estates as possible. His motives seem to have been pure enough. He hoped that once the estates passed to private hands, the Laws of the Indies, which provided for a minimum distance of two leagues between estates and villages, could be enforced, thus better protecting the Indians' milpas from intrusions by cattle. And he wanted to use the funds derived from the sale of the estates to establish educational facilities for the Indians and to create a scholarship fund to pay for them to study at the seminary.

In any event, between 1780 and 1782, 59 of the 158 cofradía estates were sold, on credit, to private individuals. Needless to say, the Indians, who had not been consulted by the Bishop, resisted the transfer of their collective property to private hands. They were supported by the Governor, Roberto Rivas Betancourt, who was already locked in a bitter dispute with Piña y Mazo and used the defense of the Indians as an issue in that political battle. Though the crown responded by suspending further sales of cofradía property, it eventually approved those already made. The result, in the end, was the sudden transfer to Spaniards of a large part of the Indians' stock-raising properties. For the Maya economy, this was a severe blow, the first of several stemming from new policies being pursued by Church and state in the late colonial period.

The Farmers

As we saw earlier, non–Indian rural people, that is, the vecinos, were not much involved in stock-raising. This shows up clearly in Table 7.12, which divides their production into the three fundamental sectors of agriculture, apiculture, and stock-raising. Their nonparticipation in ranch-

TABLE 7.12
The Structure of Production on Vecino Farms, 1777–93

Parish	No. of tithers	Total value of tithes (pesos)	Share of total production		
			Stock-raising	Apiculture	Agriculture
Sahcabchén	101	186.44	1.9%	0.4%	98.0%
Seyba Playa	147	224.79	10.9[a]	0.0	89.1
Chicbul	8	12.15	8.2	0.0	91.8
Pich[b]	33	137.81	3.5	0.9	95.6
Campeche city	69	95.73	4.2	0.0	95.8
Campeche Extramuros	84	224.79	12.4[a]	0.0	87.6
Hecelchakán	80	224.35	10.0	1.8	88.2
Calkiní	28	87.63	13.7	3.9	82.5
Maxcanú	110	338.04	3.1	2.5	94.5
Mama	80	73.68	0.8	1.4	97.8
Tekax:					
1790–91	?	175.00	32.2	11.9	55.9
1791–92	?	94.69	37.2	2.8	60.0
1792–93	?	186.44	19.5	8.2	72.3
Mochochá	27	23.06	47.7	7.0	45.3
Izamal	225	597.64	7.2	10.3	82.4
Hoctún[c]	50	72.92	17.6	10.9	71.5
Hocabá[c]	59	49.58	6.9	4.9	88.2
Homún[c]	28	21.40	2.6	2.0	95.3
Sotuta	101	191.30	2.7	4.2	93.1
Peto	74	167.85	4.7	1.0	94.3
Tahdziu	18	21.77	8.1	7.5	84.4
Tihosuco	18	34.79	4.1	5.0	90.8
Chunhuhub	9	7.06	12.4	8.0	79.6
Valladolid city	36	21.94	11.1	17.7	71.2
Sisal	11	11.88	29.5	1.1	69.5
Chemax	15	7.69	5.7	30.1	64.2
Tizimín	57	97.72	3.8	2.2	93.9
Espita	46	114.63	11.9	3.9	84.1

NOTE: For years not otherwise indicated, see Table 7.3.
[a]Includes minor quantities of apicultural production.
[b]Includes villages of Pich and Timucuy, but not Bolonchencauich. The data are for 1777–78.
[c]1777–78.

ing was undoubtedly due to the problem of procuring a license. Although the licensing law had been loosely enforced in the early colonial period, from the late seventeenth century on, as we have seen, the legally sanctioned ranchers were using their power and influence to prevent others from competing with them. They were not wholly successful, to be sure, since the law did not apply to the Indians. But Piña y Mazo effectively removed much of this competition when he sold off more than a third of the cofradía estates.

In the main, then, the village vecinos raised pigs and chickens, which were much less valuable than *ganado mayor* and therefore accounted for only a small proportion of the total value of their production. On the whole the farmers also seem to have been little involved in beekeeping, certainly less so than the haciendas, for in only nine parishes did apiculture account for 5 percent or more of the total. Nevertheless, it was of considerable importance in Tekax, Izamal, Hoctún (where the haciendas were also quite involved in honey and wax production), Valladolid, and Chemax. On the other hand, as was also true of the haciendas, apiculture was practically nonexistent among the vecinos in the Campeche jurisdictions. Finally, as noted above, the farmers tended to raise maize, cotton, beans, and squash but rarely produced cane, which except for the parish of Peto was everywhere virtually the monopoly of the large estates.

Some vecinos acquired property by purchase, but certainly many of them got their land through squatter's rights. Still others must have been renters or sharecroppers, for many haciendas had vecino as well as Indian residents.[17] (Hacendados almost always lived in the cities.) Some of these non-Indians were undoubtedly employees of the estates, but it is also possible that some received land in return for a fixed rent or proportion of the harvest. Whatever the case, among the rural vecinos, whether of villages or haciendas, agriculture was not the exclusive preserve of males, as it was among the Maya. True, most of the small farming units were run by males, but several vecinas appear in the tithe records paying religious taxes for agricultural as well as stock production. Though the number of cases is not large, for female tithe-payers appeared in only 19 of the villages in the sample, the very existence of the phenomenon is proof of an important cultural difference between the Maya and the non-Indians.

The Hacendados

Despite the great importance of the hacienda in late colonial Yucatan, we know far too little about its organization and operation. The example of Estancia Locá is of some help, but until such time as comparably full records for a privately owned estate are found, we must make do with tithe and notarial records, supplemented by census material and the occasional judicial document.

From these sources we know, first of all, that landed estates were extraordinarily numerous in Yucatan. Though the census of 1794 does not list any haciendas as such, this was apparently merely because the officials chose to use the term estancia instead. At that time, there were 862 estancias in the province, as well as 324 "ranchos dependientes," by which was meant private estates devoted mostly to agricultural activities—or a total of 1,186 landed estates, a truly enormous number given the surface area of the settled part of the peninsula.[18] We also know that, for all this, landownership was highly concentrated. Most of the estates were of very modest proportions, and many of the largest belonged to people who owned more than one hacienda. Complete information on this subject is available only for a few parishes: Mérida, Conkal, Acanceh, Tekax, Mocochá, and Izamal. But the existing records leave no doubt about the concentration of property. In fact, it is remarkable how many cases of individuals owning several estates can be found.[19]

Take Mérida's city councilmen and their relatives, for example. Regidor Manuel Bolio de la Helguera was the proprietor of one hacienda in the jurisdiction of Mérida, one in Acanceh, and three in Umán, while his cousins Luis, Miguel, and Martín owned estates in Mérida, Acanceh, Umán, and Izamal. Regidor Ignacio Rendón owned three haciendas in Umán, one in Kopomá, and one in Maxcanú, while his brother Juan José owned one in Mérida and one in Maxcanú, his brother José Augustín had two in Mérida, his sister Josefa had one in Acanceh, and his nephew José Joaquín owned one in Tunkás. Regidor Juan José Domínguez was the proprietor of one hacienda in Mérida and four in Umán. Regidor Gregorio de la Cámara owned one or possibly two estates in Mérida, one in Conkal, two in Mocochá, and at least one more somewhere in the Sierra, while his aunt Juana de la Cámara Domínguez owned one in Mérida, one in Conkal, one in Acanceh, and one in Kopomá, his cousin Cristóbal de la Cámara owned the large Estancia Hobonil in Peto, his cousins José Ignacio (a priest), Juan, and María de Lara y Cámara owned two estates in Mérida, one in Umán, and one in Tekit, and his aunt's nephew, Anastasio de Lara, owned an hacienda in Conkal. Regidor José Cano had four estates in Mérida, one in Umán, one in Hunucmá, and one in Izamal. Regidor Juan Antonio de Elizalde owned one hacienda in Mérida, one in Acanceh, and one in Izamal. And finally, all but one of the other city councilmen, as well as the elected officials, possessed at least one estate in either Mérida, Conkal, Acanceh, Mocochá, or Izamal, and since the information available is incomplete, it is very possible that they all owned more than one hacienda.

Priests were another group who frequently owned several estates. Dr. Luis Joaquín Aguilar owned no fewer than five in Mérida, as well as one in each of the parishes of Conkal, Homún, and Tekit. Two priests named Miguel and Pedro Antonio de la Paz (apparently brothers) between them owned 10 haciendas: Miguel had two in Mérida, one in Umán, one in Motul, and one in Mocochá, while Pedro Antonio's five estates were in Mérida, Conkal, Acanceh, Mocochá, and Motul. The curate of Umán, Luis de Echazarreta—who was eventually removed from his position for exacting the *ius primae noctis*—owned five haciendas, all within his own parish. And finally Pedro Faustino Brunet, a priest of the cathedral, was the proprietor of three estates, all in Mérida.

Among the largest landowners were the Peón and Quijano families, the Count and Countess of Miraflores, and the former repartimiento agent Enrique de los Reyes. In fact, in 1780 the body of estancia owners of Yucatan, called the *gremio de estancieros*, was represented before the cabildo of Mérida by the leaders of the Peón and Quijano clans and by the Count of Miraflores. The founder of the first of these families was Alonso Manuel Peón, a Peninsular Spaniard who apparently came to Yucatan to join his brother, Bernardo, a Franciscan. Peón married well and eventually came to own three haciendas near Mérida, as well as Estancia Uayalceh (one of the largest landed estates in colonial and modern Yucatan), located between Tecoh and Abalá; a sugar hacienda named Xcatmís in the Sierra; and the famous Hacienda Uxmal, near Muna. By the 1790's his son Ignacio had come to own two important haciendas near Mérida, and his son Josef owned one near Ticul. Both Alonso Manuel and Ignacio Peón served many times as elected officials of the cabildo of Mérida.

The Quijano family was founded in Yucatan by a Peninsular Spanish merchant named Juan Quijano, who set up business in Mérida in the early eighteenth century. His son, Juan Francisco, continued in commercial activities but more importantly became a landowner. At one time or other in his long life, he owned at least nine, and probably more, haciendas in Mérida, Hoctún, Hocabá, Hecelchakán, and Maní. Juan Quijano also had an adopted son named Juan Esteban Quijano, the illegitimate child of former Governor Antonio de Figueroa and Isabel Avila Ancona, a cousin of Juan Quijano's wife. Juan Esteban, who grew up to be a man of considerable importance, owned four or five haciendas in Mérida, one in Umán, and one in Hocabá, and his sons Ignacio and Juan Tomás owned four others in Mérida. Since practically all these estates were in the family's possession at the same time, the Quijanos were clearly at the top of the ranching elite. In addition, Juan Francisco and Juan Esteban held elected positions on the city council on numerous occasions, and the latter eventually became regidor. Juan Esteban Quijano also continued in the family's traditional business by maintaining a store in Mérida.

The Counts of Miraflores, as will be remembered, had originally based their fortune on the repartimiento of indulgences. In the eighteenth century, however, they balanced their religious business with ranching, and by the late eighteenth century Santiago Calderón de la Helguera, the Fifth Count, owned at least three large estancias in the Camino Real area. His wife, Ildefonsa Bermejo Solís, was the daughter of José de Bermejo Magaña, a former regidor of Mérida, and the granddaughter of Magdalena Magaña, one of the most prominent landowners in Yucatan in the early eighteenth century. Indeed, by the numbers at least, the Countess was even more important than the Count as a landowner. She had five haciendas in Mérida, two in Acanceh, one in Tekax, and one in Izamal, for a total of no fewer than nine estates. On his death—she was a widow by 1790—she was probably the most important landowner in all Yucatan.

As for the notorious Enrique de los Reyes, who was almost certainly a

Peninsular Spaniard, he had the great good luck, on coming to Yucatan to join his brother, Manuel Josef, a Franciscan, of hooking up with Governor Roberto Rivas Betancourt. Bishop Piña y Mazo claimed, in his denunciation of Rivas Betancourt, that Reyes had amassed a fortune of over 50,000 pesos as repartimiento agent and as war captain of the Sierra (where his brother served as prior of the important convent at Maní). The Bishop proved to be an inveterate liar whenever he was involved in political disputes, but in this case he may have been halfway to the truth. Reyes's eight haciendas—in which he had apparently invested most of his profits—were worth some 23,500 pesos.[20] Even this was a considerable fortune in late colonial Yucatan.

The large number of landed estates therefore should not mislead us into concluding that wealth was somehow more evenly distributed in Yucatan than in the regions of huge latifundia. But it would also be a mistake to assume that the landed elite possessed all the wealth to be had. In reality, there was room in this socioeconomic structure for the small and medium-size producer. In fact, there was even room, and limited economic opportunity, for individual Indians. Apparently some of the Maya took advantage of their right to raise cattle and did so independent of their village cofradía estancias. As we have seen, 18 Indians owned sitios in the parish of Mocochá in 1790, and although none at all were reported in many other parishes, this is likely because the tithe collectors there were less painstaking than the man who looked at his own situation in Mocochá in detail. In fact, there are a few other Indian estate owners in the records. Estancia Sacnicté, in the parish of Hocabá, was owned by Francisco Tun, an Indio Hidalgo, who in 1778 tithed 42 cargas of maize; 3 cargas, 2 *almudes*, of beans; and 5 pesos, 4 reales (for wax and honey production). His total payment, worth 18 pesos, 3 reales, was the third-largest in the Hoctún-Hocabá-Homún curacies. Several other smaller properties in this area were also owned by Indians. Even Mérida's jurisdiction included an Indian estate: Sitio Yaxchalbec, owned by Francisco Ku.[21]

The presence of Maya landowners, albeit on a modest scale, draws attention once again to the reality of the agrarian structure. There were no clear-cut categories of hacendados (large landowners), rural vecinos (small producers), and Indians (poor peasants). Divisions did exist, of course, but they were not absolute: the classes tended to blend into each other. The majority of haciendas in fact were so small that they sometimes cannot be distinguished from the properties of the vecinos, or even of the Indians.

Spanish property ownership nevertheless differed considerably from that of the Maya. This applies in the cultural as well as the economic sense. The Indians, as we have seen, maintained rigid rules about the economic roles of men and women. The rural vecinos, on the other hand, did not insist on a strict division of labor. Least rigid of all were the Spaniards. It was in fact quite common for haciendas to be owned by women. In the jurisdiction of Mérida, for example, 28 women owned no fewer than 37 of the 146 estates in the years 1790–93, which means that one out of four estates was in female hands. This was probably inevitable if, as impressionistic evidence suggests, the Spaniards in Mérida followed the pattern of the well-studied Spanish community in Buenos Aires:[22] men tended to marry at an older age than women, and to die younger. A large number of women thus became property owners through inheritance. But many seem to have been landowners in their own right, buying and selling haciendas even while their husbands were alive. All of this is in sharp contrast to what we have seen among the Maya. The Spanish and Indian Commonwealths, therefore, not only had different ideas regarding property, but operated according to different cultural principles with regard to sex roles and the organization of production.

Since the source of Spanish landed wealth was spread out all over the landscape in the form of noncontiguous haciendas, the management of property must have presented something of a problem. In fact, we know that effective administration was difficult. When Diego García Rejón, an encomendero as well as landowner, made his will in 1784, he lamented that his Hacienda Temozón, in the curacy of Hocabá, had been ruined because as a vecino of Campeche and resident of Muna he had been unable to manage his property directly. He had entrusted that task to a friend, Francisco Jorge López, a vecino of Izamal, but his friend had looted Temozón and left it with little of value except the land and license to raise cattle.[23]

Where, as here, personal oversight by the owner was not possible, many hacendados relied, as Enrique de los Reyes did, on professional managers, or mayordomos. The administrative structure he set up is revealed in the documentation on his impounded properties.[24] The records, kept by Regidor Gregorio de la Cámara, the Treasurer (*Depositario General*) of the cabildo of Mérida, cover seven of Reyes's haciendas. All of these estates (plus Estancia Pelé, which he had to sell to meet his legal expenses)—Tixcacal (near Mérida), Cibceh (in the parish of Acanceh), Pixyah (Tecoh), Aynal (apparently adjacent to Hacienda Pixyah), Bolontunil (Mama), Techoh (adjacent to Bolontunil), and Chenchac (Sacalum)—although scattered, were located either very close to Mérida or in the partido of the Sierra Baja, that is, the area between the capital and the Puuc region. This meant that Reyes had relatively easy access to the market in Mérida. But this concentration in a relatively homogeneous geographic area also meant that the estates lacked diversity in their agricultural production. They produced maize and beans, but no cane, rice, or cotton. Consequently, the conclusions to be drawn from these haciendas are valid only for estates specializing in traditional agricultural production and stock-raising.

At the top of Reyes's administrative structure were two mayordomos, named Marcelino Moguel and Lázaro Barroso. Since neither man was referred to as *don* by Cámara, who as regidor was well acquainted with matters relating to status, it is virtually certain that the two managers were mestizos or mulattoes. Their salaries do not seem to have been set formally in advance, for Moguel was paid five pesos in cash and in addition was given, in a somewhat ad hoc manner, a breeding bull worth 10 pesos. No record at all was kept of what was paid to Barroso. Since the mayordomo certainly did not work without compensation, it is likely that both managers simply negotiated their salaries over time.

Most of the other members of the labor force were Indians, as is proved by their obligation to pay the holpatán tax. The five foremen (mayorales) were paid a cash wage, but the amount varied considerably, from two to eight pesos. Those who received less apparently were given other benefits in lieu of cash, such as having their holpatán paid for them. It is also likely that all the mayorales received a maize allotment, so that their total pay was higher than the money wages alone would suggest.

The number of vaqueros on these estates varied considerably. Cibceh, with 11 in addition to a mayoral, had the largest labor force of the seven. Pixyah had five vaqueros but neither a mayordomo nor a mayoral. Bolontunil and Tixcacal each had four vaqueros as well as a mayoral, but only Bolontunil had a mayordomo. Chemchac had three vaqueros in addition to a mayoral. Finally, Techoh and Aynal each had two vaqueros; Aynal had a mayoral but no mayordomo, Techoh the reverse. Or so the records say. In reality the two mayordomos probably oversaw all the estancias, and in fact the documents specifically state that Lázaro Barroso was mayordomo of both Bolontunil and Techoh. The lack of mention of a similar arrangement for the other estates is probably due to administrator Cámara's inattention to details. It is also likely that the two estates seemingly without a mayoral were in the charge of one from an estate in close proximity. Techoh was near to the larger Bolontunil, and in any case the two estates had the same manager. And the mayoral of Aynal was almost certainly responsible for Pixyah, which was always run as a unit with Aynal: their maize rations and workers' taxes were always combined in the records.

There is enough evidence to conclude from all this that hacendados who owned several estates did attempt to centralize the administration of their properties to some degree. Many haciendas undoubtedly were run independently of each other. In fact, many had no mayordomos, for the owners, especially if they possessed no more than one estate, could have carried out the manager's functions by themselves. Mayorales, on the other hand, were always to be found when the estate was not combined administratively with another one.

The vaqueros' wages, like the mayorales', varied considerably. The highest-paid cowboy on the Chemchac estate received a wage of seven pesos, four reales, paid in part in goods (a large piece of leather). One of the other two vaqueros on the estate got five pesos in cash and a piece of leather worth one peso, four reales, for a total wage of six pesos, four reales. The third received five pesos, four reales (counting leather worth one peso, four reales). Estancia Chemchac apparently specialized in tanning, for not only was it the only estate that paid its workers in leather; it also was the only one that produced tanned leather for the market.

In addition to the cash wages, administrator Cámara paid the tribute and holpatán tax owed by the estates' Indian laborers. Moreover, most or all of the mayorales and vaqueros probably received a maize ration. In 1786 Cámara spent 10 pesos to buy 40 cargas of maize identified as the "ración de maíz" owed the workers of Estancias Pixyah and Aynal, and in 1788 the manager of Bolontunil and Techoh spent 50 pesos to buy 200 cargas for the laborers of those estates.[25] No mention is made of maize being purchased for or paid to the workers of the other haciendas, but since the estates together produced a total of only 257 cargas of maize in 1788, as against slightly more than 539 in 1787,[26] all the workers were almost certainly paid out of total agricultural production; in the event of a mediocre harvest, as in 1788 (and 1786), the estates had to make up the shortfall. These haciendas, therefore, although permanently engaged in agriculture activities, clearly did not always produce enough of a surplus for sale on the market.

As on the cofradía estancia discussed previously, debt peonage was an integral part of the labor system on de los Reyes's haciendas. Wages were paid in advance to ensure—insofar as it was possible to ensure—the service of the workers, who were called collectively sirvientes, that is, servants. Even the two mayordomos were in debt to the estate owner. Moreover, an important technique, of enormous significance for the future, had already been introduced on haciendas in Yucatan in the eighteenth century. This was the principle of the transferable debt, which enabled landowners in need of labor to buy workers from other hacendados. For example, in December 1786 administrator Cámara paid 21 pesos, 6 reales, to Bernardo Canto, owner of Estancia Xnacchén, for the debts of a vaquero named Manuel Zumbado, who then owed that amount to Enrique de los Reyes and was immediately put to work on Estancia Tixcacal.[27] The following February, Regidor José Rendón, the owner of many haciendas, drew up a statement in which he declared that his vaquero Lázaro Cob owed him 19 pesos, 3 reales, and then added, "I will give a receipt to that effect to whoever wishes to pay for him." Cámara did just that, and in addition advanced the cowboy five pesos. Cob then went to work on Estancia Cibceh owing a new total of over 24 pesos.[28]

It is important to emphasize that peonage is a somewhat general term with different meanings in the various labor systems in force in Latin America since the sixteenth century.[29] In particular, it is important not to confuse the peonage of eighteenth-century Yucatan with that existing at other times and in other places. Though there is little evidence regarding labor conditions on Yucatecan haciendas in the late colonial period, many of the practices described in the 1830's and 1840's can be presumed to have grown up earlier.[30] Hacienda peons at that time were whipped as punishment, had to address the hacendado with considerable respect and fear, and were even required to kiss the owner's hand as a sign of their inferiority. Nevertheless, the system in no way approximated the plantation slavery of Brazil, Cuba, and the Old U.S. South. Estate owners in Yucatan did not need to maximize production, and thus workers, although whipped for disobedience, were not beaten to make them work harder. Hacendados even loaned their peons money to go to the fair, and what with the throngs of people in attendance, they could have fairly easily run away and taken refuge on the southern frontier beyond the reach of governments and masters. Yet the problem of flight apparently did not exist, or at least it did not exist in the areas under the jurisdiction of Mérida and Valladolid.[31]

Perhaps the story was different in Campeche. There the smaller population and the greater availability of land meant that few Indians were being pushed out of their villages and into the hands of the estate owners. The level of indebtedness of peons seems to have been higher in Campeche, especially in the southern part of the region, than elsewhere in the peninsula.[32] This demonstrates a greater need to attract or perhaps even bind workers to the estates.

In the eighteenth century peonage was often voluntary. As early as 1723 Bishop Gómez de Parada complained that the Indians were running away not from but to the estancias because residents of the estates paid lower taxes than the Indians of the villages.[33] This complaint was repeated in 1782 by the Franciscan prior of Maní, Manuel José de los Reyes, who pointed out that the hacienda residents were also free from such burdensome civil obligations as forced work on roads, street cleaning, and mandamientos. Consequently, he wrote, "if I ask, which group of Indians are reputed by the children of our parish to be the best-off, they will answer, . . . those of the Spanish estates. And if I ask, what gives this group its great happiness, they will answer, being free from the obligations of their villages."[34]

As the crisis of production became increasingly apparent, especially in the last quarter of the century, Indians found still another advantage in taking up residence on haciendas: the owners guaranteed the workers food for survival. That is the significance of the above-mentioned "ración de maíz," and even if a complete crop failure prevented payment in grain, there was always meat to feed the workers. Indeed, the cabildo of Mérida reported that hacienda livestock as well as grain were seriously depleted during and after the famine of 1770–71 because the hacendados had to feed the residents of their estates.[35] And as we will see in the next chapter, there is evidence of a considerable reduction in the size of herds because cattle were being slaughtered faster than they could reproduce during the years of the crisis.

So security was another reason for the attractiveness of the estates. Still another was money. Villagers normally had very few opportunities to acquire cash, for their market activities were seasonal, and since the repartimiento advances were usually made precisely when taxes were due, the money almost immediately fell into the hands of the government, encomendero, or priest. On estancias, however, payments were regularly made in cash three or more times a year. With subsistence assured, estate workers could do what villagers could not. Friar Reyes at Maní tells us what money could buy: "The *vaqueros* ordinarily invest it in drunken orgies when they come to town . . . for between those Indians of the village and those of the haciendas there is this difference: the former are accustomed to having their weak moments, but ordinarily they only choose fiestas as the time to have their Bacchanalia, while those of the haciendas have no special time for their orgies, because their attitude is 'there's no time like the present.' "[36]

It is important to note, in this connection, that most of the evidence on peonage concerns the workers engaged in stock-raising in the partidos of the district of Mérida. What about agricultural labor? The documents from the cofradía estate and from Enrique de los Reyes's haciendas are completely silent on the subject. Yet there must have been agricultural laborers because those estates produced maize and beans, some of which, as we have seen, went toward the vaqueros' pay. The answer to this riddle must be that agricultural production was in the hands of luneros, that is, the Indians who colonized hacienda land in return for modest labor services performed for the owner. Theoretically, this labor was applied to land worked on the owner's behalf. Judging by the accounts of the Reyes haciendas, however, it seems likely that at times the hacendados and managers found it advantageous to collect fixed quantities or proportions of production from the luneros, thereby passing on all the problems and risks to the colonists, who became in effect renters or sharecroppers.

There is evidence for the presence of luneros on these estates despite their absence from the hacienda accounts. Estancia Pixyah, in the parish of Tecoh, employed only five vaqueros in 1788, and even when the labor force of nearby Aynal is included, the total was only seven vaqueros and one mayoral. Yet in 1803, only some 15 years later, the local curate reported that Pixyah had a resident population of 257, almost all of whom were Indians. Chemchac, in Sacalum, had only three vaqueros and one mayoral in the accounts of 1788, yet a priest's report from 1782 put the total Indian population at 94. And Bolontunil, in Mama, employing four vaqueros, a mayoral, and a mayordomo in 1788, had 183 residents in 1803. Only in the case of Estancia Cibceh, in Acanceh, do we find any rough coincidence between the total population and the workers engaged in stock-raising. In 1788 the estancia employed 11 vaqueros, a mayoral, and a mayordomo. With family members, a population of 30 Indian residents in 1782 is entirely plausible; by 1803 the figure was down to 19.[37] In all the other cases, the size of the population was much too large for the level of stock-raising carried out on the estates. Consequently, the people other than the vaqueros and their families must have been colonists who worked the land for the hacendados and, of course, for their own subsistence.

The population of many other haciendas was also much larger than that required for stock-raising. In 1803 in the Sierra Baja, for example, Estancia Ticopó (Acanceh) had 389 residents, and in Abalá parish, Uayalceh, Mukuyché, Cacao, Pebá, and Ochil had populations of 1,385, 601, 331, 385, and 284, respectively. In Tecoh, Kumcheilá had 466 people, Oxtapacab 248, Idzincab 373, and San Joaquín 259. In Mama, Cumul had 272. In Sacalum, Yuncú had 479, Citnicabchén 360, Yalkuk 260, and San Andrés 208; and in Muna, Estancias Santa Rosa, Koholchacah, and San José had 353, 309, and 252. In the partido as a whole, at least 39 estates had Indian populations exceeding 100.[38]

The same was true elsewhere. In the Camino Real Bajo, where information is available only for Umán, one hacienda, Yaxcopoíl, had 229 Indian residents in 1782 and another had over 100.[39] On the other side of Mérida, in the partido of La Costa, five estates in Conkal had Indian populations exceeding 100. The largest were Xcuyum and Sacnicté, with 400 and 235, respectively. The parishes of Mochocá, Nolo, Tixkokob, Telchac, Motul, Cansahcab, Teya, and Temax all had at least one hacienda with more than 100 Indian residents.[40] In the Sierra Alta there were fewer estates with that many Indians: Maní had only three, Ticul two, Tekax two, and Oxkutzcab four. But the average and median size of these haciendas was much larger than anywhere else. Sacpacal and San José in Tekax had populations of 691 and 908, respectively. Hacienda Tabi, in Oxkutzcab, with a population of 1,898, was the largest hacienda in Yucatan in the late eighteenth century.[41]

Finally, although the information on the partido of Beneficios Bajos is incomplete, it is clear that haciendas with populations of over 100 people were to be found in the region.[42] Beneficios Altos, on the other hand, had few private estates of any size, and in Tizimín most of the labor force was engaged in agriculture. Only in the area around Valladolid and in a few parishes of the Costa were the haciendas so small as to suggest that the bulk of the labor force might have worked in stock-raising alone.[43]

Practically everywhere else the hacienda residents were so numerous that at times they even required their own local chapels, or oratorios. Since stock-raising required a very small number of permanent workers, it could not possibly have absorbed the labor of so many people. Haciendas in effect had become major settlements composed for the most part of agriculturalists.

Most unfortunate is the lack of documentation on the Campeche region. Since many of the haciendas there tended to be dedicated overwhelmingly to agriculture, information from that area would probably tell us a great deal about the new labor system coming into existence in the eighteenth century. We do know, as already noted, that African slaves were being used on some of the Campeche estates by this time, and that mandamientos were a major source of labor for the region's sugarcane-producing haciendas. But little or no information is available about peonage and the luneros in Campeche. It is likely, though, that most or all of the laborers in the stock-raising sector were debt peons. On the other hand, the haciendas within the jurisdiction of the curacy of Campeche and in the parish if Pocyaxum were not large compared with those in other parts of the province. In 1790 only one of the 24 estates in the two parishes had a resident population of more than 100 people. This was Hacienda Xtum, near Pocyaxum, with 124.[44] Luneros, obviously so important in much of the rest of the province, were seemingly not all that significant in Campeche. Perhaps peonage had already become the major mechanism for recruiting workers.

Yucatecan haciendas, in sum, employed a variety of labor systems in the late colonial period. Peonage was one of these systems, but it was not necessarily the most important. In time, however, most of the agricultural laborers would be brought into that system. This trend was already evident in the eighteenth century, for there were some instances of people other than vaqueros who were indebted to hacendados and who were required to do field labor.[45] This trend gained momentum after 1786. Once the government made hacendados responsible for paying the luneros' tribute, that class of people sank quickly into the morass of debts and labor obligations. By the 1840's they were indistinguishable from other debt peons, and the very word lunero had all but vanished from the lexicon of agrarian life. The inability to import significant quantities of African slaves also contributed to the growing trend toward agricultural peonage, for the demand for labor was increasing while the supply of free workers was not. The stage was set, then, for the labor system that made Yucatan infamous in the era before the Revolution.

CHAPTER EIGHT

Commerce, Markets, and the Crisis of Production

STUDIES OF THE ECONOMIC history of Latin America have traditionally focused on either production or long-distance commerce, and have given little attention to the marketing systems linking the two. Moreover, since emphasis has been given to long-distance trade at the expense of local markets, the quantitatively most important part of the economy—the transportation and distribution of the goods necessary for survival—has usually been ignored. Fortunately for the economic historian, scholars have now begun to concentrate instead on markets and regional economies, and their pioneering studies have contributed significantly to our understanding of the relations between production, marketing, and consumption.[1] It is now clear that whereas an important sector of the Mexican economy was oriented toward the world market, the structure of the regional economies and societies was to a great extent determined by the demands of local markets. A study of the sector oriented toward the producing and distributing of the essentials of life can therefore at times reveal more about historical reality than an analysis of the export industries. In the case of Yucatan, it is clear that even production by haciendas was geared more to internal than to external demand, and that an understanding of the regional marketing system is crucial to an analysis of the relationship between the producers and consumers of Yucatan and the worldwide economic system to which Yucatan belonged.

World Trade

During the first half of the eighteenth century, Yucatan's external trade was limited almost entirely to the exchange of products between Campeche, Tabasco, and Veracruz. Imports consisted mostly of fine textiles, wine, rum, and cacao—the last coming from Tabasco and Guayaquil. Other imported goods were cooking oil, dried fruits, metals, and tools. The main exports, as before, were cotton textiles and thread, wax, honey, tallow, hides, logwood, and salt. Yucatan, then, continued to be tied to the Mexican economy, and its most important exports were acquired from the producers through the classic mechanisms of colonialism, namely, tribute, religious taxation, and the repartimiento.[2]

By this time a relatively large merchant class had grown up around this export-import trade. Though the villa of Campeche was certainly Yucatan's most important emporium, we have not yet found out much about the merchants there. It is known that Campeche had a number of French and Italian residents early in the century, as well as two slave-trading English factors of the Asiento.[3] With respect to Mérida there is substantial evidence attesting to the presence of foreign merchants.[4]

Nevertheless, most commerce, both within the province and with the outside world, was carried out by Spaniards, or better, by two groups of Spaniards. There were first of all the communities of Canary Islanders who resided in Campeche and Mérida. Called simply *isleños*, the Islanders dominated Yucatan's commerce with the outside world for much of the century, although their position deteriorated in the depressed years following the abolition of the repartimiento. A number of Islanders were elected to the cabildos, and the group gave rise to many of the Hispanic families of modern Yucatan. Members of this group were important in the business of supplying goods for the Fair of the Immaculate Conception in Izamal, which was of sufficient magnitude to require the presence of a notary public from Mérida. The connection between isleños and commerce was so strong that even priests from the Canaries were often merchants in clerical garb. One of them, Br. Juan Angel de la Vega, operated four stores in Mérida while serving as the head sacristan of the cathedral.[5]

Basques were the other important ethnic group engaged in long-distance trade between Yucatan and the rest of the Spanish Empire. Although Basques had been immigrating to the province since the sixteenth century, their numbers seem to have grown considerably during the governorship of Martín de Urzúa y Arizmendi, the Count of Lizarraga. A Basque himself, the Count brought many of his countrymen to Yucatan in the last decade of the seventeenth century. Like isleños, Basques were frequently elected to the cabildos and founded families whose names are still common in Yucatan.[6]

The taxes paid for licenses to run stores in Mérida provide some insight into the size of the city's mercantile class. According to the surviving records for 1752, 1754, and 1783, the number of establishments fluctuated between 72 and 81.[7] Counting family members, then, the commercial class would have comprised no fewer than 200 people, and possibly as many as 400, between the 1750's and 1780's. This is a significant number in a city with something over 28,000 inhabitants in 1794. The proportion would have been even higher, of course, in Campeche.

The family histories of the merchants reveal a process similar to that described for many other areas of colonial Spanish America: although many people returned to Spain, others settled down and founded families. Most stuck with commerce at first, but such activities became increasingly problematical as time went on because of the difficulty of maintaining personal ties with the merchant community in Spain. Many people of the commercial class and their immediate descendants then shifted their attention to landowning. Class conflict between merchants and landowners was practically nonexistent, for intermarriage fused the two groups into a single, interlocking elite. Moreover, both usually had similar interests when it came to government policy, which is what counted.[8] Only during and after Independence was this traditional class harmony disrupted.

The merchants of eighteenth-century Yucatan did much more than simply buy and sell goods. As already noted, they frequently served as bondsmen for Governors. Rodrigo Chacón, a prominent businessman in the first half of the eighteenth century, served as bondsman for cabildo officials and as business agent for moneylending priests. He also joined another merchant, Juan de Utrera Rendón, in purchasing a ship to engage in the export of salt. They thus made profits from shipping as well as from sales. Chacón or his son was also chosen in 1758 to voice the Mérida business community's unhappiness with the cabildo's plan to raise commercial taxes.[9]

Even more important, the merchants were vital links in the chain connecting the Maya peasants with the mine workers of northern Mexico—and not only in the direct sense, but because they provided the credit and business connections that stimulated production and sales. In 1729, for example, Diego Francisco Ceballos, an isleño merchant, loaned 2,235 pesos, 3 reales, and 400 cargas of cotton to Santiago Bolio Solís, a prominent encomendero who obviously was engaging in repartimientos.[10] The Basque immigrant Miguel de Zavalegui, nephew of former Governor Urzúa, loaned 1,500 pesos to the war captain of the Valladolid jurisdiction, and was repaid in kind—in wax, cotton textiles, and cloth bags—in 1728.[11] In 1734 Andrés Vázquez Moscoso, another Basque immigrant, loaned merchandise worth 280 pesos, 3.5 reales, to residents of Tizimín, who agreed to repay the loan in raw cotton, patíes, and wax. Four years later Vázquez loaned 770 pesos, 5 reales, to Br. Mateo de Arce of Tabasco, who needed the money to buy his priestly gear. Arce mortgaged his "spiritual and temporal rents" and agreed to repay the loan in cacao, which was acquired through repartimientos carried out in Tabasco and was used as currency in small transactions in Yucatan.[12]

One of the most important merchants of the middle of the century was a Basque named Joseph Augustín de Gorostieta, whose export house handled a good part of the cloth, wax, and copal sent to New Spain. He acquired those commodities not merely by buying them on the market, but also by lending his capital to small merchants who carried out repartimientos in the villages. For example, in 1759 he loaned Buenaventura Ongay, a vecino of the remote village of Ichmul, 2,000 pesos, which was to be paid back in patíes, wax, and copal. In the same year he loaned 320 pesos to Andrés Troncos, a vecino of the even more remote village of Chunhuhub, to be repaid in copal.[13]

The merchants also used their connections to channel other people's capital into commercial operations. In 1718 Juan Quijano, the founder of the Quijano commercial-landowning dynasty in eighteenth-century Yucatan, borrowed 400 pesos from the funds of the Jubilee of the Feast of Saint Francis and another 100 pesos from the Church's Chantry Fund. The Church loaned the funds at the normal rate of interest of 5 percent annually, and Quijano agreed to repay principal and interest within three years.[14] Merchants could also put the surplus capital of individual clerics to use. In 1720 Pedro Cabrera Calderón, a member of the Canary Islander commercial community, borrowed 1,000 pesos from Br. Tomás Caballero, the curate of Hunucmá. The rate of interest was again 5 percent, and the borrower agreed to repay the capital and interest within five years.[15] Here, then, we see how merchants funneled their own and other people's capital into the local economy to acquire the goods demanded outside of Yucatan, thus linking the most remote regions of the peninsula to the economy and society of New Spain and points north.

During the last three decades of the eighteenth century, the province's ties to the world economy were modified in important ways. One of the changes has already been mentioned: the decline of textile exports with the abolition of the repartimiento and the growing competition from Catalonia and Great Britain, twin blows that sent the cotton-producing regions into an economic depression from which they did not fully recover until the twentieth century. Exports of wax also declined substantially, helping to keep Yucatan's commerce as a whole in a depressed state until at least the 1790's.

But even as the traditional export economy was collapsing, a new one was emerging. This was due in part to the Bourbon Reforms. Yucatan was one of the first provinces affected by the imperial changes made during the reign of Charles III. In 1770 Libre Comercio, that is, permission to trade with most ports within the Spanish Empire, was extended to Campeche. This had an immediate impact. Until now the outward traffic from Campeche had been limited to six to eight ships bound for Veracruz, two or three for Havana, an occasional ship for Portobello, and two for the Canary Islands, and arrivals from Spain had been extremely rare; no ships at all had put into Campeche between 1758 and 1770. After 1770 Campeche's commerce increased dramatically as trade with Havana, formerly of a sporadic and frequently clandestine nature, became the cornerstone of a new export economy.[16] In 1802 the port saw the arrival and departure of 960 ships.[17]

The effect of the new dispensation was already clear to the prominent Campechano and former alcalde Juan Ignacio de Cosgaya by 1787. In his request for a license to import up to 1,000 Africans to serve as slaves in the thriving agricultural enterprises being established, Cosgaya wrote: "This franchise [Comercio Libre] introduced such dynamism into the inhabitants of this Province that, ridding themselves of the languor or apathy in which they formerly found themselves, they have exploited the well-known possibilities of the Country with the vigor and impulse that have long been clamored for."[18]

The growing importance of Campeche was soon institutionalized. The villa had requested an upgrade in status to *ciudad*, or city, as early as 1722, but the crown had rejected Campeche's precocious pretensions. When the villa renewed the request in 1772, the economic situation had changed dramatically. This time the crown acceded to the request, and in 1777 Campeche officially became a ciudad.[19] The change was more than just symbolic, for as a full-fledged city Campeche could more effectively compete with Mérida for power. The institutional basis had been laid for the struggle for power and the concomitant political instability characteristic of Yucatan after Independence.

Meanwhile Mérida was also trying to increase its status in response to the economic progress made in the late eighteenth century. The capital city, with the support of the cabildo of Valladolid, requested that Mérida be the site of a new royal audiencia and a university. Those institutions were appropriate, the supporters argued, considering the recent "increase and advance in agriculture and commerce experienced" in the province. The Council of the Indies decided that an audiencia might be something to consider in the future but rejected out of hand the request for a university. "More damage than utility" would come from this, in the council's opinion, because it would distract the people "from agriculture, professions, mechanical arts, and commerce" and thereby "increase the evils about which the Procurators are now complaining."[20] Yucatan would not have a formal university until the twentieth century.

What did it consist of, this new export economy that so boosted expectations in Campeche and Mérida? To a great extent it was based on hides, tallow, and beef, both salted and on the hoof. These were of course traditional exports. What was new was both their prominence within the export sector—replacing cotton textiles—and their quantity.[21] The major destination of these goods was Havana, for Cuba was at this time putting more land into cane and thus needed to import large quantities of food.

Another traditional export that grew in importance at this time was log-wood, used in the making of dye. This was produced in the southern part of Campeche near the Laguna de Términos, a region long coveted by English logwood interests. The dye was Yucatan's only major export that reached European markets. Another traditional export that continued to be shipped from Yucatan was salt. As before, salt was shipped mostly to Veracruz, but new markets had been opened up by now—in Coatzacoalcos and, more important, in Havana and Spanish New Orleans.

New products were also being sent to markets abroad. The most important was rice, which was shipped primarily to Havana. Yucatan also began to export timber to Cuba, to meet the sugar industry's growing demand for wood for crates. Finally, of great significance for the future was the growth of exports of articles made of henequen. These included rope, rigging, sacks, and raw fiber, which were shipped in part from Campeche but mostly from Sisal because of its proximity to Mérida and the main centers of henequen production. Thanks to this small port's leading role in the trade, henequen entered the English language with the name of sisal.[22] The export of these old and new products was facilitated by the opening of the peninsula's minor ports—Sisal, Dzilam, Río Lagartos, and Bahía de la Asención—to trade with the outside world.[23]

As for imports, the items remained much the same as always: high-quality textiles, wine, rum, cacao, oil, dried fruit, metals, and tools.[24] But there was one very important change: as the century wore on, Yucatan was forced to import maize with greater frequency. In fact, the province was becoming increasingly dependent on imports of grain, to meet the needs of the population. The true change, then, as this clearly signaled, was occurring in the internal, or domestic, economy. As we will see, the province was stricken by a crisis of production that grew progressively worse as the century proceeded.

Government policy affected Yucatan's economic development in important ways. Seventeen years after the introduction of Libre Comercio, the Bourbon monarchy established the intendancy system in Mexico. The Intendants were instructed to take vigorous measures to stimulate commerce in the areas under their control, and the first Intendant of Mérida, Lucas de Gálvez, did just that. Shortly after his arrival, he sent a message to the cabildo lamenting "the deplorable state that this City is in because of its poverty and decadence, with there being no useful commerce." As we saw in Chapter Six, Gálvez eventually blamed this not on the citizens of Mérida but on the government's suppression of the repartimiento, and recommended that the old system of business with the Indians be reinstated.[25] Though the viceregal and royal governments did not accept Gálvez's recommendation, they did respond favorably to his request for more than two tons of gunpowder to initiate the largest road construction program in the history of the colony. The new and better roads were so clear a boon to commerce that Gálvez's successors continued the program.[26]

Paradoxically, even as the Bourbon government was taking measures to stimulate commerce, it was instituting policies intended to curb important facets of it. In 1777 the crown, realizing that it could not enforce the absolute ban on cane alcohol production in Yucatan, established the Estanco de Aguardiente, a state-run enterprise designed to increase royal revenues through the monopolization of the sale of spirits distilled from sugarcane. The Estanco was supposed to buy all aguardiente produced in the province and sell it at a profit. The success of the enterprise depended on the ability to monopolize the supply. But the Estanco cut its own throat by trying to buy the alcohol below the old free-market price, whereupon the distillers undersold the government monopoly. At the same time producers in Havana, pointing out that the production of aguardiente had previously been illegal in Yucatan, complained that the Estanco was cutting into their exports.

The crown reacted to these events in a contradictory fashion. The Fiscal of the Royal Exchequer in Mexico reminded his superiors in Spain that aguardiente production in Yucatan had been banned in order to protect the Andalusian producers of alcoholic beverages. In response to this report, Charles III himself declared in 1783 that he found the whole Estanco project "most disagreeable" and ordered the Viceroy to enforce rigorously all the laws banning production and consumption in Yucatan. After a time, he changed his mind and allowed the Estanco to continue to operate in the hope that it would succeed in diminishing production. Finally, in 1790, after the accession of Charles IV, the Council of the Indies shut down the hopelessly ineffective Estanco and legalized cane alcohol production in Yucatan. The government had been unable to suppress or even control production. The distillers finally won out.[27]

The government had no greater success in its attempt to control the salt industry. In 1784 the crown created the Estanco de Sal, a royal monopoly that tried to raise revenue by buying salt from the producers in Campeche at 18 reales a fanega and then selling it in Veracruz for 32 reales. The administrators found that the only way to sell at that price in Veracruz was to hold down the supply, which meant decreasing production in Campeche. As a result, annual salt exports from Yucatan declined from 36,000 fanegas in 1783 to only 20,000 a few years later, and the number of ships engaged in the trade between Campeche and Veracruz declined from 22 to 11. The cabildo of Campeche complained bitterly as the two government Estancos took their economic toll. In 1790, the Estanco de Sal too was abolished. Yucatan's production and exports of salt quickly recovered.[28]

For reasons of its own, then, the Bourbon government did not pursue

consistent economic policies in Yucatan. On the one hand it tried to stimulate commerce; on the other it tried to impede particular kinds of commercial activity either to protect Andalusian producers or to raise revenue. It is also possible that the abolition of the repartimiento had as a goal
the destruction of the province's textile industry so as to create markets
for Spanish textiles.[29] Nevertheless, the most contradictory features of
Bourbon policy were relatively short-lived, and by the 1790's the regional
economy was less restricted than ever before. Since the liberal policies
tended to coincide with the emergence of a new regional economy based
more on private property—haciendas—and less on the Maya communities than in the past, the groundwork was being laid for the burst of economic development that would characterize Yucatan in the first half of
the nineteenth century.

The eighteenth century also saw a substantial growth in the illegal trade
between Yucatan and Great Britain. Commerce between the two had
been going on for centuries, but the establishment of a permanent British
colony at Belize, on the peninsula's southeast coast, in this period undoubtedly increased the ability of English smugglers to get their goods
to the residents of Yucatan.[30] There are of course no statistics on this illegal
commercial activity, but judging by the openness of the smugglers, significant quantities of English goods must have been entering Yucatan's
economy illegally, and possibly some goods were being routinely re-
exported to other Spanish colonies.

Despite some similarity with the past, in sum, Yucatan's commercial
ties with the world economy were changing in important ways. In the
export sector, the increased production of hides, tallow, meat, logwood,
rice, salt, and articles of henequen signified the demise of the colonial
mechanisms traditionally used to extract products from the Indian economy. Exports from now on would be based on the output of landed estates and private enterprises, and would consist not of manufactured
goods but of primary products. Yucatan, in short, was developing a neocolonial economy. At the same time, imports were coming more and
more from England without interference from the Peninsular Spanish in-
termediary. And expanded trade with Havana, the United States, and Belize, and the concomitant decline of trade with Veracruz, signified a shift
in commercial relationships. Yucatan's ties to the rest of Mexico were
being weakened, a fact that probably had much to do with the province's
well-known tendency toward separatism in the nineteenth century. Yucatan's commercial future was now pointed in another direction.

Markets and the Rhythms of Economic Activity

For all the vitality of Yucatan's export sector, the internal economy was
of greater significance, in both a qualitative and a quantitative sense. The

major structures of production—the hacienda, the ranch, the farm, and the Maya milpa and household—developed partially or wholly in response to the demands of local markets. Foremost among those demands was the demand for "el grano de primera necesidad." In a normal year, maize was cheap and in ample supply from late September through May, when most of the Indians brought their grain to the cities to sell. If shortages were to develop, as they increasingly did, it would be in the summer months as the year's harvest was gradually consumed and the Indians preoccupied themselves with the next year's crop. June, July, August, and early September, then, were generally the problem months of low supply and peak prices.[31]

As we have seen, it was the duty of the pósitos to provide for these annual ups and downs and to maintain reserves against a bad harvest. In the eighteenth century the procedure was much the same as before: the municipal grain funds acquired maize by making advance payments directly to the Maya village cabildos; the cabildos collected the grain from the producers after the harvest; and it was forwarded on to the cities at the pósitos' expense. Fortunately, for this period, unlike the earlier one, we have grain fund records for Campeche and also more complete data on Valladolid. These sources reveal that no fewer than 188 villages and parcialidades were contracted for maize by the province's three pósitos. In other words, practically every village in Yucatan was incorporated into the market economy through the system organized to provision the cities with grain.[32]

Three new features were added to the provisioning system in the second half of the century. First, the pósitos began to purchase grain with some regularity from hacendados as they moved into production to meet the increasing demand for foodstuffs. Second, as maize shortages became more frequent and more severe, the pósitos began to arrange for the regular importation of wheat flour from Veracruz and the United States. And third, during times of impending shortages, the pósitos sent out special agents, called *comisionados*, on grain-purchasing expeditions. Sometimes these agents operated within the province itself and acquired surplus maize wherever they could find it. But at times they were sent to Veracruz, Tuxpan, and even the United States.

Since trade between Yucatan and foreign countries, even in vital foodstuffs, was illegal, before importing flour from or sending comisionados to the United States, a cabildo would formally request the Governor to approve the action. Fortunately for the starving people of Yucatan, the laws were usually ignored on both sides. The Governor simply informed his superiors after the fact and justified the step on the grounds of absolute necessity; and although the crown did its best to discourage commercial contact with foreigners, it could hardly blame its local officials for doing what was necessary to prevent mass starvation.

Exports of grain, possible only in the event of an exceptionally good harvest, were prohibited not by the laws of the Spanish Empire but by the policies of the municipal governments. However, even in the best of times, merchants were rarely able to persuade the cabildos to grant permission to export grain, for municipal governments, like their medieval predecessors, were very cautious about relaxing the controls designed to ensure the provisioning of the population. In fact, free trade in grain, that is, the unhindered movement of grain into and out of the peninsula, was not established in Yucatan until the late nineteenth century.

Turning to the Maya side of things, it is important to keep in mind that during a normal year by far the largest part of the maize consumed in the cities was still being produced not by Spanish-owned haciendas but by the Indian peasantry. In 1773 the cabildo of Mérida noted this fact in its report to the King about the economy of Yucatan. It also reported that the Indian sellers came from villages as far away as 30 or more leagues (about 120 km). The pósito records of Valladolid reveal a similar radius of activity, with sellers trekking as much as 26 leagues (104 km).[33] A large part of the peasantry participated in the market economy on a regular basis apart from the system organized by the urban grain funds. For example, in 1776 the cabildo of Mérida noted that the number of maize sellers declined somewhat in February because many of them were staying at home to harvest their bean crop.[34] The producers, in short, were frequently the very people who did the selling. In 1761 the rebels led by Jacinto Canek surprised several Indians from Dzonotchel (some 130 km southeast of Mérida) as they were on their way to the capital to sell bananas.[35] Clearly, the urban markets of Yucatan affected a vast hinterland.

The muleteers, or *arrieros*, were vital links in the chain connecting the two. Because of them, the pósitos were able to extend their reach to even the remotest villages. In 1783 in the Valladolid region, for example, muleteers from Tihosuco (57 km south-southeast of Valladolid) carried grain to the villa not only from the area around their own village but also from Panabá, a pueblo 65 kilometers *north* of Valladolid. Arrieros from the villa's barrios of San Marcos, Laboríos, San Juan, and Santa Ana brought grain to the city from Telá, Celul, and Sacalaca, villages located 57, 78, and 80 kilometers, respectively, from Valladolid. In the same year the villa's pósito received grain from the muleteers of Tekom, Tekuch, Yalcón, Chichimilá, Tixcacalcupul, Chemax, Chikindzonot, Ekpedz, Tepich, and Dzonotchel. Some of these pueblos were close to the city, but others were located at some distance, and the last village was over 80 kilometers away.[36] The following year, 1784, muleteers from at least 15 villages carried grain from the pueblos of Valladolid's hinterland to the urban market.[37] Practically all of the villages around Mérida had arrieros to carry their pósito grain to the capital.

TABLE 8.1
Provenance of Maize Delivered to Mérida and Valladolid
as Indicated by Transport Costs, 1770's–80's
(Percent of total)

Freight charges per pack animal (reales)	Mérida			Valladolid		
	1782	1785	1787	1777	1778	1787
0.5–1	0.1%	0.0%	0.0%	28.1%	43.0%	64.6%
2	0.0	0.0	0.5	10.2	24.9	26.0
3	1.7	0.0	22.2	24.2	9.4	7.1
4	36.0	61.5	47.5	32.4	18.2	1.2
5	6.7	17.3	28.5	5.1	4.6	0.0
6 and over	55.4	21.2	2.9	0.0	0.0	1.0

SOURCES: *Mérida*, AAM, Libro 23, Expedientes incompletos y Acuerdos del Cabildo de el Año de 1801, fols. 6–8, Libro 16, Expedientes de Cabildos, 1785, Testimonio de las cuentas de pósito presentadas por su administrador en el año espresado, la que se sacó en el de 1791, fols. 31–38; Expedientes de Cabildos, 1787, Cuentas presentadas por el mayordomo de pósitos de esta Ciudad D. José Duarte en el año presentado, fols. 12–15. *Valladolid*, AHN, 20751, Pieza 12, Cuentas de Pósito de Valladolid, 1777–81, fols. 1–2; AGI, México 3042, 1792, Cuentas del Pócito de la Villa de Valladolid presentadas por el Ynterventor de el en el año de 1788 siendolo Don Juan Francisco Muñoz, fols. 11–17, 32.

As before, we can look to freight charges for clues to the relationship between town and country in this period. As can be seen in Table 8.1, the two cities were provisioned quite differently. Valladolid received the vast majority of its maize from nearby areas. In the three years for which information was found, it got at least 62.5 percent and as much as 97.7 percent of its grain at freight costs of three reales or less per pack animal. By contrast, Mérida got at most only 22.7 percent of its supply close by, and usually a great deal less. In 1785 all of its pósito grain came from districts with freight charges of four or more reales.

The size of the two cities certainly accounts in part for this difference. The capital had approximately three times as many mouths to feed as the eastern villa. But there were also many more Indian mouths to feed in the area around Mérida and the partidos of La Costa and the Camino Real Bajo, where a still-expanding Maya population put ever-more pressure on the land. Indeed space for milpas was in such short supply in this part of the province that the Indians could not produce any surplus at all except in years of extraordinarily good harvests. The Costa in fact sometimes had to import maize to feed itself. Mérida was therefore provisioned for the most part by the partidos of Beneficios Bajos, the Sierra Baja, and, above all, the Sierra Alta. Valladolid was in a much happier position. There the local Indians could still increase production by bringing new lands into cultivation. Nevertheless, even Valladolid had to incorporate distant villages into its provisioning system. Most importantly, Beneficios Altos, which had been incorporated into the grain-market economy only sporadically in the midcolonial era, became one of Valladolid's regular suppliers in the eighteenth century. That district also was the principal supplier for Bacalar.[38]

Since as the century progressed the pósitos contracted more and more grain to feed the expanding urban population, more and more Indians were brought into the provisioning system as producers and shippers of grain. This meant that a significant proportion of peasant income was being generated by participation, in one way or another, in marketing activities. It should be emphasized that this participation was voluntary. True, the pósito contracts prevented the peasants from making windfall profits in times of extreme shortage. Moreover, since the pósitos rarely paid more than two reales per carga of maize, what the Maya got for their efforts at best merely kept them from sinking into deeper poverty.[39] Nevertheless, the system did work to a certain extent to their advantage. With guaranteed markets for their surpluses, they could make profits even when abundant harvests drove prices down. Moreover, since the Maya had the producer's advantage, the city governments had to make participation as attractive as possible. The pósito of Valladolid thus found itself compelled at times to pay cash bonuses, called *gratificaciones*, to the village caciques to guarantee their cooperation. More important, the Indians' cash advances were never converted into a new form of repartimiento. When a peasant died before his crop was brought in, the in-kind debt was not transferred to family members or to the community; rather, the money was simply returned, something that was never permitted under the repartimiento system.[40]

In a sense, then, the Indians lived in two worlds. They continued to go their own way in many respects. At the same time, they were an integral part of and intimately affected by the colonial system, and became accustomed to buying and selling on the market in the cities of their colonial masters. This economic activity in turn had an effect on the tributary system, for it enabled the Maya to commute their tribute to cash payments. This practice became increasingly common in the late eighteenth century.

The provisioning system, as we have seen, also stimulated the development of agriculture on Spanish-owned haciendas. In practice the pósitos, rather than waiting for surplus grain to rot, lent it to producers as seed corn. The recipients were supposed to repay the loan after the next harvest, but the cabildos were usually lenient, and debtors often had a grace period of many years. This procedure dated from at least the seventeenth century but did not become common practice until the 1730's. Though the pósitos did at times advance seed corn to Maya caciques, the main beneficiaries were Spanish hacendados, who found it profitable to accept the seed and repay it in kind at their convenience.[41] In this way the pósitos served the interests of the colonial landowning elite, for these loans favored a select group of Spanish landowners, not the agricultural sector as a whole.

Nevertheless, with the instituting of the intendancy, efforts were made to improve the lot of the principal agricultural producers, namely, the Maya peasantry. Most importantly, Intendants Gálvez and O'Neil ordered the establishment of pósitos in the villages. The Indians were required to contribute a portion of their harvest to the pueblo grain funds to build up a reserve for the needy in times of shortage. Though the villagers opposed the new institution, seeing in the requirement to pay part of their produce a new and burdensome tax, the Intendants adhered to the policy, insisting on its long-term benefits. There are only a couple of references to these rural grain funds in subsequent years. In 1804 the cabildo of Mérida reported that the village pósitos were functioning adequately and were helping to relieve some of the effects of grain shortages;[42] and they are mentioned in the records of the Provincial Congress of Yucatan in the years 1813–21. So far as can be determined, they were a dead issue by the 1840's.[43]

Though not the staff of life that maize was, beef was an important article of consumption for the Spanish population, and during times of crop failure, it became one for the Indians as well. The trade in this domain was dominated by the Spaniards. Though the Maya owned a considerable quantity of livestock,[44] practically all the cattle slaughtered for the Mérida market came from the haciendas. Maya participation consisted almost entirely of sales by the estancias belonging to Indian cofradías.

Pork figured little in the market economy. Most swine were raised by the Indians who, it was said, usually kept two, three, or four pigs around the house. Consequently, what pork sales there were came largely from Maya producers.[45] However, for the most part urban consumers supplied their own needs. Like their modern descendants, most city dwellers raised pigs and other sorts of small animals in the patios of their houses, a practice the cabildo of Mérida referred to as "crianza doméstica."

Mérida, like all colonial Spanish American cities, used what was known as the *postura* system for organizing the *abasto de carne*, that is, the provisioning of the city with meat. At the beginning of every year, the cabildo held an auction in which the lowest bidder was given an exclusive contract to market meat in the city. This *obligado* (or *obligada* in the case of a woman) thereby agreed to provide as much meat as the public wished to consume, at the bid rate (the postura, or fixed price), from Easter Sunday until Shrove Tuesday of the following year, no meat being provided during Lent. Sometimes the contract specified two slightly different prices, the higher one taking into account the lack of forage until the onset of the rainy season (from Easter through September), and the lower one based on the "good season" (from October to Shrove Tuesday). The obligado also had to ensure that only fresh meat was sold, that health regulations were enforced, and that records were kept so that the proper municipal and royal taxes could be assessed.[46]

Though in some places the *abasto de carne* system may have been a monopoly, with the obligado selling only his own cattle and excluding everyone else's,[47] this was not the case in Yucatan. In Mérida the obligado issued tickets, or *boletas*, to a large number of cattle ranchers, each of whom was assigned a specific day, week, or weeks in which to bring his or her cattle to market. In this way the chaos of having all the ranchers and their cattle in town at the same time was avoided. Of course, this system also functioned to exclude non-certified cattle ranchers, for only people with proper licenses could be issued market days. The estancieros therefore were a select group, their brands having been carefully registered in a calfskin-bound volume, or Libro Becerro, kept by the Royal Exchequer. In fact these people were even said to belong to a *gremio de estancieros*, or ranchers' guild. Now, "gremio" in this sense should be interpreted not as a formal guild, which would have had statutes and a patron saint, but as an occupation. Nevertheless it does suggest that these ranchers were a rather exclusive group. The only meat sold that did not belong to members of the *gremio de estancieros* was that of the cofradía estancias. But even the cofradías had to receive a proper permit and a selling time from the obligado. In this way participation by the sodalities was sanctioned, and since most, if not all, of the cofradías in the eighteenth century were entirely Indian in membership, revenues resulting from market activities were generated for Maya cultural activities.

In addition to providing for orderly marketing and serving to exclude non-certified ranchers, the *abasto de carne* system facilitated the collection of taxes. This was because all legal slaughtering and sales of meat had to take place at one central location, where they could easily be watched over by the proper authorities. The royal government exacted the *alcabala* (sales tax) on all sales except those involving the cattle of cofradías, which as religious institutions were exempt from the tax. The municipal government collected what was called the *sisa*, a consumption tax first introduced by Spanish municipalities during medieval times.

Once again the lack of documentation makes it impossible to study in detail the marketing systems of the province's other cities. Nevertheless, surviving records from Campeche shed some light on beef consumption in one of Yucatan's urban centers. According to the municipal accounts for the years 1778/79–1783/84, 1,501, 1,480, 1,366, 1,218, 1,047, and 1,214 head of cattle were slaughtered in those six years, or an average of 1,304 head.[48] Assuming each animal yielded about 244 pounds of beef,[49] the inhabitants of the port city would have consumed some 318,000 pounds of meat in that period.

We do not have much information on the provisioning of other major towns of the peninsula, though the *abasto de carne* system was clearly functioning in Izamal as early as 1718.[50] After that the record is silent until 1792, when the Mérida notarial documents suddenly registered postura contracts for the partidos of Sierra Alta y Baja, Beneficios Bajos, Camino Real Alto y Bajo, and La Costa.[51] This was the result of the initiative of Governor-Intendant Lucas de Gálvez, who was acting in accordance with his instructions to stimulate commerce and work against nonroyal monopolies.

The marketing structure for meat permitted participation by a broader range of producers than might have been expected. But at the same time the market worked in a way that permitted the large producers to exercise considerable economic power. The mere existence of the *gremio de estancieros* illustrates that the ranchers frequently had enough group solidarity to act in concert to protect their interests. Since the seventeenth century, they had been pressuring the government to suppress unlicensed estancias in order to limit competition. In 1785–86 they participated collectively in the effort to rescind the new law that made them financially responsible for the tribute of the luneros. And in the second half of the eighteenth century, the *gremio de estancieros* acted when necessary to prop up meat prices. For example, when competitive bidding for the *abasto de carne* of Mérida began to result in lower prices during the 1750's, the important ranchers used their influence to stop the competition; the cabildo then had to assume control of the abasto, and since the stock raisers were well represented on the council, the selling prices set by the municipal government in 1763 and after were considerably higher than those prevailing during the previous 15 years.[52] In fact, as Table 8.2 and its accompanying figure demonstrate, new peaks were achieved in the late 1760's.

But in the struggle over meat prices the ranchers found the crown far less susceptible to their influence than the local city councils. This was especially true in the age of the intendancy. Lucas de Gálvez, for example, convinced that the livestock economy had recovered sufficiently from the disasters of the 1770's and 1780's to justify a reduction in meat prices, intervened to drive prices down. By the early 1790's prices were only 2 percent above the 1750 level. Moreover, as we have seen, Gálvez acted to break up the ranching oligopoly and encourage competition by instituting the *abasto de carne* system in the chief towns.

The first decade of the nineteenth century witnessed an intense struggle between the ranching elite and the royal government. Since these were years of almost continuous grain shortage, the price of meat began to rise

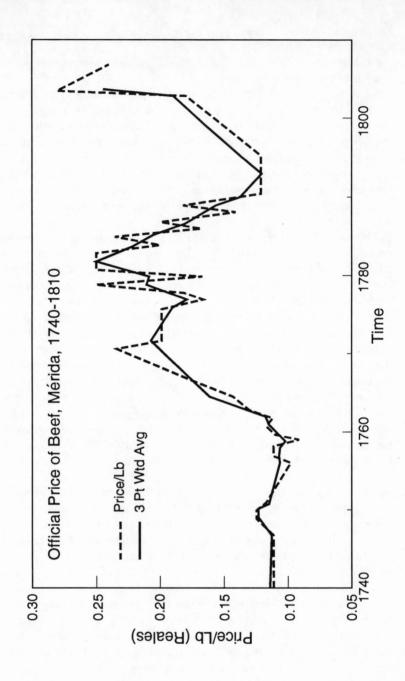

Official Price of Beef, Mérida, 1740-1810

Price/Lb
3 Pt Wtd Avg

Time

Price/Lb (Reales)

TABLE 8.2
Price Index of Beef in Mérida, 1708–1807
(1750 = 100)

Year	Pounds of beef per real	Price index[a]	Year	Pounds of beef per real	Price index
1708	7.0–8.0	106	1776	5.0	170
1719	9.0	94	1777[b]	6.0	142
1721	8.0	106	1778	5.5	155
1738	9.0	94	1779[b]	4.0	213
1747	8.5, 9.5	89	1780[b]	6.0	142
1748	8.0, 9.0	94	1781[b]	4.0	213
1749[b]	7.5, 8.5	100	1782[b]	4.0	213
1750	7.5, 8.5	100	1783	4.0	213
1751	8.0, 9.0	94	1784[b]	5.0	170
1756	10.0, 10.5	81	1785[b]	4.0, 4.5	189
1757	9.0	94	1786	6.0	142
1758	9.0	94	1787	5.0	170
1759	11.0	77	1788	7.1[c]	119
1760	9.0	94	1789	5.5	155
1761	8.0, 9.0	94	1790	8.3[c]	102
1762	9.0	94	1793	8.3[c]	102
1763[b]	7.5, 8.0	106	1795	8.3[c]	102
1765[b]	7.0	121	1803	5.6[c]	153
1771	4.0, 4.5	189	1804	3.6[c]	238
1772	5.0	170	1807[b]	4.2[c]	204

SOURCES: AGI, Escribanía 322A, Residencia de Martín de Urzúa, el Conde de Lizarraga, Pesquisa en Mérida (1708), fol. 344; ANEY, M. Montero, 3 April 1719, fols. 276–77, 2 April 1721, fol. 277; AAM, Autos y Acuerdos 1747–51, fols. 1, 53–54, 94–95, 125, 247–51, Acuerdos y Títulos 1757–60, fols. 12, 14, 15, 52–60, 149, Acuerdos 1761–66, fols. 15–16, 58–59, 97, 124, 137; AGI, México 3056, Carta del Gobernador al Rey, 23 May 1773; AAM, Acuerdos 1776–85, fols. 8, 37, 66, 90, 115, 146, 178, 202, 210–15, 242–43, 258, Acuerdos 1786–95, fols. 15, 46, 61; ANEY, J.J. Manzanilla, 1 April 1789, fol. 453; AGI, México 3073, exp. 6, carta no. 25 del Intendente Interino al Secretario del Consejo de Indias (Ventura de Taranco), 31 May 1793; ANEY, P. Barbosa, 26 March 1793, fols. 190–91, M. Palomeque, 31 March 1795, fols. 80–81; AAM, libro 21, Junta Municipal de Proprios, Acuerdos, 29 March, 1 April, 28 April 1803, 14 March 1804; Acuerdos, 14 March 1807, fols. 1–2.
  [a]Calculated from the lower rate where there are "good" and "bad" seasonal rates.
  [b]Years in which the cabildo ran the meat marketing system.
  [c]Calculated from prices per arroba (25 lbs.).

precipitously. Between 1795 and 1803 the price rose 50 percent, and in the following year, the price jumped a further 55 percent. So steep an increase—133 percent in less than 10 years—prompted the province's third Intendant, Benito Pérez, to intervene. The issue came to a head in 1807, when the cabildo of Mérida accepted a bid for the abasto that would have set prices at the same level as in 1804. At this, Pérez suspended the proceedings and took an unprecedented step: he read to the cabildo an official report from Guatemala, where in similar conditions the President of the Audiencia had declared—to the ranchers' horror—free trade in meat. This threat had the desired result. Regidor Miguel Bolio quickly stepped forward to say that such a drastic step was unnecessary, for the stock raisers were legally bound by the terms of their ranching licenses to sell at whatever postura the cabildo might set. He was willing, he said, to supply meat for four weeks at a price 25 percent below the price that had so upset the Intendant, and if no one else would commit himself to follow suit for the succeeding weeks, the cabildo should assign turns to all the licensed ranchers, who would then be required to sell at the same price "or even lower." Pérez thereupon thanked Bolio and pointed out that, although Article 37 of the Ordinances of Intendants required him to prohibit public officials from participating in the city's *abasto de carne*, he would bend the rules; the article's purpose, after all, was to prevent fraud and monopoly, but in this case Bolio's participation would bring down prices and be in the public's interest.[53]

The Intendant thus won a victory over the stock-raising elite. The former was influenced by Enlightenment thought on the value of competition, but the latter still clung to the protectionist ideology of the past. Only with Independence, which by now was close at hand, would liberalism triumph at the local level and effect the restructuring of a marketing system that was an integral feature of the colonial regime.

The Crisis of Production

In the early and middle colonial periods, Yucatan had been devastated by epidemic disease; in the eighteenth century, it was devastated once again, this time by recurring famines. Two factors were in the main responsible for Yucatan's great crisis of production in the late colonial era. First, natural catastrophes hit the province again and again. The eighteenth century witnessed a worldwide warming trend, which resulted in not only hotter but also drier conditions.[54] The crop failures of 1747, 1769, 1773, 1776, and 1809 were all caused by drought. Grain shortages also resulted from the storms, or *nortes*, that blew in from the Gulf of Mexico and seriously disrupted either the agricultural cycle or the transport of grain to market. Such storms caused a severe shortage in Mérida in 1790.[55] One of the worst crises occurred after a hurricane struck Yucatan in September 1772 and destroyed most of the crops.[56]

Certainly related to the warmer and drier conditions were the series of locust plagues that afflicted Yucatan in the second half of the eighteenth century. The famine of 1769–71, the worst in the province's history, began when locusts ravaged the milpas before the 1769 harvest could be brought in—a harvest already so meager after an exceptionally dry summer as to presage a grain shortage.[57] The insects were so numerous, people later testified, that the sun was blotted out from the sky. The result was utter disaster. The locusts returned the following year, causing another failed harvest. Fortunately for Yucatan, the voracious flying insects did not appear in large numbers in the summer of 1771, and food supplies were adequate. But then the hurricane of 1772 destroyed practically the entire harvest, and in 1773 drought and locusts again afflicted the province. Consequently, with the exception of the year 1771, there was a continuous crisis from the summer of 1769 until the fall of 1774. Thereafter the situation improved somewhat, but even so there was drought in 1776, and food supplies were inadequate in 1777. Clearly, natural phenomena were causing severe problems for a society that was already exploiting its resources to the limit. But the locust plagues, which spread death and destruction throughout southern Mesoamerica and resulted in the loss of crops in many parts of Guatemala, long-term economic decline in El Salvador, and severe famine in Chiapas as well as Yucatan, may have been in part man-made. The forest of what is now El Salvador was being rapidly cut down to make way for the production of indigo, and this may have provoked the locusts to swarm.[58]

The other main contributing factor was the new agrarian structure that had emerged in the eighteenth century. During the period of Maya population decline in the early and mid-colonial era, Spaniards had acquired large quantities of land. In the eighteenth century, when the size of the Indian population was increasing, the owners of haciendas loaned some of their property to landless people being pushed out of their villages. Many estates thus were converted into major settlements with populations numbering in the hundreds or, in a few cases, the thousands. But it is likely that not all surplus hacienda property was given over to luneros. Keeping some land idle, after all, was in the interest of the landowners because limiting production meant higher prices for their own crops. In any event, given the large proportion of the land held by the haciendas, and the noticeable increase in rents, it is clear that peasants could not colonize unused land as easily as in the past.

Transport and distribution problems exacerbated the situation. Sometimes the difficulty was not too little rain, but an overabundance, which incurred the risks of getting the grain wet. Muleteers had to suspend activities altogether during such periods. The loss of large numbers of pack animals in the several equine epidemics that occurred in the late colonial period must have made a bad situation worse.[59]

The crisis of production, in sum, was brought on by the conjuncture of two historical processes: rapid demographic expansion resulting in growing pressure on the land, which could not be easily alleviated because of the agrarian structure; and climatic change resulting in deteriorating conditions for agriculture and the greater likelihood of insect damage. The crisis was not as severe as the one that had afflicted the Maya in the eighth or ninth century and led to the decline or collapse of Classic Maya civilization. Nevertheless, it was of sufficient gravity to demonstrate once again the intimate relationship between human beings and their environment.

Grain prices, predictably, rose to extremely high levels on numerous occasions in this period. From at least 1724 on, a carga of maize "normally" (i.e. when there was no shortage) sold for two reales or less in the villages and for between two and three reales in Mérida because of added transport costs.[60] But as "normal" years became less common, so did "normal" prices. In 1773 the cabildo of Mérida reported that in previous years maize had been selling for four reales in the villages, or double the normal price.[61] In many of the years after 1750, the price of maize was well above two reales per carga. It frequently reached eight reales (one peso), sometimes went as high as 18–24, and on one occasion—in 1770, during the great famine—rose to an incredible 36 reales.[62]

Meat prices kept pace with the maize market, for in times of grain shortages the demand for a substitute increased. During the crisis of 1769–70, for example, the number of cattle slaughtered in Mérida rose to between 300 and 400 weekly, as compared with an average of 70–100 during years of adequate maize supplies.[63] Meanwhile, in the countryside hungry people stole cattle to feed themselves. Since the animals were being eaten faster than they could reproduce, the grain shortage led to the depletion of herds. The cabildo of Mérida reported that the number of cattle in the province declined from between 150,000 and 200,000 head in the 1760's to only 30,000 in 1773.[64] This may have exaggerated the situation somewhat, but it does help explain the rise of meat prices shown in Table 8.2 and the accompanying figure.

The measures taken by the cabildo of Mérida and the Governor to alleviate grain shortages were more concerned with the effects than with the causes of the crisis. And as might be expected, the cabildo's policies were strongly in the tradition of the medieval Spanish municipal controls and regulations. One main thrust was to impede the activities of engrossers. When, in 1795 and 1798, the Procurator of the cabildo reported that the grain shortages of those years were being caused by profiteers (logreros), the councilmen undertook to ensure that the selling price of pósito maize would be well below the market price and to prohibit anyone from buying large quantities of grain at one time.[65] In 1807 the situation was so bad that the Intendant threatened to publicize the names of profiteers to bring public pressure on them to sell at reasonable prices. The threat must have been effective, for at the very next meeting of the cabildo, two regidores announced that they possessed surplus grain, which they were willing to sell immediately to help alleviate the shortage.[66]

The controls on bakeries were also tightened to ensure that the bakers did not diminish the size of loaves of bread, the prices of which were fixed by the cabildo. At the same time, to ensure that the bakers got flour at reasonable cost, thereby eliminating any excuse for offering a smaller loaf for the money, the cabildo purchased flour through its comisionados and sold it to the bakers at specified prices.[67]

In times of scarcity, the city government's intervention in the grain market went beyond simply setting the price of pósito maize. At this point, pósito supplies represented a larger-than-normal proportion of the total maize for sale, so that the price set by the cabildo amounted to extensive price-fixing. More important, when the supply of grain promised to be well below what was necessary, the cabildo did not hesitate to fix prices for all the maize being sold in the market, whether of private sellers or of the pósito.[68]

In 1795 the cabildo of Mérida even attempted to ration maize. The attempt seems to have failed, and manageable shortfalls during the next several years temporarily eliminated the need for such an experiment. However, in 1804 a severe shortage forced the cabildo to revive the rationing scheme. This time it was partially successful, primarily because of adequate preparation and planning. A *padrón*, or list of residents, was drawn up, and only poor people on the list were permitted to buy maize from the pósito. Every registered poor person was given a ticket (*papeleta*) each month entitling him or her to buy one *almud* (one-twelfth of a carga) at a price of two reales (i.e., 24 reales per carga). This was a very high price indeed, but the cabildo justified it as a means of encouraging people to diminish consumption. To facilitate the orderly functioning of rationing, grain was sold at only five locations in the city and its barrios: the Alhóndiga (on the main plaza), and the churches of Santa Ana, Santiago, San Cristóbal, and the Hermita. The pastors of the four churches supervised the sales conducted there. The cabildo imposed this rationing system again in 1807 and probably in several other years for which no records have remained.[69]

The cabildo took a variety of other measures to ameliorate shortages during the last half of the eighteenth century. At least twice, in 1761 and 1795, it petitioned the Bishop for a dispensation from the Lenten prohibition against eating meat so that the residents of the city would have a substitute for maize.[70] On several occasions it ordered all muleteers to regions known to have surplus grain to ensure that the maize got to the city.[71] In 1777 it persuaded the Provincial of the Franciscans of Yucatan to donate 500 cargas to the pósito for the succor of Mérida's poor.[72] And when the pósito ran out of money for grain purchases, the cabildo frequently took out loans from the Royal Treasury, the Indian *caja de comunidad*, private parties, the Church, and other sources to fund further operations.[73]

But of all the measures taken by the cabildo, the most important was the move to import foodstuffs from abroad. Though some food may have been brought in from abroad without being mentioned in the surviving sources, the first documented case of grain imports is for 1770, the year of the worst famine in the peninsula's history. At that time the cabildo sent comisionados to Veracruz, Tuxpan, and Tampico in search of grain. Finding that those places were experiencing shortages too and had very little grain to export, the comisionados proceeded to New Orleans, at that time a Spanish colony, where maize was procured and shipped to Yucatan. There it was sold along with small quantities gathered in Veracruz.[74]

Maize of unspecified provenance was imported again the following year. Mérida and Campeche, it appears, were competing for imported grain at the time and were willing to resort to expropriation in order to obtain it, for the cabildo of Mérida specified that all grain from abroad should be imported through Sisal rather than Campeche, where it could have fallen into the hands of that city's pósito.[75] Maize was also imported in 1772 and 1773, although again the provenance of the grain was not stated.[76]

The need to import foodstuffs was becoming so common in the late eighteenth century that by 1795 the cabildo of Mérida was taking steps to arrange for suppliers abroad to provision the city on a permanent basis. It contracted a merchant in Campeche to import wheat for the capital every year. In the first year of the contract, at least 100 barrels were brought in, and apparently similar quantities were imported every year thereafter.[77]

During the first decade of the nineteenth century, as grain shortages became almost a routine fact of life, the cabildo of Mérida was forced to recognize that food imports were the only means of feeding the population. In 1800 it again empowered comisionados to buy grain in Veracruz, but once more a shortage in that port sent them on to New Orleans (which became a French colony some time in 1800, although it continued to be administered by Spain until 1802). There foodstuffs, including rice, were procured and sent back to Mérida.[78] In 1804 grain had to be imported again, though this time the comisionados were dispensed with; foodstuffs were now purchased directly from foreign ships calling at Campeche and Sisal. The origin of the food imported in 1804 is significant: it came not only from Tuxpan, but also from Matanzas (Cuba) and from New Orleans (a U.S. territory since 1803), Baltimore, and Charleston.[79] These are the first known instances of imports coming directly from the United States.

Since trade with foreign countries was illegal, the authorities were understandably nervous about approving such commerce. The grain shortage of 1805 necessitated imports of maize and wheat flour from Veracruz, but the cabildo of Mérida declined to purchase food from U.S. ships at Campeche, apparently because the shortage was not considered to be of sufficient severity.[80] But in 1807 the situation was so bad that even Intendant Pérez, despite being under strong pressure from the Viceroy to prohibit all imports of foreign goods, yielded to the pleas of the local cabildos and permitted purchases of grain from foreigners. He defended his action by reporting that such illegal imports were becoming absolutely necessary, as they had been in 1804, and that in any case he had no choice in the matter since even the 30,000 cargas he had authorized were not going to meet the province's needs.[81] Grain had to be imported from the United States in 1808 and 1809 as well, although in those years complications developed because of an embargo imposed by President Jefferson in December 1807. The Yucatecans had to use the good offices of the Consul-General of the United States, the Spanish Vice-Consul in New Orleans, and the Spanish Ambassador in Washington to get the food shipped.[82]

Since the province now had to import food on a regular basis, the cabildo of Mérida took steps to stimulate that trade. It granted licenses to merchants and either gave them monopolies over certain goods or guaranteed them high rates of profit. In 1806 it granted one merchant the right to 12 percent of the value, freight charges included, of the maize he imported.[83] The cabildo even granted special privileges to foreigners who undertook to ship grain to Yucatan. Foodstuffs were sometimes allowed to enter duty-free, and foreigners were also permitted to bring in commercial goods as long as grain was part of the cargo. On one occasion the cabildo granted some North Americans the right to export logwood without paying the usual taxes provided that they brought maize to Yucatan.[84]

Though the measures taken by the municipal government of Mérida, and undoubtedly that of Campeche and Valladolid as well, were clearly in the tradition established centuries earlier by municipalities in medieval Spain, this should not be taken to mean that the late colonial economy was essentially "feudal" in nature. For by the late eighteenth century, Yucatan, and indeed all the Spanish American colonies, had developed social and economic structures that were in no way like Europe's at any time in European, or Spanish, history. Nevertheless the continued functioning of institutions of medieval European origin is testimony to both the durability and the usefulness of those institutions. This would mean that transition to a full-fledged capitalist system would not be easy, for it would require the elimination of these features of the Spanish American ancien régime.

At the same time, the crisis of production in late colonial Yucatan marked the beginning of a new historical era. Because production could no longer keep up with growing demand, Yucatan had to enter into new commercial relationships, especially with the United States. Even before Independence the province's commerce was being oriented away from the old colonial metropolis and toward the new economic power of North America. Grain was already being imported from New Orleans, Baltimore, and Charleston. In a sense, then, Independence would merely speed up and confirm a process that began in the late eighteenth century. Consequently, the crisis of production, which was also evident in the Valley of Mexico at this time,[85] signified a partial break-up of the old colonial system and the orientation of the economy in significantly different directions.

The eighteenth century was certainly not a period of prosperity in Yucatan, especially not for those who were too poor to afford even the meager quantities of food supplied by the pósitos. And the municipal governments, dominated as they were by merchants and landowners, both of whom profited from the high prices caused by grain shortages, did nothing to eliminate the cause of the crisis of production. Instead, they continued to rely on old methods to solve a problem that, at least in Yucatan, was relatively new. Only after Independence would the elite embrace a new ideology that justified the importing of food on a permanent basis as a natural concomitant of the export of Yucatan's products. The basis of nineteenth-century Liberalism and neocolonialism was thus laid in the late colonial period. The days of the colonial regime were now numbered.

CHAPTER NINE

Rural Society

THE RAPID RATE OF economic growth in the late eighteenth century inevitably produced social change. To be sure, many things stayed the same. The Maya maintained their numerical superiority over all other groups, and the peasantry continued to be the largest social class. But the proportion of Indians resident on haciendas was increasing significantly, and in many regions, as we have seen, this social class was becoming more important than the independent peasantry. At the same time, the growth of the rural vecinos was significant, and in some regions this class of small farmers was becoming more important than the Maya peasantry.

The Maya in the Late Colonial Era

Settlement Patterns

In effect, the old colonial regime of a República de Indios and a República de Españoles was being replaced by a class system in which race, culture, and class were intimately related. But the concept of separate Indian and Spanish Commonwealths did not disappear all at once. Even in modern Yucatan the word "Indian" has real meaning. Nevertheless, the social changes evident by the late eighteenth century signified in one more way that the colonial regime was dying.

The colonial government never officially gave up trying to "civilize" the Maya by making them live in concentrated settlements. Even after the Governors had lost any hope of keeping all the Indians in their authorized villages, the crown continued to adhere to the goals of colonialism. Thus in 1731, and again in 1740 and 1742, the King ordered the reducción of the Maya of Yucatan. But the Governors and Bishops failed to comply with these orders, insisting that resistance was so strong among the Indians, only the massive application of force would have any effect at all in making them comply with the law. Since the local officials simply lacked the means to apply such force, laws were—as usual—reiterated and then ignored.[1]

The Maya, consequently, lived where they pleased. This reality was confronted in the late colonial era by still another Spanish official. When the cantankerous Bishop Luis de Piña y Mazo made his customary episcopal visitation in the 1780's, he found to his chagrin that, despite the law, many of the Maya of Yucatan were not settled in large, easily controlled villages but scattered all over the countryside in hamlets and unauthorized villages; they were, in the words of several priests at the time, *arranchados*, that is, settled in ranchos. Joseph Ortiz and Joseph Gerónimo Espínola, pastors respectively of Tizimín and Kikil (villages in the area north of Valladolid), were especially eloquent on this point in the reports they submitted to the Bishop at the time of his visitation. As Ortiz put it:

The royal provisions on the Indians' *reducción* are not observed as they should be; for in spite of so many royal directives on this matter, and in spite of what the Third [Mexican] Council provides for on the same point, I find introduced among my parishioners the pernicious abuse—universal in this Province—of the large part of the Indians being separated from their *doctrinas* [authorized villages] and living in the wilderness in some thickly forested places that are called Ranchos. . . . The Indians live without unity, order, or concert, deprived in places so distant of the prompt succor of the sacraments, of that which human necessity obliges one human being to give another, of the necessary and continued instruction in Christian doctrine and Evangelical Law.[2]

The Franciscan pastor of Maní, Fray Manuel Joseph de los Reyes (a brother of the notorious Enrique de los Reyes), was also insistent on this point, emphasizing the Indians' dispersion as a cause of the Church's failure to Christianize and civilize the Maya. He asked rhetorically, "And what can we say about the Indians' civility? . . . I will exaggerate very little if I say that they still have not been removed from their primordial rusticity in spite of their residence in population centers. For nothing is gained if the Indians have their water supply and houses in those places, when they spend most of the year in their ranchos [*arranchados*], on the lands of their *milpas*; hence they could more appropriately be called forest people than citizens."[3]

So in spite of centuries of royal and ecclesiastical policies, the Maya refused to be "reduced" and live as their colonial masters wanted. As already noted, geographic conditions worked to pull peasants out of their villages and scatter them over the countryside. Other factors tended to produce the same result. Many Indians desired to escape from civil and religious taxation, from the repartimiento, from forced labor, or from the prying eyes of the clergy. The very attitude of Spaniards toward the Maya also helped disperse the peasant population. As Fray de los Reyes explained it, the mistreatment and contempt displayed by the colonialists had caused the Indians "to aspire to an uncivil rustic life, to flee from the Spaniards, to be cautious about communicating with them, to be filled with fear at the mere sight of them, and even to desire to live buried where they will not have to see or hear them."[4]

Like the problem itself, the solutions suggested by the contemporaries of Piña y Mazo were not new. The most eloquent informant was again Fray de los Reyes, the pastor of Maní. Ideal as it would be to enforce the law, he argued—that is, to destroy the ranchos and force the Indians to live in the specified villages, adhering to the policy of reducción—that policy was impractical. Accordingly, all efforts ought to be directed toward preventing the founding of new ranchos. To that end, the wives and children of agriculturalists should be forbidden to move to the place where the head of the family had established a milpa, for once the family had been united there, a rancho had effectively been established, and it was difficult to reverse the process after it had been completed.[5]

Once again the problem for the civil and ecclesiastical authorities lay not with the policies but with the means of carrying them out. For to prevent the Indians from doing what they wanted would have required a stronger state apparatus than the crown was willing to contemplate. Failing that, there was no imminent solution to the problem of controlling the Maya population.

Still, it is important to emphasize once again that these descriptions of the Maya settlement pattern were made by Spaniards, whose own cultural background was such that they considered any population dispersion at all noteworthy. In fact, according to the government's own records, in 1784 more than 60 percent of the Indians lived in officially sanctioned pueblos, not in ranchos or hamlets.[6] True, this represents a decline from the 75 percent recorded in 1711, but much of the change can be imputed to the rise of the haciendas as population centers. In short, what provoked the commentaries of the colonial officials was deviation from the norm, not the norm itself.

Moreover, even when the Maya left their villages to settle elsewhere, they did not thereby abandon their civilization. In most cases they simply recreated their society and polity in new areas. This was inevitably admitted by the colonial officials themselves. For instance, Bishop Francisco Martínez de Tejada, who in 1748 had railed against the Maya tendency to leave their villages and found ranchos, ended up authorizing the construction of chapels in two new settlements in the parish of Yaxcabá because, as it was said, "therein is found the major part of the parish's strength."[7] What had begun as the uncontrolled dispersion of the population ended in the formation of what eventually became officially sanctioned villages.

One of the best examples of this process of the systematic recreation of Maya society in new areas is offered by the village of Cisteíl, the site of the rising of 1761. There is no record at all of that settlement in Spanish records until 1755. Yet when the village suddenly made its appearance during an inquest into the repartimiento, it already had a functioning Indian cabildo. The only deviation from the norm in government was the absence of a cacique, for Cisteíl was ruled by an official identified as a *teniente* (lieutenant).[8] But this was by no means rare, for many villages were ruled by lieutenants, a title suggesting dependence on a cacique residing elsewhere. It is likely that the cacique of Tixcacaltuyú had some authority over the new settlement, for when the rising began in 1761, Cisteíl was identified at first as a parcialidad of the larger and better known village. The evidence thus demonstrates that Cisteíl was not founded in a haphazard fashion. Rather, it is likely that an entire parcialidad of Tixcacaltuyú left that village and created a new settlement in a nearby area.

Cisteíl had been founded as a result of the normal process of Maya migration and colonization of new lands. Only one of the 258 Indians who received sentences for participating in the rising identified himself as a native of Cisteíl; everyone else, including every member of the cabildo, was from some other pueblo or rancho. Since some of these people had certainly come to the village not as colonists but as recruits joining the movement led by Jacinto Canek, the 258 rebels are not wholly representative of the colonization process. Nevertheless, an analysis of their origins provides some insight into the geographic mobility of the Maya in the middle of the eighteenth century. Not surprisingly, the best-represented village in the group, with 48 people, that is, 18.6 percent of the total, was Tixcacaltuyú, from which Cisteíl had apparently spun off. Next in importance were Tahdziu (south of Cisteíl) and Tiholop (just to the east), which contributed 10.5 and 8.9 percent (27 and 23 people), respectively. When Tahdzibichén and Tixméuac, villages that bordered on Cisteíl to the northeast and west, are grouped with the other three pueblos, only 45 percent—or well under half the group—came from the immediate vicinity.

What is significant, then, is the large number of Indians from more distant parts who had come to Cisteíl for one reason or another. A breakdown by partido of origin drives the point home. Beneficios Bajos, which included Cisteíl itself as well as Tixcacaltuyú, Tahdzibichén, Tzanlahcat, Yaxcabá, Homún and Xocchel, was the place of origin of 27.9 percent of the group; and Beneficios Altos, including Tahdziu and Tiholop as well as Tihosuco, Chikindzonot, Ichmul, Peto, Petulillo, Chacsinkín, Sacalaca, and Telá, contributed slightly more, 28.3 percent. In third place was the partido of La Costa, most importantly Tekantó, Mocochá, Temax, and Bokobá, with 16.3 percent. The Sierra Alta and the Sierra Baja, most importantly the villages of Maní and Mama, each accounted for 10.5 percent; Mérida's barrio of San Cristóbal for 3.5 percent; the Valladolid partido for 1.9 percent; and the Camino Real Bajo for 0.8 percent. Only one person—Jacinto Uc (Canek) himself—was from Campeche.

These data reveal that either the pull of colonization or recruitment for participation in the rebel cause brought in people from a wide area. The group from Beneficios Altos was probably largely made up of people drawn to the rising from relatively close-by settlements. Some of those from the Sierra Alta, which bordered Cisteíl on the west, were probably also recruits to the cause. But it is notable that so many of the convicted rebels came from the Costa and the Sierra Baja, both of which were becoming overpopulated by the middle of the eighteenth century. That, along with the fact that only five people came from Valladolid and none at all other than Canek from Campeche, jurisdictions that were less densely populated, suggests that a significant proportion of the Indians colonizing new lands—like the area around Cisteíl—came from the Costa, the Sierra Baja, and probably the Sierra Alta.

It is important to note that these colonists, apparently without any encouragement or interference from the Spanish authorities, had founded a replica of other Maya villages, complete with alcaldes, regidores, an alguacil, *tupiles* (deputy constables), and an *escribano* (secretary). All of these officials were originally from other villages. By the time of the uprising, a church complex and a cemetery had been constructed in the center of the settlement, and important religious posts open to the Maya, like *fiscal de doctrina* (catechism instructor), *teniente de coro* (choirmaster), *cantor* (member of the choir), and mayordomo of the cofradía, had been filled. Cisteíl's teniente was even recognized as a *don*, as was traditional in the case of the chief political official of a village. Nearby Rancho Nenelá, whose residents joined in the rising, also had a functioning Indian cabildo despite being an unauthorized settlement.[9]

The Maya population was therefore not as dispersed as one might think at first glance. Many people abandoned their home villages only to create new communities elsewhere. Relatively few people actually fled their society to live beyond the pale of civilization. Even some of the participants in the rising of 1761, instead of fleeing to the bush, chose to return to their original villages despite the certainty of capture and punishment. In 1786 both Bishop Piña y Mazo and Governor José Merino y Ceballos informed the crown that the frontier area to the south of the province's permanent villages was unpopulated.[10] This was not entirely accurate, for the region did in fact have a small number of subsistence farmers who eked out a living free from the control of Church and state—something the state government of Yucatan would discover only after Independence.[11] Nevertheless, the vast majority of the Maya of Yucatan lived in villages or on haciendas subject to civil and ecclesiastical authority. In effect, Maya "dispersion" was often merely a step toward the founding of new villages by a society in a continual state of flux. The settlement pattern, in sum, was characterized by substantial concentration as well as by dispersion.

Social Groups, Stratification, and Leveling Tendencies

The Maya continued to preserve many of the elements of their own social structure despite more than two centuries of colonialism. Many of the parcialidades mentioned in the late seventeenth or early eighteenth century were still in existence in the late colonial period. In some cases, these units still preserved their own Indian governments. For example, when the Indians of Tahdzibichén joined the rising of 1761, they did so as members of two separate parcialidades, each led by its own cacique.[12] The reducción of the sixteenth century may have succeeded in relocating some people, but it failed to eliminate their sense of identity.

Also surviving into the late colonial period was considerable social stratification. Distinctions were still made between Indios Hidalgos and commoners.[13] In fact, one of the questions to which the parish priests had to respond at the time of Piña y Mazo's episcopal visitation was whether or not the rights and privileges of the nobles were being protected and enforced in the villages. Most priests replied in the affirmative, and indeed in other contemporary documents, there are numerous cases in which the writer carefully distinguished between commoners and nobles, the latter always being called *don*. But if the Hidalgos had a higher status, they were also more heavily burdened with religious taxes than the commoners were. Maya nobles since the Conquest had been exempt from tribute, both civil and religious, but from 1699 on, they were subject to the tithe, which was considered to be a heavier financial burden than tribute. Moreover, Hidalgos had to pay higher rates for the sacraments, in practice only slightly less than what Spaniards were charged.[14]

The native nobility survived the centuries of colonialism because it was an important element of the Maya social structure. The status of Hidalgo was so significant that people were willing to pay the bribes the Spanish Governors routinely collected for the confirmation of noble titles.[15] But the native nobility also survived because the colonial authorities found the Indios Hidalgos useful. The nobles performed valuable military service for the Spaniards. They participated in the *entradas* made into the Montaña in the seventeenth century. In the eighteenth century they carried out coast-watching activities in places like Chuburná Puerto, and after 1752 every able-bodied male Hidalgo was required to have a firearm and be ready to serve His Majesty at a moment's notice. This requirement was maintained even after the rising of 1761, and the Hidalgo companies continued to exist at least until the 1790's.[16] (Those companies even gave their name to a part of the capital: the plaza in Mérida that served as their mustering point is still known as the Plaza Hidalgo.)

It is impossible to determine how large a class the nobles were. Two extant *padrones* are most illustrative because they caution against hasty generalization: in Tekuch (nine km east of Valladolid) Hidalgos accounted for only 3.8 percent of the Indian population; but in Temozón (12 km north of the city) the percentage was 27.4. Just which of these two figures is closer to the average is a matter of speculation. The official inspectors sent to Yucatan at the time of the general visitation of José de Gálvez reported that the number of Indios Hidalgos was very high relative to the commoner population. Impressionistic assessments by other contemporaries suggest that in general 10 percent or so of the Indians were nobles.[17]

In addition, as we have seen, a new elite had grown up around the holding of cabildo and cofradía offices and the ownership of property. By now, in fact, landed property, as well as the accumulation of personal possessions and of capital goods like horses and mules, had created considerable economic inequality among the Maya. Consequently, despite the natural leveling tendency that accompanied Spanish colonialism, important class differences still survived among the Maya well into the nineteenth century.[18]

On the other hand, the position of both the old and the new elite had unquestionably declined to a considerable extent by the late colonial period. The destruction of many of the Indian cofradías by the Church, the Bourbon government's looting of the funds of the Indian *cajas de comunidad,* and the natural leveling process inherent in Spanish colonialism all contributed to the destruction of the positions traditionally exercised by the Maya elite. The bases of social stratification, in short, were being undermined.[19] The process was a slow one and was still under way at Independence. As late as the 1840's, the Hidalgos were included in the tax lists with the vecinos, for any attempt to "include or mix them with the Indians" was thought to be a potential cause of unrest.[20] Nevertheless, by the late eighteenth century the status of the Maya elite was clearly even worse than it had been in the mid-colonial period. Colonialism inevitably erodes the society of the colonized.

The base of the Maya social structure continued to be the peasants. These were the people whose tribute and taxes were the major source of revenue for both Church and state, and whose labor was a vital element in the production of the goods and services consumed by the colonialists. Though religious taxation was still not completely regularized, with two or more tribute schedules in use,[21] at the time of the Piña y Mazo episcopal visitation of 1782–87, most parishes were using the schedule introduced in the 1750's by Bishop Ignacio Padilla Estrada: 12.5 reales a year for adult males, with nine usually paid in silver and the rest in maize and beans, and nine reales a year for adult females, with 5.5 usually paid in silver and the rest in kind (a fowl and a quantity of woven cotton). Children gave the local priest an egg every Thursday, although this exaction was said to be customary and was not included in the tribute schedule. As before, Indians had to tithe for the "products of Castile," that is, for nonindigenous animals like chickens, cattle, and pigs.

Even though the commoners got off easier in this respect than the Hidalgos, who had to tithe on all their income, these religious taxes were far more of a burden on a family than civil or encomienda tribute, which was levied only on adult males. Tribute cost a married couple only 14 reales a year (one peso, six reales), compared with a religious tax of 21.5 reales (two pesos, 5.5 reales), plus the value of whatever they may have tithed. When marriage and baptism fees (10 and three reales, respectively) are added in, it is clear that the Maya paid dearly for the benefits of Christianity.

But as we have seen, this all-important prop of the colonial regime—the independent peasantry—was being whittled away by the rise of two new classes, namely, the rural vecinos (farmers) and the dependents of haciendas. In many areas, especially in the northwestern part of the peninsula, the free peasants were by now outnumbered by the people who rented land from hacendados, and in some places, they were even outnumbered by the vecinos. This displacement of the independent peasantry, which was one of the most significant changes taking place in the late colonial period, was to be temporarily reversed after 1847 by the Caste War. Once resumed, the process then continued unabated until the Revolution.

This process in fact helped to undermine the colonial regime. The Church, one of the traditional supports of colonialism, was based to a great extent on the independent peasantry. Parish priests depended almost entirely on the religious taxes paid by this class, and consequently the declining importance of the free peasants meant a crisis of major proportions for one important branch of the ecclesiastical establishment. True enough, the Cathedral Chapter prospered during these years because it received its income from tithe revenues, which were on the rise. But the good fortune of the handful of chapter members—most of whom were Castilian-born rather than creole—was more than offset by the declining economic base of the curates and their assistants. In short, still another branch of the colonial regime was withering away. This process made it easier for liberal reform, in the post-Independence era, to deliver the coup de grace to the social and political power of the Church.

Non-Indian Society

By the late eighteenth century the colonial estate system of Indian and Spanish Commonwealths was no longer a close approximation of reality. According to the census of 1779, mestizos, pardos, and *negros* made up 10.7, 8.1, and 0.7 percent, respectively, of the adult population, for a combined total of almost 20 percent; people classified as Spaniards accounted for only 7.7 percent.[22] By 1791 the proportion of non-Indians was slightly higher on the whole, and substantially so in the case of mulattoes and *negros*, whose combined share now stood at 12.4 percent.[23] The racial structure and geographical distribution of the population in 1779 is shown in Tables 9.1 and 9.2.[24]

What is perhaps most surprising about these statistics is the large number of people who were partly or wholly of African descent; their population share was now larger than the Spaniards'. In earlier times, free blacks and pardos had tended to be concentrated in the cities. In Mérida the area around the Church of Jesus (one block north of the *plaza mayor*) was populated to a great extent by pardos, and in 1722 Bishop Gómez de Parada instituted reforms that provided the people of that parish with a special schedule of religious taxes, lower than those for whites but higher than those for the Indians. This was thought to be appropriate for a parish "in which the sacraments are administered to blacks, mulattoes, *chinos* of both sexes, and the Indian and mestizo women married to them."[25]

By the late colonial period there were substantial pardo communities in the villages as well. At the time of Piña y Mazo's episcopal visitation (1782–87), for example, pardos accounted for a fair share of the baptisms, marriages, and burials in the parishes of Tixkokob and Campeche Extramuros (see Table 9.3).

By and large, outside the provincial capital, people of African descent tended to settle down in the western part of the peninsula. To be sure, Mérida continued to be a favored location. In 1794 the city and its barrios, plus six nearby villages, had a total mulatto population of 3,416 or 12.3 percent of the area's total population. In addition, many of the 6,250 people classified as "otras castas" in that year's census were undoubtedly part African.[26] But according to the same census, pardo militia companies, each with 85 fully armed men, were to be found in Izamal, Muna, Hunucmá, Maxcanú, Calkiní, Tenabo, Seyba Playa, and Pocyaxum.[27] Of these, all but Izamal are in the western half of the peninsula, especially in what is now the Mexican state of Campeche. Indeed, Campeche alone contained almost three-quarters of all the *negros* and over one-quarter of all the people of African descent, compared with 15.4 and 10.5 percent, respectively, for Mérida (Table 9.2). Also noteworthy is the large proportion of *pardos* in Sahcabchén and Hunucmá, as indicated in Table 9.1. To be sure, people of African descent were to be found in significant numbers in central and eastern Yucatan, especially in the large Sierra towns, in Izamal, in Sotuta, and in Tizimín. Nevertheless, the vast majority lived in the west.

What accounts for this settlement pattern? First of all, it seems clearly related to maritime activities and commercial contact with the Caribbean

TABLE 9.1

Racial Structure of the Population of Yucatan by Political District, 1779

District	Total population	Spaniards No.	Pct.	Pardos No.	Pct.	Negros No.	Pct.	Mestizos No.	Pct.	Indians No.	Pct.
Sahcabchén	5,152	295	5.7%	874	17.0%	11	0.2%	735	14.3%	3,237	62.8%
Campeche	23,479	5,211	22.2	4,033	17.2	1,101	4.7	3,070	13.1	10,064	42.9
Camino Real (Alto)	20,274	851	4.2	951	4.7	12	0.1	809	4.0	17,651	87.1
Hunucmá (Camino Real Bajo)	20,899	211	1.0	2,184	10.5	3	–	1,785	8.5	16,716	80.0
Mérida	15,821	3,311	20.9	1,774	11.2	230	1.5	4,351	27.5	6,155	38.9
Sierra	44,583	1,590	3.6	2,117	4.7	6	–	4,855	10.9	36,015	80.8
Dzidzantún (Costa)	21,876	2,404	11.0	1,356	6.2	32	0.1	3,327	15.3	14,667	67.3
Sotuta (Beneficios Bajos)	28,063	855	3.0	1,527	5.4	6	–	1,584	5.6	24,091	85.8
Tihosuco (Beneficios Altos)	11,198	205	1.8	344	3.1	6	0.1	697	6.2	9,946	88.8
Valladolid	11,332	1,008	8.9	694	6.1	14	0.1	1,066	9.4	8,550	75.5
Tizimín	11,771	459	3.9	1,534	13.0	14	0.1	900	7.6	8,864	75.3
Bacalar	4,025	432	10.7	208	5.2	55	1.4	292	7.3	3,038	75.5

SOURCE: AGI, México 3061, Superior Gobierno, Año de 1785, no. 1, Testimonio del Expediente que trata sobre poner en la Villa de Cordova una fábrica de Chinguirito para proveer el Estanco de Yucatan, fol. 16.

NOTE: The census of 1779 uses political rather than ecclesiastical districts, and thus the names used here and in Table 9.2 differ from those used in previous tables. But in fact there was a perfect correspondence between the partidos of Hunucmá and the Camino Real Bajo, between Dzidzantún and La Costa, between Sotuta and Beneficios Bajos, and between Tihosuco and Beneficios Altos. The two differences are (1) the Sierra Baja and the Sierra Alta, which were ecclesiastically separate, composed one political district; and (2) the villages of what would later become the partido of Bolonchencauich were divided in 1779 among the districts of Sahcabchén, Campeche, and the Camino Real, but it is not clear how.

TABLE 9.2
Distribution of Racial Groups by Political District, 1779
(Percent)

District	Spaniards	Pardos	Negros[a]		Mestizos	Indians
Sahcabchén	1.8%	5.0%	0.7%	[4.6]	3.1%	2.0%
Campeche	31.0	22.9	73.9	[26.9]	13.1	6.3
Camino Real	5.1	5.4	0.8	[5.0]	3.4	11.1
Hunucmá	1.3	12.4	0.2	[11.5]	7.6	10.5
Mérida	19.7	10.1	15.4	[10.5]	18.5	3.9
Sierra	9.4	12.0	0.4	[11.1]	20.7	22.7
Dzidzantún	14.3	7.7	2.1	[7.3]	14.2	9.2
Sotuta	5.1	8.7	0.4	[8.0]	6.7	15.2
Tihosuco	1.2	2.0	0.4	[1.8]	3.0	6.3
Valladolid	6.0	3.9	0.9	[3.7]	4.5	5.4
Tizimín	2.7	8.7	0.9	[8.1]	3.8	5.6
Bacalar	2.6	1.2	3.7	[1.4]	1.2	1.9

SOURCE: Same as for Table 9.1.
[a]Figures in brackets combine the pardo and negro populations.

TABLE 9.3
Racial Structure of Tixkokob and Campeche Extramuros Parishes
as Indicated by Church Rites, 1769–87

				Campeche Extramuros, 1781–87			
	Tixkokob, 1769–85			Cabecera San Francisco and Santa Lucía	Lerma and Sambula	Hampolol	San Diego and Cholul
Rite	Cabecera	Ekmul	Euan				
Baptism							
Spaniards	25.0%	0.0%	0.0%	0.0%	3.8%	14.4%	4.4%
Pardos	1.2	3.7	0.0	0.0	5.5	13.5	0.0
Indians	75.8	96.3	100.0	100.0	90.7	72.1	95.6
Marriages							
Spaniards	20.3	0.0	0.0	3.7	7.4	13.8	7.9
Pardos	6.5	6.0	0.0	4.3	5.9	12.6	5.3
Indians	75.2	94.0	100.0	92.0	86.7	75.6	86.8
Burials							
Spaniards	27.2	0.0	0.0	0.0	4.9	12.7	7.4
Pardos	7.9	6.7	0.0	0.0	4.9	11.5	6.4
Indians	62.9	93.3	100.0	100.0	90.2	75.8	86.2

SOURCE: AME, Visitas Pastorales, Tixkokob, 24 Feb. 1785, San Francisco de Campeche (Extramuros), 1787.

and the Gulf of Mexico. Practically all the province's commerce passed through the ports of Campeche and Sisal, which came to be tied, especially in the late colonial era, to several Caribbean ports inhabited mostly by people of African descent; Campeche was the region in which commercial agriculture on haciendas was most developed in the eighteenth century; and significant numbers of Africans, both slave and free, worked in the shipyards that began operating in Campeche in the seventeenth century. The relatively small Maya population of the Campeche region may also have figured in, for there would have been plenty of land for newcomers to colonize.

The pardos in rural Yucatan were part of that larger society of non-Indians known as vecinos. It was a substantial society. By the 1780's some vecino communities were of town size. We have had some inkling of the numerical importance of non-Indians outside the Spanish cities in Table 9.3. Similar data are available for Izamal and Cacalchén.[28] In Izamal, vecinos accounted for 38.7 percent of the baptisms performed in the parish between 1769 and 1784, and for 39.3 percent of the marriages; and in Cacalchén they accounted for 17.1 percent of baptisms and 23.2 percent of marriages. The proportion of vecinos in the visitas was usually much less than in the chief villages of the parishes. Detailed information about the vecino population of Yucatan, drawn from several sources, is summarized in Appendix B.

Several important patterns are evident in Tables 9.1 and 9.2 and in the Appendix B data. First, the non-Indian population was not scattered haphazardly throughout the peninsula. Rather, it tended to congregate in particular regions and kinds of settlements. The truly large communities—Hunucmá, Maxcanú, Oxkutzcab, Ticul, Tekax, and Muna—are all located in the western half of the peninsula, either in the Sierra or along major roads connecting Mérida to the sea. Economic opportunity clearly played a crucial role in attracting so many non-Indians to these places.

The only exception to this settlement pattern was Izamal (63 km east of Mérida), the site of what was probably the largest non-Indian rural community in Yucatan at the time.[29] Economics played a role here as well. The village was located on a major line of communications; market goods passed along the main road from Valladolid and along the secondary roads from Beneficios Altos and Beneficios Bajos on their way to Mérida, Sisal, and Campeche. In addition, Izamal was well located for provisioning the capital with maize and cattle. In fact, the parish contained no fewer than 49 estates—an extraordinarily large number. Finally, the village's development was stimulated by the series of fairs held there annually in honor of the Blessed Virgin, the most important of which took place in December. Thousands of people, mostly Indians, attended the Izamal fairs, and must have given commercially minded people plenty of opportunities to make profits (as the presence of royal notaries from Mérida attests). All these factors contributed to the development in Izamal of what was becoming a regional creole elite distinct from that of Mérida, Campeche, and Valladolid.

The non-Indian communities of secondary importance, those of between 200 and 400 heads of families, generally conform to this same pattern. Like the larger settlements, they were to be found either in the Sierra (Maní), or along the Camino Real between Mérida and the sea (Umán and Calkiní). The sole exception was Champotón, a coastal town 65 kilometers south of Campeche. But again commerce was a crucial factor in determining the settlement pattern, for Champotón's hinterland was becoming a major producer of rice and sugar in the late colonial period, and the village itself had maritime communications with Campeche to the north and with Carmen and Palizada to the south.

The situation is less clear-cut for the many small vecino communities comprising 100–200 heads of families. These were to be found in almost all parts of the peninsula: in the Campeche region (Seyba Playa, Tenabo, and Hool), along the Camino Real (Samahil, Kopomá, and Opichén), east of the Sierra in the thick of Indian territory (Sotuta and Ichmul), north of the large Sierra towns (Teabo and Tekit), and in the thinly populated region north and northwest of Valladolid (Tizimín, Sucilá, and Espita). The factors that brought all these communities into existence were as varied as their locations. Again, some of them were well located for trade with Mérida and Campeche. Tizimín, Sucilá, and Espita, in the heart of the cotton-producing region, owed their existence to the demand for raw cotton. Since the Maya population in this part of the province was quite small, Tizimín was one of the regions where many villages had more vecinos than Indians. And since small producers could successfully compete with the owners of haciendas in the cotton economy, its agrarian structure was characterized by the predominance of small farmers, who were more important economically than either Spanish hacendados or Maya peasants. Or more important, at least, until the abolition of the repartimiento system in 1782 sharply reduced the demand for raw cotton and led to the collapse of their economic base. However minuscule their numbers—in 1787 Tizimín and Espita had only 156 non-Indian family heads, and Sucilá only 157—they represent an almost forgotten class of small farmers in colonial Yucatan.

Another discernible pattern is the tendency for non-Indians to congregate in the cabeceras and in most cases to be totally absent from one or more of the visitas (see Appendix B). In the parishes where the populations of both classes of villages are known, over 70 percent of the non-Indians lived in cabeceras. The partido with the highest percentage was the Camino Real Alto, with 86.2; Campeche had the lowest, 26.3. Since the rate in all the other partidos was between 63.8 percent (Tizimín) and 82.0 percent (the Sierra), it is clear that Campeche was widely divergent in this regard. In fact, if it is left out of the computation, the overall figure on non-Indians residing in the cabeceras rises to 76.9 percent.

Campeche diverged from the general pattern primarily because it was an area of heavy concentration of small farmers. In many of the other non-Indian communities, a large number of the vecinos were engaged in commerce, much of which was probably carried out with, or at the expense of, the Indians. But in Campeche the local Maya population was small: only 8.3 percent of the province's Indians lived in the districts of Campeche and Sahcabchén in 1779, and they made up only 46.5 percent of the population (see Tables 9.1 and 9.2). The area of the modern state of Campeche (districts of Campeche, Sahcabchén, and the Camino Real) contained only 19.4 percent of the province's Indians. Opportunities to do business with the native people were therefore limited. In any case, most of the vecinos here worked the soil themselves and so had good reason to live closer to their land, which is to say outside the cabeceras. In sum, the nature of the soil, which permitted production of a wider variety of crops than elsewhere, combined with the small size of the native population and the availability of land, helped produce a distinct settlement pattern for the non-Indian population of Campeche.

Several important regions, including most notably the partidos of Sotuta (Beneficios Bajos) and Tihosuco (Beneficios Altos), had very small populations of vecinos. Opportunities for commercial agriculture were limited in these areas, located well away from urban markets. Moreover, since large parts of these districts were densely populated with Indians, it was more difficult to acquire land than in thinly populated regions like Campeche. This was a factor of great importance, for even in the area east, west, and south of the villa of Valladolid, also densely populated by Indian peasants, vecinos were unable to take advantage of the inviting city market. The Maya of this region defended their land with great tenacity well into the nineteenth century.[30] In short, vecino settlement patterns were directly related to the nature of Maya society in Yucatan.

The non-Indian communities were supported by a varied economic base. Trade conducted by small merchants had always attracted people to live outside the cities. But the great development of the vecino communities in the eighteenth century was based even more importantly on commercial agriculture. Tithe records provide some insight into the distribution of the benefits of production, since the ability to pay religious taxes was directly related to the ownership of property and control of labor. Table 9.4 shows the regional variations in median and average payments for several years. Let me emphasize again that tithe records cannot be used to compare data from different years because the value of payments in kind changed from one year to the next. In many of the villages shown in Table 9.4, for example, the payments made in 1778 were worth twice as much as those made in 1777 because a bad harvest had driven prices up. The only safe comparisons, consequently, are those made for different places in the same year.

With this caveat in mind, it can be concluded from Table 9.4 that the

TABLE 9.4
Regional Variations in Tithe Payments, 1777–95

Partido and village	Number of tithers	Payment in reales		Average payment	
		Median	Average	Highest decile	Lowest decile
1777					
Sahcabchén					
Champotón	69	14.0	21.6	89.8	3.1
Sahcabchén	32	16.0	26.8	94.9	3.7
Chicbul	8	11.3	12.2	24.0	1.5
Campeche, Pich					
and Tixmucuy	33	16.3	33.4	184.6	0.8
Camino Real Bajo,					
Maxcanú	110	13.4	24.6	124.7	2.5
Beneficios Bajos					
Hoctún and					
visitas	50	6.5	11.7	39.9	1.5
Hocabá and					
visitas	59	4.0	6.8	24.2	1.3
Homún and					
visitas	28	4.0	6.1	18.1	1.3
Sotuta and					
visitas	101	8.0	15.1	66.8	2.2
Beneficios Altos					
Peto	70	10.4	18.2	84.8	2.2
Tahdziu	18	4.8	9.7	34.0	2.1
Tihosuco	18	10.0	15.5	48.8	1.8
Chunhuhub	8	5.0	6.3	15.5	2.0
1778					
Campeche					
Pocyaxum	43	8.0	10.8	32.2	3.0
Hampolol	61	8.7	12.8	37.6	1.9
Camino Real Alto,					
Hecelchakán	17	21.5	36.1	146.0	7.0
Sierra Alta, Dzan	20	4.5	5.5	13.8	1.1
1787					
Valladolid					
Valladolid	54[a]	7.0	35.1	216.3	1.3
Sisal	11[a]	3.0	8.6	32.0	2.0
Chemax	15[a]	4.0	4.1	6.8	1.3
Tizimín					
Tizimín	57[a]	5.5	13.7	68.9	1.5
Espita	46[a]	7.0	19.9	107.0	2.0
1790					
Costa					
Mocochá	27	4.0	6.8	26.5	1.0
Izamal	83	12.0	19.4	81.0	1.5
Sitilpech	36	14.0	26.5	103.8	2.1
Pixilá	63	14.0	24.1	92.4	3.1
Sudzal	21	11.0	15.4	53.5	6.0
Xanabá	10	15.0	20.6	54.0	5.0
Kantunil	12	10.0	14.0	62.0	3.3
1795					
Beneficios Bajos,					
Tixcacaltuyú and					
Tahdzibichén	43	6.0	9.6	45.7	2.5

SOURCES: BCAA, Manuscripts, Diezmos, 1777–87, Special Collection, libros 19, Diezmos de los curatos de Acanceh, Mérida, Tekax e Izamal, 1791–94, and 20, Diezmos de Tixcacaltuyú, 1795–98.
[a]Includes hacendados as well as vecinos.

vecino communities were by no means all alike. In some regions they were much better off economically than in others. Consider the figures for 1777. Judging by the median payments, the vecinos in the Campeche region (partidos of Campeche and Sahcabchén) and the adjoining area to the northeast (the village of Maxcanú, in Hunucmá, formerly the ecclesiastical partido of Camino Real Bajo) were the most prosperous, those of Beneficios Bajos (Sotuta district), especially the area around Hoctún, Hocabá, and Homún the least, and those of Beneficios Altos (Tihosuco district) somewhere in between. These trends were undoubtedly the result, first, of the greater availability of land in Campeche and, second, of limited agricultural possibilities in Beneficios Bajos.

On the other hand, the wealthier regions in 1777 seem to have been characterized by greater extremes of wealth and poverty. True, all regions contained poor people, as is revealed by the very low average payments made by the poorest decile of the tithe-paying population, but the gap between the poor and the "rich"—the difference between the average payments of the poorest and richest deciles, as well as the difference between the median and the wealthy payments—was far less marked in Beneficios Bajos than in the Campeche region. In other words, the wealth of the western regions was not shared by all, whereas poverty was rather equally distributed in Beneficios Bajos. Still, given the median and the average payments of the lowest decile in the west, the poor there (with the exception of the area around Pich) were probably somewhat better off than their Beneficios Bajos counterparts. The poor were also probably better off in some parts of Beneficios Altos.

The figures for 1778 are scanty, and in any case the year's higher prices make comparisons risky. Nevertheless, the data once again suggest that Campeche was the most important region of commercial agriculture in the province. Moreover, agricultural production by vecinos was important not just in the area around the city of Campeche and in Sahcabchén but also in the settlements along the Camino Real leading to Mérida.

For 1787, information is available only for the Valladolid and Tizimín regions. Moreover, the data demonstrate just how difficult it is to distinguish between wealthy vecinos and middling hacendados. Usually the distinction, however misleading, was made in the records themselves. But in this case all tithe-payers were lumped together with no property ownership stated. For this reason, as one would expect, Valladolid demonstrates extreme inequalities of wealth. By contrast, the village of Chemax, to the northeast of the villa, had possibly the most equitable distribution of wealth in the province; everyone was poor. It is also notable that even with the inclusion of hacendados in the records, the extremes of wealth and poverty were not nearly so marked in Tizimín and Espita as they were in Valladolid. To be sure, these two villages unquestionably had their share of poor people. But the gap between the average and the median payments, and even that between the median and the average payment of the highest decile, was far narrower than in Valladolid. The farming society of Tizimín and Espita was characterized by social stratification but not by mass poverty.

The figures for 1790 are derived exclusively from the partido of La Costa (Dzidzantún district). The Mocochá picture is especially interesting. As we saw in Chapter Seven, the Indians of that village owned considerable quantities of livestock and were undoubtedly quite prosperous by Indian standards. The village vecinos, it seems, did not share in that prosperity. The rest of the data from 1790 are derived from the parish of Izamal, which had one of the largest vecino communities in the province. The cabecera showed extremes of wealth and poverty, as did Sitilpech, which seems to have had one of the wealthiest vecino communities in Yucatan. Much more equality was evident in Kantunil, and especially in Sudzal and Xanabá. But on the basis of this admittedly sketchy data, it appears that the poorest one-tenth of the population of Sudzal and Xanabá, and to a lesser extent the poorest in Kantunil, were among the better off of the province's poor vecinos.

Finally, the figures from 1795 demonstrate the dangers of comparing data from different years. At first glance one might conclude that the villages of Beneficios Bajos were becoming more prosperous because the average payment of the poorest decile was higher than in 1777. But 1795 was a year of poor harvests, and the figures reflect a rise in prices. Moreover, the vecinos were almost certainly worse off in 1795 because their own crops would have been diminished. Many farmers undoubtedly could not pay their tithes at all. Total tithe revenues might not have decreased because of the increased value of what was paid, but the economic condition of the farmers as a whole might well have deteriorated in a way not reflected in tithe records.

It is unfortunate that so little is known about the farming class in late colonial Yucatan. What few passing comments we have from priests and government officials tend to be filled with the characteristic European contempt for these mostly racially mixed people. Piña y Mazo ended up harping on one of the themes that had struck Bishop Gómez de Parada earlier in the century: the vecinos' preference for the Mayan language. Although Spanish seems to have been in general use in the largest non-Indian communities, in some of the smaller ones the non-Indians spoke only Maya. This was especially true in the eastern and southeastern parts of the peninsula, although all over, even in Mérida, Spaniards and other non-Indians reportedly could communicate in Maya and usually did so when conversing with the Indians. As Pedro de Alarcón, the curate of Espita (a village with a high percentage of non-Indians) explained, "The

Spaniards who live among the Indians, even though they be Europeans and outsiders, apply themselves to this Mayan language, and they speak it not only with the Indians but also among their domestic servants and their own children, giving as an excuse that it is an easier and more flexible language to use."[31]

Despite these fears of the total Mayanization of the non-Indians, in the long run the vecinos, even in the most rural areas, came to represent the spread of Hispanic culture in Yucatan. Perhaps this was due in part to their continued contact, commercial and otherwise, with the cities. Moreover, relations between the rural vecinos and the urban centers of Spanish society were not carried out through institutionalized intermediaries like caciques and the Tribunal de Indios, as in the case of the Maya. This might have encouraged the rural non-Indians to maintain cultural affiliation with the Spanish world. By the late eighteenth century, Izamal, one of the largest vecino communities, possessed a resident royal notary—a clear sign of the perceived need to maintain Spanish cultural norms. Early in the next century, notaries were to be found in many of the other non-Indian communities as well. Since Indian cabildos had formerly conducted notarial affairs, this meant the replacement of the Maya cabildos as agents for the conducting of official business.

In the era of Independence, local political elites would take the next logical step: the replacement of the Maya cabildos by village councils open to vecinos. The new bodies would be called *ayuntamientos*, in order to distinguish them from the previous municipal institutions.[32] Shortly after Independence the largest of the villages would be given the official status of cities.

In other words, the emergence of the vecino communities meant the further advance of Hispanic civilization and the concomitant retreat of the Maya. For example, in Izamal and Tizimín—two of the most important non-Indian communities of Yucatan—the parish priests reported in the 1780's that the village Indians understood Castilian, although they had an aversion to speaking it.[33] In many ways this social, economic, political, and cultural advance of the non-Indians was just as important as the establishment of Spanish-owned landed estates. Both processes were undermining the colonial regime and preparing the way for neocolonialism.

From the point of view of the Latin Americanist, what is significant about the class of rural vecinos in Yucatan is its very existence. The historiography has tended to work with the *a priori* assumption that the agrarian structure was composed of a landed elite and a mass of either Indian peasants or African slaves, with the further implication that such rigidly stratified societies were less conducive to the development of democracy and modern capitalism than the small-farming societies of English North America. In fact, however, it is now clear that all over Latin

America rural society was made up of several strata that could be called classes, and among them was a class of small farmers distinct from both the landed elites and the Indian peasants or African slaves. The historical problem, then, is not to account for the absence of a rural middle class, but to explain why this class, after growing considerably in the late colonial era, failed to expand and become predominant in the nineteenth century, and why the small farmers fared so poorly vis-à-vis the great bourgeoisie in the age of export-led agricultural growth.

Conclusion

Yucatan's history is unique because the specific combination of ecological, socioeconomic, and cultural factors present there are found nowhere else. But the same could be said of every society. All are shaped by unique ecological and human forces, and therefore scholars must try to do more than merely demonstrate how generalizations about Latin America as a whole do not apply to a specific case (or as Steve Stern has said of the historiography, to prove that a general model "does not apply to the case of sarsaparilla exports from Santa Rosa de la Frontera de la Oscuridad").[1] Historians must also formulate hypotheses that incorporate the varieties of unique experiences into a common framework of historical interpretation.

This is especially important now that our knowledge of colonial Latin America is no longer restricted to the few so-called "core" (mining and urban) areas. Indeed, we now know enough about the "peripheral" areas to conclude that many of them were not peripheral at all. They frequently contained large populations, and were vital and integral parts of an imperial and international system of trade and division of labor.

The history of Yucatan and of other regions demonstrates the inadequacy of one of the most time-honored of theses, namely, that colonial Latin America can be understood as a manifestation of an American variety of feudalism. The idea of a feudal Latin America has impeccable Marxist origins. After all, it was advanced by Marx himself and accepted by dedicated followers like José Carlos Mariátegui.[2] It was also used by at least one left-wing regime to justify large-scale land reform as part of a program of economic modernization.[3] This Marxist interpretation was then taken up by capitalists and became the intellectual basis of the developmental schemes of the 1950's and 1960's. The reason for this seeming paradox is clear: if Latin America has feudal structures, then capitalism is progressive.[4] Though the idea of a feudal Latin America subsequently came under attack by adherents of the dependency school, feudalism made a theoretical recovery in the 1970's as the result of new formulations of the concept.[5]

The idea that feudalism characterized Latin American history is therefore by no means dead. It continues to be important in European historiography.[6] Moreover, there are not a few scholars and intellectuals in Latin America whose profession to Marxism binds them to this interpretation and to the use of other typical phrases like modes of production and class struggle.

In my own view, it is time to bury the feudal interpretation of Latin American history once and for all. It is based on the assumption that the fundamental characteristic of feudalism was the landed estate worked by a dependent peasantry.[7] To be sure, some Latin Americanists who favor this interpretation would broaden their definition to include more than just the landed-estate-cum-unfree-peasantry as the essential element.[8] Nevertheless, the feudal hacienda is still central to the argument, and is that argument's Achilles' heel. In fact, in colonial Latin America the rural population was for the most part a free peasantry. This was not true everywhere, of course, for a serflike system of labor was found in practically every region of Latin America, and in some areas the unfree workers greatly outnumbered the free. Nevertheless, in the most advanced regions—Mexico and Peru—as well as in supposedly backward areas like Yucatan and Central America, a free peasantry predominated, and even on the haciendas some of the workers were free wage laborers. The most important form of unfree labor was found in the plantation system, which can hardly be classified as feudal.

If the feudal interpretation greatly overestimates the importance of landed estates worked by serflike laborers, it at the same time underestimates or misinterprets the importance of commercial activity in these enterprises. *All* landed estates, whether highland haciendas, lowland plantations, or Yucatecan estancias, came into existence for the purpose of producing for markets, and none succeeded in becoming, or even pretended to become, self-sufficient. They were part of an economic system that was both commercialized and monetized. Even the free peasantry was brought into the commercial economy either voluntarily, through local or regional markets (which in the case of Mesoamerica antedated the colonial regime), or involuntarily, through the commercial repartimiento. Most marketing systems were of course regional in nature and somewhat independent of each other, but their reach into the countryside was considerable and resulted in the incorporation of a large hinterland into marketing activities. Moreover, there also existed, albeit on a limited scale, a "national" (i.e., multi- and interregional) market, which was integrated through trade not only in imported luxury goods but also in livestock, wheat and wheat flour, cacao, wax, salt, rice, sugar, spices, cane alcohol, and American- and Asian-made textiles.[9] "Natural" economies existed only in frontier areas.[10] In short, colonial Latin America was anything but feudal in the generally accepted sense of the term.

But if colonial Latin America cannot be considered feudal, does that mean that it was capitalist? To judge by the vocabulary of many postwar U.S. studies,[11] it would seem that the theory of a capitalist colonial Latin America is about to triumph—once again. It is at least a more defensible theory than feudalism: land, though subject to a variety of restrictions, was in fact bought and sold, and landed estates in particular changed hands with considerable frequency; property was purchased for the purpose of producing goods for sale on the market; capital was borrowed and invested to expand production; producers used a variety of economically rational means to maximize profits; and goods were produced and sold through a largely monetized marketing system that integrated the regional, "national," and international economies.

Such an interpretation is typically popular in the United States, where the intellectual tradition is anti-Marxist and dominated by functionalism, neoclassical economics, and empiricism. But before this line of thought is allowed to triumph, some accommodation must be made to the fact that colonial Latin America had many characteristics that do not accord well with capitalism.[12] Much capital that was accumulated was in fact wasted because of an ideology concerned with salvation. Merchants, in true medieval fashion, tried to create scarcities with a view to making a large profit on each transaction and ignored the promise of the money to be made in a large volume of transactions. Despite the presence of free wage labor in some sectors of the economy and in some regions, most people did not voluntarily sell their labor for wages, either because as free peasants they chose not to participate or because as slaves or peons they were unfree. And finally, most scholars who argue for a capitalist colonial economy erroneously equate capitalism with money and markets.

True, some historians attempt to get around the problem by resorting to the well-worn concept of "commercial capitalism" to account for a market-oriented mode of production based on something other than wage labor.[13] But this ignores the fact that commercial capitalism so defined was found in practically all ancient civilizations: money, markets, merchant classes, and "commercial capitalism" have existed almost since the rise of civilization and are not by themselves sufficient criteria for classifying an economy as capitalist.

In any case, what is clear is the following: despite the presence of "capitalistic" economic characteristics, the Latin American social structure was not consistent with what is normally thought of as capitalist society. In short, while the colonial *economy* may have had elements of capitalism, colonial *society* did not; or at least it had very few.

Since colonial Latin America is hard to classify as feudal or capitalist, some scholars have contended that several modes of production were present at the same time. These were feudalism (especially noteworthy in the system of landed estates), capitalism (evident in mining and to a lesser extent in the *obrajes*), and the tributary or "Asiatic" mode of production (the tribute-paying free peasantry).[14] One scholar has gone so far as to argue that all three operated side by side in central Mexico even *before* the Spanish Conquest.[15] (Perhaps we should call this the tutti frutti mode of production.) But such a formulation would make sense only if one mode eventually emerged as predominant. Otherwise, one can speak meaningfully only of different sectors of a socioeconomic formation, not of one or more modes of production, which by definition must be predominant within the socioeconomic structure or else are not modes of production.[16]

In reality, of course, no single sector emerged as predominant in colonial Latin America. The so-called Asiatic or tributary mode survived not only the sixteenth century but the three succeeding centuries as well; the free peasantry was not really destroyed until liberal regimes deprived the villages of their lands in the late nineteenth and early twentieth centuries. Latin American "feudalism"—landed estates worked by unfree labor—far from disappearing in the colonial era, spread in the nineteenth century and lasted well into the twentieth. And colonial "capitalism," rather than triumphing, all but died after Independence. The capitalism that eventually triumphed did not grow out of the colonial "capitalist" sector of silver mining and *obrajes* but emerged *de novo* out of agriculture and manufacturing; it became truly dominant, therefore, only in the twentieth century.

The problem, then, is that the mode of production of colonial Latin America was neither feudal nor capitalist. Moreover, efforts to interpret the socioeconomic formation as a three-in-one mode are the theoretical equivalent of the Holy Trinity—resistant to rational analysis. What is the theoretical solution? Stern has recommended that historians "return to the drawing board" in a search for appropriate analytical categories. He has even suggested that scholars seriously consider "a theory of colonial modes of production."[17] But *which* "colonial" socioeconomic formation should be used? After all, colonialism existed not only in Latin America but also in Asia and Africa, and even in Ireland. This would mean, then, not two or three but hundreds of "colonial modes of production."

Therefore, instead of going back to the drawing board, perhaps we should go back to the graveyard and bury all typologies of modes of production alongside the theories of Latin American feudalism and colonial capitalism. A careful analysis of European history reveals that at no time since the emergence of civilization did a single predominant mode of production exist. Europe was always characterized by a variety of socioeconomic formations, and therefore it is arbitrary to define any one of them as *the* mode of production. The solution is surely not to identify each individual socioeconomic formation and define each one as a type of mode of production. For why should the list stop with Europe? In fact the world as a whole must have contained thousands of socioeconomic formations throughout history. Categorizing them all ad infinitum is nothing but cataloguing ad absurdum.

In the end, the search for a truly dominant mode of production is likely to be futile except in the case of modern industrial capitalism. Historical reality is much too diverse to be forced into the straitjacket of the long-cherished typology of modes of production. Even a province as small as Yucatan was divided into several regions of different socioeconomic structures. It would be difficult to define any one of them as dominant. And what is true for Yucatan is *a fortiori* true for the rest of Latin America. Modern historiography, with its great emphasis on socioeconomic history and regional studies, has clearly demonstrated this. And at the same time this expansion of knowledge has revealed just how little was known about social and economic history at the time of the theoretical formulations of "dependency" and modes of production. Some of the revisions I have suggested—especially regarding social stratification, the formation of a "national" economy, and the articulation of relations between localities, regions, and conglomerations of regions[18]—point the way to future lines of research.

Reference Matter

Estimated Population of Indian Settlements, 1700 and 1716

Information on the village population in the early eighteenth century is scarce. The *matrícula* of 1688 cannot be used for this purpose because the data are organized by encomienda, and the vast majority of encomiendas included people from more than one village. The data gathered in the table that follows comes from two sources: the Franciscan report of 1700 and the documents on the investigation of the Santa Cruzada repartimiento in 1716.

Neither source is entirely satisfactory. The Franciscan report covers only 105 rural settlements at a time when the villages numbered between 190 and 200. But it does have the virtue of providing almost complete information on the districts of the Sierra, the Costa, and Valladolid, and on over half the villages of the Camino Real and Campeche. It thus takes in well over half the rural population. The report is also relatively reliable, permitting us to establish reasonably accurate parameters of settlement sizes.

The repartimiento data present considerable problems for analysis. The quantities of wax contracted cannot be used because wax was not always contracted in all regions. Consequently, I have relied on the textile repartimiento, which was carried out in practically all the villages of the province except for part of Campeche. The cloth was contracted in terms of both patíes and mantas, at the rate of four reales per patí and two pesos per manta. To unify the information, I have converted mantas to patíes at the rate of one to four.

In theory textiles were contracted at the rate of one-half patí per woman, but it is certain that some repartimiento agents overburdened the villages in their districts, and others may have underburdened the Indians in theirs. These variations unquestionably undermine the validity of the data. Nevertheless, I have tried to relate them to the 1700 report to arrive at a ratio of patíes to people. Information from 58 settlements for which both population and repartimiento data are available resulted in a conversion factor of 5.31 (i.e., one patí equaled 5.31 persons). I then applied this factor to the number of textiles contracted in 1716 for a rough estimate of the village populations in that year.

The 1700 totals are based on a different conversion factor. The Franciscans counted only *indios de confesión* (people old enough to receive the sacrament of confession). To calculate the total Indian population, I have used a conversion factor of 1.67, a figure that Cook and Borah derive from considerable evidence and vigorously defend for its reliability.

Because the repartimiento was not carried out consistently, and because the 1716 totals were derived using two conversion factors (1.67 to convert *indios de confesión* to total population, a figure that was then used to arrive at the 5.31 persons per patí), the results are far from trustworthy. A comparison of the population estimates for both years reveals many similarities but also many differences. Consequently, the 1716 figures should be employed only with the greatest caution. I have used them here simply for a general notion of the situation in areas left out of the Franciscan report, namely, Beneficios Bajos, Beneficios Altos, and Tizimín.

Finally, for the purposes of comparison with later periods, the data are organized according to the districts of ca. 1780. The administrative districts of 1700 and 1716 were fewer in number and covered more territory. And since the Franciscans did not always distinguish parcialidades from each other, the settlements in the table refer to all the people occupying a given site.

Partido and village	1700		1716	
	Indios de confesión	Total population	Textiles (in patíes)	Total population
La Costa				
Conkal	372	621	145	770
Cholul	379	633	169.5	900
Sicpach	124	207	59.5	316
Chicxulub	540	902	332.5	1,766
Chablekal	49	82	–	–
Mocochá	442	738	248	1,317
Baca	788	1,316	508	2,697
Ixil	729	1,217	620	3,292
Tixkumcheíl	351	586	170	903
Motul	700	1,169	240	1,274
Ucí	736	1,229	220	1,168
Kiní	448	748	125	664
Muxupip	216	361	43	228
Telchac	350	585	270	1,434
Dzemul	772	1,289	560	2,974
Sinanché	406	678	83	441
Dzidzantún	376	628	175	929
Yobaín	398	665	175	929
Dzilam	136	227	67	356
Temax	354	591	142.5	757
Tekal	104	174	32.5	173
Buctzotz	86	144	25	133
Dzoncauich	180	301	45.5	242
Teya	368	615	156	828
Tepakán	472	788	135.5	720
Cansahcab	400	668	133	706
Suma	348	581	125	664
Tekantó	668	1,116	380	2,018
Kimbilá	283	473	108	573
Citilcum	277	463	83	441
Tixculum-Tixcoch	198	331	45	239
Izamal	490	818	148	786
Sitilpech	78	130	24	127

Partido and village	1700		1716	
	Indios de confesión	Total population	Textiles (in patíes)	Total population
Pixilá	149	249	66	350
Kantunil	86	144	56	297
Sodzil	201	336	82	435
Xanabá	209	349	58	308
Cacalchén	515	860	180	956
Bokobá	317	529	97	515
Tixkokob	–	–	140	743
Euan	–	–	57.5	305
Ekmul	–	–	63.5	337
Yaxkukul	–	–	37.5	199
Nolo	–	–	201	1,067
Tixpéual	–	–	83.5	443
Mérida				
Kanasín	126	210	–	–
Itzimná	154	257	–	–
Ucú	80	134	–	–
Caucel	114	190	–	–
Chuburná	96	160	–	–
Camino Real Bajo				
Maxcanú	406	678	95	504
Kopomá	72	120	24	127
Opichén	370	618	203	1,078
Halachó	774	1,293	290	1,540
Umán	–	–	107	568
Samahil	–	–	25	133
Bolonpoxché	–	–	50	266
Chocholá	–	–	15	80
Hunucmá	–	–	186.5	990
Kinchil	–	–	119	632
Tetiz	–	–	45	239
Camino Real Alto				
Bécal	707	1,181	330	1,752
Nunkiní	410	685	208	1,104
Tepakán	355	593	142	754
Calkiní	1,112	1,857	354	1,880
Dzitbalché	958	1,600	440	2,336
Hecelchakán	–	–	77	409
Tenabo	–	–	26	138
Pocboc	–	–	37	196
Pocmuch	–	–	100	531
Bolonchén	552	922	–	–
Hopelchén	219	366	–	–
Dzibalchén	224	374	–	–
Campeche				
Lerma	126	210	–	–
Samulá	18	30	–	–
San Diego	56	94	–	–
Cholul	20	33	–	–
Tixmucuy	38	63	–	–
Hampolol	13	22	–	–
Bolonchencauich	129	215	–	–

Partido and village	1700		1716	
	Indios de confesión	Total population	Textiles (in patíes)	Total population
Cauich	57	95	–	–
Sierra Baja				
Muna	306	511	110	584
Sacalum	303	506	114	605
Abalá	81	135	42	223
Teabo	952	1,590	390	2,071
Pencuyut	682	1,139	168	892
Chumayel	307	513	150	797
Xaya	125	209	20	106
Mama	–	–	533	2,830
Tekit	–	–	424	2,251
Tecoh	–	–	30	159
Telchaquillo	–	–	18	96
Acanceh	–	–	72.5	385
Timucuy	–	–	32	170
Sierra Alta				
Ticul	1,006	1,680	250	1,328
Pustunich	257	429	82	435
Nohcacab	969	1,618	275	1,460
Oxcutzcab	1,949	3,255	550	2,921
Yotolín	190	317	155	823
Akil	499	833	195	1,035
Maní	1,281	2,139	360	1,912
Chapab	225	376	52	276
Tipikal	323	539	155	823
Dzan	377	630	67	356
Tekax	1,781	2,974	300	1,593
Tixcuitún	178	297	75	398
Ticum	421	703	210	1,115
Tixméuac	342	571	60	319
Beneficios Bajos				
Hoctún	–	–	40	212
Tahmek	–	–	40	212
Xocchel	–	–	30	159
Seyé	–	–	61	324
Hocabá	–	–	50	216
Sahcabá	–	–	25	133
Huhí	–	–	25	133
Sanlahcat	–	–	50	266
Homún	–	–	60	319
Cuzamá	–	–	66	350
Sotuta	–	–	246	1,306
Bolon-Tabi	–	–	60	319
Tabi	–	–	96	510
Cantamayec	–	–	82	435
Usih	–	–	50	266
Tibolón	–	–	124	658
Tixcacaltuyú	–	–	320	1,699
Tahdzibichén	–	–	207	1,099
Yaxcabá	–	–	140	743
Mopilá	–	–	85	451

Partido and village	1700		1716	
	Indios de confesión	Total population	Textiles (in patíes)	Total population
Beneficios Altos				
Peto	–	–	100	531
Tzucacab	–	–	50	266
Chacsinkín	–	–	53	281
Tahdziu	–	–	115	611
Tixualahtún	–	–	120	637
Chikindzonot	–	–	121	643
Ekpedz	–	–	84	446
Sacalaca	–	–	80	425
Petul	–	–	30	159
Dzonotchel	–	–	80	425
Tihosuco	–	–	224	1,189
Telá	–	–	146	775
Ichmul	–	–	90	478
Celul	–	–	13	69
Tiholop	–	–	140	734
Tinum	–	–	45	239
Uaymax	–	–	80	425
Sabán	–	–	90	478
Tituc	–	–	30	159
Valladolid				
Yalcón	–	–	80	425
Kanxoc	–	–	140	734
Tixualahtún	–	–	260	1,381
Tikuch	–	–	90	478
Tesoco	–	–	97.5	518
Tahmuy	–	–	72	382
Popolá	1,608	2,685	432.5	2,297
Pixoy	496	828	177	940
Temozón	400	668	119.5	635
Chemax	–	–	230	1,221
Cenotillo	206	344	60	319
Dzitás	232	387	68.5	364
Tunkás	312	521	60	319
Tixbahá	116	194	–	–
Tepich	64	107	–	–
Uayma	292	494	65	345
Tinum	357	596	100	531
Cuncunul	320	534	14.5	77
Kaua	240	401	31.5	166
Chichén Itzá	138	230	–	–
Tixcacalcupul	790	1,319	140	743
Tekom	520	868	200	1,062
Chichimilá	934	1,560	250	1,328
Xocén	977	1,632	480	2,549
Ebtún	360	601	123.5	656
Sismopó	328	548	98	520
Tizimín				
Tizimín	–	–	62	329
Sucopó	–	–	20	106
Sodzil	–	–	24	127

| Partido | 1700 | | 1716 | |
and village	Indios de confesión	Total population	Textiles (in patíes)	Total population
Espita	–	–	62.5	332
Kikil	–	–	40	212
Sucilá	–	–	50	266
Calotmul	–	–	75	398
Tahcabo	–	–	20	106
Tzabcanul	–	–	44	234
Nabalam	–	–	24	127
Tixcancal	–	–	20	106
Yalcobá	–	–	50	266
Hunukú	–	–	45	239
Chancenote	–	–	25	133
Tixmukul	–	–	13	69
Cehac	–	–	20	106
Chanchanhá missions	392	655	–	–

SOURCE: AGI, México 1035, Matrícula y razón individual del número fijo de los indios tributarios . . . , 28 June 1700; AGI, Escribanía de Cámara 327, Causa criminal . . . contra el Tesorero de la Santa Cruzada (1716), fols. 9–285.

Non-Indians in the Villages
of Yucatan, 1777–91

Incomplete as these data are—the lack of information on La Costa and Valladolid is particularly unfortunate—and despite substantial inconsistencies between sources in some cases, I believe the following table is a useful, if rough, indicator of the importance of the vecino societies in the villages of Yucatan in the late colonial period. As indicated in the column heads, it is based on three sources:

1. The documents prepared by local priests for the visitation of Bishop Piña y Mazo, AME, Visitas Pastorales, 1782–87;

2. "Expediente formado para el establecimiento de escuelas en Yucatán y Campeche, 1782–1805," in Rubio Mañé, ed., *Archivo de la historia de Yucatán, Campeche y Tabasco*, 3 (México, 1943): 159–303;

3. Two sets of tithe records in BCCA: Manuscripts, Diezmos, 1777–87; and Special Collection, libro 19, Diezmos de los curatos de Acanceh, Mérida, Tekax e Izamal, 1791–94.

Cabeceras and visitas	(1) Vecinos as pct. of total, 1782–87	(2) Vecino family heads, 1789	Vecinos as pct. of total	(3) No. of vecino tithers, 1777–91[a]
Sahcabchén	–	51	30.7%	32
Holaíl	–	0	0.0	0
Champotón	–	208	78.2	69
Chicbul	–	76	40.2	8
Seyba	–	70	31.4	25[b]
Xkeulil	–	25	23.6	10[b]
Seyba Playa	–	182	54.8	70[b]
Hool	–	133	68.9	34[b]
Sihochac	–	30	27.0	8[b]
Campeche San Francisco (Extramuros)	–	–	–	–
Hampolol	–	70	85.4	61[b]
Lerma	–	39	27.8	–
Samulá	–	7	14.9	–
San Diego	–	8	9.9	–
Cholul	–	7	14.9	–
Pocyaxum	–	52	44.8	43[b]
Santa Rosa	–	0	0.0	0[b]

Cabeceras and visitas	(1) Vecinos as pct. of total, 1782–87	(2) Vecino family heads, 1789	Vecinos as pct. of total	(3) No. of vecino tithers, 1777–91[a]
Chiná	–	29	33.3	1[b]
Kulán	–	0	0.0	0[b]
Pich	–	30	21.6	21
Tixmucuy	–	15	22.4	12
Bolonchen-cauich	–	9	12.6	9
Cauich	–	20	12.9	–
Bolonchenticul	–	–	–	77
Hopelchén	–	–	–	49
Dzibalchén	–	–	–	0
Bécal	–	50	12.5	45
Nunkiní	–	0	0.0	0
Tepakán	–	0	0.0	0
Calkiní	–	200	33.3	28[b]
Dzitbalché	–	40	7.4	0[b]
Hecelchakán	–	–	–	17[b]
Pocboc	–	0	0.0	0[b]
Pocmuch	–	0	0.0	0[b]
Tenabo	–	150	61.7	38[b]
Tinum	–	40	31.0	25[b]
Hunucmá	–	400	57.2	139
Tetiz	–	10	4.8	0
Kinchil	–	0	0.0	0
Umán	–	300	54.6	57
Samahil	–	150	60.0	64
Kopomá	–	150	64.7	34
Chocholá	–	78	40.2	37
Opichén	–	150	33.3	64
Maxcanú	–	400	39.1	110
Halachó	–	85	12.1	55
Mérida	–	–	–	–
Caucel	–	–	–	16[b]
Ucú	–	–	–	16[b]
Chuburná	–	–	–	3[b]
Kanasín	–	–	–	5[b]
Teabo	–	125	26.3	30[b]
Chumayel	–	25	20.0	14[b]
Pencuyut	–	30	7.9	25[b]
Xaya	–	4	10.0	0[b]
Mama	–	82	22.4	31[b]
Tekit	–	150	49.7	49[b]
Tecoh	–	70	14.9	–
Telchaquillo	–	5	4.5	–
Acanceh	–	54	41.8	56[c]
Timucuy	–	5	4.5	23[c]
Abalá	–	10	10.3	–
Sacalum	20.2	60	19.3	–
Muna	–	400	40.0	–
Oxkutzcab	–	460	43.4	–
Xul	–	40	23.5	–

Cabeceras and visitas	(1) Vecinos as pct. of total, 1782–87	(2) Vecino family heads, 1789	Vecinos as pct. of total	(3) No. of vecino tithers, 1777–91[a]
Akil	–	39	12.7	–
Yotholín	–	22	17.3	–
Ticul	40.5	600	37.5	–
Nohcacab	6.9	110	14.9	–
Pustunich	11.3	12	8.8	–
Tekax	–	500	50.0	–
Tixméuac	–	26	12.6	11[b]
Tixcuytún	–	28	21.9	4[b]
Ticum	–	28	15.7	7[b]
Maní	–	200	33.3	49[b]
Chapab	–	23	22.5	9[b]
Tipikal	–	4	3.2	0[b]
Dzan	–	11	10.3	20[b]
Motul	47.8	–	–	–
Ucí	8.3	–	–	–
Kiní	17.2	–	–	–
Muxupip	36.8	–	–	–
Nolo	14.7	–	–	–
Yaxkukul	0.0	–	–	–
Tixpéual	0.0	–	–	–
Tekantó	37.4	–	–	–
Kimbilá	11.8	–	–	–
Tixkoch	0.0	–	–	–
Citilcum	0.0	–	–	–
Temax	51.1	–	–	–
Buctzotz	83.8	–	–	–
Dzoncauich	0.0	–	–	–
Tekal	54.1	–	–	–
Mocochá	10.6	–	–	27[d]
Baca	18.5	–	–	–
Tixkumcheil	8.0	–	–	–
Tixkokob	53.9	–	–	–
Euan	0.0	–	–	–
Ekmul	31.0	–	–	–
Teya	36.2	–	–	–
Tepakán	1.9	–	–	–
Izamal	–	–	–	83, 53[e]
Sitilpech	–	–	–	36, 43[e]
Pixilá	–	–	–	63, 78[e]
Sudzal	–	–	–	21, 28[e]
Xanabá	–	–	–	10, 8[e]
Kantunil	–	–	–	12, 17[e]
Sotuta	–	110	–	71
Tabi	–	6	–	4
Bolón	–	–	–	18
Cantamayec	–	–	–	8
Yaxcabá	44.9	–	–	51
Mopilá	50.0	–	–	0
Tixcacaltuyú	–	50	5.9	23
Tahdzibichén	–	40	16.7	17

Cabeceras and visitas	(1) Vecinos as pct. of total, 1782–87	(2) Vecino family heads, 1789	(2) Vecinos as pct. of total	(3) No. of vecino tithers, 1777–91[a]
Hoctún	–	90	48.9	44
Tahmek	–	9	12.3	1
Seyé	–	28	19.7	10
Xocchel	–	1	0.7	0
Hocabá	–	76	32.5	31
Tzanlahcat	–	21	15.1	3
Huhí	–	11	52.4	16
Sahcabá	–	10	18.9	9
Homún	23.9	43	26.2	17
Cuzamá	8.8	9	7.4	5
Tihosuco	21.3	90	17.5	18
Telá	0.0	0	0.0	0
Tepich	0.0	0	0.0	0
Ichmul	37.2	191	41.3	48
Celul	4.2	0	0.0	1
Uaymax	8.2	18	8.0	3
Sabán	2.4	7	2.3	2
Tinum	3.0	2	0.8	0
Tiholop	5.8	23	3.3	2
Sacalaca	25.8	38	16.0	28
Dzonotchel	23.8	39	16.8	19
Petul	0.0	0	0.0	0
Chunhuhub	–	18	10.7	8
Polyuc	–	11	5.2	0
Tituc	–	8	4.0	0
Peto	–	–	–	70
Tzucacab	–	–	–	0
Chacsinkín	–	2	1.1	–
Tahdziu	–	80	16.0	18
Tixualahtún	–	0	0.0	0
Chikindzonot	18.0	42	12.1	14
Ekpedz	0.0	0	0.0	0
Tixcacalcupul	16.2	–	–	–
Tekom	1.1	–	–	–
Uayma	26.3	–	–	–
Tinum	2.3	–	–	–
Kaua	36.6	–	–	–
Pisté	4.3	–	–	–
Tikuch	–	–	–	5[f]
Sisal	–	–	–	5[f]
Chichimilá	–	–	–	0[c]
Chemax	–	–	–	15[c]
Tizimín	85.8	156	76.1	57[c]
Sucopó	75.0	31	66.0	–
Dzonotaké	52.1	4	11.8	–
Kikil	60.0	60	67.4	–
Loché	65.6	41	50.0	–
Panabá	60.2	33	63.5	–
Sucilá	85.6	157	87.7	–
Espita	36.8	156	38.3	46[c]

| Cabeceras and visitas | (1) Vecinos as pct. of total, 1782–87 | (2) | | (3) No. of vecino tithers, 1777–91[a] |
		Vecino family heads, 1789	Vecinos as pct. of total	
Calotmul	–	65	55.1	–
Tahcabo	–	8	12.7	–
Nabalam	60.7	26	42.6	–
Hunukú	26.8	15	34.1	–
Yalcobá	29.0	10	28.6	–
Sisbicchén	0.0	0	0.0	–
Chancenote	45.3	98	44.7	–
Tixcancal	28.4	28	25.9	–
Xcan	–	16	7.2	–

[a]Unless otherwise indicated, the figures are for 1777.
[b]1778. [c]1787. [d]1790.
[e]1790 and 1791. [f]1782.

Notes

For complete authors' names, titles, and publication data on works cited in short form, see the Works Cited, pp. 303–14. The following abbreviations are used in the Notes:

AAM   Archivo del Ayuntamiento de Mérida (BCCA, Special Collection), Mérida
AGEY   Archivo General del Estado de Yucatán, Mérida
AGI   Archivo General de Indias, Seville
AGN   Archivo General de la Nación, México
AHH   Archivo Histórico de Hacienda, Mexico
AHN   Archivo Histórico Nacional, Madrid
AME   Archivo de la Mitra Emeritense (Cathedral Archives), Mérida
ANEY   Archivo Notarial del Estado, Mérida
BCCA   Biblioteca "Crescencio Carrillo y Ancona," Mérida
DHY   *Documentos para la historia de Yucatán.* 3 vols. Mérida, 1936–38
MARI   Middle American Research Institute, Tulane University, New Orleans
RPP   Registro Público de la Propriedad, Hipotecas, Mérida
RY   Relaciones de Yucatán, I and II (Real Academia de la Historia, *Colección de documentos inéditos relativos al descubrimiento, conquista y organización de las antiguas posesiones españolas de ultramar.* Vols. 11 and 13. Madrid, 1898)

Introduction

1. Karl Marx and Friedrich Engels, *The German Ideology*, in Marx, *Pre-capitalist Economic Formations*, pp. 135–36.

2. Karl Marx and Friedrich Engels, "The Manifesto of the Communist Party," in Marx and Engels, *Basic Writings*, p. 8.

3. See, especially, Frank, "Development of Underdevelopment"; Stein and Stein, *Colonial Heritage*; and Chilcote and Edelstein, "Alternative Perspectives."

4. Wallerstein, *Modern World-System*, vols. 1 and 2.

5. Here I am alluding of course to the well-known book by the Uruguayan writer Eduardo Galeano, *Las venas abiertas de América Latina.*

6. Braudel, *Civilisation matérielle*, 1: 39.

7. *New York Times*, 6 Feb. 1983. For a forceful argument of the same position as mine, see Stern, "Feudalism, Capitalism, and the World-System," and especially the commentary by Immanuel Wallerstein and Stern's reply, pp. 873–97.

8. For good historiographical essays discussing the nature of the research, see Gibson, "Writings on Colonial Mexico"; Grieshaber, "Hacienda-Indian Community Relations"; Van Young, "Mexican Rural History"; Keen, "Main Currents"; Bronner, "Urban Society"; and Kicza, "Social and Ethnic Historiography."

9. Van Young, "Mexican Rural History," p. 26.

10. For an introduction to some of the issues of the historical geography of Latin America, see Robinson, "Introduction to Themes and Scales." For a recent example of this genre of research, see Lovell, *Conquest and Survival in Colonial Guatemala*. Interestingly, this discipline, once practiced to a great extent by U.S. geographers, is now pursued mostly by scholars from France, the United Kingdom, and the British Commonwealth countries.

11. For a pioneering essay clarifying many theoretical issues, see Van Young, "Haciendo historia regional."

12. The major monographs are García Bernal, *Sociedad de Yucatán*; Hunt, "Colonial Yucatan"; García Bernal, *Yucatán*; González Cicero, *Perspectiva religiosa*; Thompson, "Tekantó in the Eighteenth Century"; Patch, "Colonial Regime"; Farriss, *Maya Society*; Clendinnen, *Ambivalent Conquests*; Jones, *Maya Resistance*; and Quezada, "Pueblos y caciques." Modern Yucatan has been well studied, too. See especially Joseph, *Revolution from Without*; Wells, *Yucatán's Gilded Age*; and Joseph, *Rediscovering the Past*.

Chapter One

1. RY, II: 16.

2. RY, I: 45–46.

3. Secretaría de la Presidencia, Dirección de Planeación, Comisión de Estudio del Territorio Nacional y Planeación, *Carta de Climas*, 1970; Roys, *Indian Background*, pp. 9–10.

4. On the rise of Maya civilization, see Adams, *Origins of Maya Civilization*.

5. Landa, *Relación*, p. 40.

6. See Patch, "Decolonization."

7. Conklin, "Ethnoecological Approach"; Watters, "Nature of Shifting Cultivation"; Geertz, *Agricultural Involution*, pp. 15–28; Nettings, "Maya Subsistence"; Harrison and Turner, *Pre-Hispanic Maya Agriculture*; Flannery, *Maya Subsistence*; Pohl, *Prehistoric Lowland Maya Environment*.

8. Moreno Toscano, *Geografía económica*.

9. Chamberlain, *Conquest*, pp. 275–76.

10. RY, I: 61.

11. See García Bernal, "Pérdida de la propiedad indígena."

12. Cline, "Sugar Episode," p.85.

13. Cook and Borah, *Essays*, 2: pp. 22–38.

14. RY, I: 57–59, 69–71, 87, 95–96, 105, 125–26, 151–52, 282, II: 34, 37–38, 57, 83, 116, 125; Roys, *Indian Background*, pp. 46–56; Blom, "Commerce"; Gaspar Antonio Chi, "Relación," in Tozzer, *Landa's Relación*, pp. 230–32, n. 26; Mc-

Bryde, *Cultural and Historical Geography*; Chapman, "Port of Trade Enclaves"; Scholes and Roys, *Maya Chontal Indians*, pp. 83–86.

15. Roys, *Political Geography*.

16. Still the best treatments of the pre-Hispanic Maya are the two Roys books: *Indian Background* and *Political Geography*.

17. Martínez Hernández, *Diccionario*, cited in Roys, *Indian Background*, p. 46, from which the quote in the text is taken.

18. See Villa Rojas, "Notas sobre la tenencia." The same kinds of property seem to have existed in the highland Maya area as well. See Zamora Acosta, *Mayas*, pp. 193–205.

19. See the numerous descriptions of the pre-Hispanic tribute system in the *relaciones* of 1579–81, in RY, I and II passim.

Chapter Two

1. Semo, *Historia*, pp. 115–16.

2. García Bernal, *Yucatán*, pp. 27–143, 159–63, including table 10, p. 160.

3. Cook and Borah, *Essays*, 2: 177–79; García Bernal, *Yucatán*, pp. 27–143, 159–63, including table 10 (p. 160).

4. Cook and Borah, *Essays*, 2: 40–48, 55–75. See also the comments made in the early seventeenth century by Sánchez de Aguilar, *Informe*, pp. 4–5.

5. Newson, "Indian Population Patterns."

6. Borah, *Justice by Insurance*, especially pp. 351–68. On the founding of the Tribunal de Indios in Yucatan, see AGI, México 3056, Expediente sobre la creazion del Juzgado de Yndios de Yucatan, 1771–73, and Carta del Gobernador al Rey, 8 Nov. 1767.

7. Roys, *Indian Background*, pp. 148–60. Farriss, *Maya Society*, p. 109, identifies the Indios Hidalgos as the descendants of the Mexican Indians who came to Yucatan to fight on the side of the Spaniards in the conquest of the Maya. However, the AGI documents she cites are ambiguous on this point. Sergio Quezada has pointed out (personal communication) that since the pre-Conquest Maya elite claimed descent from Mexicans, the fact that the Hidalgos continued to do so in the colonial period does not prove they were descendants of the Spaniards' Mexican allies. Moreover, Farriss's thesis is contradicted not only by Roys but also, more recently, by Thompson; see his "Tekantó," pp. 46–52, 197–222.

8. My interpretation of the impact of colonialism on the Maya elite differs from that in Farriss, *Maya Society*, pp. 227–55. I find more convincing the older interpretation put forth by Roys in *Indian Background*, pp. 129–71, which has recently been reaffirmed not only by Thompson (see preceding note) but also by Quezada (in "Encomienda, cabildo y gobernatura indígena").

9. Clendinnen, "Yucatec Maya Women."

10. Gibson, *Aztecs*, pp. 153–57.

11. For detailed studies demonstrating the survival of the Indian nobility long after the European invasion, see Taylor, *Landlord and Peasant*, pp. 35–66; Spalding, "Social Climbers"; Spalding, "Kurakas"; and Stern, *Peru's Indian Peoples*.

12. In this case I generally agree with the interpretation in Farriss, *Maya Society*, pp. 176–86.

13. Ibid., pp. 187–92, 231–37.

14. Villa Rojas, "Notas," pp. 34–42; Farriss, *Maya Society*, pp. 132–34, 177–87.

15. Roys, *Political Geography*, passim; López de Cogolludo, *Historia*, 5: cap. 16; *DHY*, 1: 78, 2: 55–63; RY, I: 49, 146–47, 265–75, II: 69, 101, 120–21, 132, 188; Lizana, *Historia*, pp. 11–14.

16. See the complaints by officials in *DHY*, 2: 148, 152–53.

17. López de Cogolludo, *Historia*, 11: cap. 8. For some examples of anti-Spanish resistance, see ibid., 5: caps. 5, 7–8, 7: cap. 11, 9: cap. 1; Sánchez de Aguilar, *Informe*, p. 83; and Molina Solís, *Historia*, 2: 129–37, 292, 299.

18. Barabas, "Profetismo."

19. See, for example, *Libro de Chilam Balam*, pp. 26, 68–69, 110.

20. On cofradías and cofradía estates in Yucatan, see Farriss, "Propiedades"; and Negroe Sierra, "Cofradía de Yucatán."

21. For information on wax and cotton collection and textile production in the last half of the seventeenth century, see AGI, Escribanía 326A, Testimonio a la letra . . . sobre agravios y vejaciones hechas a los Indios por el Sr. Gl. D. Antonio de Laiseca Alvarado . . . (1678), Pieza 6, Qno. 3; and AGI, México 1035, Certificaciones originales de los agravios irreparables y Vejaciones impuestas que padecen los Yndios de la Provincia de Campeche . . . (1700).

22. Cook and Borah, *Essays*, 2: 8–14; García Bernal, *Yucatán*, pp. 57, 82–83.

23. García Bernal, *Yucatán*, p. 389.

24. Ibid., pp. 388–94.

25. Farriss, *Maya Society*, pp. 40–41; BCCA, Special Collection, Libro 12, Synodo Diocesano . . . (1722), fols. 245–49; AME, Visitas Pastorales, Izamal 10 May 1784, Hoctún 14 May 1784, Ichmul 12 March 1784.

26. See sources cited in previous note. According to the computation in Farriss, *Maya Society*, table 1.1, p. 41, each tributary paid an average of 34.5 reales in religious taxes annually over a 20-year period. Her computation assumes, in that period, "one wedding with matrimonial inquiries, six baptisms, three confirmations, and two adult burials with *testamentos* (prescribed bequests for various pious works) for the couple's parents (assuming an equal share with other siblings)."

27. García Bernal, *Yucatán*, p. 389; Farriss, *Maya Society*, pp. 40, 264.

28. See the sources cited in n. 6.

29. García Bernal, "Servicios personales."

30. López de Cogolludo, *Historia*, 7: caps. 3–4.

31. Farriss, *Maya Society*, pp. 48–56.

32. The term repartimiento had several different meanings in colonial Spanish America. At first it meant essentially the same thing as encomienda, i.e. a grant of Indians from whom labor and tribute could be demanded. Once labor services came to be separated from grants of encomienda, the meaning changed in Mexico and Central America, now referring to the labor drafts of Indians who were allocated to individual Spaniards by the Spanish state. (But in Peru it was still used to refer to the institution known elsewhere as the encomienda.) In the second half of the sixteenth century, still another meaning emerged, namely, the unequal commercial dealings that Spaniards had with Indians. Henceforth in this study, I use repartimiento in the third, i.e. commercial, sense of the term, and refer to the forced labor institution (draft) as the labor repartimiento.

33. For full-scale studies of the repartimiento system in Peru, see Moreno Cebrián, *Corregidor de indios*; and Golte, *Repartos y rebeliones*. On the system in Mexico, see Pietschmann, "Repartimiento-Handel"; and Pastor, "Repartimiento."

34. See Hamnett, *Politics*, pp. 5–23; MacLeod, *Spanish Central America*, pp. 316–17, 344; MacLeod, "Papel social," pp. 78–80; Wortman, *Government*, pp. 27–31; Hunt, "Colonial Yucatan," pp. 465–88. Regarding Chiapas, Robert Wasserstrom has published the same study in three different places: *Class and Society*, pp. 35–37, 43–49, 54, 60–61, 63–64; "Spaniards and Indians," pp. 97ff; and (with Brooke Larson) "Consumo forzoso," pp. 383ff. I would like to thank Beatriz Cáceres Menéndez for information on the Philippines.

35. See Ascensio, "Report on Cozumel," p. 26.

36. López de Cogolludo, *Historia*, 7: caps. 12, 15; 10: cap. 7.

37. Ibid., 11: caps. 3, 8–13.

38. See, for example, ibid., 10: cap. 7, for the text of the *real cédula* of 17 March 1627, which states that wine was being forcibly sold to the Indians.

39. Borah and Cook, "Despoblación," pp. 9–10.

40. Miranda, *Tributo*, pp. 45–143.

41. West, *Mining Community*, pp. 81–82; Bakewell, *Silver Mining*, p. 75.

42. Blair and Robertson, *Philippine Islands*, 27: 198–203; 29: 308; 30: 64–65, 96–97; 42: 155.

43. For the period 1584–1653, the Chaunus estimate that gold and silver accounted for 84.35 percent of the total value of Spanish American exports to Spain (*Séville*, 6.1: table 217A, pp. 462–63). For the second half of the seventeenth century, Everaert estimates the percentage at between 85 and 90 ("Commerce colonial," p. 48). And finally, for 1717–78, García-Baquero estimates that gold and silver made up 77.6 percent of Spanish American exports (*Cádiz*, 1: 349).

44. See Farriss, *Maya Society*, pp. 30–39; and Farriss, "Indians," pp. 6–12.

45. RY, I: 57–58, 69–71, 87, 92, 95–96, 105, 125–26, 151–52, 172, 190, 196, 207, 219, 230, 249, 274, 282, 305; II: 30, 34, 37–38, 57, 87, 125.

46. Scholes and Adams, *Don Diego Quijada*, 2: 98–105; "La Visita de García de Palacios," *Boletín del Archivo General de la Nación*, 11 (1940): 406, 432, 467.

47. Farriss, *Maya Society*, pp. 44–47.

48. Sánchez de Aguilar, *Informe*, pp. 148–50.

49. The history of the encomienda in Yucatan is well studied in García Bernal's *Sociedad de Yucatán* and *Yucatán: Población y encomienda*.

50. Vázquez de Espinosa, *Compendio*, pp. 116–19; Cárdenas Valencia, *Relación*, pp. 99–110; López de Cogolludo, *Historia*, 4: caps. 19–20.

51. Chevalier, *Formation*, pp. 59–85; Medina Rubio, *Iglesia*, pp. 111–31; Keith, *Conquest*, pp. 80–105.

52. RY, I: 38.

53. Carta de Fray Lorenzo de Bienvenida a S.A. el Príncipe Don Felipe, 10 Feb. 1548, in Ministerio de Fomento, *Cartas de Indias*, p. 74.

54. Chevalier, *Formation*, p. 88; Ruz, "Añil."

55. López de Cogolludo, *Historia*, 7: caps. 3–4; DHY, 2: 53; Chevalier, *Formation*, p. 88; Ruz, "Añil."

56. RY, II: 70.

57. This topic is dealt with in detail in Chap. 4. For an introduction to the

stock-raising industry, see Chevalier, *Formation*, pp. 102–45; Bishko, "Peninsular Background"; Matesanz, "Introducción"; Dusenberry, *Mexican Mesta*; Hunt, "Colonial Yucatan," pp. 372–463; and Patch, "Colonial Regime," pp. 94–126.

58. RY, II: 57. This statement was repeated almost word for word by Juan Benavides, encomendero of Temul (RY, II: 124–25).

59. RY, I: 198. For an almost word-for-word statement by Juan Bote, encomendero of Teabo, see RY, I: 291–92.

60. Andrews, *Maya Salt Production*, pp. 130–31, 136–38; García Fuentes, *Comercio*, pp. 187–88, 204–6, 327–30.

61. See Coatsworth, "Obstacles," pp. 92–97.

62. Aguirre Beltrán, *Proceso de aculturación*, pp. 83ff. Cf. Semo, *Historia*, pp. 150–61.

63. *Cambridge Economic History of Europe*, 3: 171–79, 285, 399–406; Lacarra, "Villes-frontière," pp. 214–15; Valdeavellano, *Curso de historia*, pp. 241–42, 469–70.

Chapter Three

1. López de Cogolludo, *Historia*, 12: cap. 12.

2. For Mexican demographic history, see Cook and Borah, *Indian Population*; Cook and Borah, *Essays*, vol. 1; Gibson, *Aztecs*, pp. 136–44; Vollmer, "Evolución cuantitativa"; and Malvido, "Factores de despoblación." The trend toward demographic expansion in the seventeenth century is well documented in Calvo, "Demographie historique"; and Morin, "Population."

3. Cook and Borah, *Essays*, 2: 179.

4. Vivo Escoto, "Weather and Climate." See also Wagner, "Natural Vegetation."

5. C. W. Dixon, *Smallpox* (London, 1962), p. 304, cited in Joralemon, "New World Depopulation," p. 119.

6. There were a few instances in Cholula, but all the cases involved people already infected who were fleeing from Veracruz. See Malvido, "Factores de despoblación," pp. 83, 92.

7. Curtin, *Image of Africa*, pp. 483–87; Curtin, "Epidemiology."

8. Murdo MacLeod has already drawn attention to the similarity between Yucatan's and Chiapas's demographic histories ("Outline," pp. 8–9).

9. López de Cogolludo, *Historia*, 12: caps. 12–14.

10. Ibid., cap. 21.

11. For references to plague and famine, see AGI, Escribanía 322B, Residencia de Roque Soberanis, Pesquisa en Mérida (1709), fols. 219ff; AGI, México 1035, Certificaciones originales de los agravios . . . (1700), Maxcanú, no fol.; AGI, Escribanía 323A, Residencia de Fernando y Alonso Meneses, Pesquisa en Mérida (1721), fols. 23ff.

12. López de Cogolludo, *Historia*, 7: cap. 6.

13. García Bernal, *Yucatán*, pp. 75–77.

14. García Bernal's estimate of the population in 1688 may be too low, for it relies on a conversion factor derived from data on family size from the 1660's. If it is true, as she herself notes, that the population had already begun to increase in 1688, then it is likely that family size—abnormally low in the 1660's—had also

increased. This in turn would have led to a higher conversion factor and a correspondingly higher population figure for 1688.

15. Hunt, "Colonial Yucatan," pp. 165–67 and fig. 2, p. 241.

16. López de Cogolludo, *Historia*, 12: cap. 23.

17. See especially Calvo, "Demographie historique," pp. 12–14; Morin, "Population," pp. 45–47; and Malvido, "Factores de despoblación," pp. 90–95.

18. AGI, México 891, Carta del Tribunal de Indios al Rey, 1 July 1728.

19. Cook and Borah, *Essays*, 2: 96–114.

20. García Bernal, *Yucatán*, p. 143.

21. Farriss, "Nucleation," pp. 199ff.

22. Braudel, *Mediterranée*, 1:27–36.

23. Jones, "Agriculture and Trade"; Jones, "Last Maya Frontiers"; Farriss, *Maya Society*, pp. 152–55.

24. Jones, "Last Maya Frontiers," especially pp. 65–72, 84–88; Scholes and Thompson, "Francisco Pérez *Probanza.*"

25. López de Cogolludo, *Historia*, 9: caps. 2, 4–10, 12–13; 10: caps. 2–3; 11: caps. 12–17; 12: cap. 23.

26. García Bernal, "Gobernador," pp. 135–40.

27. Baudot, "Dissidences."

28. AGI, Escribanía 326A, Testimonio a la letra de la informazion hecha . . . (1678), fols. 72ff, Residencia de Antonio de Layseca, Sentencia y Autos en Mérida (1682), fol. 62.

29. AGI, Escribanía 326A, Residencia de Antonio de Layseca, Sentencia y Autos en Mérida (1682), fol. 62; W. B. Stephens Collection, Nettie Lee Benson Library, University of Texas, Austin, ms. no. 655, Documentos relativos al comercio entre Veracruz y Yucatán, 1676–79, fols. 123ff.

30. Documents regarding the entrada were presented in a petition for an encomienda by a descendant of Juan del Castillo y Toledo (AGI, México 997, Encomienda de Sismopó y Navalam, 1754, fols. 231–85).

31. The standard account of the campaign and conquest is Villagutierre y Sotomayor, *Historia de la conquista.*

32. Farriss, *Maya Society*, pp. 16–20. For reports on the population free from civil and religious control, see AGI, México 3050, Año de 1761, Testimonio de Autos hechos sobre la Sublevación . . . , fols. 90–92; AGI, México 3027, Cuad. 3, Testimonio de los Ynformes que los Sres. Curas . . . , 12 Sept. 1795, fols. 8ff; AGEY, Poder Ejecutivo, Oficio del Jefe político de Tekax al Srio. gral. de Gob., 29 Dec. 1841, and Oficio de la Autoridad 1a. Municipal de Maní al Srio. gral. de Gob., 10 Oct. 1844. On the final triumph of Western civilization over the Maya, see Vos, *Paz de Dios y del Rey.*

33. Phelan, *Hispanization*, pp. 44–49; Elliott, *Old World*, pp. 19–20; Cushner, *Landed Estates*, p. 11.

34. See the various articles in Willey, *Prehistoric Settlement Patterns.* On Yucatan, see Roys, *Titles of Ebtún*, pp. 12–13, 73–77, 81; Garza T. and Kurjack, "Organización social"; and Ashmore, *Lowland Maya Settlement Patterns.*

35. For discussions of reducción in general, see Gibson, *Aztecs*, pp. 281–87; MacLeod, *Spanish Central America*, pp. 120–23; Gerhard, "Evolución," especially the map, p. 571; Cline, "Civil Congregations"; and Lovell, *Conquest*, pp. 75–94.

For a good introduction to the reducción of the Yucatec Maya in the sixteenth century, see Roys, *Political Geography*.

36. Roys, *Political Geography*, pp. 19, 89. According to Roys, the inhabitants of Nunkiní were eventually permitted to return to the site of their original village. But a settlement of that name also continued to exist at Calkiní.

37. *DHY*, 2: 55–63.

38. Patch, "Colonial Regime," p. 150.

39. For a somewhat different interpretation of the conflict between the reducción policy and Maya culture, see Farriss, "Nucleation," pp. 195–205.

40. Roys, *Political Geography*, pp. 3–10; Villa Rojas, "Notas," pp. 29–37.

41. Roys, *Political Geography*, pp. 15–23. Guatemala is an even more extreme case of extensive resettlement resulting in the grouping of numerous parcialidades, which in the Guatemalan context were the equivalents of the Mexican *calpullis*. See Lovell, *Conquest*, pp. 80–82; and Hill, "*Chinamit and Molab*."

42. Farriss, *Maya Society*, p. 163, states that parcialidades "vanished from documentary view" around the middle of the seventeenth century, and then uses this assumption to argue that residence alone defined the identity of villagers. The evidence does not support this conclusion.

43. An excellent description of this process is contained in two letters submitted by the Subprefect of Temax, José Castellanos, shortly after Independence. See AGEY, Poder Ejecutivo, Carta del Subprefecto de Temax al Jefe político de Izamal, 12 July 1837, cited in Carta del Jefe político de Izamal al Srio. gral. de Gob., 18 July 1837, and Carta del Subprefecto de Temax al Jefe político de Izamal, 6 Nov. 1838. See also Farriss, *Maya Society*, pp. 199–223, 355–88; Farriss, "Nucleation," pp. 187–216; and Patch, "Decolonization."

44. Farriss distinguishes three kinds of population movement, which she categorizes as flight, dispersal, and drift ("Nucleation," pp. 202ff). For a statistical analysis of population movement from village to village, see Robinson and McGovern, "Migración regional yucateca."

45. *DHY*, 2: 148.

46. López de Cogolludo, *Historia*, 9: cap. 1.

47. AGI, México 1037, Testimonio . . . del Tribunal de los Yndios, Mérida, 15 Sept. 1711.

48. See, for example, AGI, México 1039, Testimonio nos. 4 (1722) and 5 (1723).

49. AGI, Escribanía 321C, Residencia de Juan Joseph de Bárcena, Autos en Valladolid (1693), fols. 29ff.

50. AGI, México 891, Visita del Gobernador Antonio de Cortaire a Valladolid y la Costa (1722), and, Carta del Gobernador al Rey, 12 Feb. 1723.

51. Ibid., Carta del Gobernador al Rey, 11 Feb. 1723.

52. BCCA, Special Collection, Libro 12, Synodo Diocesano (1722), fol. 10.

53. AGI, México 892, Carta del Gobernador al Rey, 14 Feb. 1729. Also cited in García Bernal, *Sociedad de Yucatán*, pp. 94–95.

54. AGI, México 1035, Matrícula y razón individual del número fijo de los indios tributarios . . . , 28 June 1700.

55. For a brief overview of salt production in colonial Yucatan, see Andrews, *Maya Salt Production*, pp. 22–30, 34–37, and Appendix A, pp. 136–38.

56. AGEY, Poder Ejecutivo, Expediente de Cristóbal Espínola, 15 April 1845.

57. On the Maya states, see Roys, *Political Geography*, passim. For the importance of social integration in surviving colonialism, see Newson, "Indian Population Patterns."

58. For the classic formulation of the concept, see Wolf, "Closed Corporate Communities." See also the same author's *Sons of the Shaking Earth*, pp. 211–31.

59. Farriss, "Nucleation," pp. 203ff; Patch, "Colonial Regime," pp. 404ff; Farriss, *Maya Society*, pp. 221–22.

60. Hill, "*Chinamit* and *Molab.*"

61. See Roys, *Titles of Ebtún*, passim; and Villa Rojas, "Notas."

Chapter Four

1. Wolf, "Types of Latin American Peasantry"; Wolf, *Peasants*; Foster, "Introduction: What is a Peasant?"; Redfield, "Social Organization of Tradition"; Fallers, "Are African Cultivators to Be Called 'Peasants'?"; Nash, "Organization of Economic Life"; and Ford and Douglas, "Primitive Economics."

2. Yucatan's first Bishop, Fray Francisco de Toral, noted that unlike the Indians of New Spain, those of Yucatan "do not pay quitrent [*terrazgo*] to their lords" (Scholes and Adams, *Don Diego Quijada*, 2: 39). On highland Mexico, see Olivera, *Pillis*, pp. 113–22; and Martínez, *Tepeaca*.

3. Villa Rojas, "Notas"; Zamora Acosta, *Mayas*, pp. 188–205. See also Thompson, "Tekantó," pp. 111–92, for an idea of the complexities of Maya land tenure in the eighteenth century.

4. MARI, Títulos de Tabi, 1: 10 Feb. 1651. I would like to thank Raquel Barceló for permitting me to consult her photocopy of these documents.

5. Roys, *Titles of Ebtún*, pp. 16–19, 94–103, 111–13.

6. AGI, México 1039, Testimonio no. 4 (1722), fol. 24; AGI, México 3050, Año de 1761, Testimonio de Autos hechos sobre la Sublevación . . . , fol. 189.

7. Roys, *Titles of Ebtún*, pp. 14, 23, 83–85, 431.

8. MARI, Títulos de Tabi, 1: 16 March 1569.

9. ANEY, J. A. Baeza, 11 Sept. 1689, fols. 69–70.

10. Ibid., 8 Oct. 1692, fols. 577–79.

11. ANEY, P. Barbosa, 18 March 1796, fols. 7–24.

12. MARI, Títulos de Tabi, 1: 15 April 1624.

13. Ibid., 10 Oct. 1708. The *h* used in the text is the Maya article designating masculine gender.

14. Ibid., 1 Oct. 1733.

15. ANEY, M. Montero, 18 Nov. 1719, fols. 571–72.

16. ANEY, F. A. Savido, 20 Nov. 1738, fols. 222–24.

17. Ibid., 11 Sept. 1737, fols. 422–23.

18. ANEY, M. Montero, 2 Nov. 1737, no fol.

19. ANEY, F. A. Savido, 20 Aug. 1738, fols. 173–75.

20. ANEY, M. Montero, 18 Jan. 1718, fols. 16–18.

21. ANEY, J. A. Baeza, 11 Feb. 1692, fols. 431–36.

22. ANEY, M. Montero, 25 June 1732, fols. 205–7.

23. MARI, Títulos de Tabi, 1: 15 April 1624.

24. Ibid., 28 July 1791.

25. Ibid., 20 May 1718.

26. ANEY, M. Montero, 20 May 1719, fols. 339–42.

27. Ibid., 16 Oct. 1719, fol. 525.

28. MARI, Títulos de Tabi, 1:6 March 1640.

29. Ibid., 26 March 1738.

30. ANEY, J. A. Baeza, 27 Dec. 1692, fols. 509–11.

31. See Patch, "Decolonization." For a different interpretation, see Farriss, *Maya Society*, p. 165.

32. Florescano, *Precios del maíz*, pp. 140–79.

33. Taylor, *Landlord and Peasant*, pp. 121–27; Mörner, *Perfil*, pp. 64–71.

34. Florescano, *Precios del maíz*, pp. 88–97.

35. Van Young, *Hacienda and Market*.

36. AGI, Escribanía 323B, Residencia de Fernando y Alonso de Meneses, Pesquisa en Valladolid (1721), fols. 252ff; López de Cogolludo, *Historia*, 4: cap. 10.

37. AGI, Escribanía 323B, Residencia de Fernando y Alonso de Meneses, Autos en Valladolid (1721), fols. 83ff.

38. Ibid., 323A, Residencia de Fernando y Alonso de Meneses, Pesquisa en Mérida (1721), fol. 229.

39. Ibid., 322A, Residencia de Martín de Urzúa y Arizmendi, Pesquisa en Mérida (1708), fols. 298–99; AGI, México 1039, Testimonios nos. 10 and 11 (1721).

40. AAM, Acuerdos, 27 Sept., 1 Oct. 1748, 15 Sept. 1750.

41. ANEY, M. Montero, 7 Dec. 1721, fols. 372–75. See also the *real cédula* of 1 July 1731, copied in the reports from Yucatan in AGI, México 1579, Testimonio del Expte. formado en virtud de Orden circular de 16 de Diciembre . . . (1797), no fol.

42. Recopilación de las Leyes de Indias, Ley 10, Libro 1, Título 20, cited in AGI, Escribanía 323B, Demanda hecha por el Conde de Miraflores (1721), fols. 128–29.

43. Ibid., fols. 320–23.

44. Ibid., fols. 131–35. The Count's costs can be roughly estimated from the data in the 1700 Franciscan report. At that time he and others acquired raw cotton at four reales per carga of 32 pounds (i.e. one-eighth real per pound). Since the same rates were in effect in 1716–18 and 1720–22, and since there is no evidence of a prolonged rise in the price of raw cotton in the intervening years, it is safe to assume that the Count paid the same rate in 1704–14.

45. AGI, México 1035, Certificaciones originales de los agravios . . . (1700), report from Chichimilá; AGI, Escribanía 326A, Testimonio a la letra de la informazion hecha . . . (1678), fols. 35ff.

46. García Bernal, *Sociedad de Yucatán*, pp. 132–33.

47. Ibid., pp. 63–64.

48. AGI, México 1035, Certificaciones originales de los agravios . . . (1700), reports from Cuncunul, Tekax, Muna, and Izamal. See also México 1039, Carta del Gobernador al Rey, 2 July 1723.

49. AGI, Escribanía 326A, Sentencias (1682), fols. 47ff.

50. AGI, México 1039, Testimonio no. 26 (1723).

51. Ibid., Carta del Gobernador al Rey, 2 July 1723.

52. AGI, México 1035, Certificaciones originales de los agravios . . . (1700), report from Opichén.

53. ANEY, M. Montero, 25 Jan. 1721, fols. 270–71.

54. AGI, Escribanía 323B, Demanda hecha por el Conde de Miraflores . . . (1721), fols. 213ff. When these loans were brought up in several complaints lodged against Meneses, the Governor did not deny the allegations.

55. AGI, México 1039, Testimonio no. 26, 28 July 1723.

56. AGI, Escribanía 326A, Testimonio a la letra de la informazion hecha . . . (1678), fols. 26–27, 34, 53, and Pieza 6, Cuad. 3 (1682), fols. 45ff; ibid., 321B, Residencia de Juan Bruno Tello de Guzmán, Pesquisa en Valladolid (1687), fols. 11–15, 74ff; AGI, México 1039, Carta del Gobernador al Rey, 2 July 1723, and Testimonio no. 2, 29 Aug. 1722, México 1020, Carta de Juan de Zuazúa al Rey, 4 Sept. 1723.

57. AGI, Escribanía 321B, Residencia de Juan Bruno Tello de Guzmán, Pesquisa en Valladolid (1687), fols. 11–15, 74ff, 321C, Residencia de Juan Joseph de Bárcena, Autos en Valladolid (1692), fols. 92ff; AGI, México 1035, Certificaciones originales de los agravios . . . (1700), reports from Sisal, Uayma, and Cacalchén; AGI, Escribanía 323A, Residencia de Fernando y Alonso de Meneses, Pesquisa en Mérida (1721), fols. 221ff.

58. AGI, México 1035, Certificaciones originales de los agravios . . . (1700).

59. AGI, Escribanía 326A, Testimonio a la letra de la informazion hecha . . . (1678), fols. 35–102, and Sentencias (1682), fols. 30ff; ibid., 323A, Residencia de Fernando y Alonso de Meneses, Autos en Campeche y Mérida (1715–21), fol. 475; AGI, México 1020, Carta de Juan de Zuazúa al Rey, 4 Sept. 1723.

60. See the sources cited in no. 56–58, above; in addition, see AGI, Escribanía 326A, Pieza 6, Cuad. 3 (1682), fols. 45ff; and AGI, México 1039, Carta del Gobernador al Rey, 2 July 1723.

61. AGI, Escribanía 326A, Testimonio a la letra de la informazion hecha . . . (1678), fols. 24–27, 33–34, 102, Pieza 6, Cuad. 3 (1682), fols. 45ff; and Sentencias (1682), fols. 1–12.

62. AGI, Escribanía 323A, Residencia de Fernando y Alonso de Meneses, Autos en Mérida y Campeche (1715–21), fols. 469–77, and Pesquisa en Mérida (1721), fols. 13ff, 529–44; ibid., 323B, Información hecha por el Capitan Francisco Mendicuti (1721), fols. 6ff.

63. The repartimiento was often denounced for these abuses during the colonial period. For examples, see especially the inquest on Governor Layseca (AGI, Escribanía 326A), the Franciscan report of 1700 (AGI, México 1035), and the residencia of Fernando and Alonso de Meneses (AGI, Escribanía 323A and 323B). See also the *real cédula* of 1 July 1731 (copied in AGI, México 1579), which summarizes many of the abuses discovered over the years.

64. AGI, Escribanía 323B, Demanda hecha por el Conde de Miraflores (1721), fols. 131–35, ibid., 327, Causa criminal fulminada . . . contra el Tesorero de la Santa Cruzada . . . (1716–17), fols. 332–43.

65. AGI, Escribanía 327, Causa criminal fulminada . . . (1716–17), fols. 344–79.

66. Ibid., 324A, Residencia de Antonio de Cortaire, Autos generales (1726), fols. 21, 112–13; AGI, México 892, Carta del Gobernador al Rey, 14 Aug. 1739, and Informe de Eloy Clemente de Cuenca, 4 Aug. 1739.

67. ANEY, J. A. Baeza, 13 Aug. 1692, fols. 541–43; AGI, México 1039, Carta del Gobernador al Rey, 2 July 1723.

68. AGI, Escribanía 323B, Demanda hecha por el Conde de Miraflores (1721), fol. 274.

69. Gibson, *Aztecs*, p. 96.

70. Bakewell, *Silver Mining*, p. 75; West, *Mining Community*, p. 81; Boyd-Bowman, "Two Country Stores." See also Blair and Robertson, *Philippine Islands*, 27: 199–200.

71. For information on Oaxaca, see Hamnett, *Politics*, pp. 5–23. I intend to study the repartimiento system in the Kingdom of Guatemala in a future manuscript.

72. AGI, Escribanía 326A, Testimonio a la letra de la informazion hecha . . . (1678), fols. 98–100. Presumably the figure of 272 pueblos includes all the parcialidades.

73. A similar point is made in Enrique Tandeter, "Forced and Free Labour."

74. Anhang I, in Pietschmann, "*Alcaldes Mayores*," p. 254.

75. García Bernal, *Yucatán*, pp. 112–15.

76. AGI, México 1035, Certificaciones originales de los agravios . . . (1700), report by the curate of Bolonchenticul.

77. Roberto Rivas Betancourt (1777–82) was apparently the first Governor who succeeded in carrying out repartimientos in the Campeche jurisdiction. See AHN, 20750, Residencia de Roberto Rivas Betancourt, Autos en Mérida (1786), fols. 199ff.

78. Blair and Robertson, *Philippine Islands*, 29: 308; 30: 64–65, 96–97; 42: 155; 45: 38–40, 64, 83–84.

79. For the argument that long-distance trade involved only luxury goods, see Ouweneel and Bijleveld, "Economic Cycle," pp. 486–87.

80. See Smith, "Examining Stratification Systems."

Chapter Five

1. Cook and Borah, *Essays*, 2: 75–83; García Bernal, *Yucatán*, pp. 149–54.

2. *DHY*, 2: 52.

3. Hunt, "Colonial Yucatan," pp. 87–97, 386–88, 410–15, 442–47, 506–10; Solano y Pérez Lila, *Estudio socioantropológico*, p. 30.

4. The source for the following is ANEY, Notarías, 1689–1738.

5. ANEY, M. Montero, 1 Jan. 1733, fols. 283–84; 4 May 1732, fols. 163–64, 18 July 1732, fols. 217–18; 27 March 1734, fols. 411–12, 28 May 1734, fols. 455–56.

6. BCCA, Special Collection, Libro 12, Synodo Diocesano (1721–22), fols. 210–11.

7. García Bernal, *Sociedad de Yucatán*, pp. 17–18; Solano y Pérez Lila, *Estudio socioantropológico*, p. 30.

8. BCCA, Special Collection, Libro 12, Synodo Diocesano (1721–22), fols. 210–11.

9. Cited in García Bernal, *Sociedad de Yucatán*, p. 19.

10. Ibid., pp. 55–62.

11. Derived from "Incorporación a la Real Corona."

12. Chamberlain, *Conquest*, pp. 23–35, 59, 149, 200, 203, 226; García Bernal, *Sociedad de Yucatán*, p. 46.

13. García Bernal, *Yucatán*, pp. 425–74; García Bernal, *Sociedad de Yucatán*, pp. 69–92.

14. *Colección de documentos inéditos*, 18: 106–7.

15. *DHY*, 3: 92.

16. Patch, "Colonial Regime," pp. 83–90, 97–99.

17. García Bernal, *Sociedad de Yucatán*, pp. 55, 63.

18. Ibid., p. 76.

19. "Incorporación a la Real Corona."

20. AGI, México 1035, Certificaciones originales de los agravios . . . (1700), reports by priests in Teya, Tekax, and Izamal; ibid., 3048, Testimonio hecho en virtud del despacho del Gobernador . . . (1755), fol. 6; AGI, Escribanía 321B, Residencia de Juan Bruno Tello de Guzmán, Autos en Valladolid (1687), fols. 106–17; ibid., 323B, Residencia de Fernando y Alonso de Meneses, Autos en Valladolid (1721), fols. 48–49.

21. ANEY, J. A. Baeza, 11 April 1691, fols. 256–61, 24 Dec. 1691, fols. 402–3; AGI, México 1039, Testimonio no. 4 (1722), fol. 18.

22. AGI, México 1035, Certificaciones originales de los agravios . . . (1700), report by priest in Tekantó; BCCA, Special Collection, Libro 12, Synodo Diocesano (1721–22), fols. 114–15.

23. For examples, see AGI, México 1035, Certificaciones originales de los agravios . . . (1700), reports by priests in Tekantó and Oxkutzcab; and México 1039, Testimonio no. 4 (1722), fols. 6, 10.

24. For examples in addition to those cited below, see ANEY, M. Montero, 22 July 1722, fols. 462–63, 5 Oct. 1722, fols. 554–55, and 20 March 1734, fol. 407. See also RPP, 1736–71, which includes numerous cases.

25. AGI, México 1039, Testimonio no. 26 (26 June 1723). Data for the tribute of encomiendas are listed in García Bernal, *Yucatán*, p. 496, and *Sociedad de Yucatán*, pp. 146–47.

26. ANEY, M. Montero, 5 Nov. 1722, fols. 547–48. The encomienda data are from García Bernal's *Yucatán*, p. 502, and *Sociedad de Yucatán*, p. 156.

27. ANEY, B. Magaña, 26 March 1729, no fol.; García Bernal, *Sociedad de Yucatán*, p. 139, for encomienda income.

28. For examples, see ANEY, M. Montero, 7 Dec. 1720, fols. 244–46, B. Cetina, 3 Jan. 1721, fols. 255–56, B. Magaña, 7 March 1728, no fol., 13 Jan. 1729, no fol.; and RPP, 17 Feb. 1742, fol. 25.

29. ANEY, B. Magaña, 7 March 1728, no fol.

30. ANEY, M. Montero, 16 Nov. 1722, fols. 560–61, F. A. Savido, 28 June 1738, fols. 135–37; RPP, 17 Feb. 1742, fol. 25.

31. ANEY, J. A. Baeza, 11 April 1691, fols. 256–61; AGI, México 1039, Testimonio no. 26 (26 June 1723); RPP, 17 Nov. 1740, fol. 18.

32. For examples of encomienda mortgages involving important creditors like Lucas de Villamil, Francisco de Solís, and Eloy Clemente de Cuenca—all deeply involved in the repartimiento—as well as Canary Island merchants, see ANEY, M. Montero, 7 Dec. 1720, fols. 244–46, B. Cetina, 3 Jan. 1721, fols. 255–56, M. Montero, 5 Nov. 1722, fols. 547–48, B. Magaña, 13 Jan., 26 March, 12 Nov. 1729, no fols., M. Montero, 20 March 1734, fols. 405–6, F. A. Savido, 14 Nov. 1735, fol. 156; and RPP, 15 Oct. 1739, fol. 10.

33. ANEY, J. A. Baeza, 20 March 1692, fols. 453–54.

34. The cabildo session is in ANEY, M. Montero, 23 Feb. 1720, fols. 20–24.

35. BCCA, Manuscripts, Documentos inéditos de la Hacienda Chichí (1765).

36. Miranda, "Función económica del encomendero." See also the discussion in Chevalier, *Formation*, pp. 152–57. For an overview of the historiography, see Lockhart, "Encomienda and Hacienda." For other evidence of the relationship between the encomienda and the hacienda, see Gibson, *Aztecs*, p. 275; Riley, "Land in Spanish Enterprise"; Góngora, *Encomenderos*, pp. 4–9; Marzahl, *Town in the Empire*, p. 21; Davies, *Landowners*, pp. 18–27; and Ramírez, *Provincial Patriarchs*, pp. 35–61.

37. See García Bernal, *Yucatán*; García Bernal, *Sociedad de Yucatán*; Valdés Acosta, *A través de las centurias*.

38. Hunt, "Colonial Yucatán," pp. 451–52.

39. AGN, Tierras, vol. 483, exp. 2 (1700), fols. 47–48; ANEY, M. Montero, 17 May 1720, fols. 103–4.

40. ANEY, M. Montero, 30 Oct. 1737, no fol., A. de Argaíz, 18 Nov. 1784, fols. 434–37, M. Montero, 1 Aug. 1738, no fol.; RPP, 20 Aug. 1740, fol. 17; BCCA, Manuscripts, Diezmos, Comprobantes de la Media Sierra . . . (1779), fols. 3, 4, 30.

41. ANEY, M. Montero, 22 Oct. 1721, fols. 362–64, S. Ph. de Zavala, 16 Nov. 1770, fols. 407–12, B. Magaña, 30 March 1729, no fol., M. Montero, 13 Sept. 1719, fols. 471–74, 20 Jan. 1721, fols. 269–70.

42. AGI, México 1035, Certificaciones originales de los agravios . . . (1700), reports by priests in Tekantó and Oxkutzcab; ibid., 1039, Testimonio no. 4 (1722), fols. 6, 10; "Incorporación de encomiendas en la Provincia de Yucatán y Tabasco," *Boletín del Archivo General de la Nación*, 9 (1938): 646.

43. BCCA, Special Collection, Libro 12, Synodo Diocesano (1721–22), fol. 164; AGI, Escribanía 324B, Residencia de Antonio de Figueroa, Autos en Vallodolid (1734), fols. 108ff.

44. ANEY, J. A. Baeza, 29 May 1692, fols. 484–85.

45. Chevalier, *Formation*, p. 122; Lockhart and Otte, *Letters and People*, pp. 71–72; Carta de Bernal Díaz del Castillo al Rey, 20 Feb. 1558, in Ministerio de Fomento, *Cartas de Indias*, pp. 38–47; Martin, *Rural Society*, p. 16.

46. AGN, Tierras, vol. 483, exp. 2 (1700), fols. 43–45; AGI, Escribanía 306A, Pleito no. 11, Bernardo Magaña con Don Ignacio de Vázquez [*sic*] y el Sr. Fiscal Sobre el goce de unas tierras (1662). For the estate after the liquidation, see ANEY, B. Magaña, 16 Nov. 1728, no fol. Magaña's connections with one royal Governor are mentioned in García Bernal, "Gobernador," p. 134. For his loan to Layseca, see AGI, Escribanía 326A, Testimonio a la letra de la informazion hecha . . . (1678), fols. 62, 74.

47. AGN, Tierras, vol. 483, exp. 2 (1700), fols. 1–77.

48. Ibid., fols. 51–60.

49. Mérida, Títulos de la Hacienda San Pedro Timul, 1701–02.

50. Bishko, "Peninsular Background."

51. Ibid., p. 514.

52. For examples of royal land grants in Yucatan, see BCCA, Manuscripts,

Documentos inéditos de la Hacienda Chichí (1765); the citations in Chardon, *Geographic Aspects*, pp. 82–83, 173–75, and Stephens, *Incidents of Travel in Yucatán*, 1: 196–98.

53. AGI, Escribanía 306A, Pleito no. 11 (1662), fols. 108ff.

54. ANEY, M. Montero, 5 Aug. 1720, fols. 156–60.

55. ANEY, N. F. de Córdoba, 4 Dec. 1737, no fol.

56. Roys, *Titles of Ebtún*, p. 17.

57. ANEY, F. A. Savido, 4 Nov. 1735, fols. 157–60.

58. Archivo de la Secretaría de la Reforma Agraria (Mexico City), exp. 23: 5576 (25 Aug. 1914), fols. 111–29; ANEY, J. A. Baeza, 7 Dec. 1691, fols. 368–70.

59. ANEY, M. Montero, 22 May 1718, fols. 61–64, 13 Aug. 1718, fols. 112–13 (Cacalchén), 18 Nov. 1719, fols. 571–72 (Sitio Ya), 25 June 1732, fols. 205–7 (Sitio Xuxá), 20 May 1719, fols. 339–42, 23 May 1719, fols. 349–51 (Kalax); ANEY, F. A. Savido, 11 Sept. 1737, fols. 422–23 (Sitio Xaxá); ANEY, M. Montero, 2 Nov. 1737, no fol. (Sitio S. Antonio Hiciná).

60. ANEY, M. Montero, 22 April 1719, fols. 295–97.

61. ANEY, A. de Argaíz, 13 Aug. 1756, fols. 152–53, F. A. Savido, 20 Nov. 1738, fols. 222–24.

62. AGN, Tierras, vol. 483, exp. 2 (1700), fols. 77ff.

63. AGI, México 3069, Exte. no. 1 de 1788, Testimonio no. 1 (1782), fols. 2–8, includes a report by the Vicar-General of the Diocese on this matter.

64. ANEY, J. A. Baeza, 23 Jan. 1692, fols. 423–24, B. Magaña, 22 Aug. 1728, no fol.

65. ANEY, M. Montero, 22 March 1720, fols. 36–39, 5 Sept. 1720, fols. 179–81, 3 Aug. 1722, fols. 465–66, B. Magaña, 30 Nov. 1728, no fol.

66. ANEY, M. Montero, 6 April 1722, fols. 416–19, 30 Aug. 1732, fols. 228–30, 9 Oct. 1721, fols. 356–57, 17 June 1720, fols. 89–92, 18 Nov. 1720, fols. 215–16, 9 Oct. 1719, fols. 512–14, 6 Sept. 1729, fols. 80–83, 25 May 1718, fols. 65–67; ANEY, F. A. Savido, 28 Feb. 1736, fols. 277–81, 6 Feb. 1738, fols. 11–16; AGI, Escribanía 323B, Demanda puesta por el Capitán Gaspar de Salazar . . . (1721).

67. BCCA, Manuscripts, Documentos inéditos de la Hacienda Chichí (1765); AGEY, Planos, Mérida nos. 9, 10.

68. Hunt, "Colonial Yucatan," pp. 401–3.

69. AGEY, Planos, Mérida no. 70.

70. See AGI, Justicia 252, Residencia de Diego de Santillán, Autos de 27 Oct. 1568, 8 Nov. 1568, 8 Aug. 1569, fols. 707–11. I would like to thank Sergio Quezada for calling my attention to this document.

71. BCCA, Manuscripts, Documentos inéditos de la Hacienda Chichí (1765).

72. Hunt, "Colonial Yucatan," pp. 402–3.

73. Ibid., pp. 376–77.

74. Chevalier, *Formation*, pp. 345–63.

75. Hunt, "Colonial Yucatan," pp. 398–405.

76. AGI, Escribanía 323B, Demanda hecha por el Conde de Miraflores (1721), fol. 299, Demanda puesta por el Capitán Gaspar de Salazar . . . (1721).

77. AGN, Tierras, vol. 483, exp. 2 (1700), fols. 46–48, 60–68, 130.

78. AGI, México 1039, Carta del Gobernador al Rey, 2 July 1723, México 892, Carta del Gobernador al Rey, 14 Feb. 1729.

79. ANEY, J. M. Mendoza, 8 Sept. 1846, fols. 242–45.

80. ANEY, M. Montero, 18 Nov. 1720, fols. 215–16.

81. Ibid., 17 May 1720, fols. 103–4.

82. Ibid., 12 Aug. 1719, fols. 438–41.

83. See, for example, ANEY, J. A. Baeza, 29–30 Nov. 1691 (executed in Yax-cabá), fols. 394ff, for the will of a stock owner who "loaned" his mules and horses to others, apparently because he had no right to raise them himself.

84. For examples of the new attempts to raise *ganado menor*, see ibid.; and ANEY, J. A. Baeza, 16 Dec. 1691, fols. 373–75, 14 Dec. 1692, fols. 602–4.

85. AGI, México 1579, Testimonio del Expte. formado . . . , *real cédula* of 1 July 1731.

86. See Hunt, "Colonial Yucatan," pp. 404–15 passim, 634, and all of chap. 4, for an intelligent discussion of the kinds of estancias and the origins of the latifundium.

87. RY, I: 48; "Relación de las cosas que sucedieron al Padre Fray Alonso Ponce," pp. 425–26.

88. Molina Solís, *Historia*, 1: 291. This historian of the late nineteenth and early twentieth centuries had the opportunity to examine the first volume originally registered with the Registro Público de la Propiedad. Unfortunately, this volume is no longer to be found in that archive.

89. "Relación de las cosas que sucedieron al Padre Fray Alonso Ponce," pp. 396–400.

90. Hunt, "Colonial Yucatan," pp. 163–65.

91. Ibid., pp. 277–80, 286–96.

92. ANEY, Notarías 1718–38. The statistics are not complete because of gaps in the notarial records; the major one is for the years 1724–27.

93. ANEY, M. Montero, 3 Aug. 1722, fols. 465–66.

94. ANEY, B. Magaña, 22 Aug. 1728, no fol.

95. ANEY, M. Montero, 15 May 1720, fols. 95–98.

96. García Bernal, "Comerciantes estancieros," p. 9.

97. Hunt, "Colonial Yucatan," pp. 439–42.

98. The turn to cotton in the Valladolid region is suggested in AGI, Escribanía 326A, Testimonio a la letra de la informazion hecha . . . (1678), fol. 102.

99. AGI, Escribanía 321, Residencia de Antonio de Layseca, Autos en Valladolid (1683), fols. 65–66, 322A, Residencia de Martín de Urzúa, Autos generales (1708), fols. 240, 251, for pósito records mentioning the lending of seed corn to non-Indians. Most of the pósito documents make it clear that normally only Indian producers were contracted for grain.

100. AGI, México 1035, Certificaciones originales de los agravios . . . (1700), reports by priests from Telchac, Oxkutzcab, Tekax, and Bolonchenticul, México 3070, Carta del Cabildo Eclesiástico de Mérida al Rey, 5 Dec. 1710, México 891, Carta del Sargento Mayor Juan Josef de Castro al Rey, 28 Dec. 1722, México 1039, Testimonio no. 4 (1722), fols. 6, 10, and Testimonio no. 5 (1723).

101. AGI, México 891, Visita del Gobernador Cortaire a Valladolid y la Costa,

1722; Hunt, "Colonial Yucatan," pp. 440–42; García Bernal, "Comerciantes estancieros," p. 9.

102. ANEY, Notarías 1718–38. Several estancias appear more than once in the notarial records, thus raising the problem of which of several values to use in the statistics. I chose to use the value given when the estate first appeared.

103. ANEY, M. Montero, 17 Sept. 1720, fols. 185–87; A. de Argaíz, 6 Oct. 1769, fols. 702–6.

104. García Bernal, "Comerciantes estancieros," p. 12; BCCA, Manuscripts, Documentos inéditos de la Hacienda Chichí (1765).

105. BCCA, Special Collection, Libro 19 (1790–94); BCCA, Manuscripts, Diezmos, 1777–79; Rubio Mañé, ed., *Archivo*, 1:207–34.

106. ANEY, M. Montero, 15 May 1720, fols. 95–98, B. Magaña, 22 Aug. 1728, no fol., F. A. Savido, 10 Jan. 1736, fols. 227–32, 4 Sept. 1738, fols. 179–81, 6 Sept. 1738, fols. 186–90.

107. Patch, "Una cofradía y su estancia."

108. BCCA, Special Collection, Libro 12, Synodo Diocesano (1721–22), fol. 138.

109. Góngora, "Urban Social Stratification," p. 431.

110. See Patch, "Colonial Regime," pp. 176–80.

111. Molina Solís, *Historia*, 2:302; Sierra O'Reilly, *Indios*, 2: appendix 2.

112. See, for example, ANEY, J. A. Baeza, 21 Jan. 1692, fols. 421–22, 14 Dec. 1692, fols. 602–4; and RPP, 1736–71, 6 July 1740, fol. 16.

113. ANEY, J. A. Baeza, 14 Dec. 1692, fols. 602–4.

114. ANEY, M. Montero, 17 May 1734, fols. 434–47.

115. Ibid., 26 Sept. 1738, foliation illegible.

116. García Bernal, *Yucatán*, pp. 247–73; García Bernal, *Sociedad de Yucatán*, pp. 33–40.

117. The government of Flores de Aldana is well discussed in García Bernal, "Gobernador."

118. AGI, Escribanía 326A, Testimonio a la letra de la informazion hecha . . . (1678), Pieza 4, Cuads. 1 and 2 (1682); 321A, Residencia de Antonio de Layseca Alvarado (1683).

119. For a good analysis of the residencia system elsewhere in Spanish America at roughly the same time, see Marzahl, *Town in the Empire*, pp. 123–36. Much of what Marzahl says about Popayán applies to Yucatan as well. He notes, for example, that on appointment a new Governor underwent something of a learning process, in which he became informed about the business opportunities awaiting him in his new post.

120. AGI, Escribanía 321B, Residencia de Juan Bruno Tello de Guzmán, Autos en Mérida (1687), fol. 8.

121. AGI, Escribanía 326A, Testimonio a la letra de la informazion hecha . . . (1678), fol. 101; ibid., 321B, Residencia de Juan Bruno Tello de Guzmán, Pesquisa en Mérida (1687), fols. 200 ff, 220 ff, 230, 259; ibid., 322A, Residencia de Roque de Soberanis, Autos generales (1704, 1709), fol. 15.

122. Ibid., 321C, Residencia de Juan Joseph de Bárcena, Autos generales en Mérida (1692), fol. 10.

123. Ibid., 322A, Residencia del Conde de Lizarraga, Martín de Urzúa y Ariz-

mendi, Autos generales (1708), fols. 18–21, 88, 91. Juan de Vergara is identified as war captain in AGI, México 1035, Certificaciones originales de los agravios . . . (1700), report by friar in Teya.

124. AGI, México 1020, Declaración del Cabildo de Valladolid, 4 March 1686, and Carta del Cabildo de Valladolid al Virrey, 20 Aug. 1720; AGI, Escribanía 321B, Residencia de Juan Bruno Tello de Guzmán, Pesquisa en Valladolid (1687), fols. 15ff, 26, 74ff, 78, 321C, Residencia de Juan Jose Barcena, Autos en Valladolid (1692), fols. 101–3, 322A, Residencia de Martín de Urzúa y Arizmendi, Pesquisa en Valladolid (1708), fols. 113ff, 322B, Residencia de Alvaro de Rivaguda, Pesquisa en Valladolid (1709), fols. 36ff, 79ff, and Residencia de Roque de Soberanis, Autos en Valladolid (1709), fol. 80ff.

125. ANEY, J. A. Baeza, 20 April 1689, fols. 32–33.

126. ANEY, 30 Oct. 1689, fols. 89–90, 6 Oct. 1690, fols. 171–72, 28 Nov. 1690, fols. 193–95, 20 April 1691, fols. 266–67, 13 Dec. 1691, fols. 372–73, 8 June 1692, fols. 491–92, 27 Dec. 1692, fols. 507–9.

127. AGI, México 1035, Carta del Comisario general de Yndias de la Orden de San Francisco al Señor Don Manuel de Aperrigui, in Madrid, 14 Feb. 1704.

128. Pietschmann, "*Alcaldes Mayores,*" p. 254.

129. AGI, Escribanía 323A, Residencia de Fernando y Alonso de Meneses, Autos en Campeche y Mérida (1715–21), fol. 85.

130. Ibid., 324A, Residencia de Juan Joseph Vertiz, Autos generales (1723), fols. 1–8.

131. Ibid., 322B, Pleito contra el Gobernador Fernando Meneses Bravo de Sarabia (1709), 323B, Demanda hecha por el Conde de Miraflores (1721), fols. 15, 279.

132. Ibid., 323A, Residencia de Fernando y Alonso Meneses, Autos en Campeche y Mérida (1715–21), fols. 469–72.

133. Ibid., 322A, Pleito entre Juan Manuel Carrillo de Albornoz y el Conde de Lizarraga (1708), fol. 251.

134. The information for what follows is found in AGI, Escribanía 323A, Residencia de Fernando y Alonso de Meneses, Autos en Campeche y Mérida (1715–21), and Pesquisa en Mérida (1721), Escribanía 323B, Demanda hecha por el Conde de Miraflores (1721), and Documentos relativos a los cargos hechos por los Procuradores de Mérida (1715–16), Escribanía 323C, Residencia de Fernando Meneses, Autos en Mérida (1715), and Instrumentos de Composición y Averío que hicieron los Regidores . . . (1715); and AGI, México 1037, Testimonio de el sumaria hecha sobre los crecidos repartimientos del Governador . . . , 1711.

135. AGI, México 3070, Carta del Cabildo Eclesiástico de Mérida al Rey, 5 Dec. 1710.

136. Ibid., 3076, Indice de Expedientes Diarios, 1720. The cabildo's letter is registered in the index, but I was unable to locate it.

137. AGI, Escribanía 324A, Residencia de Juan Joseph Vertiz, Autos generales (1724), fols. 38, 47, 55–58, and Pesquisa en Mérida (1725), fols. 11ff, 140ff; ibid., 323C, Residencia de Fernando y Alonso Meneses, Pieza de 1721.

138. Ibid., 323A, Residencia de Fernando y Alonso Meneses, Pesquisa en Mérida (1721), fols. 451–52.

139. Ibid., fols. 861–86.

140. What follows is based on AGI, Escribanía 324A, Residencia de Antonio Cortaire, Pesquisa en Mérida (1726); AGI, México 1020, Carta de Juan de Zuazúa al Rey, 4 Sept. 1723, México 1039, Carta del Gobernador al Rey, 2 July 1723, and Carta del Gobernador al Rey, 21 July 1724, México 891, Carta del Tribunal de Indios al Rey, 1 July 1728; and Sierra O'Reilly, *Indios*, 2: appendix 2, pp. 57–102. The last is a copy of the Fiscal's lengthy report.

141. Sierra O'Reilly, *Indios*, 2: appendix 2, p. 66.

142. AGI, Escribanía 324B, Residencia de Antonio de Figueroa, Autos generales (1734), fols. 32, 47.

143. AGI, México 892, Carta del Gobernador al Rey, 14 Feb. 1729.

144. Ibid., 1579, Testimonio del Expediente formado . . . , copy of the *real cédula* of 1 July 1731.

145. Ibid.

Chapter Six

1. Lenski, *Power and Privilege*, p. 77.

2. For analyses of race, class, and estate in colonial Latin America, see Chance and Taylor, "Estate and Class"; Chance, *Race and Class*; McCaa, Schwartz, and Grubessich, "Race and Class"; Seed, "Social Dimensions"; and McCaa, "*Calidad, Clase*, and Marriage."

3. Patch, "Decolonization."

4. AGI, México 3047, Informes sobre los subdelegados, 14 May 1796, fols. 78ff.

5. Ibid., 3050, Año de 1761, Testimonio de Autos hechos sobre la Sublevación . . . , fol. 103, México 3057, Año de 1775, Cuad. 2, Testimonio de la Información . . . , fols. 19ff.; AAM, Acuerdos, 10 Dec. 1806, fol. 31.

6. AME, Visitas Pastorales, 1803.

7. In addition to the sources cited in Table 6.1, see AAM, Acuerdos, 15 June 1807, fol. 11.

8. AAM, Despachos, 7 March 1774, fol. 228.

9. Patch, "Colonial Regime," pp. 339–44; AGI, Escribanía 324B, Residencia de Antonio de Figueroa, Autos Generales (1734), fols. 122–24.

10. Folan et al., "Paleoclimatological Patterning." The locust plagues in fact struck a large area in Central America and Chiapas as well as Yucatan. See Wortman, *Government*, pp. 127, 166, 185.

11. For the "crisis of production" in Yucatan in the last half of the eighteenth century, see Patch, "Colonial Regime," pp. 331–46, 409–17; for prices after 1813, see Cline, "Regionalism," pp. 407, 728.

12. AGI, Escribanía 324B, Residencia de Antonio de Figueroa, Autos en Valladolid (1734), fols. 72ff, Autos Generales (1734), fols. 131, 135ff, 181ff.

13. AAM, Acuerdos, 5 April 1800, fols. 11–12, 16 April 1800, fol. 12, 29 April 1800, fol. 16.

14. BCCA, Manuscripts, Diezmos, Hecelchakán, 1778–79, fol. 15, Diezmos, Campeche, 1779, fols. 1–4, 14–15, Diezmos, Comprabantes de la Media Sierra, 1779, fols. 26–27. See also *DHY*, 3: 62–63; AME, Asuntos Terminados, caja 2, exp. 34, Razón de los frutos de prosperidad en la Provincia de Yucatán rendida por Joseph de Cicero, 1785; and AAM, Acuerdos, 5–29 April 1800, fols. 11–16.

For import and export statistics, see Pérez-Mallaina Bueno, *Comercio y autonomía*, pp. 62–116; and Rubio Mañé, "Movimiento marítimo."

15. Pérez-Mallaina Bueno, *Comercio y autonomía*, pp. 62–116; Rubio Mañé, "Movimiento marítimo"; Farriss, "Propiedades," pp. 193–95.

16. For some examples of estates, see ANEY, A. de Argaíz, 20 Sept. 1756, fols. 176–78, D. Villamil, 11 March 1759, no fol., and T. Baeza, 31 July 1761, no fol. On production, see BCCA, Manuscripts, Diezmos, Beneficios altos y bajos, 1777–78, Diezmos, Campeche, 1778–79, Diezmos, Hecelchakán, 1778–79, and especially Diezmos, Valladolid, 1783–88.

17. Hunt, "Colonial Yucatan," pp. 433–35.

18. For 1758–59, see Quezada, "Commercio marítimo." The information for 1788 is from AAM, Correspondencia de Cabildos, 1788, Cuenta de proprios [*sic*] de esta Capital, 1788, fols. 8–29. See also Pérez-Mallaina Bueno, *Comercio y autonomía*, pp. 62–116; and Rubio Mañé, "Movimiento marítimo."

19. AGI, México 3061, Expediente sobre el estanco de aguardiente, Informe del Consejo de Indias al Rey, 22 Sept. 1797, and Testimonio no. 1 del Expediente que trata sobre poner en la Villa de Córdova una fabrica de Chinguirito para proveer el Estanco de Yucatán, Año de 1785.

20. AAM, Acuerdos, 17 July 1781, fols. 149–53.

21. AHH, Intendencias, leg. 1038–68, Petition of D. Juan Ignacio de Cosgaya to the Alcalde de Primera Elección de Campeche, 8 April 1785.

22. AGI, México 3042, Residencia de José Merino y Ceballos, Memorial ajustado . . . (1791), fol. 53.

23. A similar change in terminology occurred in the Mexican Bajío at the time (see Brading, *Haciendas and Ranchos*, p. 63). But even within Yucatan there were local variations in nomenclature. In southern Campeche, in the southern Sierra area, and around Valladolid, the agricultural estates emerging in the eighteenth century were at first called ranchos, not haciendas. Formerly, the term rancho had been used only to refer to unauthorized settlements of Indian agriculturalists, and it was probably because of this connection with agriculture that the term began to be applied to the new kind of private estates. By the latter part of the century, however, the term hacienda was also in use in these areas, and in the next century, it finally replaced "rancho" altogether. Since the eighteenth-century Yucatecan rancho was not the equivalent of the Mexican property of the same name, to avoid confusion I have chosen to use "hacienda," which in any case was the more commonly employed term.

24. AAM, Despachos, 18 May 1773, fols. 208–9, 215.

25. AME, Visita Pastoral, Umán, 17 March 1782.

26. "Incorporación de encomiendas," p. 646. See also AGI, México 3139, Expediente sobre la incorporación de las encomiendas, Informe no. 9 del Contador Oficial Real de la Provincia de Yucatán al Marqués de Sonora, 28 Feb. 1787.

27. ANEY, Notarías, 1756–1803. I used a random sample for the analysis here because the large number of extant notarías precluded examining all the records, as was done for the 1718–38 period.

28. In 1718–38, the average value of estancias was 1,471 pesos, 2.5 reales, and the median was 1,175 pesos. In 1756–1803, the average and median values were 2,329 pesos, 5.5 reales, and 1,958 pesos, respectively.

29. In the second half of the century, horses on the whole increased 16 percent in value, *plantas* 7 percent, and cows and bulls 5 percent. At the same time, the value of mules decreased 1 percent, stud donkeys 12 percent, and apiaries 19 percent. Agricultural produce did not show any change over the two periods.

30. As in the case of inventory evaluations, tithe records are not precise measurements of the relative importance of the stock-raising, agricultural, and apicultural sectors of the hacienda economy; but in the absence of information on the income derived from sales, they can be used as rough indicators of the relative importance of the sectors, as well as reasonably reliable guides to temporal and spatial differences in the structure of production.

31. Cline, "Aurora Yucateca."

32. AHH, Intendencias, leg. 1038–68, Petition of Cosgaya to the Alcalde de Campeche, 8 April 1785.

33. AGI, México 3047, Informes sobre los subdelegados, Diligencias 14 May, 15 July 1796, Informes del Consejo de Indias, 4 Feb., 28 April 1797, Cuad. de 16 June 1796, fols. 18–113, Informe del Gobernador al Rey, 27 Aug. 1796; AGEY, Colonial, Bandos y Ordenanzas, vol. 1, exp. 4, Bando de Gobernador Benito Pérez Valdelomar con disposiciones para las siembras anuales de maíz, 27 May 1808, Ayuntamientos, vol. 1, exp. 5, Representaciones de los alcaldes y vecinos contra el subdelegado del Camino Real Alto y otras personas por abusos cometidos, 1811.

34. "Incorporación de encomiendas," pp. 646–47.

35. Ibid., p. 661.   36. Ibid., pp. 660–61.

37. Ibid., p. 636.   38. Ibid., pp. 633, 640–41, 642–47.

39. Ancona, *Historia de Yucatán*, book 6: 123.

40. "Incorporación de encomiendas," pp. 631, 640.

41. Farriss, "Nucleation," pp. 213–14.

42. Ibid., p. 213; Patch, "Colonial Regime," pp. 106–8, 117–18.

43. Farriss, "Nucleation," pp. 195–213; Patch, "Colonial Regime," pp. 361–63, 383–87, 404–9, 417–20.

44. Granado Baeza, "Informe dado por el cura de Yaxcabá," pp. 174–75.

45. Hernández, "Las indias"; AGEY, Poder Ejecutivo, Oficio del Jefe Político de Motul al Secretario General del Gobierno, 13 June 1843.

46. "Incorporación de encomiendas," p. 623.

47. AME, Visitas Pastorales, 1781–87, 1803. For a discussion of these documents and an explanation of the methods used to interpret the data, see Patch, "Colonial Regime," pp. 225–45. The interpretation of these data has been refined by further research in tithe and notarial records and in late colonial censuses (AGEY, Colonial, Censos y Padrones, vols. 1 and 2), and by an examination of a list of cofradía estates in AGN, Cofradías y Archicofradías, vol. 18, exp. 9, Petition of José de la Luz Nájera to the Viceroy, Mérida, 27 Sept. 1787.

48. This is the thesis argued in Cline, "Regionalism."

49. Van Young, "Mexican Rural History," p. 25.

50. Geertz, *Agricultural Involution*, pp. 1–11.

51. See Frank, "Development of Underdevelopment"; Stein and Stein, *Colonial Heritage*; Chilcote and Edelstein, "Alternative Perspectives"; and Halperín-Donghi et al., "Symposium." For a study of the rise of the hacienda in eighteenth-

century Chile as a result of primarily external stimulus, see Mario Góngora, *Origen de los "inquilinos"*; and Carmagnani, *Mécanismes de la vie économique.*

52. ANEY, A. de Argaíz, 1 Oct. 1756, fol. 179.

53. ANEY, S. Ph. de Zavala, 28 March 1767. For more examples of the mortgage of encomiendas, see RPP, 1736–71, fols. 10, 18, 21, 23, 25.

54. *DHY*, 3: 18.

55. AGI, México 892, Carta del Gobernador al Rey, 22 Jan. 1737, Marginal notes on Carta del Gobernador al Rey, 8 July 1738, Carta del Gobernador al Rey, 14 Aug. 1739; AGI, Escribanía 325, Residencia de Antonio de Benavides, Pesquisa en Mérida (1750), fol. 19.

56. *DHY*, 3: 20; AHN, 20751, Residencia de Roberto Rivas Betancourt, Pieza 23, Carta del Obispo a José de Gálvez, 17 May 1782, Carta del Abogado de los Naturales al Rey, 3 Aug. 1782, fol. 33.

57. AGI, México 1579, Testimonio del Expte. formado . . . , Informe del Intendente de Mérida, 3 Nov. 1792; AGI, Escribanía 325, Residencia de Antonio de Benavides, Cuad. 15 (1750); AGI, México 3048, Testimonio hecho en virtud del despacho del Gobernador . . . (1755), fols. 7–14; AHN, 20743, Residencia de Manuel Salcedo, Cuad. 4 (1744), fols. 26–28, Residencia de Alonso Fernández de Heredia, Cuad. 5 (1768–74), fols. 13–15.

58. AHN, 20743, Residencia de Manuel Salcedo, Autos en Mérida (1744), fol. 10.

59. Ibid., Autos en Valladolid (1744), fols. 39–42.

60. AGI, México 3048, Testimonio hecho en virtud de un despacho del Gobernador . . . (1755), fols. 2ff.

61. Ibid., passim.

62. AGI, México 3050, Año de 1761, Testimonio de Autos hechos sobre la Sublevación . . . , fols. 13, 32, 155, 157, 232ff, 274, 295ff.

63. The following discussion is based on AGI, México 3080, Expediente sobre la Santa Cruzada, Testimonios nos. 1–7 (1757–59), especially nos. 1 and 2.

64. AGI, México 3005, Consulta no. 32, 23 May 1793.

65. AGI, Escribanía 325, Residencia de Antonio Benavides, Pesquisa en Mérida (1750), fols. 54ff.

66. *DHY*, 3: 19, 55–57; Blair and Robertson, *Philippine Islands*, 45: 36–37, 83–84; Valdés Lakowsky, *De las minas al mar*, pp. 188–92, 254–59. On the Mexican cotton textile industry in the colonial period, see Salvucci, *Textiles and Capitalism*, pp. 9–31. See also Hamnett, *Politics*, pp. 21–22. In a future monograph I intend to analyze textile production in Chiapas in the eighteenth century.

67. La Force, *Development of the Spanish Textile Industry*, pp. 13–19, 165–66; Ortiz de la Tabla, *Comercio exterior*, pp. 37–54; Anes, *Antiguo régimen*, pp. 204–17; Salvucci, *Textiles and Capitalism*, pp. 160–69.

68. *DHY*, 3: 18–19, 54–55.

69. AGI, Escribanía 325, Residencia de Antonio de Benavides, Pesquisa en Mérida (1750), fols. 54ff.

70. AGI, México 3048, Testimonio hecho en virtud del despacho del Gobernador . . . (1755), fols. 12ff; ibid., 3080, Expediente sobre la Santa Cruzada, Testimonio no. 1 (1759), fols. 21ff, Testimonio no. 2 (1758), fols. 35ff.

71. García Bernal, *Sociedad de Yucatán*, p. 46; "Incorporación de encomiendas," p. 650.

72. AGI, México 3057, Año de 1775, Testimonio . . . sobre la falta de tributarios . . . , fols. 49–50.

73. Ibid., fols. 2ff, 22; AAM, Despachos, 7 March 1774, fol. 230.

74. AAM, Despachos, 7 March 1774, fol. 230.

75. AGI, México 3004, Consulta 28 Jan. 1778, ibid., 3057, Expediente sobre la prolongación de las encomiendas, Informe del Fiscal y Consulta del Consejo, 14 Jan. 1778.

76. Much of what follows is based on Stein, "Bureaucracy and Business." See also Navarro García, *Intendencias*; and Moreno Cebrián, *Corregidor de indios*, pp. 295–316.

77. J. R. Fisher, *Government and Society*, pp. 15–24; Moreno Cebrián, *Corregidor de indios*, pp. 586–614.

78. AHN, 20750, Residencia de Roberto Rivas Betancourt, Autos en Valladolid y Mérida (1786), Pieza 8, fols. 79–88, Pieza 4, fols. 55–114, 162–67, Pieza 23, Carta del Obispo a José de Gálvez, 17 May 1782, fols. 4–13, Carta del Abogado de los Naturales al Rey, 3 Aug. 1782, fol. 33, Pieza 24, fols. 59–199; AME, Visitas Pastorales, Ticul 4 Feb. 1782, Sacalum 9 Feb. 1782, Umán 20 March 1782, Uayma 1 April 1784.

79. AGI, México 3005, Consulta no. 4, 19 June 1787; ibid., 3063, Carta del Obispo al Rey, 10 June 1782.

80. AGI, Indiferente General 100, exp. 663, Carta de Diego de Lanz al Intendente del Ejército, 27 Aug. 1780, Carta de Pedro Antonio Cosío a José de Gálvez, 22 Sept. 1780. I would like to thank Jorge González Angulo for calling my attention to these documents.

81. AGI, México 3041, Residencia de José Merino y Ceballos, Pieza 1, Autos generales (1791), fol. 47, Pieza 2, Pesquisa Secreta en Valladolid (1791), fols. 167ff; AGEY, Colonial, Reales Cédulas, vol. 1, exp. 21 (1783). For Gálvez's personal involvement, see AGI, México 3087, Carta de José de Gálvez al Secretario del Consejo de Indias (Antonio Ventura de Tarranco), 30 Sept. 1783.

82. AGI, México 3005, Consulta no. 36, 4 June 1794. On the continuation of the encomienda pensions, see AGI, México 3073, exp. 3, Carta del Gobernador al Rey, 7 Jan. 1794, and México 3015, Carta del Cabildo de Mérida al Virrey, 20 Aug. 1805.

83. AHN, 20750, Residencia de Roberto Rivas Betancourt, Pieza 6, Sentencia (1786), fols. 2–12, Pieza 4 (1786), fols. 120, 129, Pieza sin número (1786), fols. 121–31, 137–41.

84. AGI, México 1579, Testimonio del Expte. formado . . . , Informe del Intendente de Mérida, 20 June 1790. On the defense of Enrique de los Reyes, see AHN, 20750, Residencia de Roberto Rivas Betancourt, Pieza 4 (1786), fols. 148–51.

85. AGI, México 1579, Testimonio del Expte. formado . . . , Informe del Intendente de Mérida, 20 June 1790.

86. Ibid., 3042, Residencia de José Merino Ceballos, Memorial ajustado . . . (1791), fols. 48–52.

87. Ibid. 1675, Carta Reservada no. 162, de Revillagigedo a López de Llerena, México, 26 Nov. 1790; Díaz-Trechuelo Spínola et al., "El Virrey Don Juan Vicente de Güemes Pacheco," pp. 166–71.

88. AGI, Lima 1119, Informe de los Señores Contadores Generales de 30 de Diciembre de 1800, paragraphs 342, 495. See also AGI, México 1675, Informe de la Audiencia de México, 13 July 1797.

89. AGI, Lima 1119, Informe de los Señores Contadores Generales de 30 de Diciembre de 1800, paragraph 504.

90. AGI, México 1675, Carta de Branciforte al Rey, Aranjuez, 18 May 1800.

91. AGI, México 3041, Residencia de José Merino y Ceballos, Pesquisa en Valladolid (1791), México 3015, Representación no. 671, Informe de Juan Antonio Elizalde, Doctor Pedro Faustino Brunet, Alonso Manuel Peón, et al. al Gobernador-Intendente Interino, 5 March 1793, México 3015, Carta del Cabildo de Mérida al Rey, 28 Nov. 1795, México 3047, Informes sobre los subdelegados, 31 Dec. 1795, fols. 91–104.

92. AGI, México 3027, Carta del Cabildo de Campeche al Rey, 25 Sept. 1795, Testimonio no. 1 (1795), fols. 2, 65ff, Testimonio no. 2 (1795).

93. Ibid., 3047, Informes sobre los subdelegados, 12 Feb. 1796, fols. 39–56.

94. Ibid., 3027, Cuad. 3, Testimonio de los Ynformes que los Señores Curas . . . , 12 Sept. 1795.

95. Díaz-Trechuelo et al., "El Virrey Don Juan Vicente de Güemes Pacheco," pp. 169–71; Navarro García, Intendencias, p. 109.

96. AGI, México 3047, Diligencias, Informe de Don Agustín Crespo, 6 May 1796, Informes sobre los subdelegados, 14 May 1796, fols. 78ff.

97. Ibid., Informes sobre los subdelegados, 1795–1976, fols. 34ff.

Chapter Seven

1. AGEY, Iglesia, vol. 1, exp. 3, Diezmos, Cuadrantes de los diezmos del Obispado de Yucatán, 1795–97, fols. 4–11.

2. AME, Representaciones y Ynformes del Yllmo. y Rmo. Señor D. Fr. Luis de Piña y Mazo Digmo. Obispo de estas Provincias de Yucatán al Rey Ntro. Señor en su Real y Supremo Consejo de las Yndias, y En la Real Audiencia de Mexico. Desde el año de 1780 (hereafter cited as Piña y Mazo), Informe de 10 June 1782, fol. 67.

3. Rubio Mañé, Archivo, 1:231.

4. Ibid., p. 218.

5. AGI, México 3047, Informe del Protector de los Naturales, 12 Feb. 1796, fol. 56.

6. Ibid., 3027, Representación no. 33, del Gobernador al Secretario de Estado de la Guerra, 20 Mar. 1799, doc. 12 (Carta de José Antonio de Bobes al gobernador, 28 Dec. 1797); ibid., 3047, Documentos relativos a los subdelegados, 16 June 1796, Informe del Protector de los Naturales, 14 May 1796, fols. 78ff.

7. Ibid., 3047, Informe del Protector de los Naturales, 12 Feb. 1796, fols. 39ff.

8. Strictly speaking, hacendados, who mostly lived in the cities, were vecinos, a term that by the late colonial period applied to all non-Indians who were not slaves. However, for purposes of analysis I distinguish between urban and village

vecinos; the bulk of the non-Indians who lived in the countryside were small farmers. Also, in the following analysis 30 Indios Hidalgos are included among the village vecinos because, unlike macehuales, who did not have to pay tithes for products native to Yucatan (including their main crop, maize), the nobles had to pay on the same formula as non-Indians. Besides, at this point they were becoming more and more like the vecinos anyway. The inclusion of so small a number of Indians does not change the statistics in any appreciable way.

9. ANEY, M. Palomeque, 5 Jan. 1795, fols. 5–6; AGEY, Iglesia, vol. 1, exp. 3 (1795–97), fols. 4ff.

10. Cline, "Aurora Yucateca," pp. 30–60.

11. Redfield, *Folk Culture*, pp. 155–228.

12. BCCA, Manuscripts, Año de 1773, Cuenta del depócito de D. Bernardo Josef Dafrota de compras de maises que hizo; 1774, Cuentas presentadas por D. Bernardo Dafrota, en virtud de la comision que se le dio para el acopio de maiz del posito de esta Ciudad.

13. Ibid., Diezmos, Mocochá 1791–92, fols. 3–7. Not included in the analysis were 11 people who, though of Hispanic surname, may have been Indians rather than vecinos. Also left out were 5 people of Maya surname who tithed in maize. Since all 5 were of the same surname—Pech—they were probably Indios Hidalgos, who were required to tithe for all their agricultural production.

14. See Trautmann, *Transformaciones*, pp. 112–15.

15. What follows is from AME, Libros de Cofradías, no. 16, Libro de la Cofradía de la Purísima Concepción de Tixkokob (1707–86).

16. AME, Piña y Mazo (as cited in no. 2, above), fols. 8–45.

17. In the Visitas Pastorales of 1782–85 and 1803, it is usually made clear that most of the residents of the estates were Indians, but on occasion the priests identified the people simply as "inhabitants" rather than as Indians. For an example of a parish report carefully distinguishing between the vecino and Indian residents, see AME, Visitas Pastorales, Homún, 16 Feb. 1784.

18. Rubio Mañé, *Archivo*, 1: 209–34.

19. What follows is derived from BCCA, Special Collection, Libro 19, Diezmos 1791–94; BCCA, Manuscripts, Diezmos 1777–79; and AME, Visitas Pastorales, Umán, 20 March 1782.

20. AGI, México 3069, Año de 1788, Autos obrados en virtud de Real Cédula . . . para la libertad de D. Enrique de los Reyes, fols. 39–45.

21. BCCA, Manuscripts, Diezmos, Beneficios Altos y Bajos, 1778, Special Collection, Libro 19, Diezmos de Mérida, 1791–94. Since macehuales did not have to tithe in grain, all the Indian estate owners who made their payments in maize were probably Indios Hidalgos.

22. Socolow, "Marriage, Birth, and Inheritance."

23. ANEY, A. de Argaíz, 12 Aug. 1784, fols. 456–60 (executed in Muna).

24. What follows is taken from AGI, México 3069, Año de 1788, Autos obrados en virtud de Real Cédula . . . para la libertad de Don Enrique de los Reyes.

25. Ibid., fols. 38, 46.   26. Ibid., fols. 30–32.

27. Ibid., fol. 34.   28. Ibid., fol. 36.

29. A different school of thought on the significance and nature of peonage in

Latin American history has grown up in the last several years. See, in particular, Bauer, "Rural Workers"; Loveman and Bauer, "Forum"; and Knight, "Mexican Peonage."

30. For conditions on haciendas in Yucatan in the 1830's and 1840's, see the classic works of John Lloyd Stephens, *Incidents of Travel in Central America, Chiapas and Yucatan,* and *Incidents of Travel in Yucatan.*

31. Stephens, *Incidents of Travel in Yucatan,* 1: 110–15.

32. Luis Millet Cámara, "De las estancias y haciendas en el Yucatán colonial," in Cámara et al., *Hacienda y cambio,* p. 33.

33. AGI, México 1021, Carta del Obispo al Rey, 30 May 1723.

34. AME, Visitas Pastorales, Maní, 17 Jan. 1782.

35. AAM, Despachos, 18 May 1773, fols. 207–8.

36. AME, Visitas Pastorales, Maní, 17 Jan. 1782.

37. AME, Visitas Pastorales, Tecoh 19 April 1803, Mama 22 April 1803, Sacalum 9 Feb. 1782, Acanceh 7 Jan. 1782, 16 April 1803.

38. Ibid., Acanceh 7 Jan. 1782, 16 April 1803, Abalá 28 May 1803, Tecoh 19 April 1803, Mama 22 April 1803, Sacalum 9 Feb. 1782, 6 May 1803, Muna 23 May 1803.

39. Ibid., Umán 20 March 1782.

40. Ibid., Conkal 22 Jan. 1785, 5 Oct. 1803, Mocochá 20 Jan. 1785, Nolo 28 Feb. 1785, Tixkokob 24 Feb. 1785, Telchac 4 Feb. 1785, 24 Sept. 1803, Motul 31 Jan. 1782, Cansahcab 6 Feb. 1785, Teya 18 Feb. 1785, 11 Sept. 1803, Temax 12 Feb. 1785, 16 Sept. 1803.

41. Ibid., Maní 17 Jan. 1782, Ticul 4 Feb. 1782, 5 May 1803, Tekax 2 May 1803, Oxkutzcab 8 May 1803.

42. Ibid., Sotuta 23 Feb. 1784, Homún, 16 Feb. 1784.

43. Ibid., Valladolid and Sisal 5 April 1784, Cenotillo 8 May 1784.

44. AME, Concursos a Curatos, 1790, Exp. 73, fol. 17.

45. Millet Cámara, "De las estancias," in Millet Cámara et al., *Hacienda y cambio,* pp. 30–35.

Chapter Eight

1. See especially Florescano, *Precios del maíz;* and Van Young, *Hacienda and Market.*

2. Quezada, "Comercio marítimo," chaps. 2, 3.

3. See, for example, AGI, México 891, Carta del Gobernador al Rey, 16 Aug. 1721.

4. See, for example, the will of a Genoese merchant in Mérida in ANEY, M. Montero, [1720], fols. 192–95.

5. For examples of the activities of the Canary Islanders, see, in ANEY, M. Montero, 8 Dec. 1720, fols. 246–48, 16 April 1720, fols. 54–60, 7 Dec. 1721, fols. 272–375, B. Magaña, 8 Oct. 1728, no folio, and A. de Argaíz, 29 July 1756, fols. 132–38. In 1762 and 1782, the Governor and the Bishop, respectively, noted the prominence of the isleños in Yucatan's commerce (AGI, México 3080, Carta del Gobernador al Secretario de Estado de Indias [Julián de Arriaga], 1 July 1762; AHN, 20751, Residencia de Roberto Rivas Betancourt, Pieza 23, Carta del Obis-

po a José de Gálvez, 17 May 1782, fol. 9). On the decline of the Islanders, see AGI, México 3015, Breve Exordio sobre la importancia del comercio, [ca. 1793] (report written by Eugenio Rubio).

6. On the Basque merchants in Yucatan in the seventeenth and eighteenth centuries, see ANEY, J. A. Baeza, [1691], fols. 332–34; and AGI, Escribanía 323A, Residencia de Fernando y Alonso Meneses, Autos en Campeche y Mérida (1715–21), fols. 122–23.

7. BCCA, Manuscripts, Año de 1753, Cuenta de propios del espresado año, fols. 1–2, Año de 1753, Licencias de Tiendas dadas por los Señores Regidores D. Juan José de Bergara y D. Diego de Aranda y Cano en dicho año de 53 . . . , fols. 1–5; AHN, 20751, Residencia de Roberto Rivas Betancourt, Pieza 20, Cuentas del Mayordomo de Proprios D. Andrés de Cervera (1783), fols. 66–67.

8. Brading, *Miners*, pp. 95–128, 253–57; Góngora, "Urban Social Stratification," pp. 436–41; Socolow, *Merchants of Buenos Aires*, pp. 12–33; Van Young, *Hacienda and Market*, pp. 142–60; Lindley, *Haciendas and Economic Development*, pp. 43–53.

9. ANEY, M. Montero, 25 Jan. 1720, fol. 6, 8 Feb. 1720, fol. 17, 15 April 1722, fols. 405–7, A. de Argaíz, 17 Oct. 1758, fols. 240–42.

10. ANEY, B. Magaña, 13 Jan. 1729, no fol.

11. Ibid., 18 July 1728, no fol.

12. ANEY, M. Montero, 19 Dec. 1734, fols. 490–92, 26 Sept. 1738, illegible folio.

13. Quezada, "Comercio marítimo," passim; ANEY, A. de Argaíz, 22 Sept. 1759, fols. 406–7, 29 Oct. 1759, fols. 426–27.

14. ANEY, M. Montero, 30 March 1718, fols. 49–50, 28 Aug. 1718, fols. 116–20.

15. Ibid., 19 Sept. 1720, fol. 188.

16. "Incorporación de encomiendas," pp. 650–51.

17. AGI, México 3015, Representación del Cabildo de Mérida al Rey, 14 Dec. 1804.

18. AHH, 1038–68, Solicitud de Juan Ignacio de Cosgaya al Alcalde de Campeche, 4 May 1787.

19. AGI, México 3004, Consultas, 17 July 1777.

20. Ibid., Remisiones al Consejo, 27 May 1797.

21. Farriss, *Maya Society*, pp. 366–70; AAM, Correspondencia de Cabildos, 1788, fols. 8–29.

22. *DHY*, 3:60–63.

23. AGI, México 3015, Representación del Cabildo de Mérida al Rey, 14 Dec. 1804.

24. AAM, Correspondencia de Cabildos, Cuentas de Proprios de esta Capital, 1788, fols. 8–29; Rubio Mañé, "Movimiento marítimo."

25. AAM, Acuerdos, 10 July 1789, fol. 101.

26. AHH, 1038–70, Carta del Intendente al Virrey, 21 May 1788, Parecer del Fiscal de la Real Hacienda, 30 June 1788. See AAM, Acuerdos, 5 Nov. 1793, fol. 258, and 13 May 1806, fols. 15–16, for the activities of Governors-Intendants Arturo O'Neil and Benito Pérez in stimulating road construction.

27. For the history of the Estanco de Aguardiente, see AGI, México 3061, In-

forme del Consejo al Rey, 22 Sept. 1797, and Superior Govierno, Año de 1785, no. 1, Testimonio del Expediente que trata sobre poner en la Villa de Cordova una fabrica de Chinguirito para proveer el Estanco de Yucatán. See also AAM, Acuerdos, 17 July 1781, fols. 149, 151–53.

28. On the Estanco de Sal, see AGI, México 3139, Expediente sobre extinguir el estanco de sal en Veracruz, dejando en entera libertad a los vecinos de Yucatán y Campeche para llevarlas como antes del establecimiento del referido Estanco, [ca. 1790].

29. This motive for the attack on Yucatan's textile production is suggested by crown policy in Peru, where the government also undertook measures to contain the local textile industry while stimulating most other branches of commerce (Fisher, *Government and Society*, p. 126).

30. *DHY*, 3: 31–35.

31. For contemporary accounts of this agricultural cycle and the movement of prices, see AAM, Despachos, 18 May 1773, fols. 207–9, 7 March 1774, fols. 226–31; AAM, Acuerdos, 6 Feb. 1776, fol. 5; and the Governor's report of 1809 published as "Maíz para Yucatán en 1809," in *Novedades de Yucatán*, 18 May 1975.

32. BCCA, Manuscripts, Cuentas de Pósito y Alhóndiga, 1747–48, 1749, 1754, 1757, 1759, 1761–63, 1768, 1772, 1774, 1781; AAM, Libro 13 (1767), Libro 16 (1785, 1787); AAM, Expedientes incompletos y Acuerdos del Cabildo del Año de 1801; AHN, 20751, Residencia de Roberto Rivas Betancourt (1786), Pieza 12, 20752, Residencia de Roberto Rivas Betancourt (1786), Pieza 6; AGI, México 3042, Cuentas de Pósito, 1782–85, 1788, 1790, 1791.

33. AAM, Despachos, 18 May 1773, fols. 208–9.

34. AAM, Acuerdos, 6 Feb. 1776, fol. 5.

35. AGI, México 3050, Año de 1761, Testimonio de Autos hechos sobre la Sublevación . . . , fol. 145.

36. AHN, 20751, Pieza 12, Cuentas de Pósito de Valladolid, 1777–83, fols. 77–87.

37. AGI, México 3042, Año de 1791, Cuentas del Pócito de la Villa de Valladolid precentadas por su Administrador Don Jph. Triay de los años de 1784 y 1785.

38. Ibid., 3061, Superior Govierno, Año de 1785, no. 1, Testimonio del Expediente que trata sobre poner en la Villa de Cordova una fabrica de Chinguirito para proveer el Estanco de Yucatán, fol. 15; ibid., 3047, Informe sobre los subdelegados, 12 Feb. 1796, fols. 39–56.

39. Patch, "Colonial Regime," pp. 314–19.

40. AGI, México 3042, 1792, Cuentas del Pócito de la Villa de Valladolid presentadas por el Ynterventor de el en el año de 1788 siendolo Don Juan Francisco Muñoz, fols. 14, 32.

41. For some of the many examples of such seed corn transactions and of the problems resulting from them, see AAM, Acuerdos, 12 March 1777, fol. 38, 14 Jan. 1780, fol. 105, Jan.–March 1783, fols. 195–99, 30 April 1793, fol. 250, 17 Jan. 1794, fol. 268; and BCCA, Manuscripts, 1758, Cuentas de Alhóndiga del presente año, presentadas por D. Francisco Anguas, fols. 4–5 and 1759, Providencias dadas por el M. Y.C. de esta Ciudad en favor de su pósito y alhóndiga a pedimiento de los mayordomos que lo administraron, fols. 12–14, 19.

42. AGEY, Colonial, Ayuntamientos, vol. 1, exp. 2 (1790); AGI, México

3047, Informe sobre los subdelegados, 16 June 1796, fols. 18ff, 3015, Representación del Cabildo de Mérida al Rey, 14 Dec. 1804.

43. See the reports on village pósitos in the Motul area in AGEY, Poder Ejecutivo, Exp. de la vicita practicada por el Gefe político subalterno del partido de Motul en los meses de Abril y Mayo de 1846.

44. AAM, Despachos, 18 May 1773, fols. 207–8.

45. Ibid., fols. 208, 215.

46. For an example of the obligado's duties, see AAM, Acuerdos, 20 March 1776, fol. 8.

47. See, for example, Van Young, *Hacienda and Market*, pp. 49–52.

48. AHN, 20752, Residencia de Joseph Merino y Ceballos, Pieza 5a, Cuentas de Proprios, 1778–83.

49. AGI, México 3069, Año de 1788, Autos obrados en virtud de Real Cédula dirigida al Sor. Yntendente de Yucatan, y en su defecto al Sor. Tente. y Auditor de Guerra para la libertad de D. Enrique de los Reyes . . . , fol. 16, shows 33 head yielding 8,040 pounds of beef.

50. ANEY, M. Montero, 28 March 1718, fol. 48.

51. ANEY, A. de Argaíz, 19 April 1792, fols. 38–39, 20 April 1792, fols. 39–40, 5 May 1792, fols. 42–44, 9 May 1792, fols. 45–46.

52. The problem of the abasto system in this period is found in AAM, Acuerdos y Títulos, 1757–60, and Acuerdos, 1761–66.

53. AAM, Acuerdos, 14 March 1807, fols. 1–2.

54. Folan et al., "Paleoclimatological Patterning."

55. AAM, Acuerdos, 22 Dec. 1790, fol. 145.

56. AAM, Despachos, 7 March 1774, fol. 227.

57. Ibid., fols. 227–28.

58. Wortman, *Government*, pp. 127, 166, 185. On Chiapas, see AGI, Guatemala 554, exp. 12, Cuads. 3 (1771) and 4 (1772).

59. AAM, Acuerdos, 15 June 1807, fol. 11.

60. BCCA, Special Collection, Libro 12, Synodo Diocesano (1721–22), fol. 115, for prices in the early eighteenth century. For the later period, see AAM, Despachos, 7 March 1774, fol. 227; BCCA, Manuscripts, Cuentas de Alhóndiga, 1758, fols. 4–5, Providencias dadas por el M.Y.C. de esta Ciudad en favor de su pósito y Alhóndiga a pedimiento de los mayordomos que lo administraron (1759), fols. 11, 13, 29, Cuentas del depócito y Alhóndiga (1761–63), fols. 10, 14, Cuentas de Alhóndiga (1768), fols. 5, 53, Cuentas de pócito (1772), fols. 56–57, Cuentas presentadas por D. Bernardo Dafrota (1774), fols. 8–14; AME, Libros de Cofradías, no. 16; and AAM, Acuerdos, 23 May 1764, fols. 128–29, 30 Jan., 14 Feb. 1787, fols. 43, 44, 11 Dec. 1793, fol. 263. A few notary records bear out these values: ANEY, A. de Argaíz, 16 Aug. 1769, fols. 659, 669, 21 Feb. 1792, fols. 21–23, and 15 June, 1792, fols. 48–50, 53.

61. AAM, Despachos, 18 May 1773, fols. 208, 215.

62. See AAM, especially the years 1752, 1769–73, 1777, 1780, 1786–87, 1790–91, 1793, 1795, 1798–1802, 1804, 1807; AME, Libros de Cofradías, no. 16; BCCA, Manuscripts, Cuentas de Alhóndiga, especially 1761–62, 1772–73; ANEY, A. de Argaíz, 30 April 1783, fol. 219, P. Barbosa, 10 Dec. 1803, fols. 312–15; "Maíz para Yucatán en 1809," *Novedades de Yucatán*, 18 May 1975; BCCA, Spe-

cial Collection, Libro 39, Archivo de la Excelentísima Diputación Provincial, 5 July 1813, fol. 51.

63. AAM, Autos y Acuerdos, 20 Jan. 1751, fol. 246, Despachos, 18 May 1773, fols. 207–8.

64. On this interaction between the maize and cattle economies, especially the impact of grain shortages on the supply of beef, see AAM, Despachos, 18 May 1773, fols. 207–8, 210, 214, Acuerdos, 7 Aug. 1783, fols. 212–14, 14 March 1807, fol. 1; AME, Piña y Mazo (1780–82; see n. 2, above), fol. 83, Libros de Cofradías, no. 16; ANEY, S. Ph. Zavala, 20 Dec. 1770, fol. 430; and "Incorporación de encomiendas," p. 636.

65. AAM, Acuerdos, 3 Feb. 1795, fol. 298, 14 April 1795, fol. 303, 18 May 1795, fol. 304, 24 April 1798, fols. 8–9, 5 May 1798, fol. 9.

66. Ibid., 2 June 1807, fol. 10, 15 June 1807, fol. 12.

67. Ibid., especially the years 1795, 1804, 1806–8.

68. On price-fixing for all marketed maize, see, for example, ibid., 22 July 1808, fols. 31–33.

69. Ibid., 11 Feb., 1 March, 10 April, 24 April, 26 June 1804, fols. 10, 15, 22–23, 26, 40, 15 June 1807, fols. 11–12.

70. Ibid., 27 Jan. 1761, fol. 5, 10 Feb. 1795, fol. 299.

71. AAM, Autos y Acuerdos, 27 Sept. 1748, fol. 70; AAM, Acuerdos, 14 March 1804, fol. 18, 2 June 1807, fol. 10, 15 June 1807, fol. 11.

72. AAM, Acuerdos, 14 June 1777, fols. 39–40.

73. Ibid., 18 April 1795, fol. 303, 3 April 1799, fol. 38, 17 March 1807, fol. 3; AAM, Despachos, 11 May 1770, fols. 92–93.

74. AAM, Despachos, 5 May 1770, fols. 90–91, 7 March 1774, fol. 228.

75. Ibid., 9 March 1771, fols. 103–4.

76. BCCA, Manuscripts, Cuentas de pócito (1772), fols. 57, 59; AAM, Acuerdos, 16 July 1776, fol. 19.

77. AAM, Acuerdos, 20 Jan. 1795, fol. 296, 8 April 1795, fol. 301.

78. Ibid., 13 Jan., 11 March, 28 March, 5 April, 1800, fols. 4, 9, 11.

79. Ibid., 10 April, 28 May, 5 June, 14 July, 17 July, 31 July 1804, fols. 23, 31, 34, 43, 44, 48.

80. Ibid., 21 March, 30 April, 10 May, 18 June 1805, fols. 84–85, 91, 92, 98.

81. AHH, 733–38 (23 May 1807); AAM, Acuerdos, 27 Feb., 3 March 1807, fols. 46, 47.

82. AAM, Acuerdos, 1 Feb., 11 March 1808, fols. 8, 12; "Maíz para Yucatán en 1809," *Novedades de Yucatán*, 18 May 1975.

83. AAM, Acuerdos, 23 Dec., 1806, fol. 34.

84. Ibid., 11 Feb. 1804, fol. 10; "Maíz para Yucatán en 1809," *Novedades de Yucatán*, 18 May 1975.

85. Florescano, *Precios del maíz*, pp. 180–97.

Chapter Nine

1. Patch, "Colonial Regime," pp. 384–85.

2. AME, Visitas Pastorales, Tizimín 30 April 1784. The report from Kikil (1 May 1784) is word for word the same on this point. Apparently the two reports were either written in collaboration or composed by the same person.

3. Ibid., Maní 17 Jan. 1782. See also Conkal 22 Jan. 1785, and Yaxcabá 27 Feb. 1784.

4. Ibid., Maní 17 Jan. 1782.

5. Ibid.

6. AGI, México 3139, Estado del Número de Mantas . . . , 14 July 1784.

7. AME, Visitas Pastorales, Yaxcabá 27 Feb. 1784.

8. AGI, México 3048, Testimonio hecho en virtud de un despacho del Gobernador . . . sobre el repartimiento . . . (1755), fol. 75.

9. Ibid., 3050, Autos criminales . . . sobre la Sublevación . . . (1761), fols. 227–95, 337.

10. AGI, Guatemala 572, Carta del Obispo de Yucatán al Rey, 27 June 1786, Carta del Gobernador de Yucatán al Rey, 29 July 1786. In these documents it is revealed that one of the two Indian rulers of the Petén was named Pedro Canek(!) Bisnieto ("great-grandson").

11. Patch, "Decolonization."

12. AGI, México 3050, Año de 1761, Testimonio de Autos hechos sobre la Sublevación . . . , fol. 26.

13. My interpretation of the Indios Hidalgos differs from Farriss's because of a different reading of the documents, especially those in the Visitas Pastorales and in AGI, México 3139, Informe no. 9, del Contador Real de la Provincia de Yucatán al Marqués de Sonora, 28 Feb. 1787. Cf. Farriss, *Maya Society*, pp. 227–55. See above, Chap. 2, nn. 7 and 8.

14. AME, Visitas Pastorales, Yaxcabá 27 Feb. 1784, Tihosuco 25 March 1784, Espita 3 May 1784; BCCA, Special Collection, Synodo Diocesano (1722), fol. 114; Archivo General del Arzobispado, Izamal, Difunciones, vol. 3, 1755–92; BCCA, Manuscripts, Año de 1773, Cuenta del Depócito de D. Bernardo Josef Dafrota . . . , fol. 2.

15. On this procedure, see AHN, 20751, Residencia de Roberto Rivas Betancourt, Pieza 23, Carta del Obispo al Secretario de Indias, 17 May 1782, fol. 8, and Autos en Mérida, 1786, fols. 70–110.

16. BCCA, Manuscripts, Cuenta de pósito . . . (1747 and 1748), fol. 5 (for mention of the coast-watchers). For reference to the Companies of Hidalgos, see AGI, Escribanía 325, Residencia de Antonio Benavides, Autos en Valladolid (1750), fol. 112; and BCCA, Manuscripts, Cuarenta Manuscritos varios del Capitán General, Oficio del Teniente veterano de Maxcanú al Sr. Yntendente Gobernador y Capitán General, 2 July 1797. See also Roys, *Indian Background*, p. 143.

17. *DHY*, 3: 10; AME, Visitas Pastorales, Tekuch 5 April 1784, Sisal 5 April 1784.

18. See Chaps. 7–8; and Thompson, *Tekantó*, pp. 111–241.

19. See Farriss, *Maya Society*, pp. 356ff.

20. AGEY, Poder Ejecutivo, Oficio de la Comicion de Matrículas del Partido de Yzamal al Secretario General de Gobierno, 21 Oct. 1844.

21. For what follows I used practically all the Visita Pastoral documents in the Archivo de la Mitra Emeritense. See also "Incorporación de encomiendas," pp. 599–600.

22. AGI, México 3061, Superior Govierno, Año de 1785, no. 1, Testimonio del Expediente que trata sobre poner en la Villa de Cordova una fabrica de Chinguirito para proveer el Estanco de Yucatan, fol. 16.

23. Rubio Mañé, *Archivo*, 1:250.

24. The 1779 census is flawed by a large number of arithmetic errors. Nancy Farriss (*Maya Society*, p. 59) accepts the totals, thereby rejecting the individual figures. I chose instead to accept the individual figures as a basis for the percentages. In any case, the document is so imperfect that neither Farriss nor I would trust it for purposes of computing sex and age ratios. On the other hand, though the racial data may not be exact, they are still useful to indicate the general shape of the population in 1779.

25. Hunt, "Colonial Yucatan," pp. 88–97, 386–87, 410–44, 506–12, 529–36; BCCA, Special Collection, Libro 12, Synodo Diocesano (1721–22), fols. 226–27. It is not clear what exactly the Bishop, a native of Guadalajara, New Galicia, meant by the term *chino*. He was possibly referring to people of mixed African and Indian ancestry.

26. Rubio Mañé, *Archivo*, 1:211.

27. Ibid., pp. 216–43.

28. AME, Visitas Pastorales, Izamal 10 May 1784, Cacalchén 21 Feb. 1785.

29. "Expediente formado para el establecimiento de escuelas en Yucatán y Campeche, 1782–1805," in Rubio Mañé, *Archivo*, 3: 159–303, shows Izamal as having 505 male and 383 female non-Indian children "appropriate for school." Even allowing for the subdelegados' inconsistent manner of defining "appropriate," it had by far the most children of any village.

30. Roys, *Titles of Ebtún*, offers numerous examples of the Maya villagers' defense of their land against both Indian and Spanish interlopers.

31. AME, Visitas Pastorales, Yaxcabá 27 Feb. 1784, Espita 3 May 1784. See also Tihosuco 25 March 1784 and Sacalum 9 Feb. 1782.

32. For the beginnings of rural ayuntamientos in Yucatan, see BCCA, Special Collection, Actas de la Diputación Provincial de Yucatán, 29 April 1813, fol. 6, and 21 May 1813, fol. 22.

33. AME, Visitas Pastorales, Izamal 10 May 1784, Tizimín 30 April 1784.

Conclusion

1. Stern, "Feudalism, Capitalism, and the World-System," p. 848.

2. Toledo, *México en la obra de Marx y Engels*; Marx and Engels, *Materiales para la historia de América Latina*; Mariátegui, *Siete ensayos de interpretación*, pp. 35–39. See also the discussion of this topic in Stern, "Feudalism, Capitalism, and the World-System," pp. 832ff.

3. President Jacobo Arbenz of Guatemala stated in 1951 that one of the goals of his administration was "to transform our nation from a backward nation with a predominantly feudal economy to a modern capitalist country." Quoted in Jonas, "Guatemala," p. 156.

4. See the analysis in Chilcote and Edelstein, "Alternative Perspectives," pp. 5–14.

5. Ibid.; Frank, "Development of Underdevelopment"; Kula, *Teoría económica del sistema feudal*.

6. Carmagnani, *Formación y crisis de un sistema feudal*; Morin, *Michoacán*; Romano, "American Feudalism."

7. Kula, *Teoría económica*, p. 22.

8. Laclau, "Feudalism and Capitalism," p. 28; Semo, *Historia*, pp. 132–33; Carmagnani, *Formación y crisis*, pp. 31–44; Romano, "American Feudalism," p. 123.

9. For a different interpretation, see Ouweneel and Bijleveld, "Economic Cycle," pp. 486–89. Those authors assign almost no importance to large-scale livestock production in New Galicia and northern Mexico for markets in central and southern Mexico, or to textile production in Oaxaca, Chiapas, Yucatan, and the Philippines for central and northern Mexico. For evidence to the contrary, see above, chaps. 4, 6; Serrera Contreras, *Guadalajara ganadera*; pp. 75–118; Harris, *Mexican Family Empire*, pp. 79–86, 109; Hamnett, *Politics*, pp. 5–23; Morin, *Michoacán*, pp. 141–202; Floyd, "Guatemalan Merchants"; Prado, *Colonial Background of Modern Brazil*, pp. 213–41; Boxer, *Golden Age of Brazil*, pp. 226–45; and Assadourian, *Sistema de la economía colonial*, pp. 155–254.

10. Some historians (e.g. Carmagnani, Morin, Romano) have argued that colonial Latin America had a natural, and therefore noncapitalist, economy because money was scarce and was used in very limited ways. According to these scholars, credit, bills of exchange, I.O.U.'s, etc., are nonmonetary in nature; apparently, the only real form of money is cash. But by this criterion, the twentieth-century U.S. economy—in which cash is only one-seventh of the money supply—would have to be considered noncapitalist. Moreover, it is ethnocentric to classify cacao, in the case of Mesoamerica, as a "money substitute." In fact, cacao was money, and had been money long before the European invasion.

11. See, for example, Lockhart, *Spanish Peru*, p. 77; Lockhart and Otte, *Letters and People*, p. 39; Chance and Taylor, "Estate and Class," 456, n. 3; Cushner, *Farm and Factory: The Jesuits and the Development of Agrarian Capitalism in Colonial Quito, 1600–1767*; and Salvucci, *Textiles and Capitalism*.

12. For another criticism of this concept, see Stern, "Feudalism, Capitalism, and the World-System," especially pp. 865–71.

13. For a recent application of this concept, see Larson, *Colonialism*, pp. 43–91. At the same time it should be noted that Steve Stern—wisely in my opinion—refuses to fall into this kind of analysis. See his *Peru's Indian Peoples*, pp. 35–40.

14. Semo, *Historia*, especially pp. 13–19, 230–60. See also Wolf, *Europe*, pp. 73–100.

15. Olivera, *Pillis y macehuales*.

16. For a criticism of the use of the term "mode of production," see Chiaramonte, *Formas de sociedad*, pp. 99–166, where the author argues that the concept of mode of production in fact played little or no role in Marx's analysis but was incorporated into Marxist thought after his death.

17. Stern, "Feudalism, Capitalism, and the World-System," pp. 871–72.

18. For an introduction to the study of regions, see Van Young, "Haciendo historia regional."

A Note on the Primary Sources

This study is based on manuscript sources found in both Mexico and Spain. The most important single site for research was Mérida, Yucatan, the location of many archives and manuscript collections. First in order of importance for research was the Notarial Archive (Archivo Notarial del Estado; ANEY), which contains the notarized records of wills, sales of real estate, dowries, contracts, and even renunciations from office and formal protests and acts by the cabildo and by members of the community. The holdings of the ANEY are by no means complete; they date only from 1689, and there are no records at all for the years 1700–1718 and 1724–27. Thereafter the documentation improves considerably, and there is a plethora of records for the second half of the eighteenth century. The holdings of the ANEY are also quite good for the nineteenth and twentieth centuries.

Second in importance in Mérida was the Cathedral Archive, or Archivo de la Mitra Emeritense (AME; which has recently been renamed). The Episcopal Visitations (Visitas Pastorales) section contains useful information about the culture, economy, and society of the second half of the eighteenth century but is of little value for the nineteenth—a reflection of the declining importance of the Church after Independence. Also useful in the Cathedral Archive are the Cofradías and Capellanías sections, and some of the documents found in the sections enigmatically entitled Asuntos Terminados (Finished Matters) and Asuntos Pendientes (Pending Matters). Most of the AME documents seem to date only from the eighteenth century, although I did not have time to investigate all the archive's holdings.

Third, the manuscript collection of the State Library Crescencio Carrillo y Ancona (BCCA) proved to be invaluable. Among these documents are almost all the surviving tithe records of the archdiocese (which seem to have gotten here as part of the private papers of Bishop Carrillo y Ancona) and the Archive of the Cabildo of Mérida (Archivo del Ayuntamiento de Mérida; AAM). Most of the library's manuscripts are from the eighteenth and nineteenth centuries; the AAM dates only from 1747, and is by no means complete even after that.

The remaining source material in Mérida is scattered throughout various collections. The State Archive (Archivo General del Estado; AGEY) has meager holdings for the colonial period, although it is rich in materials for the nineteenth and twentieth centuries. The Public Registry of Property (Registro Público de la Propiedad; RPP) is so badly maintained that it is quite difficult to use or even know the contents of its collection. Perhaps a persistent, and patient, scholar will some day discover something of value there. The General Diocesan Archive (Archivo General del Arzobispado) contains mostly the records of baptism, marriage, and last rites. These are invaluable for the demographic historian but were little used in my research. Finally, private papers, especially hacienda deeds, belonging to members of the current or former elite are useful to consult because they provide concrete examples of hacienda land acquisition and inheritance. Rarely, however, do private papers shed much light on the economy of the landed estates. In any case, access to these materials is restricted.

Outside of Mérida, the source material is meager. The archives of Campeche are hardly available for consultation, and the would-be researcher must be prepared to play the role of prospector. In the states of Yucatan and Campeche, and in Mexico as a whole, municipalities rarely keep any records at all *in situ;* what is available is usually placed—or perhaps more accurately stated, dumped—in state archives. On the other hand, with its continuing classification of documents, the very well-run Mexican National Archive (Archivo General de la Nación; AGN) in Mexico City has come to have increasing importance for historians of Yucatan. Also in Mexico City is the Archivo de la Secretaría de la Reforma Agraria (ASRA), which includes the files, organized by *municipio,* relating to land reform carried out since the Revolution. The records often include maps and copies of old hacienda deeds, but since the ASRA is not run for scholars, the archive, though valuable, is difficult to use.

The second-most-important site for research for this book was not Mexico City but Seville, the location of the General Archive of the Indies (Archivo General de Indias; AGI). Because of the paucity in Mexico of materials relating to seventeenth-century Yucatan, the holdings of the AGI were invaluable because they allowed me to extend the time frame of study. The collections in this archive are arranged chronologically by the source and type of document, but not by topic, and the guides and indexes of the AGI were compiled by people with little or no interest in Indians or socioeconomic history; archival organization and administration, in short, reflect the interests of traditional Spanish historiography. As a result, the non-Spanish researcher is usually in the role of a prospector searching for gold. That influence has its advantages, however, for the rococo qualities of the AGI have protected valuable materials from discovery by other scholars. In short, the General Archive of the Indies is a gold mine of information for the person with time, patience, and good eyes. The most important sections for me were the Audiencia de México—which includes reports and correspondence submitted by Governors, Bishops, city councils, and the Audiencia in Mexico City— and Escribanía de Cámara. The latter contains residencias and lawsuits for the era 1640–1740; the information that can be acquired from such sources is much more important than is often suspected. Unfortunately, many documents from the Contaduría section—exchequer accounts—were destroyed or damaged in a fire.

The second archive consulted in Spain was the Archivo Histórico Nacional (AHN) in Madrid. This is of much less importance than the AGI for the Latin Americanist, but it does contain many residencias of Governors from the 1730's to the 1780's. The AHN also contains a great deal of information about the Society of Jesus, although in my case most of the materials were of very limited value because the Jesuits were not very important in Yucatan. I did not consult the Archivo General in Simancas because that archive's holdings relate mostly to financial, state, and military affairs. However, other scholars may one day find valuable information there.

Works Cited

I have used the abbreviations *HAHR* (*Hispanic American Historical Review*) and *LARR* (*Latin American Research Review*) in the entries.

Adams, Richard E. W., ed. *The Origins of Maya Civilization.* Albuquerque, N.M., 1977.

Aguirre Beltrán, Gonzalo. *El proceso de aculturación.* México, 1957.

Ancona, Eligio. *Historia de Yucatán.* 4 vols. Mérida, 1917.

Andrews, Anthony P. *Maya Salt Production and Trade.* Tucson, Ariz., 1983.

Anes, Gonzalo. *El antiguo régimen: Los Borbones.* Madrid, 1976.

Ascensio, Cristóbal de. "Report on Cozumel, 1570," in Ralph L. Roys, France V. Scholes, and Eleanor B. Adams, eds., "Report and Census of the Indians of Cozumel, 1570," Carnegie Institution of Washington, Publication no. 523, *Contributions of American Anthropology and History,* vol. 6 (1940), 23–29.

Ashmore, Wendy, ed. *Lowland Maya Settlement Patterns.* Albuquerque, N.M., 1981.

Bakewell, Peter J. *Silver Mining and Society in Colonial Mexico: Zacatecas, 1546–1700.* Cambridge, Eng., 1971.

Barabas, Alicia M. "Profetismo, milenarismo y mesianismo en las insurrecciones mayas de Yucatán," Instituto Nacional de Antropología e Historia, Dirección de los Centros Regionales, *Cuadernos de los Centros,* no. 5 (n.d. [1974]), 1–30.

Baudot, Georges. "Dissidences indiennes et complicité filibustières dans le Yucatan du XVIIe siècle," *C.M.H.L.B. Caravelle,* no. 46 (1986), 21–33.

Bauer, Arnold J. "Rural Workers in Spanish America: Problems of Peonage and Oppression," *HAHR,* 59.1 (1979), 34–63.

Bishko, Charles Julian. "The Peninsular Background of Latin American Cattle Ranching," *HAHR,* 32.4 (1952), 491–515.

Blair, Emma Helen, and James Alexander Robertson, eds. *The Philippine Islands, 1493–1898.* 55 vols. Cleveland, Ohio, 1903–7.

Blom, Franz. "Commerce, Trade and Monetary Units of the Maya," *Middle American Research Series,* no. 4 (1932), 531–66.

Borah, Woodrow. *El gobierno provincial en la Nueva España.* México, 1985.

———. *Justice by Insurance: The General Indian Court of Colonial Mexico and the Legal Aides of the Half-real.* Berkeley, Calif., 1983.

Borah, Woodrow, and Sherburne F. Cook, "La despoblación del México central en el siglo XVI," *Historia Mexicana,* 12.1 (1962), 1–12.

Boxer, Charles R. *The Golden Age of Brazil, 1695–1750: Growing Pains of a Colonial Society*. Berkeley, Calif., 1962.

Boyd-Bowman, Peter. "Two Country Stores in XVIIth-Century Mexico," *The Americas*, 27.3 (1972), 241–48.

Brading, D. A. *Haciendas and Ranchos in the Mexican Bajío: León, 1700–1860*. Cambridge, Eng., 1978.

———. *Miners and Merchants in Bourbon Mexico, 1763–1810*. Cambridge, Eng., 1971.

Brannon, Jeffery T., and Gilbert M. Joseph, eds. *Land, Labor, and Capital in Modern Yucatán: Essays in Regional History and Political Economy*. University, Alabama, 1991.

Braudel, Fernand. *Civilisation matérielle et capitalisme*. 3 vols. Paris, 1967.

———. *La Mediterranée et le monde mediterranéen à l'époque de Philippe II*. 2 vols. Paris, 1966.

Bronner, Fred. "Urban Society in Colonial Latin America: Research Trends," *LARR*, 21.1 (1986), 7–50.

Calderón Quijano, José Antonio, ed. *Los virreyes de Nueva España en el reinado de Carlos IV*. 2 vols. Seville, 1972.

Calvo, Thomas. "Demographie historique d'une paroisse mexicaine: Acatzingo (1606–1810)," *Cahiers des Amériques Latines*, no. 6 (1972), 7–41.

The Cambridge Economic History of Europe from the Decline of the Roman Empire. 8 vols. Cambridge, Eng., 1942–89.

Cárdenas Valencia, Francisco. *Relación historial eclesiástica de la provincia de Yucatán . . . año de 1639*. México, 1937.

Carmack, Robert M., John Early, and Christopher Lutz, eds. *The Historical Demography of Highland Guatemala*. Albany, N.Y., 1982.

Carmagnani, Marcelo. *Formación y crisis de un sistema feudal: América Latina del siglo XVI a nuestros días*. México, 1976.

———. *Les Méchanismes de la vie économique dans une société coloniale: Le Chili (1680–1830)*. Paris, 1973.

Chamberlain, Robert S. *The Conquest and Colonization of Yucatan*. Washington, D.C., 1948.

Chance, John K. *Race and Class in Colonial Oaxaca*. Stanford, Calif., 1978.

Chance, John K., and William B. Taylor, "Estate and Class in a Colonial City: Oaxaca in 1792," *Comparative Studies in Society and History*, 19.4 (1977), 454–87.

Chapman, Anne M. "Port of Trade Enclaves in Aztec and Maya Civilizations," in Karl Polanyi, Conrad Arensberg, and Harry W. Pearson, eds., *Trade and Markets in the Early Empires* (Glencoe, Ill., 1957), 114–50.

Chardon, Roland Emmanuel Paul. *Geographic Aspects of Plantation Agriculture in Yucatan*. Washington, D.C., 1961.

Chaunu, Huguette, and Pierre Chaunu. *Séville et l'Atlantique (1504–1650)*. 8 vols. Paris, 1955–59.

Chevalier, François. *La Formation des grands domaines au Mexique: Terre et société aux XVIe–XVIIe siècles*. Paris, 1952.

Chiaramonte, José Carlos. *Formas de sociedad y economía en Hispanoamérica*. México, 1983.

Chilcote, Ronald H., and Joel C. Edelstein, "Alternative Perspectives of Development and Underdevelopment in Latin America," in Ronald H. Chilcote and Joel C. Edelstein, eds., *Latin America: The Struggle with Dependency and Beyond* (Cambridge, Mass., 1974), 1–87.

———. eds. *Latin America: The Struggle with Dependency and Beyond.* Cambridge, Mass., 1974.

Clendinnen, Inge. *Ambivalent Conquests: Maya and Spaniard in Yucatan, 1517–1570.* Cambridge, Eng., 1987.

———. "Yucatec Maya Women and the Spanish Conquest: Role and Ritual in Historical Reconstruction," *Journal of Social History*, 15 (1982), 427–41.

Cline, Howard F. "The 'Aurora Yucateca' and the Spirit of Enterprise in Yucatan, 1821–1847," *HAHR*, 27.1 (1947), 30–60.

———. "Civil Congregations of the Indians in New Spain, 1598–1606," *HAHR*, 29.3 (1949), 349–69.

———. "Regionalism and Society in Yucatan, 1825–1847. A Study of 'Progressivism' and the Origins of the Caste War," Ph.D. diss., Harvard University, 1947.

———. "The Sugar Episode in Yucatan, 1825–1850," *Inter-American Economic Affairs*, 1.4 (1948), 79–100.

Coatsworth, John H. "Obstacles to Economic Growth in Nineteenth-Century Mexico," *American Historical Review*, 83.1 (1978), 80–100.

Colección de documentos inéditos relativos al descubrimiento, conquista y colonización de las antiguas posesiones españolas de ultramar. 25 vols. Madrid, 1885–1932.

Conklin, Harold C. "An Ethnoecological Approach to Shifting Cultivation," *Transactions of the American Academy of Sciences*, series 2, 17 (1954), 133–42.

Cook, Sherburne F., and Woodrow Borah. *Essays in Population History.* 3 vols. Berkeley, Calif., 1971–79.

———. *The Indian Population of Central Mexico, 1531–1610.* Ibero-Americana, no. 44. Berkeley, Calif., 1960.

Curtin, Philip D. "Epidemiology of the Slave Trade," *Political Science Quarterly*, 83 (1968), 190–216.

———. *The Image of Africa: British Ideas and Action, 1780–1850.* Madison, Wis., 1964.

Cushner, Nicholas P. *Farm and Factory: The Jesuits and the Development of Agrarian Capitalism in Colonial Quito, 1600–1767.* Albany, N.Y., 1982.

———. *Landed Estates in the Colonial Philippines.* New Haven, Conn., 1976.

Dalton, George, ed. *Tribal and Peasant Economies.* Garden City, N.Y., 1967.

Davies, Keith A. *Landowners in Colonial Peru.* Austin, Tex., 1984.

Díaz-Trechuelo Spínola, María Lourdes et al. "El Virrey Don Juan Vicente de Güemes Pacheco, Segundo conde de Revillagigedo," in José Antonio Calderón Quijano, ed., *Los virreyes de Nueva España en el reinado de Carlos IV* (Seville, 1972), vol. 1, 85–366.

Dusenberry, William H. *The Mexican Mesta: The Administration of Ranching in Colonial Mexico.* Urbana, Ill., 1963.

Elliott, J. H. *The Old World and the New, 1492–1650.* Cambridge, Eng., 1970.

Everaert, John. "Le Commerce colonial de la nation flamande à Cádiz sous Charles II," *Anuario de Estudios Americanos*, 28 (1971), 139–51.

Fallers, L. A. "Are African Cultivators to Be Called 'Peasants'?," in Jack M. Potter, May N. Díaz, and George M. Foster, eds., *Peasant Society: A Reader* (Boston, 1967), 35–40.

Farriss, Nancy M. "Indians in Colonial Yucatan: Three Perspectives," in Murdo J. MacLeod and Robert Wasserstrom, eds., *Spaniards and Indians in Southeastern Mesoamerica* (Lincoln, Neb., 1983), 1–39.

————. *Maya Society Under Colonial Rule: The Collective Enterprise of Survival.* Princeton, N.J., 1984.

————. "Nucleation Versus Dispersal: The Dynamics of Population Movement in Colonial Yucatan," *HAHR*, 58.2 (1978), 187–217.

————. "Propiedades territoriales en Yucatán en la época colonial: Algunas observaciones acerca de la pobreza española y la autonomía indígena," *Historia Mexicana*, 29.2 (1980), 153–208.

Fisher, J. R. *Government and Society in Colonial Peru: The Intendant System, 1784–1814.* London, 1970.

Flannery, Kent V., ed. *Maya Subsistence.* New York, 1982.

Florescano, Enrique. *Precios del maíz y crisis agrícola en México (1708–1810).* México, 1969.

Floyd, Troy S. "The Guatemalan Merchants, the Government, and the *Provincianos*, 1750–1800," *HAHR*, 41.1 (1961), 90–110.

Folan, William J., Joel Gunn, Jack D. Eaton, and Robert W. Patch. "Paleoclimatological Patterning in Southern Mesoamerica," *Journal of Field Archaeology*, 10 (Winter 1983), 453–68.

Ford, Daryll, and Mary Douglas. "Primitive Economics," in George Dalton, ed., *Tribal and Peasant Economies* (Garden City, N.Y., 1967), 13–28.

Foster, George M. "Introduction: What Is a Peasant?," in Jack M. Potter, May N. Díaz, and George M. Foster, eds., *Peasant Society: A Reader* (Boston, 1967), 2–13.

Frank, Andre Gunder. "The Development of Underdevelopment," *Monthly Review*, 18 (Sept. 1966), 17–31.

Galeano, Eduardo. *Las venas abiertas de América Latina.* Buenos Aires, 1971.

García Bernal, Manuela Cristina. "Los comerciantes estancieros en Yucatán y la gran propiedad de Nohpat," *Temas Americanistas*, No. 4 (1984), 8–14.

————. "El Gobernador de Yucatán Rodrigo Flores de Aldana," in *Homenaje al Dr. Muro Orejón* (Seville, 1979), 123–72.

————. "La pérdida de la propiedad indígena ante la expansión de las estancias yucatecas (siglo XVI)," in *Actas de las VIII Jornadas de Andalucía y América: Propiedad de la tierra, latifundios y movimientos campesinos* (Seville, 1991), 55–90.

————. "Los servicios personales en Yucatán durante el siglo XVI," *Revista de la Universidad de Yucatán*, no. 110 (1977).

————. *La Sociedad de Yucatán.* Seville, 1972.

————. *Yucatán: Población y encomienda bajo los Austrias.* Seville, 1978.

García Fuentes, Lutgardo. *El comercio español con América, 1650–1700.* Seville, 1980.

García Márquez, Gabriel. Address, published in *The New York Times*, Feb. 6, 1983.

García-Baquero González, Antonio. *Cádiz y el Atlántico (1717–1778).* Seville, 1976.

Garza T., Silvia, and Edwardo Kurjack. "Organización social y asentamientos mayas prehispánicos," *Estudios de Cultura Maya*, 15 (1984), 301–27.

Geertz, Clifford. *Agricultural Involution: The Process of Ecological Change in Indonesia*. Berkeley, Calif., 1963.

Gerhard, Peter. "La evolución del pueblo rural mexicano: 1519–1975," *Historia Mexicana*, 24.4 (1975), 566–79.

Gibson, Charles. *The Aztecs Under Spanish Rule: A History of the Indians of the Valley of Mexico, 1519–1810*. Stanford, Calif., 1964.

———. "Writings on Colonial Mexico," *HAHR*, 55.2 (1975), 297–300.

Golte, Jürgen. *Repartos y rebeliones: Tupac Amaru y las contradicciones de la economía colonial*. Lima, 1980.

Góngora, Mario. *Encomenderos y estancieros*. Santiago, 1970.

———. *Origen de los "inquilinos" de Chile central*. Santiago, 1960.

———. "Urban Social Stratification in Colonial Chile," *HAHR*, 55.3 (1975), 421–48.

González Cicero, Stella María. *Perspectiva religiosa en Yucatán, 1515–1571*. México, 1978.

Granado Baeza, Bartolomé del. "Informe dado por el cura de Yaxcabá . . . sobre el manejo, vida y costumbres de los indios. 1 de abril de 1813," *Registro Yucateco*, 1 (1845), 165–78.

Grieshaber, Erwin P. "Hacienda-Indian Community Relations and Indian Acculturation: An Historiographical Essay," *LARR*, 14.3 (1979), 107–28.

Halperín Donghi, Tulio, et al. "Symposium," *LARR*, 17.1 (1982), 115–71.

Hamnett, Brian R. *Politics and Trade in Southern Mexico, 1750–1821*. Cambridge, Eng, 1971.

Harris, Charles H., III. *A Mexican Family Empire: The Latifundio of the Sánchez Navarros*. Austin, Tex., 1975.

Harrison, Peter D., and B. L. Turner, eds. *Pre-Hispanic Maya Agriculture*. Albuquerque, N.M., 1978.

Hernández, Juan José. "Las indias de Yucatán," *Registro Yucateco*, 3 (1846), 290–98.

Hill, Robert M., II. "*Chinamit* and *Molab*: Late Postclassic Highland Maya Precursors of Closed Corporate Community," *Estudios de Cultura Maya*, 15 (1984), 301–21.

Homenaje al Dr. Muro Orejón. Seville, 1979.

Hunt, Marta Espejo-Ponce. "Colonial Yucatan: Town and Region in the Seventeenth Century," Ph.D. diss., University of California, Los Angeles, 1974.

"Incorporación a la Real Corona de las encomiendas de Yucatán. Distrito de las Reales Cajas de Mérida y Campeche," *Boletín del Archivo General de la Nación*, 9.3 (1938), 469–567.

"Incorporación de encomiendas de la Provincia de Yucatán y Tabasco," *Boletín del Archivo General de la Nación*, 9.3 (1938).

Jonas, Susanne. "Guatemala: Land of Eternal Struggle," in Ronald H. Chilcote and Joel C. Edelstein, eds., *Latin America: The Struggle with Dependency and Beyond* (Cambridge, Mass., 1974), 89–216.

Jones, Grant D. "Agriculture and Trade in the Colonial Period Southern Maya Lowlands," in Kent V. Flannery, ed., *Maya Subsistence* (New York, 1982), 275–93.

———. "The Last Maya Frontiers of Colonial Yucatan," in Murdo J. MacLeod and Robert Wasserstrom, eds., *Spaniards and Indians in Southeastern Mesoamerica* (Lincoln, Neb., 1983), 64–91.

———. *Maya Resistance to Spanish Rule: Time and History on a Colonial Frontier.* Albuquerque, N.M., 1989.

———, ed. *Anthropology and History in Yucatan.* Austin, Tex., 1977.

Joralemon, Donald. "New World Depopulation and the Case of Disease," *Journal of Anthropological Research,* 38 (1982), 108–27.

Joseph, Gilbert M. *Rediscovering the Past at Mexico's Periphery.* University, Alabama, 1986.

———. *Revolution from Without: Yucatan, Mexico, and the United States, 1880–1924.* New York, 1982.

Keen, Benjamin. "Main Currents in United States Writings on Colonial Spanish America, 1884–1984," *HAHR,* 65.4 (1985), 657–82.

Keith, Robert G. *Conquest and Agrarian Change: The Emergence of the Hacienda System on the Peruvian Coast.* Cambridge, Mass., 1976.

Kicza, John E. "The Social and Ethnic Historiography of Colonial Latin America: The Last Twenty Years," *William and Mary Quarterly,* 45.3 (1988), 453–88.

Knight, Alan. "Mexican Peonage: What Was It and Why Was It?," *Journal of Latin American Studies,* 18 (May 1986), 41–74.

Kula, Witold. *Teoría económica del sistema feudal.* México, 1976. Originally published in Polish in 1962 and translated into Spanish from the French edition of 1970.

Lacarra, José María. "Les Villes-frontière dans l'Espagne des XIe et XIIe sìecles," *Le Moyen Age,* 69 (1963), 205–22.

Laclau, Ernesto. "Feudalism and Capitalism in Latin America," *New Left Review,* 67 (May–June 1971), 19–38.

La Force, James Clayburn, Jr. *The Development of the Spanish Textile Industry, 1750–1800.* Berkeley, Calif., 1965.

Landa, Diego de. *Relación de las cosas de Yucatán.* México, 1959.

Larson, Brooke. *Colonialism and Agrarian Transformation in Bolivia: Cochabamba, 1550–1900.* Princeton, N.J., 1988.

Larson, Brooke, and Robert Wasserstrom. "Consumo forzoso en Cochabamba y Chiapa durante la época colonial," *Historia Mexicana,* 31.3 (1982), 361–408.

Lenski, Gerhard E. *Power and Privilege: A Theory of Social Stratification.* New York, 1966.

El Libro de Chilam Balam de Chumayel. México, 1973.

Lindley, Richard B. *Haciendas and Economic Development: Guadalajara, Mexico, at Independence.* Austin, Tex., 1983.

Lizana, Fray Bernardo de. *Historia de Yucatán, devocionario de Ntra. Sra. de Izamal, y conquista espiritual.* México, 1893.

Lockhart, James. "Encomienda and Hacienda: The Evolution of the Great Estate in the Spanish Indies," *HAHR,* 49.3 (1969), 411–29.

———. *Spanish Peru, 1532–1560: A Colonial Society.* Madison, Wis., 1968.

Lockhart, James, and Enrique Otte, eds. *Letters and People of the Spanish Indies: The Sixteenth Century.* New York, 1976.

Lombardi, John V. *People and Places in Colonial Venezuela*. Bloomington, Ind., 1976.

López de Cogolludo, Diego. *Historia de Yucatán*. México, 1957.

Lovell, W. George. *Conquest and Survival in Colonial Guatemala: A Historical Geography of the Cuchumatán Highlands, 1500–1821*. Kingston, Ont., 1985.

Loveman, Brian, and Arnold J. Bauer, "Forum," *HAHR*, 59. 3 (1979), 478–89.

McBryde, F. W. *Cultural and Historical Geography of Southwest Guatemala*. Washington, D.C., 1945.

McCaa, Robert. "*Calidad, Clase,* and Marriage in Colonial Mexico: The Case of Parral, 1788–90," *HAHR*, 64. 3 (1984), 477–501.

McCaa, Robert, Stuart B. Schwartz, and Arturo Grubessich. "Race and Class in Colonial Latin America: A Critique," *Comparative Studies in Society and History*, 21. 3 (1979), 421–42.

MacLeod, Murdo J. "An Outline of Central American Colonial Demographies: Sources, Yields, and Possibilities," in Robert M. Carmack, John Early, and Christopher Lutz, eds., *The Historical Demography of Highland Guatemala* (Albany, N.Y., 1982), 3–18.

———. "Papel social y económico de las cofradías indígenas en la colonia en Chiapas," *Mesoamérica*, 5 (June 1983), 64–86.

———. *Spanish Central America: A Socioeconomic History, 1520–1720*. Berkeley, Calif., 1973.

MacLeod, Murdo J., and Robert Wasserstrom, eds., *Spaniards and Indians in Southeastern Mesoamerica*. Lincoln, Neb., 1983.

"Maíz para Yucatán en 1809," *Novedades de Yucatán*, May 18, 1975.

Malvido, Elsa. "Factores de despoblación y reposición de la población de Cholula (1641–1810)," *Historia Mexicana*, 23. 1 (1973), 52–106.

Mariátegui, José Carlos. *Siete ensayos de interpretación de la realidad peruana*. Santiago, 1955.

Martin, Cheryl English. *Rural Society in Colonial Morelos*. Albuquerque, N.M., 1985.

Martínez, Hildeberto. *Tepeaca en el siglo XVI: Tenencia de la tierra y organización de un señorío*. México, 1984.

Martínez Hernández, Juan, ed. *Diccionario de Motul: Maya-Español*. Mérida, 1929.

Marx, Karl. *Pre-capitalist Economic Formations*. New York, 1965.

Marx, Karl, and Friedrich Engels. *Basic Writings on Politics and Philosophy*. Ed. Lewis S. Feuer. Garden City, N.Y., 1959.

———. *Materiales para la historia de América Latina*. México, 1975.

Marzahl, Peter. *Town in the Empire: Government, Politics, and Society in Seventeenth-Century Popayán*. Austin, Tex., 1978.

Matesanz, José. "Introducción de la ganadería en la Nueva España, 1521–1535," *Historia Mexicana*, 14.4 (1965), 533–66.

Medina Rubio, Arístides. *La iglesia y la producción agrícola en Puebla, 1540–1795*. México, 1983.

Millet Cámara, Luis, et al. *Hacienda y cambio social en Yucatán*. Mérida, 1983.

Ministerio de Fomento. *Cartas de Indias*. Madrid, 1877.

Miranda, José. "La función económica del encomendero en los orígenes del régimen colonial de Nueva España (1525–1531)," *Anales del Instituto Nacional de Antropología e Historia*, 2 (1941–46), 421–62.

———. *El tributo indígena en la Nueva España*. México, 1952.

Molina Solís, Juan Francisco. *Historia de Yucatán durante la dominación española*. 4 vols. Mérida, 1904–13.

Moreno Cebrián, Alfredo. *El corregidor de indios y la economía peruana en el siglo XVIII. (Los repartos forzosos de mercancías)*. Madrid, 1977.

Moreno Toscano, Alejandra. *Geografía económica de México (siglo XVI)*. México, 1968.

Morin, Claude. *Michoacán en la Nueva España: Crecimiento y desigualdad en una economía colonial*. México, 1979.

———. "Population et épidemies dans une paroisse mexicaine: Santa Inés Zacatelco (XVIe–XIXe siècles)," *Cahiers des Amériques Latines*, no. 6 (1972), 43–73.

Mörner, Magnus. *Perfil de la sociedad rural del Cuzco a fines de la colonia*. Lima, 1978.

Nash, Manning. "The Organization of Economic Life," in George Dalton, ed., *Tribal and Peasant Economies* (Garden City, N.Y., 1967), 3–11.

Navarro García, Luis. *Intendencias en Indias*. Seville, 1959.

Negroe Sierra, Genny Mercedes. "La cofradía de Yucatán en el siglo XVIII," Tesis de Licenciatura, Escuela de Ciencias Antropológicas, Universidad Autónoma de Yucatán, 1984.

Nettings, R. M. "Maya Subsistence: Mythologies, Analogies, Possibilities," in R. E. W. Adams, ed., *The Origins of Maya Civilization* (Albuquerque, N.M., 1977), 299–333.

Newson, Linda. "Indian Population Patterns in Colonial Spanish America," *LARR*, 20.3 (1985), 41–74.

Olivera, Mercedes. *Pillis y macehuales: Las formaciones sociales y los modos de producción de Tecali del siglo XII al XVI*. México, 1978.

Ortiz de la Tabla, Javier. *Comercio exterior de Veracruz, 1778–1821: Crisis de dependencia*. Seville, 1978.

Ouweneel, Arij, and Catrien C. J. H. Bijleveld. "The Economic Cycle in Bourbon Central Mexico: A Critique of the *Recaudación del diezmo líquido en pesos*," *HAHR*, 69.3 (1989), 479–530.

Pastor, Rodolfo. "El repartimiento de mercancías y los alcaldes mayores novohispanos: un sistema de explotación, de sus orígenes a la crisis de 1810," in Woodrow Borah, ed., *El gobierno provincial en la Nueva España* (México, 1985), 201–36.

Patch, Robert W. "Una cofradía y su estancia en el siglo XVIII: Notas de investigación," *Boletín de la Escuela de Ciencias Antropológicas de la Universidad de Yucatán*, 8 (Jan.–April 1981), 56–66.

———. "A Colonial Regime: Maya and Spaniard in Yucatan," Ph.D. diss., Princeton University, 1979.

———. "Decolonizaton, the Agrarian Problem, and the Origins of the Caste War of Yucatán, 1812–1847," in Jeffrey T. Brannon and Gilbert M. Joseph, eds., *Land, Labor, and Capital in Modern Yucatan: Essays in Regional History and Political Economy* (University, Alabama, 1991), 51–82.

Pérez-Mallaina Bueno, Pablo Emilio. *Comercio y autonomía en la Intendencia de Yucatán, 1797–1814*. Seville, 1978.

Phelan, John Leddy. *The Hispanization of the Philippines: Spanish Aims and Filipino Responses, 1565–1700*. Madison, Wis., 1967.

Pietschmann, Horst. "*Alcaldes Mayores, Corregidores* und *Subdelegados*: Zum Problem der Distriktsbeamtenschaft im vizekönigreich Neuspanien," *Jahrbuch für Geschichte von Staat, Wirtschaft und Gesellschaft Lateinamerikas*, 9 (1972), 173–270.

————. "Der Repartimiento-Handel der Distriksbeamten im Raum Puebla im 18 Jahrhundert," *Jahrbuch für Geschichte von Staat, Wirtschaft und Gesellschaft Lateinamerikas*, 10 (1973), 236–50.

Pohl, Mary, ed. *Prehistoric Lowland Maya Environment and Subsistence Economy*. Papers, Peabody Museum of Archaeology and Ethnology, Harvard University, 77 (1985).

Polyani, Karl, Conrad Arensberg, and Harry W. Pearson, eds. *Trade and Markets in the Early Empires*. Glencoe, Ill., 1957.

Potter, Jack M., May N. Díaz, and George M. Foster, eds. *Peasant Society: A Reader*. Boston, 1967.

Prado, Caio, Jr. *The Colonial Background of Modern Brazil*. Berkeley, Calif., 1971.

Quezada, Sergio. "El comercio marítimo entre Sisal y Campeche a mediados del siglo XVIII," Tesis de Licenciatura, Escuela Nacional de Economía, Universidad Autónoma Nacional de México, 1977.

————. "Encomienda, cabildo y gobernatura indígena en Yucatán, 1541–1583," *Historia Mexicana*, 34.4 (1985), 662–84.

————. "Pueblos y caciques yucatecos, 1550–1580." Ph.D. diss., El Colegio de México, 1990.

Ramírez, Susan E. *Provincial Patriarchs: Land Tenure and the Economics of Power in Colonial Peru*. Albuquerque, N.M., 1986.

Redfield, Robert. *The Folk Culture of Yucatan*. Chicago, 1941.

————. "The Social Organization of Tradition," in Jack M. Potter, May N. Díaz, and George M. Foster, eds., *Peasant Society: A Reader* (Boston, 1967), 25–34.

"Relación de las cosas que sucedieron al Padre Fray Alonso Ponce en las Provincias de La Nueva España," *Colección de documentos inéditos para la historia de España*, vol. 43. Madrid, 1872.

Riley, G. Michael. "Land in Spanish Enterprise: Colonial Morelos, 1522–1547," *The Americas*, 27.3 (1971), 233–51.

Robinson, David J. "Introduction to Themes and Scales," in David J. Robinson, ed., *Social Fabric and Spatial Structure in Colonial Latin America* (Ann Arbor, Mich. 1979), 1–24.

————, ed. *Social Fabric and Spatial Structure in Colonial Latin America*. Ann Arbor, Mich., 1979.

Robinson, David J., and Carolyn G. McGovern. "La migración regional yucateca en la época colonial: El caso de San Francisco Umán," *Historia Mexicana*, 29.1 (1980), 99–125.

Romano, Ruggiero. "American Feudalism," *HAHR*, 64.1 (1984), 121–34.

Roys, Ralph L. *The Indian Background of Colonial Yucatan*. Washington, D.C., 1943.

————. *The Political Geography of the Yucatan Maya*. Washington, D.C., 1957.

————. *The Titles of Ebtún*. Washington, D.C., 1939.

Roys, Ralph L., France V. Scholes, and Eleanor B. Adams, "Report and Census of the Indians of Cozumel, 1570," Carnegie Institution of Washington, Publication no. 523, *Contributions of American Anthropology and History*, 6 (1940), 1–29.

Rubio Mañé, J. Ignacio, ed. *Archivo de la Historia de Yucatán, Campeche y Tabasco.* 3 vols. México, 1942.

——, ed. "Movimiento marítimo entre Veracruz y Campeche, 1801–1810," 3 parts, *Boletín del Archivo General de la Nación*, 24 (Oct.–Dec. 1953), 597–676; 25 (Jan.–March 1954), 91–146; 26 (April–June 1954), 237–335.

Ruz, Mario Humberto. "El añil en el Yucatán del siglo XVI," *Estudios de Cultura Maya*, 12 (1979), 111–56.

Salvucci, Richard J. *Textiles and Capitalism in Mexico. An Economic History of the Obrajes, 1539–1840.* Princeton, N.J., 1987.

Sánchez de Aguilar, Pedro. *Informe Contra Idolorum Cultores del Obispado de Yucatán.* México, 1937.

Scholes, France V., and Eleanor B. Adams, eds. *Don Diego Quijada, Alcalde Mayor de Yucatán, 1561–1565.* 2 vols. México, 1938.

Scholes, France V., and Ralph L. Roys. *The Maya Chontal Indians of Acalán-Tixchel.* Washington, D.C., 1948.

Scholes, France V., and Sir Eric Thompson. "The Francisco Pérez *Probanza* of 1654–1656 and the *Matrícula* of Tipu (Belize)," in Grant D. Jones, ed., *Anthropology and History in Yucatan* (Austin, Tex., 1977), 43–68.

Seed, Patricia. "Social Dimensions of Race: Mexico City, 1753," *HAHR*, 62.4 (1982), 569–606.

Semo, Enrique. *Historia del capitalismo en México: Los orígenes, 1521/1763.* México, 1973.

Sempat Assadourian, Carlos. *El sistema de la economía colonial: El mercado interior, regiones, y espacio económico.* México, 1983.

Serrera Contreras, Ramón. *Guadalajara ganadera: Estudio regional novohispano, 1760–1805.* Seville, 1977.

Sierra O'Reilly, Justo. *Los indios de Yucatán.* 2 vols. Mérida, 1954.

Smith, Carol A. "Examining Stratification Systems Through Peasant Marketing Arrangements: An Application of Some Models from Economic Geography," *Man*, 10.1 (1975), 95–122.

Socolow, Susan Migden. "Marriage, Birth, and Inheritance: The Merchants of Eighteenth-Century Buenos Aires," *HAHR*, 60.3 (1980), 387–406.

——. *The Merchants of Buenos Aires, 1778–1810.* New York, 1978.

Solano y Pérez Lila, Francisco de. "Estudio socioantropológico de la población rural no indígena de Yucatán, 1700." Mérida, 1975.

Spalding, Karen. "*Kurakas* and Commerce: A Chapter in the Evolution of Andean Society," *HAHR*, 53.4 (1973), 581–99.

——. "Social Climbers: Changing Patterns of Mobility Among the Indians of Colonial Peru," *HAHR*, 50.4 (1970), 649–63.

Stein, Stanley J. "Bureaucracy and Business in the Spanish Empire, 1759–1804: Failure of a Bourbon Reform in Mexico and Peru," *HAHR*, 61.1 (1981), 2–28.

Stein, Stanley J., and Barbara H. Stein. *The Colonial Heritage of Latin America: Essays on Economic Dependence in Perspective.* New York, 1970.

Stephens, John Lloyd. *Incidents of Travel in Central America, Chiapas and Yucatan.* 2 vols. New York, 1841.

———. *Incidents of Travel in Yucatan.* 2 vols. New York, 1843.

Stern, Steve J. "Feudalism, Capitalism, and the World-System in the Perspective of Latin America and the Caribbean," *American Historical Review*, 93.4 (1988), 829–72.

———. *Peru's Indian Peoples and the Challenge of Spanish Conquest: Huamanga to 1640.* Madison, Wis., 1982.

Tandeter, Enrique. "Forced and Free Labour in Late Colonial Potosí," *Past and Present*, no. 93 (1981), 98–136.

Taylor, William B. *Landlord and Peasant in Colonial Oaxaca.* Stanford, Calif., 1972.

Thompson, Philip C. "Tekantó in the Eighteenth Century," Ph.D. diss., Tulane University, 1978.

Toledo, Domingo P. de. *México en la obra de Marx y Engels.* México, 1939.

Tozzer, A. M., ed. *Landa's Relación de las Cosas de Yucatán: A Translation.* Papers, Peabody Museum of Archaeology and Ethnology, Harvard University, 18 (1941).

Trautmann, Wolfgang. *Las transformaciones en el paisaje cultural de Tlaxcala durante la época colonial: Una contribución a la historia de México bajo especial consideración de aspectos geográficos y sociales.* Wiesbaden, 1981.

Valdeavellano, Luis G. de. *Curso de historia de las instituciones españolas.* Madrid, 1968.

Valdés Acosta, José María. *A través de las centurias.* 3 vols. Mérida, 1979.

Valdés Lakowsky, Vera. *De las minas al mar: Historia de la plata mexicana en Asia, 1565–1834.* México, 1987.

Van Young, Eric. *Hacienda and Market in Eighteenth-Century Mexico: The Rural Economy of the Guadalajara Region, 1675–1820.* Berkeley, Calif., 1981.

———. "Haciendo historia regional: Consideraciones teóricas y metodológicas," Instituto de Estudios Históricos y Sociales (Tandil, Argentina), *Anuario*, 2 (1987).

———. "Mexican Rural History Since Chevalier: The Historiography of the Colonial Hacienda," *LARR*, 18.3 (1983), 5–46.

Vázquez de Espinosa, Antonio. *Compendio y descripción de las Indias Occidentales.* Washington, D.C., 1948.

Villa Rojas, Alfonso. "Notas sobre la tenencia de la tierra entre los Mayas de la antigüedad," *Estudios de Cultura Maya*, 1 (1961), 21–46.

Villagutierre y Sotomayor, Juan de. *Historia de la conquista de la provincia de el Itzá (1701).* Guatemala, 1933.

Vivo Escoto, Jorge A. "Weather and Climate of Mexico and Central America," *Handbook of Middle American Indians*, 1 (1964), 187–215.

Vollmer, Gunter. "La evolución cuantitativa de la población indígena en la región de Puebla (1570–1818)," *Historia Mexicana*, 23.1 (1973), 43–51.

Vos, Jan de. *La paz de Dios y del Rey: La Conquista de la Selva Lacandona.* México, 1980.

Wagner, Philip L. "Natural Vegetation of Middle America," *Handbook of Middle American Indians*, 1 (1964), 216–63.

Wallerstein, Immanuel. *The Modern World-System: Capitalist Agriculture and the Origins of the European World-Economy in the Sixteenth Century.* New York, 1974.
——. *The Modern World-System, II: Mercantilism and the Consolidation of the European World-Economy, 1600–1750.* New York 1980.
Wasserstrom, Robert. *Class and Society in Central Chiapas.* Berkeley, Calif., 1983.
——. "Spaniards and Indians in Colonial Chiapas, 1528–1790," in Murdo J. MacLeod and Robert Wasserstrom, eds., *Spaniards and Indians in Southeastern Mesoamearica* (Lincoln, Neb., 1983), 92–126.
Watters, R. F. "The Nature of Shifting Cultivation: A Review of Recent Research," *Pacific Viewpoint,* 1.1 (1960), 59–99.
Wells, Allen. *Yucatán's Gilded Age: Haciendas, Henequen, and International Harvester, 1860–1915.* Albuquerque, N.M., 1985.
West, Robert C. *The Mining Community in Northern New Spain: The Parral Mining District.* Ibero-Americana, no. 30. Berkeley, Calif., 1949.
Willey, Gordon, ed. *Prehistoric Settlement Patterns in the New World.* Viking Fund Publications in Anthropology, no. 23. New York, 1956.
Wolf, Eric R. "Closed Corporate Communities in Meso-America and Central Java," *Southwestern Journal of Anthropology,* 13 (Spring 1957), 1–18.
——. *Europe and the People Without History.* Berkeley, Calif., 1982.
——. *Peasants.* Englewood Cliffs, N.J., 1966.
——. *Sons of the Shaking Earth.* Chicago, 1959.
——. "Types of Latin American Peasantry: A Preliminary Discussion," *American Anthropologist,* 57 (1955), 452–71.
Wortman, Miles L. *Government and Society in Central America, 1680–1840.* New York, 1982.
Zamora Acosta, Elías. *Los Mayas de las tierras altas en el siglo XVI.* Seville, 1985.

Index

In this index an "f" after a number indicates a separate reference on the next page, and an "ff" indicates separate references on the next two pages. A continuous discussion over two or more pages is indicated by a span of page numbers, e.g., "pp. 57–58." *Passim* is used for a cluster of references in close but not consecutive sequence. The following descriptive abbreviations are used with personal and place names: b = barrio; B = Bishop; e = estancia, estate; F = Franciscan; G = Governor; h = hacienda; I = Intendant; p = priest; s = sitio; v = village or parcialidad.

Library of Congress Cataloging-in-Publication Data

Patch, Robert.
    Maya and Spaniard in Yucatan, 1648–1812 / Robert W. Patch.
      p.   cm.
    Includes bibliographical references (p.   ) and index.
    ISBN 0-8047-2062-2 (acid-free paper) :
    1. Mayas—Economic conditions.   2. Mayas—Government relations.
    3. Mayas—History.   4. Yucatán (Mexico : State)—Economic
    conditions.   5. Yucatán (Mexico : State)—Politics and government.
    6. Mexico—History—Spanish colony, 1540–1810.   I. Title.
    F1435.3.E27P37   1993
    972'.02—dc20
    92-25923   CIP

⊗ This book is printed on acid-free paper.